Count Us In

Count Us In

The Struggle to Free Soviet Jews

A Canadian Perspective

by
Wendy Eisen

foreword by
Martin Gilbert

Burgher Books
10 Edmund Avenue
Toronto, Ontario
M4V 1H3 Canada

Canadian Cataloguing in Publication Data

Eisen, Wendy
Count us in: the struggle to free Soviet Jews – a Canadian perspective

Includes bibliographical references and index.
ISBN 1-896176-05-4 (bound) ISBN 1-896176-04-6 (pbk.)

1. Jews – Soviet Union – History. 2. Jews – Persecutions – Soviet Union. 3. Refusniks. 4. Canada – Foreign relations – Soviet Union. 5. Soviet Union – Foreign relations – Canada. 6. Soviet Union – Emigration and immigration – Government policy. I. Title

DS135.R92E57 1995 323.1'1924947 C95-931024-X

Endpaper photo: Ben-Gurion Airport, October 26, 1989: El Al flight 008 brings 205 Soviet Jews from the transit point in Budapest, to Israel, marking the start of "Operation Exodus." [Joe Malcolm]

Distributed by:
Raincoast Books Limited
8680 Cambie Street
Vancouver, B.C.
V6P 6M9
Toll-free order line: 1 800 663 5714

Printed and bound in Canada

95 96 97 98 99· 5 4 3 2 1

This book is dedicated to the former refuseniks and Prisoners of Zion who were courageous enough to protest, when it was so much safer to remain silent.

Contents

	Foreword	ix
	Preface	xi
	Acknowledgments	xv
1	Historical Background	1
2	Stirrings of Canadian Support	9
3	Jewish Consciousness Awakens	24
4	The Canadian Community Organizes	37
5	A Movement Emerges	47
6	Eye Witnesses	56
7	International Accountability	60
8	The 35s	63
9	Some Success	75
10	A Global Gathering	85
11	Soviet Repression – Creative Responses	90
12	The Helsinki Process	100
13	Arrests and Trials . . . The Circle Widens	105
14	Sharansky's Long Road To Judgment	117

15 To See for Ourselves 133

16 The Noose Tightens . . . Activists Respond 146

17 Everyone Is Involved 158

18 Emigration Grinds To a Halt 170

19 New Hopes . . . New Recruits 177

20 Accountability Is Working 183

21 From the Gulag to Jerusalem 190

22 Activity Escalates . . . But No Results 205

23 Parliamentary Trips to the USSR 215

24 A Matter of Life or Death 223

25 The Iron Gates Begin to Part 231

26 The Reality of Glasnost 245

27 Operation Exodus 260

Epilogue 268

Notes 274

Index 322

Foreword

Those who were active in the campaign to allow Jews to leave the Soviet Union, and to release those who were in prison and labour camps, were invariably impressed when they came in contact with their Canadian opposite numbers. The Canadian dimension to the campaign in all its aspects was formidable. The involvement of the Canadian government, whose relations with the Soviet Union were unusually less abrasive than that of other Western governments, was continually and effectively enlisted by the Canadian Jewish activists.

The Canadian Jewish population was scarcely a quarter of a million when the campaign began in Canada in 1956, the year with which Wendy Eisen begins her pioneering study. It is pioneering because, although there are a number of good and informative books which examine the Soviet Jewry campaign, this is the first full length, fully documented account of our national effort. That effort was a remarkable one, drawing out considerable reserves of tenacity, ingenuity, sheer hard work, and inspiration, from leaders and followers alike. By 1989, the year in which Wendy Eisen's account comes to a close, the task had been achieved. Soviet Jews were free to leave, the prisoners were being released, and the network of contacts, co-activists and beneficiaries had been moulded into a unique family of friends in Israel and throughout the Jewish world.

This books makes the fullest use of documentary evidence and personal recollections, and is a testament to the importance of contemporary record and accurate detail. Wendy Eisen, herself a campaigner of distinction, has undertaken a painstaking and complex task, and has carried it out triumphantly. Her book will, one hopes, serve as a model for others of its kind about national campaigns elsewhere. It also presents an unanswerable case for activism and perseverance wherever human rights are abused. I will remember the times when the situation seemed hopeless for Soviet Jews: no way out, no light at the end of the tunnel, no hope for those incarcerated, nothing but the bonds of sympathy and clandestine contact. That situation only changed because of the efforts of many individuals and groups worldwide, including Canada.

The remarkable efforts of Canadian Jews receive their full acknowledgment here, not by generalized praise, but through a detailed description of their day-to-day work. This book is sleuth-like in its unravelling of what happened. It contains a roll call of honour, in which non-Canadian activists will recognize many friends and discover many new faces. It is much more than a roll of honour, however. It is a comprehensive description of how a campaign was begun and conducted, how it grew, how it struggled against the hostility of a totalitarian opponent, and how it refused to allow either its practical methods or its emotional zeal to weaken, despite many set backs and bad moments.

What never failed was the will to succeed, a will based upon the firm belief that all Jews are responsible for the well-being of their fellow Jews, and have a part to play in ameliorating the situation of those who are in darkness or danger. Having read every word of this book, I felt a sense of urgency and involvement during the many years of struggle, a warm glow of emotion at the triumphs, and a debt of gratitude to the Canadian activists who never grew tired, and who never faltered, until the task was done.

Wendy Eisen's vivid, often dramatic account will stir the memories of all those who were involved, and will open a window of inspiration to those who today are fighting new causes for human rights and dignities, in the Jewish world and beyond.

MARTIN GILBERT
Fellow, Merton College
Oxford

Preface

In 1950, Canada was home to two hundred thousand Jews, most of whom could trace their roots back one or two generations to Russia or Poland. By the early 1980s, Canada's Jewish population had grown to three hundred and thirty thousand. Canadian Jews were free to live where they chose, work in any profession, practice and teach their religion and culture. By contrast, the three million Jews in the Soviet Union – a country that had been home to Jews for five centuries – had none of those freedoms.

The persecution of Soviet Jews by their own totalitarian government was but one chapter in the history of the Jewish people in the twentieth century. With the other chapters – the Holocaust, the creation of a Jewish homeland and Israel's struggle against hostile neighbours – it underscored the importance of the ancient Talmudic precept: *Kol Yisroel arevim ze bazeh,* All Jews are responsible for one another. Thus, many Western Jews vowed to liberate their brothers and sisters from the Soviet Union.

Advocacy on behalf of Jews in the Soviet Union grew from individual, unco-ordinated concern for their plea for freedom, and developed into a powerful international movement. It began in the 1960s – a time of protest, demonstrations and civil unrest throughout the world. Activists coalesced to effect change in the oppressive policies of the Soviet government by non-violent, legal means. They recruited people who shared their goals, regardless of religious or ethnic background.

This book chronicles the Canadian contribution to the emergence, development and eventual disappearance of a social movement, the goal of which was to rescue Jews from the USSR. Using many of the freedoms denied to Soviet Jews – freedom of speech, freedom of the press, freedom to travel, access to a responsible government – Canadian activists fought to change the human rights policies of the Soviet Union, particularly those that oppressed Soviet Jews. At the same time, they helped to ensure the viability of one-quarter of the world's Jewish population.

Soviet Jewry advocacy took place against the backdrop of the Cold War between the USSR and the United States, when many Soviet allies were enemies of the state of Israel. Relations between Canada and the USSR, by comparison, were relatively cordial. Canada's importance as a Soviet trading partner provided the Canadian government with some political leverage.

Count Us In ties the stories of Soviet Jews to the hearts of Canadians. It is a study in social action. It demonstrates the capacity of ordinary citizens to influence government leaders and to mobilize thousands of others. It documents the role that the Canadian community played in the global effort to free Soviet Jews and highlights the singular efforts of individuals who struggled tenaciously, until the Jews of the Soviet Union were free to choose their own destiny and achieve their ultimate victory – unrestricted emigration from the Soviet Union.

Soviet Jews were not the only beneficiaries of the movement's achievements. Canadian Jews with different ideologies, united by a common purpose, were rewarded immeasurably by their efforts.

I, a Jewish mother with a young family, was one such activist. I worked as a volunteer in Montreal and in Toronto with The 35s - Women's Campaign for Soviet Jewry and the Soviet Jewry Committees of the Canadian Jewish Congress. I was enriched by people who shared my convictions, both in Canada and in other countries. The Soviet Jewry movement led me to a new appreciation of my heritage and strengthened my own Jewish identity.

The research material used to trace the development of the movement was found in community, government and personal archives. I conducted interviews with more than one hundred Canadian activists and with many activists in the United States, England and Israel. Their comments expanded my understanding of the commitment of so many caring men and women to the international struggle to free Jews from the Soviet Union.

Count Us In is a narrative written in the third person with several first-person anecdotal references. It is a tribute to every Canadian who ever signed a petition, wrote a letter, sent a cable, made a telephone call, painted a sign, marched or stood at a demonstration in support of Soviet Jewry. It is about people who believed in the words of poet Robert Frost: "I have promises to keep and miles to go before I sleep."

Acknowledgments

I wish to express a deep debt of gratitude to those who have helped in the preparation of this book.

To Irving Abella, my friend and mentor, whose encouragement from the outset gave me the confidence to undertake this project.

To Martin Gilbert, whose foreword lends credence to the Canadian effort.

To Bonnie Goldberg, my research assistant, whose expertise in transcribing interviews, researching, collating and summarizing the voluminous material, spared me years of additional labour.

To Janice Rosen, director of archives, Canadian Jewish Congress, whose assistance in obtaining necessary documentation was invaluable.

To Lawrence Tapper and Ed Atkinson for facilitating access to the National Archives in Ottawa.

To the federal Ministry of Multiculturalism for their generous grant.

To Phyllis and Shmuel Segev who encouraged and directed me during the embryonic stage of the manuscript.

To C. Peter Herman and Marsha Slavens who permitted me to impose upon their friendship and who reviewed the entire manuscript.

To Ian Montagnes, whose comprehensive critique afforded the opportunity to re-organize the manuscript into a more readable form.

To Matthew Gibson and Howard Aster for their editorial suggestions.

To Lorne Vineberg who voluntarily shared his expertise and to

Lani Alexandroff, Barbara Bank, Taffy Cass, Elliott Eisen, Sherry Kaufman, Gloria Lepofsky, Glennie Lindenberg, Helen Redner, Karen Serafin, Lorne Vineberg, Maxine Wintre and Carole Herman Zucker who each read a few chapters and made suggestions to tighten the prose.

To Julius Ciss for the image of the "Torah in Chains" and to Lawrie Raskin who incorporated it into a cover design.

I owe a great vote of thanks to Ann Newton whose editorial contribution was invaluable to the flow of the book and to Joshua Samuel of Burgher Books who looked at the manuscript and said, "yes."

My deep appreciation goes out to the leaders of the Soviet Jewry movement in Canada, the United States, England and Israel, who granted me interviews and willingly gave of their time and their files to make this book as accurate a document as possible.

I thank my parents, Allie and Bernie Herman, who taught me to carry the treasure of my heritage with pride and encouraged me to do my part to ensure the survival and continuity of the Jewish people.

I am appreciative of my daughters, Tammy, Jodi, Robin and Jennifer Litwack who, during their formative years, understood their mother's need to fulfil a dream.

I am deeply grateful to my husband Elliott Eisen who, during the six years of writing, read and re-read drafts, suggested valuable changes and encouraged me with his advice, support and love.

I wish to extend my deep appreciation to the following people, whose recollections provided information that was integral to *Count Us In:*

Bill Attewell, Brenda Barrie, Ruth Bar-On, Gerald Batist, William Bauer, Yosef Begun, Renee Bellas, Ruth Berger, Judith Bloom, Sylviane Borenstein, Andrea Bronfman, Edward Bronfman, Nani Beutel, Charles Caccia, June Callwood, Judy Feld Carr, Charles Chaplin, Rena Cohen, Rita Cohn, Irwin Cotler, Penny Collenette, Rev. Roland DeCorneille, Ian Deans, Frank Dimant, Sheldon Disenhouse, Oded Eran, Rita Eker, Joyce Eklove, Eric Fawcett, Sam Filer, Sheila Finestone, John Fraser, Gerda Freiberg, Barbara Glass,

Jerry Goodman, Simone Goldberg, Jeanette Goldman, Baruch Gur, Shirley Hanick, John Harker, Elaine Dubow Harris, Milton Harris, Hon. Justice Sydney Harris, Goldie Hershon, Dr. Gerhard Herzberg, Genya Intrator, Father Barry Jones, Serge Joyal, Sol Kanee, Robert Kaplan, Ben Kayfetz, David Kilgour, Gloria Landis, Herb Landis, Tina Lerner, Reverend James E. Leland, Nechemiah Levanon, Dr. Reverend Stanford Lucyk, The Hon. Flora MacDonald, Hon. Justice Mark MacGuigan, Rabbi Shlomo Noach Mandel, The Hon. Paul Martin, The Hon. Justice Ted Matlow, The Hon. Barbara McDougall, Alan McLaine, Alexander Mariasin, Frank Medjuck, Susan Mersky, Ruth Rayman Morrison, Peter Newman, Esther Nobleman, Rick Orzy, Rabbi Martin Penn, Jim Peterson, Ben Prossin, Mayor Yitzhack Rager, Bert Raphael, Alan Raymond, Zvi Raviv, Carol Reiter, Sam Resnick, Avrum Richler, Glenn Richter, Nelson Riis, R. Louis Rogers, Moshe Ronen, Alan Rose, Ambassador Meir Rosenne, Rabbi Stuart E. Rosenberg, David Rotenberg, Sheila Roth, Janice Rotman-Goldstein, David Sadowski, Joseph B. Salsberg, David Satok, Avital Sharansky, Natan Sharansky, The Hon. Mitchell Sharp, Max Shecter, Debbie Shecter, Michael Sherbourne, Hannah Sherebrin, Myrna Shinbaum, Cecile Shore, Barbara Shumiatcher, Israel Singer, Marsha Slavens, Marsha Slivka, The Hon. David Smith, Frederick Smith, Ellen Smiley, Gene Sosin, Debby Solomon, Stan Solomon, Barbara Stern, Susan Taerk, H. Wayne Tanenbaum, Ronnie Tessler, Bracha Tritt, Stan Urman, Inna Uspensky, Morley Wolfe, Sharon Wolfe, Mark Zarecki, Sheila Zittrer.

Chapter 1

Historical Background

On October 18, 1990, just as the sun rose over the eastern horizon, an El Al jet carrying 247 passengers from Riga, Minsk, Vilnius and Odessa taxied to a stop at Ben-Gurion Airport in Israel. Wearing fur hats and heavy winter coats, the men and women disembarked. Some were carrying bundles wrapped in brown paper, and others held infants in their arms. One elderly woman could barely walk.

Standing on the tarmac, waving miniature Israeli flags, was a group of Canadians, who, along with Israelis of all ages, joined in the singing of the Hebrew song of welcome, *Haveinu Shalom Alecheim*, that was played and amplified over a public address system.

The bewildered immigrants were ushered toward chairs that faced a raised platform over which a banner with the words "Keren Hayesod – Exodus '90 – Welcome to Israel," written in Hebrew, English and Russian, was strung.[1] After a brief greeting by Keren Hayesod officials, a teenage girl stepped forward and in accented English exclaimed, "I am here in Israel. It looks very beautiful. I start my new life tomorrow with Jewish people. I love you, Israel."[2]

After seventy years of living under a regime of enforced atheism, the hopes and dreams of Soviet Jewry were fulfilled. What had begun as a trickle in the early 1970s had become an exodus of historic proportions. The Jewish exiles from Russia were returning to their ancient homeland.

When the modern Soviet Jewry movement began in the early 1970s, the nations with the largest Jewish population were the United States, five million eight hundred thousand, the Soviet Union, three million and Israel, two million eight hundred thousand. Since that time, more than one million Jews have emigrated from the Soviet Union, most of them settling in Israel. This emigration movement challenges in size the biblical exodus and represents the largest immigration of Jews to Israel in Jewish history:

> The history of Russian Jewry is a troubled and tragic one. It was and remains a story of suffering and achievement, of longing and fulfillment, of hope and disappointment. Terrible incidents haunt its path. Deeds of sublime heroism, and acts of vile barbarism, serve both as its hallmark and as its curse. Yet throughout, the Jews of Russia preserved their humanitarian instincts, their love of learning, and their vision of a better world.[3]

In order to comprehend the contemporary awakening of Jewish consciousness in the Soviet Union, one must understand that for hundreds of years, Russia was a bastion of anti-Semitism. From the sixteenth century onward, the saga of the Jews under Czarist rule in Russia was one of unmitigated oppression. The anti-Semitic doctrine of the Russian Orthodox church encouraged the Czars to find in the Jew an ideal scapegoat for the miseries inflicted on the Russian peasantry.

In the early 1700s, all Jews were banished from Russia. Most fled to the Polish territories. Later in the century, when Poland was conquered by Russia, laws were passed creating the Pale of Settlement, a region beyond which Jews were not permitted to live. More than five million Jews, representing 94 per cent of Russian Jewry, resided in this district which covered nine hundred and fifty-three thousand square kilometres from the Baltic Sea to the Black Sea. Within the "Pale" were small, confined areas called *shtetls*. Each shtetl had at least one small synagogue where Jews gathered to socialize as well as to pray.

Under the rule of Czar Alexander II (1855–1881), peasant serfdom was abolished and prosperous Jewish merchants were permitted to live "beyond the Pale." The Czar's assassination by a revolutionary's bomb on March 1, 1881, was followed by a virulent anti-Semitic campaign carried out by a population who blamed the Jews for the Czar's death. The first wave of pogroms that raged through south-western

Russia from 1881 to 1884 resulted in the looting of Jewish shops and synagogues and the destruction of property owned by Jews.[4]

Alexander's successor, Czar Alexander III, introduced the discriminatory "May Laws" of 1882 that imposed severe economic, social, academic and political restrictions on the Jewish population. He mandated that one-third of the Jewish population be annihilated, one-third convert and one-third emigrate.[5] These restrictions and the fear of more pogroms led to a massive migration of Russian Jewry that continued, unabated, until 1914. Two million Jews emigrated to North America, two hundred thousand to Great Britain and sixty thousand, drawn by their desire to return to the land of their forefathers, emigrated to Palestine.

The first settlers in Palestine inhabited mostly wasteland, sand dunes and malarial marsh that they drained, irrigated and began to farm.[6] This wave of Russian emigration carried Jewish leaders who were to become world renowned: Chaim Weizmann, Zalman Shazar, Moshe Sharett and Levi Eshkol.[7]

For those Jews who remained in Russia, life under Czarist rule became more oppressive. The theory of a Jewish conspiracy to control the world was legitimized by the publication, in 1895, of *The Protocols of the Elders of Zion*, one of the most infamous anti-Semitic documents in history.[8] Purported to be the minutes of clandestine meetings of the first World Jewish Congress, it was concocted and circulated by Russian secret service agents.[9] This obscene treatise further incited anti-Jewish hatred.

During the same period, anti-Semitic incidents in France, as typified by the Dreyfus case, convinced Theodor Herzl, a journalist from Vienna, that survival for Diaspora Jewry was precarious. Obsessed with the vision of a renewed Jewish homeland, Herzl became the moving spirit for the first Zionist Congress held in Basel, Switzerland, in 1897. In that assembly, two hundred delegates proclaimed their Zionism to the world. Their aim was the creation of a home for Jews in Palestine, a land to which they had not held title for two thousand years.[10] Zionism became the national liberation movement of the Jewish people.

The second wave of pogroms began in Kishinev in 1903, resulting in the deaths of forty-nine Jews. In addition to the killings and lootings involved in the six hundred pogroms that took place during the next three years, the most disquieting feature was the endorsement of these pogroms by the Russian government. It was revealed that the pamphlets calling for the attacks had been printed on the press of the Czar's secret police.[11] The terror of the pogroms, coupled with the 1912 trial of Mendel Beilis, a Kiev Jew who was charged with the alleged ritual murder of a Christian child, caused a major upsurge in Jewish support for Zionism.[12] This prompted the second large migration to Palestine known as the *Second Aliyah*.

In October 1917, the Bolsheviks, led by Leon Trotsky and Vladimir Lenin, seized power in Russia and created the Union of Soviet Socialist Republics (USSR) with Lenin as leader.

Most Jews had welcomed the Communist Revolution, supporting any movement to overthrow the Czar. A sudden flourishing of Zionist youth groups and the publication of Yiddish books suggested that the situation for Jews was improving; however, true equality continued to elude them. When Lenin was asked by the Bund, Russia's largest Jewish organization, where the Jews would fit into his new society, his answer was, "emancipation and assimilation." The Jews were to disappear.

Anti-Semitism persisted in Communist Russia and the Ukraine with increasing fervour. In 1919, Jews once again became targets of terrifying pogroms. This news was met with fury in the free world. The Canadian Jewish Congress (CJC), created that same year to deal with problems of relief and resettlement for Jewish refugees from Eastern Europe, at the request of its president, Montreal's Lyon Cohen, organized a mass protest against the pogroms. "We all remember the touching demonstrations which were organized in Montreal, Toronto, Winnipeg and the other cities all over the Dominion," wrote H. M. Caiserman, secretary of the CJC, in his first annual report, "protests which together with the demonstrations in all other countries had partially, at least, stopped the pogroms."[13] The demonstrations served to reinforce the CJC's position as the unifying assembly responsible for a wide program of action of national and international concern to the Canadian Jewish community.

In 1924, Josef Stalin rose to power in the USSR and immediately expunged the Politburo of his Jewish rivals – Trotsky, Kamenev and Zinoviev.[14] Hebrew and Yiddish publications were officially banned. Synagogues were converted into storehouses. Jewish schools and clubs were shut down. All attempts to promote Zionism were repressed.

Karl Marx, the founder of Communist theory, was the grandson of two Orthodox rabbis. Converted to Christianity as a young child by his father, Marx became a virulent anti-Semite.[15] His dictum, "religion is the opium of the people," inspired the Soviet Politburo to introduce a state doctrine of atheism.[16] This doctrine to eradicate religious belief was promoted by a mass educational campaign and enforced by deportation, exile and imprisonment.

Jews became targets of this hostile stance. Although recognized as a Soviet nationality, sixteenth in size among the hundred nationalities of the Soviet Union, Jews were suppressed by an atheistic state that, on one hand, sought their total assimilation, and on the other, singled them out as Jews. Unlike Ukrainians, Estonians, Armenians and many other ethnic groups, Jews lacked an indigenous region where they could speak their own language, practice their religion and teach their cultural heritage to their children.[17]

As a solution to Russia's Jewish problem, Stalin proposed Birobidjan, a sparsely populated rural area in the Soviet Far East, as the Jewish autonomous region, and in 1934, Birobidjan was assigned as a Jewish homeland. Some Canadian Jews believed that Soviet Jews were well served by Birobidjan and offered to assist them financially. In April 1937, a campaign in the Montreal Jewish community raised $5,000 to purchase a Linotype for the Birobidjan Jewish community.[18]

Geographic isolation and a harsh climate with heavy rains and infestations of insects discouraged settlement. Only fifty thousand of a projected three hundred thousand Jews settled in Birobidjan, with many becoming absorbed into the general population.[19]

On June 22, 1941, the Soviet Union was invaded by Nazi Germany under the command of Adolph Hitler. Of the half-million Jews who served in the Red Army against the Nazis, more than two hundred thousand fell in battle. Known to be loyal soldiers, many Jews were declared war-heroes and as such, were decorated by the Soviet government after the war.

Between 1939 and 1945, six million Jews, most of whom were from Eastern Europe, were systematically annihilated by the Nazis, in what is considered to be the lowest point in the moral history of mankind. At that time, nothing about the "Holocaust" was reported in the Soviet press.

When news of Hitler's deeds reached the West, pressure was brought to bear at the United Nations to establish a homeland for the Jewish people. On November 29, 1947, the UN General Assembly voted on the partition of Palestine into separate Jewish and Arab states. The draft resolution was approved by thirty-three countries in a vote that took three minutes. Thirteen nations voted against the resolution and ten abstained. With the exception of Cuba and Greece, every state that voted against partition was either Muslim or Asian. Since the Soviet Union was still revelling with the allies in the glory of victory over the Nazis, Soviet ambassador Andrei Gromyko voted with the Western countries.[20]

In January 1948, Solomon Mikhoels, a prominent Jewish actor and director of the Moscow Yiddish Theatre, was murdered by Stalin's secret police. This marked the beginning of an intensely anti-Semitic phase in Stalin's policy. Within days of Mikhoel's death, the Yiddish Theatre and all Jewish schools were closed. Linotype machines, on which Hebrew books were set, were smashed and more than four hundred leading Jewish writers and scientists were arrested and sent to labour camps.[21]

Israel came into existence through a fortuitous window in history, which opened for a few months between 1947 and 1948. The Jewish state declared its independence on May 14, 1948 and Israeli flags were raised in nations around the globe.

On the heels of the declaration of Israeli statehood, six Arab armies invaded the new country.[22] The major handicap facing Israel was a nearly worldwide boycott of armament sales. Through a historical quirk, Soviet dictator Stalin allowed Israel to purchase arms through his satellite state, Czechoslovakia.[23] Although the loss of six thousand lives (1 per cent of Israel's population) was devastating, when the final cease-fire was declared by the United Nations in January 1949, Israel was in control of the Negev in the south and the Galilee in the north. Jerusalem was divided in two, with the new neighbourhoods under Jewish control, and the Old City, including the Western Wall, Judaism's holiest site, ruled by Jordan.[24]

David Ben-Gurion, Israel's founding prime minister, invited Russian-born Golda Meir[25] to serve as Israel's first ambassador to the Soviet Union. Meir recalled the Israeli delegation's visit to the Moscow synagogue on the eve of Rosh Hashana (the Jewish New Year) in 1948. "Instead of the two thousand Jews who usually came to the synagogue on the holidays, a crowd of close to fifty thousand people was waiting for us . . . Within seconds they had surrounded me, lifting me bodily, almost crushing me, saying, 'Nasha Golda, Our Golda,' over and over again. Eventually they parted ranks and let me enter the synagogue, but there too, the demonstration went on . . . Without speeches or parades, without any words at all really, the Jews of Moscow were proving their profound desire – and their need – to participate in the miracle of the establishment of the State of Israel and I was the symbol of the State for them."[26]

Following the demonstration in Meir's honour by Jews who exhibited a profound loyalty to the Jewish homeland, Stalin reversed his support for an independent Jewish state and condemned Zionists as "enemies of the people." He disbanded the Jewish anti-Fascist committee and encouraged the systematic persecution of Jews, purging them from public office and deporting them in large numbers to Siberia.

From the end of 1948 until his death in 1953, Stalin's paranoia about a Jewish capitalist conspiracy resulted in a vituperative anti-Semitic campaign in the Soviet press. Anti-Semitism became state policy. Jews were identified as aliens, rootless "cosmopolitans" and Zionist agents of American imperialism.[27]

News of the Soviet dictator's anti-Semitic invective reached the West. In June 1951, Israel's foreign minister Moshe Sharett declared over Kol Yistoel radio that Israel had not forgotten the Jews in the Soviet Union. Immediately after his announcement, the Israeli Embassy in Moscow received its first request for an emigration visa. It was from Tova Lerner, a 76-year-old woman from Czernowitz, in the Ukraine. Her Israeli passport was stamped "Tel Aviv, June 19, 1951."[28]

The Soviet campaign to liquidate Jewish cultural leaders peaked on August 12, 1952, with the murder of twenty-six prominent Yiddish writers. The best known of these were Dovid Bergelson, Itzik Feffer, Peretz Markish, Dovid Hofstein and Leib Kvitko. The writers were imprisoned, tortured and killed in secrecy in the basement of Moscow's notorious Lubianka Prison, headquarters of the dreaded Ministry of State Security, precursor of the KGB.[29]

Five months later, on January 13, 1953, fourteen Jewish doctors were arrested and charged with a conspiracy to poison Stalin and other Communist Party leaders. When the alleged "Doctors' Plot" was reported by Moscow news services it commanded immediate international attention.[30] "Tomorrow may be too late," was the headline of an article written by US Senator Herbert H. Lehman, that appeared in many North American newspapers. It concluded, "We who enjoy the blessings of free America, must protest on behalf of those millions whom terror has silenced. We must express our anger and resentment against the most brutal tyranny of our time . . . We should expose all the criminal acts the Kremlin has committed against millions of people, for the Jews are only the latest victims."[31] Stalin's sudden death on March 6, 1953 rescued the doctors from their probable fate.

A meeting that had been planned weeks earlier was held on March 8 at Her Majesty's Theatre in Montreal. Monroe Abbey, chairman of the CJC's Eastern Region, presided over two thousand Montreal Jews who had come to demonstrate against "Anti-Semitism in Russia and Satellite Countries." The English and Yiddish banner that was strung across the stage read: "We protest red slurs against the Jewish people. All Jews are Brothers. We condemn the new false accusations about the blood conspiracy of the twentieth century."[32]

The resolution adopted that evening declared solidarity with Israel. It called upon the Soviet authorities to facilitate the exit of Jewish residents to join their brothers in other countries and it appealed to the Canadian government to raise the issue of Soviet anti-Semitism at the United Nations.[33]

Chapter 2

Stirrings of Canadian Support

For a few months after Stalin's death, under the leadership of Georgi Malenkov, the repressive measures against Soviet Jews abated. When Nikita Khrushchev was appointed head of the Communist Party in 1954, he systematically destroyed what little organized Judaism had survived the Stalinist era. Anti-Jewish policies were restored and synagogues, once too numerous to count, were reduced to a mere handful.

The fate of Soviet Jewry was not a priority on the Western Jewish agenda. Most Jewish leaders were convinced that the Iron Curtain was impenetrable. The government of Israel, however, did not share this belief. The Soviet Union had the second largest Jewish population in the world and Israeli leaders felt responsible for its survival. In an attempt to reach out to Soviet Jews, Israeli prime minister David Ben-Gurion sent Nechemiah Levanon, a Jew of Baltic origin, on a secret mission to Moscow. Levanon was a member of Kibbutz Kfar Blum in northern Israel. His fluency in Russian and his experience as the farm manager of Kfar Blum made him an ideal choice as the agricultural attaché with the Israeli Embassy. Even his fellow kibbutz members were unaware that Levanon's real responsibility in the Soviet Union was to communicate with Jews.

In Moscow, Nechemiah Levanon and his team of diplomats attended concerts and other cultural events. They discovered that by walking with a Hebrew newspaper folded under their arms during intermission, Jews would approach them, albeit cautiously, and meetings could be arranged. During a two-year period, the Israelis met with Jews in the privacy of their own homes, in a dozen Soviet cities. However, their operation was not as covert as they had believed. In

July 1955, Levanon was caught in a Soviet Jew's apartment. That same evening, about thirty Jews were arrested in Moscow and several other cities. Later, Levanon and two of his colleagues were accused of "anti-Soviet" activity and were expelled from the Soviet Union.[1]

Nechemiah Levanon brought evidence back to Prime Minister Ben-Gurion that the Soviet regime condemned the Jews to total alienation from their culture, heritage and language. He had discovered that despite a virulent anti-Semitic propaganda campaign, more and more Soviet Jews sought to maintain their identity and learn about Israel and Jews in the Diaspora. Levanon suggested that the time had come to initiate in the West, a campaign on behalf of Soviet Jews.[2]

Lishkat Hakesher, Hebrew for "liaison bureau," became the Israeli government office in the Foreign Ministry from which the entire Soviet Jewry campaign was orchestrated. The office had been created by Shaul Avigur in 1952 for the redemption of Eastern European Jews.[3] At Ben-Gurion's request, Nechemiah Levanon was entrusted with the responsibility of establishing a special department for Soviet Jewry within Lishkat Hakesher. It was to operate under secrecy and make its reports available only to the prime minister. Western activists referred to Lishkat Hakesher as "the secret office" or "the office without a name."

The first step in implementing global efforts on behalf of Soviet Jewry was to enlarge Israel's diplomatic corps. Soviet Jewry desks were established within the Israeli Embassies in London and Paris and the Israeli Consulate in New York. The task of the emissaries who were dispatched to these posts was to develop personal contacts with the heads of Jewish organizations and sensitize them to the issue of Soviet Jewry.[4]

By 1956, the Soviet Jewry department with its own office within Lishkat Hakesher was established and Levanon returned to his kibbutz. As the magnitude of the task became known, he was recalled to the Tel Aviv office in 1959 to direct the entire campaign in the West.[5] Thus began a career for Nechemiah Levanon that ultimately earned him the unofficial title of "godfather" of the Soviet Jewry movement.

International opinion concerning Soviet Jewry had been roused in February 1956 through articles in the Warsaw Yiddish Communist newspaper *Folkshtime*. They noted that when Khrushchev denounced Stalin at the twentieth congress of the Communist party, he had glossed over the fact that Jews had been persecuted and murdered. That, coupled with Khrushchev's anti-Jewish and anti-Zionist policies, made it abundantly clear that the attitude toward Jews had not changed.

In the summer of 1956, Joseph B. Salsberg of Toronto, who had served in the Legislative Assembly of Ontario as a member of the Communist Party from 1943 to 1955, visited the Soviet Union with three of his colleagues. On his first trip in 1939, he had discussed the deterioration of Soviet Jewish life with the head of the International Communist Party, but had not been able to pursue the issue because World War II intervened.

"I had a personal agenda on my second trip," recalled Salsberg. "It was to discuss the Jewish question with Soviet leaders."[6] During Salsberg's meetings in Moscow, Khrushchev's junior ministers admitted that Jews were being dismissed from positions of prominence in republics and replaced with Soviet intelligentsia. "The final session of those talks took place in the presence of Mr.Khrushchev in his own office," Salsberg said. "When I asked him directly about his speech at the twentieth congress, Khrushchev responded by saying: 'Our enemies are trying to exploit my speech to create anti-Soviet and anti-communist sentiment. But another month, and another month, and it will be forgotten.'"[7]

Salsberg was convinced that deep anti-Semitic views had penetrated the Soviet leadership. Upon his return to Canada, he renounced his Communist party affiliation and refused to run in the next provincial election. He wrote a series of articles in the Canadian Yiddish weekly *Vokhenblat* and in the American and Canadian Communist press, expounding the dangers to the Soviet Jewish community.[8]

The existence of a community of Jews in the USSR forty years after the Bolshevik revolution was a contradiction in terms. In truth, the Jews should have been absorbed into the mainstream of Soviet communist society. A combination of cultural peculiarities, audacity and a vibrant, unconquerable spirit kept Judaism alive under the yoke of Soviet tyranny.

It was difficult to estimate exactly how many Jews were living in the Soviet Union at that time. The 1959 census recorded 2,267,814 persons of Jewish nationality. It was presumed that many Jews preferred to declare they were Russians by nationality. They could freely do so because the census takers did not ask for documented proof. A verbal statement was sufficient. It is estimated that there were more than three million Jews in the USSR in 1959, and although the Jews represented only 1 per cent of the total population, it was suggested that they comprised 5 per cent of the intelligentsia.

The first international conference on Soviet Jewry took place on September 15, 1960, in Paris. It was organized by Meir Rosenne, who was serving as first counsellor responsible for Soviet Jewry with the Israeli Embassy. The Paris conference was frostily received by American Jewish leaders, in particular by Nahum Goldmann, president of the World Jewish Congress. Goldmann attended the Paris conference only after much persuasion by Ben-Gurion. Vehemently opposed to public advocacy, Goldmann believed that the Soviet Union would not respond to external pressure. He thought that Jews should not risk responsibility for reversing the process of *détente* and that any Western protests would result in serious repercussions against individual Soviet Jews.

In 1961, Meir Rosenne was transfered to the consulate general of Israel in New York, where he assumed the position he had held in Paris. Until that time, there had been no attempt by Israel's Soviet Jewry emissaries to initiate activity in Canada. Rosenne broke the pattern. He travelled to Montreal to meet with Saul Hayes, executive director of the CJC.[9] Although Hayes personally favoured speaking out on behalf of Soviet Jewry, since the CJC was an affiliate of the World Jewish Congress, he was obliged to endorse the diplomatic strategies of Nahum Goldmann.[10]

"The Canadians who were supportive of Soviet Jewry at that time could be counted on one hand," recalled Rosenne, many years later. "In Montreal, there was Rabbi David Hartman, who encouraged students to demonstrate outside the ship *Leningrad* that was docked in Montreal's harbour; Irwin Cotler, a law student who organized a student demonstration at McGill University; and Pinchas Eliav, the Israeli consul general posted in Montreal. In Toronto, there was community leader Nat Silver, the CJC's director of the Joint Community Relations Committee, Ben Kayfetz, and the spiritual leader of Beth Tzedec synagogue, Rabbi Stuart E. Rosenberg."[11]

Rabbi Rosenberg's interest in Soviet Jewry had been piqued by Joe Salsberg's articles and by reports of a delegation of the New York Board of Rabbis who had also visited the Soviet Union in 1956. Anxious to see for himself how Jews were faring under Communist rule, in 1957 Rosenberg applied for a visa to travel to the USSR. Each year thereafter he applied again, but did not receive a reply. Not until 1961 did the Soviets grant him a tourist visa.

Rabbi Rosenberg's trip to the USSR was the first such trip by a Canadian Jewish leader. He consulted with Saul Hayes and Meir Rosenne before his departure. Although Hayes was personally supportive of Rosenberg's trip, he reminded the rabbi that the CJC president Michael Garber endorsed WJC president Goldmann's opposition to "rattling" the Russians. "They want to deal quietly with Moscow behind the scenes and not pull the bear's tail," Hayes cautioned Rosenberg, "so when you return and speak or write about your trip, my advice is to soft-pedal your criticism of Soviet policy on the Jews."[12] Rosenne, on the other hand, gave Rosenberg one hundred Russian-Hebrew Jewish calendars and an El-Al flight bag to carry around in the streets – a sure way to attract Jews.

During his two weeks in Russia, Rabbi Rosenberg discovered that the policy of the Soviet government was aimed at the extinction of Jews as a national group through the prohibition of Jewish cultural, educational and religious institutions. "No words could convey the fantastic fright," recalled Rosenberg, "which has reduced these people to human caricatures and robbed them of their personality as individuals."[13]

When Rosenberg questioned a group of older men in Moscow's Choral Synagogue, they were quick to say that they received ample old age pensions, were free to practice their religion and that they possessed all the prayerbooks and religious articles they needed. Only when another man appeared from behind and whispered, "not a word of what they say is true," did Rosenberg comprehend the carefully inscribed hand-lettered Hebrew sign hanging prominently on the synagogue wall. The English translation was: "The world only subsists because of him who can keep his tongue in a time of controversy."[14]

The meeting that Rosenberg managed to arrange with Moscow's Rabbi Yehudah Leib Levin was one of the most unforgettable of his life. "Rabbi Levin removed a large brass ring from his pocket, packed tight with a bunch of keys, and led me to the entrance of his office," Rosenberg recalled. "First, one door was unlocked and we entered. Then he locked and bolted it. Then a second door and again the same procedure. The room was tiny, but lined with old editions of Jewish religious texts. We began bantering in Yiddish, exchanging small pleasantries. Levin repeated that Jewish life was better now under Khrushchev – whom he called our 'Great Leader for world peace' – than it was under 'the Terrible One,' Stalin. He sprinkled his conversation liberally with phrases like 'capitalist imperialism' and 'scientific socialism.'

"I plied him with questions, asking about Jewish rights in the Soviet Union and other questions that seemed to embarrass him. Then, suddenly without warning, switching from Yiddish to Hebrew, he dropped this 'bomb.' 'If you want to talk about "things in the world" we'll talk in Yiddish, but if you want to talk about the weather – "our Russian weather" – we must speak in Hebrew, which nobody here understands.'"[15]

In faltering, medieval Hebrew, Levin fired a series of questions at his visitor about Jewish life in Canada. Rosenberg began to describe the variety and richness of life for Jews in North America – the Jewish day schools, the institutes of higher learning, the growing number of Judaic scholars, the gifted Jewish writers and outspoken Jewish political leaders.

"As I continued," recalled Rosenberg, "Levin was becoming a strange mixture of emotions. His sad blue eyes were misting and filling up with tears, while a small hesitant smile was settling on his face. And then, the moment of truth. He stood up and moved toward me. I rose and we embraced tearfully. And the only words he said as he patted my back warmly were these: 'So you have a great and strong community of Jews in America. You must continue to be strong. We have no voice and your Jews do. You must never forget us. We will be finished if you do.'"[16]

The Soviet officials whom Rosenberg met spewed the party line. A. P. Sokolov, editorial secretary of *Moscow News*, informed Rosenberg that nobody wanted to leave Russia. "Here a man can fulfill his dream and become a total man, happy and free. Here all cultures can aspire and prosper. The only reason Jews have no cultural institutions today is that they don't want them . . . Jews are Russians and they have no need to be Jews."[17]

Sokolov's opinion was not shared by all the Jews. One evening Rosenberg walked with a Jew in a dimly lit street, far from the eyes and ears of others. Speaking in halting Yiddish, the young man said, "We have no Jewish schools, no Jewish newspapers, no Jewish theatres, no Jewish clubs, no Jewish organizations, but Jews can never give up their sense of belonging to the Jewish people."[18] He stealthily removed his "internal passport," a document that every Soviet citizen was required to carry at all times, from his pocket. On the line denoting "nationality" he pointed to *Yevrai,* the word identifying him as a Jew.

"I am sixty-three years old, tired and worn," said another man to Rabbi Rosenberg as they walked along quiet streets at midnight, "but I'd walk all the way to Israel with pack in hand and so would hundreds of thousands of other Jews, if we only had the chance."[19]

The basic question Rosenberg posed everywhere he went was, "Will Jews survive as Jews?" There were two firm and confident answers to this query. Russian officials answered, "They can but they won't," and Jews said, "We dare not, but we will!"[20]

These stories appeared in "A Rabbi Reports from Russia," an eight-part series written for *The Toronto Star.* The series was syndicated in newspapers across Canada and the United States and translated into Hebrew for publication in *Ma'ariv*, Israel's largest circulation daily newspaper.

Rosenberg contended that the time had come for activity on behalf of Soviet Jewry to be initiated in Canada, but he was thwarted by CJC leaders, who, like their American counterparts, were paralyzed into inaction by Nahum Goldmann's position.[21] Frustrated, Rosenberg approached Canadian prime minister John Diefenbaker, who agreed to champion the issue.

"On the international stage, the USSR pretends that it abhors discrimination. The record, however, speaks to the contrary," stated Diefenbaker in a speech to the Canadian Association for Labor Israel on the occasion of its presentation to him of the "Histadrut Society Humanitarian Award." "Why should a powerful nation stoop to deprive its citizens of their religion and of the traditional symbols used in religious observances? What justification can there be to deprive Jews of unleavened bread at the Passover? The Soviet leaders must not be allowed to conclude that the world outside is indifferent. Silence in the face of injustice will be taken as acquiescence."[22]

Diefenbaker addressed the issue of Soviet Jewry with Jewish audiences and also raised the subject with Soviet ambassador Miroshnichenko, later that year. He was presumed to have been the first world leader to do so.[23]

In August 1962, Rabbi Rosenberg attended a meeting in New York City that featured, as its guest speaker, the renowned American Jewish philosopher Rabbi Abraham Joshua Heschel. Heschel drew attention to the fact that one-third of the world's Jewish population was denied the right to live as Jews or to return to their homeland. "Political experts may rebuke us for calling attention to a minor issue when major issues are at stake," Heschel professed, "yet the process of liquidating a great Jewish community is not a minor issue. Should we not be ready to go to jail in order to end the martyrdom of our Russian brethren . . . to arrange sit-ins, protests, days of fasting and prayer, public demonstrations to which even Russian leaders will not remain indifferent? The voice of our brother's agony is crying to us! How can we be silent? How can we remain passive? How can we have peace of mind or live with our conscience?"[24]

Fuelled by Heschel's words, Rosenberg carried on his crusade from the pulpit at Beth Tzedec synagogue and through articles in the press. Editorials about the Soviet treatment of its Jewish population began to appear in Toronto newspapers. "Premier Khrushchev has repudiated Stalin, but the spirit of Stalin lives on in the Soviet policy toward the Jews . . . Jews find themselves in an inextricable vise. They are not allowed to assimilate or to live full Jewish lives, or to emigrate to Israel or other countries where they may live freely as Jews."[25]

Between July 1961 and March 1963 in the Soviet Union, death sentences were imposed for "economic crimes," which included "currency speculation," "embezzlement of foodstuffs," "counterfeiting of coins," "speculation in fruit," "speculation in footwear" and "plundering of public property." Of the one hundred and ten citizens sentenced to death by shooting, sixty-eight were Jews.[26]

In the fall of 1963, news reached the West that a Soviet rabbi had been sentenced to death. The CJC president Michael Garber asked the secretary of state for external affairs, Paul Martin, to raise the issue with the Soviets. Martin's written response indicated that he was uncertain of the effectiveness of such representation. Garber responded to Martin's skepticism:

> Since receipt of your letter of October 30, 1963, I have pondered the view expressed that any representations you might make to the Soviet government on behalf of a rabbi condemned to death would emphasize the foreign ties and might provoke a renewed drive against the Jews.
>
> The Soviet government knows, of course, that the Jews of Russia have no foreign ties. The Soviet press gives wide publicity to the discriminatory and harsh treatment of the Jews. This has called forth protests throughout the civilized world, including governments . . . There is reason to believe that the Soviet government is now eager to create a favourable image in the eyes of Western governments and might listen to the criticisms of its seemingly anti-Jewish policies . . . somehow, I dread the ineluctable conclusion that the civilized world should remain silent in the face of acts of an oppressor for fear that any criticism might lead to greater oppression. It is more likely that silence might lead to greater severity of treatment.[27]

Garber's letter convinced Martin to alter his position and he brought the Canadian government's concern to the attention of the Soviet ambassador. The Soviet response was one that Martin became accustomed to hearing during his tenure from 1963 to 1968 in Prime Minister Lester Pearson's cabinet. "You deal with the internal policies of your country and we will deal with ours."[28]

Soviet Jewry interest was sparked in the United States on October 21, 1963, when the Jewish Minorities Research Bureau, under the direction of Moshe Decter, held a conference in New York on "The Status of Soviet Jews."[29] It was sponsored by many American political and religious luminaries.[30] The conference drew from a wide spectrum of Jews and non-Jews in the New York area and became a springboard for the planning of a nation-wide symposium scheduled to take place a few months later in Washington.

Rabbi Stuart Rosenberg was still seeking support from the Canadian Jewish community and implored Saul Hayes to embrace tangibly the issue of Soviet Jewry.[31] His persistence finally bore fruit. Hayes convinced Rabbi S. M. Zambrowsky, chairman of CJC's National Religious Welfare Committee, to convene a country-wide conference of rabbis to deal with the troubling issue of Soviet Jewry.

In January 1964, more than sixty rabbis from across Canada travelled to Ottawa to attend an All-Canadian Rabbinic Conference: "Jews in the Soviet Union." It was chaired by Rosenberg and had as its special guest The Honourable Paul Martin. Rabbi Rosenberg cited examples of how the observance of both religious and secular life for Jews living in Communist Russia was increasingly restrictive. Martin showed great sensitivity to the issue and expressed a deep understanding of Soviet discrimination against its Jewish population. "I give you this assurance," Martin said, "that the Canadian government is concerned with this matter and will continue to make known its feelings on the subject."[32]

A resolution, calling for equal religious rights for Jews of the USSR, was passed that day and submitted to the Soviet ambassador in Ottawa along with the request for a private meeting. The meeting took place on March 10, 1964, when Rabbi Zambrowsky, Rabbi

Rosenberg and Sam Lewin, director of CJC's Eastern Region, were received by Counsellor A.Y. Popov of the Soviet Embassy. The purpose of their visit was to discuss anti-Semitic propaganda in Soviet literature and the media and the absence of religious articles necessary for prayer in synagogues.

After listening respectfully to their presentation, Popov asked the group to identify in writing the religious articles to which they referred. He presented his guests with an English language copy of a recent Soviet publication, "The Soviet Union Today," which included a photograph of Jews in a Moscow synagogue.

A few days later, Rosenberg documented the issues of Jewish concern in a letter addressed to Popov. He enclosed an anti-Semitic article from a Minsk newspaper and referred to *Judaism without Embellishment,* written by Nazi collaborator Trofim Kichko, which depicted Judaism as a philosophy of hypocrisy, bribery and greed.

The Rabbi also drew attention to the photograph taken in Moscow's Choral Synagogue, which had appeared in the material given him by Popov. "You will come to understand in visual terms, with the aid of your own photograph, that more than two-thirds of the worshippers shown do not have prayer shawls. Even Soviet Jews who obviously wish to preserve the Jewish religion under the free Soviet constitution do not possess the elementary religious articles required for the practice of their faith." Rosenberg's letter concluded: "One of our purposes in Ottawa was to discuss the possibility of Canadian Jews sending such articles to the Jews of Russia. Your response was that they did not need them. Your own photograph, however, reveals the true nature of the situation."[33]

Rabbi Rosenberg continued his private advocacy campaign. He asked John Diefenbaker, then leader of the opposition, to address the issue of the Soviet Union's refusal to permit the importation of matzah for Passover. The former prime minister appealed to Prime Minister Lester Pearson to raise the issue with Soviet authorities.[34]

The Washington symposium on Soviet Jewry that took place in April 1964 was co-chaired by Senator Jacob Javits, Senator Abraham Ribicoff and Rabbi Abraham Joshua Heschel. It attracted leaders from major American Jewish organizations, as well as the CJC.[35] The American Jewish Conference on Soviet Jewry was born at that meeting.[36]

Another energetic American force in the emerging campaign to free Soviet Jews was Jacob Birnbaum, who founded the Student Struggle for Soviet Jewry (SSSJ) that same year. This group of student activists, headed by Glenn Richter, was dedicated to public protest with grassroots support. After staging Soviet Jewry rallies, marches and demonstrations at American universities, the SSSJ began to send information about their activities to Jewish organizations on Canadian campuses.

The first Canadian branch of the SSSJ was formed at McGill University at the end of 1964. Among the organizers of the first Canadian-initiated Soviet Jewry program was Irwin Cotler, a law student with a reputation as an outstanding university debater. Held at McGill's Redpath Hall in December 1964, the event featured Moshe Decter as guest speaker. It attracted five hundred students.

"Soviet leaders are becoming increasingly sensitive to Western public opinion," Decter told the students that afternoon. "If sufficiently pressured, they might change their policies. The fate of Soviet Jewry is partly in your hands."[37]

Answering Decter's appeal, the McGill students passed a resolution condemning the Soviet government's persecution of Jews and demanded that they be permitted the same rights enjoyed by other minority groups.

"This event presaged the activist era that was to follow," recalled Cotler, many years later. "It reflected the importance of students as advocates of the Soviet Jewry movement and served as a program of action that had a relevance far beyond the 1960s."[38]

Canadian Jewish community leaders were still divided over the most effective method of dealing with the Soviet Jewish problem.[39] Michael Garber was still convinced that the interests of Soviet Jews were best served through private discussions with Soviet government leaders. Stuart Rosenberg believed that the issue of Soviet Jewry should be transferred from the diplomatic arena into the streets.

In November 1964, a successful political coup in the Soviet Union ousted Khrushchev. For a short time, Leonid Brezhnev, Alexei Kosygin and Nikolai Podgorny shared power, until Brezhnev emerged as sole leader. The implications of these events for Soviet Jews were unclear. What was becoming clear to the Israeli government, however, was that in order to effect change in Soviet policy, the American administration would have to become involved.

In the spring of 1965, Nechemiah Levanon left the Lishkat Hakesher office in Tel Aviv to serve as first counsellor responsible for Soviet Jewry at the Israeli Embassy in Washington, D.C.[40] In this capacity, he established contact with American government representatives, but was careful always to remain behind the scenes.

Soon after his arrival, Levanon was responsible for a mass demonstration in support of Soviet Jewry in Lafayette Square. "I stood all excited, trembling," remembered Levanon. "Thousands of Jews were there. Not just Washington Jews. These were Jews who came from the entire East coast. This great demonstration came about after many years of great hardships. It was a long, long journey to lead Jews out of the wilderness of ignorance, apathy and disbelief in the possible success of the struggle for Soviet Jews and the redemption of our brethren in the Soviet Union."[41]

In Canada, Rosenberg's tenacity was beginning to pay off. In May 1965, the issue of Soviet Jewry was raised at the fourteenth plenary assembly of the Canadian Jewish Congress. Discussions centred around the anti-Jewish attitude of the Soviet authorities, the closing of synagogues and the few remaining Jewish schools, obstacles to the baking of matzah, the isolation of Russian Jews from their brethren in the rest of the world and their inability to join their families in Israel and in other countries. Five resolutions dealing with these issues were raised and passed as CJC policy and the national executive was urged to take all steps that would help to alleviate the plight of Jews in the Soviet Union.[42]

CJC president Michael Garber began to compromise his position. In April 1966, he chaired the National Leadership Conference, "Jews in Russia," attended by three hundred delegates from Montreal,

Ottawa, Kingston, Cornwall, Toronto and Winnipeg. It involved the participation of The Right Honourable John Diefenbaker, MP James Walker, MP David Lewis, Rabbi Stuart Rosenberg. and Claude Ryan, editor of *Le Devoir.*

A resolution was passed that day, calling upon the Soviet government to restore cultural and religious rights to Soviet Jews.[43] According to Rosenberg, the meeting was "unenthusiastic and overly cautious when it came to putting forward a program of action."[44] It was recommended that a national committee on behalf of Soviet Jewry be established, but the idea was not pursued actively.[45]

Resolutions passed at conferences attended by a small number of Jews were not enough to propel a Soviet Jewry campaign. Rosenberg tried to awaken the Toronto Jewish community. In the fall of 1966, he invited Elie Wiesel to address a city-wide meeting at his synagogue. Wiesel's recently published *The Jews of Silence* was earning him international acclaim.

Speaking before an overflow audience, Wiesel described how during Simchat Torah 1965, thousands of Jews had gathered outside Moscow's Choral Synagogue to mark the completion of the reading of the Torah for the year and its beginning anew. Inside, there were processions and communal singing. "Men who had not seen a Torah all year long were embracing and kissing it with a love bequeathed to them from generations past," he said. "Old men lifted their grandchildren onto their shoulders saying: 'Look and remember'."[46]

Wiesel explained that the crowd spilled out onto the street and into the courtyards, joining thousands of men, women and children who were dancing and singing, all demonstrating their unshakable solidarity with the Jewish people. He wandered from one to the other, shaking hand after hand. "Thank you," he said to them. "Thank you for remaining Jewish."[47]

Elie Wiesel's speech struck a tender chord. "I went to Russia," he murmured to the Toronto audience, "drawn by the silence of its Jews and I brought back their cry. What torments me most is not the 'Jews of Silence' I met in Russia, but the silence of the Jews I live among today."[48]

A few months before Rabbi Stuart Rosenberg's death in 1989, he commented about the early stirrings of Canadian support. "Activity in Canada was really no different than in other countries. In the mid-1960s, the average Jew was sleeping on the Soviet Jewry issue, but later, Soviet Jewry became a moving vehicle for the Jewish community world-wide. A great deal of Jewish activity in North America needs a motor that is dramatic, exciting and salvational. This motor took over the entire Jewish community."[49]

Rabbi Stuart Rosenberg's initiatives resulted in a full-scale Canadian effort to liberate Jews from the Soviet Union.

Chapter 3

Jewish Consciousness Awakens

Article 12/2 of the Universal Declaration of Human Rights, enacted on December 10, 1948, states: "Everyone has the right to leave any country, including his own, and to return to his country."[1] Although the Soviet Union was signatory to this article, it did not abide by it. Anyone wishing to leave was viewed by the Soviets as a traitor. The few emigration visas issued annually were generally given to pensioners who were a drain on the state anyway. Officially, emigration from the USSR was not permitted.

The first indication that the USSR might revise its closed-door emigration policy arose from a response by Soviet premier Alexei Kosygin during a press conference in Paris on December 3, 1966. When asked about the possibility of the reunification of Soviet families separated by World War II, Kosygin replied: "We, on our side, shall do all possible, if some families want to meet or even if some among them would like to leave us, to open for them the road."[2]

Viewed as an important departure from Khrushchev's policies, this statement was reported in the international press and appeared on the front page of *Izvestia*, the official organ of the Soviet government. Almost immediately, Soviet Jews began arriving at passport offices in many Soviet republics with copies of *Izvestia* under their arms.

Within weeks the Soviet government launched a domestic propaganda campaign which depicted frightful conditions awaiting Jews who wanted to emigrate to Israel. Two show trials were hastily mounted against Solomon Dolnik, a sixty-year-old pensioner, and his protégé Valentin Prussakov, arrested on charges of anti-Soviet agitation. They were sentenced to brief prison terms for distributing *samizdat* (underground) literature about Israel. The press reports labelling them as traitors for disseminating Zionist booklets obtained from Israeli diplomats were interpreted by Moscow's Jews as a sharp warning to avoid contact with foreigners.

Ironically, the propaganda campaign fueled the very feelings it set out to quash, especially among the younger generation of Jews. These feelings manifested themselves in public gatherings outside the Moscow synagogue on Jewish festivals and in the clandestine study of Hebrew which, for many, heightened the desire for *aliyah*.

The process of applying for a visa, however, was designed to thwart most potential applicants. Among the many conditions that had to be met were a *visov* (invitation) from Israel, a character reference from one's place of employment, official permission from living parents, formal withdrawal of children from school, and the payment of 900 roubles (US$1,000) for each family member who wished to emigrate. This fee represented more than one year's wages for the average Soviet citizen.

After all requirements were satisfied, the applicant submitted his documents to OVIR (Office for Visa Registration) along with a letter, requesting an emigration visa. If approved by OVIR, the visa was issued by the Dutch Embassy, Israel's diplomatic surrogate in Moscow. Most requests for a visa were denied and one had to wait six months to reactivate the entire process.

Political events in the Middle East gave the fledgling Soviet Jewry movement focus and drive. On June 5, 1967, Egypt and Syria, rich with Soviet-supplied military hardware and reinforced by a last-minute alliance with Jordan, attacked Israel. Within six days, Israel's army and air force inflicted an overwhelming defeat on the Arab armies on all three fronts, destroying hundreds of Russian-built tanks and MIG fighters.

While Jews the world over exploded with pride over Israel's victory in the Six Day War, Soviet delegate Nikolai Federenko branded Israel the aggressor in the United Nations Security Council. Kosygin announced the termination of diplomatic relations with Israel and revoked the visas of forty Jews, all of whom had given up their flats, sold their belongings and purchased airline tickets to Tel Aviv.

On June 13, 1967, his twentieth birthday, Yasha Kazakov, a Moscow engineering student, responded to his government's actions against Israel by renouncing his Soviet citizenship. "I ask to be freed from the humiliation of being considered a citizen of the Union of Soviet Socialist Republics," he wrote to the Soviet authorities. "I am a Jew, and as a Jew I feel that the State of Israel is my homeland . . . and like any other Jew, I have the inalienable right to live in that state." [3]

When there was no reply to his letter, Kazakov wrote another, this time to U Thant, secretary general to the United Nations, and delivered it to the U.S. Embassy. Aware that he was being followed, Kazakov was not surprised when he was arrested as he left the Embassy. This was the first of countless arrests, interrogations and harassments, all of which served to harden the young man's resolve.

At the same time, in Kiev, thirty-year-old radio engineer Boris Kochubievsky, publicly rejected a resolution citing Israel as the aggressor in the Six Day War. He was denounced by his colleagues at work and subjected to months of psychological harassment until he was forced to resign. During a routine search of Kochubievsky's apartment, the KGB found an essay he had written, "Why I am a Zionist."

A few days later, Kochubievsky wrote a letter to Communist party chief Brezhnev, declaring his desire to emigrate. "As long as I live, as long as I am capable of feeling, I shall devote all my strength to obtain an exit permit for Israel. And even if you should find it possible to sentence me for this, I shall anyway, if I live long enough to be freed, be prepared even then to make my way even on foot, to the homeland of my ancestors."[4] Copies of the letter were smuggled to the West.

Kazakov and Kochubievsky were two men in a vast network of courageous Jewish activists, which by the beginning of 1968 stretched from the Baltics to central Asia. Given the intense scrutiny of the KGB, communication between these Jews was a formidable achievement. Their educational system was a secret Hebrew school, their contact was coded telephone messages and their history and culture were expressed through *samizdat* literature. In this self-renewing organization, no member was indispensable. Whenever leaders departed for Israel, others took their place.

Jewish articles and books were passed among the activists from hand to hand. For many years, American author Leon Uris's *Exodus* was the Soviet Jew's strongest identification with Judaism and Israel. There were three different handwritten Russian versions in Riga alone, each translated by a different group, unaware of the others' existence.[5] *Exodus* became known as "the book," read in a single night by candle-light and passed from parent to child. "Never in my wildest fantasy," related Uris thirty-two years after the book was published, "did I believe my words would reach out and find the lost tribe of Israel, entombed in the Soviet Union."[6]

In the aftermath of the Six Day War, there was an outpouring of anti-Semitic propaganda, hatred and vindictiveness in the Soviet press. This prompted Charles A. Kent, chairman of Toronto's newly-created "Committee of Concern for Soviet Jewry," to convene a meeting with community leadership to discuss the possibility of protest.[7]

Young Canadians seized the moment and took to the streets. "March with Hundreds of Canadian Jewish Youth in Ottawa to protest the suppression of Jewish life in the Soviet Union," headlined flyers distributed among Jewish youth groups in Montreal and Toronto.[8] On November 5, 1967, students travelled by bus from Toronto and Montreal to join their Ottawa counterparts in a march from the Jewish Community Centre to the Soviet Embassy.

In the Fall of 1968, in Riga, a small group of Jews with Zionist leanings began to submit applications through their local OVIR. For some reason, the visas were approved and within weeks, several leaders were making arrangements to leave for Israel. Among this group were Dov Shperling and Leah Slovina, who arrived in Israel in January 1969.

If the Soviet strategy behind permitting some troublemakers from Riga to emigrate was to prevent the Zionist influence from spreading, it had the opposite effect. Jews in major cities in the Soviet Union began telephoning their relatives in Israel for an *invitation*, the treasured document that would initiate emigration proceedings.[9] The Soviet government had misjudged the suppressed Jewish identity. Instead of leaving the sea calm, the exit of the fortunate few rippled the entire ocean, creating waves of new applicants.[10]

For Yasha Kazakov, the twenty-year-old radio engineer, a year of interrogations, harassment and negative responses to his requests to emigrate caused him to change his tactics. He wrote a letter detailing the history of his emigration requests to Nechemiah Levanon, who was working the Soviet Jewry desk at the Israeli Embassy in Washington, and requested that the letter be publicized. Kazakov made seven copies of the letter that he entrusted to seven tourists to take out of the USSR, hoping that at least one would reach its destination.[11]

Upon receiving Kazakov's letter, Levanon submitted it to the editor of *The Washington Post*. It was published December 19, 1968. The text was reprinted and broadcast around the world. There was global fascination with the young man who had the courage to pit himself against the mighty Soviet bear. Two months later, the war between Yasha Kazakov and the Soviet Union ended. Kazakov departed Moscow for Israel on February 19, 1969.

Kiev activist Boris Kochubiyevsky was not so fortunate. He was brought to trial on May 13, 1969, on charges of "slandering the Soviet Socialist system" and sentenced to three years at hard labour. The evidence used against him was his essay, "Why I am a Zionist." The prosecution contended that the defendant had falsely declared that Jews were oppressed in the Soviet Union.

Details of Kochubiyevsky's trial were secretly documented and smuggled abroad by visiting tourists. Following the appearance of his story in *The New York Times*, a group of Jews picketed the Soviet Consulate in New York. The movement had acquired its first symbolic hero.

The few *olim* (immigrants) who had been active in the Soviet Union were not content to remain passive in Israel. Dov Shperling, Leah Slovina and Yasha Kazakov met with Shaul Avigur, who was still a significant power in Lishkat Hakesher in Tel Aviv. They hoped to convince him that Kol Yisroel radio should broadcast less socialist and kibbutz lore into the Soviet Union and more about Jewish history, Zionism and the meaning of Jewish festivals. Avigur explained that transmitting Jewish cultural information to the USSR would be regarded as anti-Soviet. They argued for the need to switch from quiet diplomacy to an aggressive worldwide campaign to force open the Iron Curtain. "Why is it," questioned Kazakov, "that Russian Jews are not afraid to risk their lives by sending letters and petitions to the West, yet the Israelis, living in safety and freedom, are fearful of publishing them?" Avigur was adamant. He refused to change his strategy. Secret negotiations with Soviet authorities had resulted in the emigration of a small number of Soviet Jews and he feared that publicity might terminate the whole process.[12]

In May 1969, Kazakov and Shperling approached Yona Ya'hav, chairman of the National Union of Israeli Students, and implored him to use university campuses to expose and promote the plight of Soviet Jewry. Ya'hav broached the subject with Avi Plaskov and Zvi Raviv, student heads of the foreign affairs committees at the Tel Aviv and Hebrew Universities. Raviv and Plaskov eagerly accepted the challenge and used the summer to plan for action in the fall.[13]

On August 19, 1969, Kazakov, Shperling and Slovina met with Prime Minister Golda Meir to try to persuade her to "go public" with the Soviet Jewish problem. The meeting was a dismal failure. The prime minister declared that "any Jew coming to Israel from the USSR should hang seven locks on his tongue to insure that the meager immigration would not stop."[14]

A few days later, Golda Meir received a letter signed by eighteen Jewish families from Tbilisi, Georgia, imploring the Israeli government to help them achieve their goal to emigrate. The letter ended by saying: "We will wait months and years, we will wait all our lives if necessary, but we will not renounce our faith and our hopes."[15] They asked that their letter be released to the Israeli media. No action was taken.

On October 16, 1969, classes at the Hebrew University in Jerusalem were suspended for two hours to enable students to attend the first campus demonstration for Soviet Jewry. Speakers Dov Shperling and

Yasha Kazakov informed their audience of the Soviet attitude toward Jews who desired to emigrate to Israel and declared that the time had come for vociferous demonstrations.

"The State of Israel is committing a crime," cried Zvi Raviv from the speakers' platform, "by behaving as though Stalin were still alive, and not recognizing that Russia wants acceptance by Western nations." He accused the Israeli government of inflexibility for not adjusting its policies to the new realities.

The demonstration was widely broadcast over Israeli radio. This led to an immediate reprimand of the student leaders by government officials, who threatened that if demonstrations continued, the leaders would be sent to the Sinai for four months of army duty. Undeterred, the students requested a meeting with the prime minister.

On October 27, 1969, the three Israeli student leaders were granted a meeting with Golda Meir and her aide, Simcha Dinitz. They informed the prime minister that they intended to organize demonstrations for Soviet Jewry on university campuses and to use recently arrived *olim* as speakers.

When Meir enquired as to why they felt compelled to demonstrate, Raviv remarked: "Twenty years from now, when my children ask me what I did for Soviet Jewry, I will have an answer for them, unlike my father's generation, who knew what the Nazis were doing to the Jews and did nothing."

"That's not true," retorted Golda Meir. "We sent paratroopers."

"Yes," Raviv replied, "thirty-seven of them."

The prime minister responded indignantly, "We didn't have a country."

"Right," Raviv answered softly. "But we do now."

A moment passed, and then Golda Meir turned to the students and asked,

"What is it that you want?"

On October 31, Dinitz contacted Yona Ya'hav and informed him that the Israeli government had changed its policy. It would promote the plight of Soviet Jewry and allow the prime minister, cabinet ministers and public officers to appear at public rallies with Soviet *olim*.[16]

Within days the Israelis were tested. Golda Meir received another letter from the Georgian families, as did Israel's ambassador to the United Nations, Yosef Tekoah. Both letters, like the first, urged the Israeli government to fight for the families' right to emigrate to Israel. From his office in Washington, Nechemiah Levanon entreated his prime minister to publicize the letter.

On November 10, 1969, Golda Meir broadcast the appeal of the Georgian Jews over Kol Yisroel radio. It was re-broadcast by Radio Liberty, The Voice of America and the BBC, and reported in *The New York Times,* which interpreted Israel's shift in policy as a "new phase in the struggle for Soviet Jewry."[17]

The Georgian Jews had set a new trend. Letters began to reach international bodies from many groups of Soviet Jews. These public appeals to the highest Soviet, Israeli and world authorities contradicted the Soviet contention that Jews were completely integrated into Soviet society and no longer identified with world Jewry.

"Had anyone predicted that there would be hunger strikes abroad, letters sent to the UN and the foreign press, demands for language and religious rights and emigration to Israel as recently as even two years ago, the prophecies would have been laughed off as wishful thinking," wrote CJC director Ben Kayfetz in Toronto's *Jewish Reporter.* "That Jews living in this milieu have had the fortitude to stand up and tell the world of their plight is the most welcome news we have heard in many years."[18]

In March 1970, as a protest against the Soviet government's denial of visas to his family in Moscow, Yasha Kazakov embarked on a hunger strike at the United Nations Plaza in New York. His action was opposed by the Israelis but supported enthusiastically by American Soviet Jewry activists, who came in large numbers to join him in his effort. The event received wide media coverage.

The Israeli government was embarrassed by charges that their lack of support for Kazakov reflected indifference toward the plight of Soviet Jews. After eight days of heated debate in the Knesset, UN ambassador Tekoah was instructed to petition the Soviet ambassador on Kazakov's behalf. The Soviets replied that the Kazakov family's application would be reviewed.[19]

Kazakov ended his hunger strike. He had secured victory on two fronts. The Israeli government had completely abandoned its policy of quiet diplomacy and the Soviet government had responded to a protest in an international forum.

Advocacy now went public in America. A "Declaration of Solidarity with Soviet Jews" was signed by thirteen hundred faculty members from universities across North America and appeared as an advertisement in *The New York Times*.[20] The ad concluded with these words: "We say to the Soviet government: for those who wish to live as Jews in the USSR, let them enjoy the full range of rights to which they are entitled. And for those who wish to leave for Israel or elsewhere to unite families and achieve personal fulfilment, we say, Let them go!"[21]

The Soviets began to issue public declarations repudiating claims that Jews were demanding exit visas. This outraged a group of Jews from Riga and Leningrad. They conceived a desperate plot to seize an aircraft at Leningrad's Smolny airport. Some members of the group purchased tickets to board the plane in Leningrad, while the rest planned to join them at an intermediate stop, take possession of the plane, and with group member Mark Dymshitz as their pilot, fly to Helsinki, and freedom.[22]

Neither plan nor plane got off the ground. On June 15, 1970, the morning of the operation, all sixteen members of both groups were arrested by Soviet police before they had even made a bid to seize the airplane.[23] Eleven people were brought to trial in Leningrad on December 15, 1970. The remaining five were to be tried at a later date. The charges brought against the first group were "preparing or attempting to commit treason, theft of State property on a large scale and anti-Soviet agitation and propaganda."[24]

There was no doubt that the defendants had committed offences under Soviet law, but none of these charges had ever earned lengthy prison terms.[25] The Soviet press portrayed the activists as agents of the Mossad, Israel's secret service agency. Motives for the attempted escape were not mentioned, nor that most members of the accused group had repeatedly and legally requested permission to emigrate to Israel.[26]

During the seven-day trial, only the defendants' immediate relatives were allowed to enter the courtroom. News correspondents and Western observers were denied access. Before the sentences were announced each defendant was permitted to make a brief statement. Sylva Zalmanson, the only female in the group, faced her accusers and declared, "I am stunned by the penalties the procurator has demanded, for something that has not been done . . . I don't think that Soviet law can consider anyone's intention to live in another country as treason . . . Israel is the country to which we Jews are bound spiritually and historically. Even now I do not doubt for a minute that sometime I will live in Israel." Zalmanson concluded her remarks by quoting Psalm 137, "If I forget thee, O Jerusalem, let my right hand lose its cunning."[27]

The eleven defendants and their relatives began chanting in Hebrew *Am Yisrael Chai* (The people of Israel live), followed by the recitation of the watchword of the Jewish people, *Sh'ma Yisra'el, Adonai Eloheinu, Adonai Echad* (Hear, O Israel, the Lord our God, the Lord is One).[28]

The Leningrad trial verdicts were announced on December 24, 1970. Eduard Kuznetsov, who had served seven years in prison for circulating *samizdat* literature and for taking part in unauthorized public poetry readings, and the pilot, Mark Dymshitz, were sentenced to death.[29] Kuznetsov's wife, Sylva Zalmanson, Josef Mendelevich, Uri Fedorov, Alexei Murzhenko, Leib Khnokh, Anatoly Altman, Boris Penson and Israel Zalmanson received sentences varying from eight to fifteen years of "strict regime" in labour camps.[30]

Within hours of the verdicts from Leningrad, thousands of messages and cables were dispatched to the Kremlin. Soviet embassies and consulates all over the world were besieged with demonstrators demanding commutation of the death sentences. Western communist and international socialist parties joined in the protest. The official newspaper of the French Communist party, *L'Humanité,* wrote, "We don't believe that an abortive attempt should be penalized by a death sentence which we hope – and we say it again – will not be applied."[31]

In a cable addressed to Soviet president Nikolai Podgorny, CJC president Monroe Abbey implored that the death sentences be commuted. As well, he requested intervention by the Canadian government. Under-secretary of state for external affairs A.E. Ritchie responded, "The Canadian government expressed to the Soviet government, through the Soviet ambassador in Ottawa, Mr. Boris T. Miroshnichenko, its concern on humanitarian grounds over the death sentence imposed on two of the accused in the Leningrad trials. Mr. Miroshnichenko has undertaken to report our views at once to Moscow."[32]

Canadians took to the streets to protest the harsh sentences. On December 30, 1970, thousands gathered in sub-zero weather in Toronto's Nathan Phillips Square where Rabbi W. Gunther Plaut, spiritual leader of Holy Blossom Temple, proclaimed, "We are free men here in this great land but as long as our brothers are in chains, we too are prisoners . . . We too have stood with our brothers in the dock at Leningrad . . . and awaited the verdict as if it were spoken to us. Brothers in Russia," continued Plaut . . . "when the Soviet state says: Forget God, forget your heritage, forget Israel, you say NO – and in saying NO, we say NO with you."[33]

The Jewish community of Ottawa staged a demonstration outside the Soviet Embassy. Members of Winnipeg's Jewish community held a candlelight vigil on the steps of their provincial legislature. Special services were held in synagogues in Halifax and Edmonton. There were rallies in Calgary and Vancouver and in the outlying regions of southwestern Ontario, including Hamilton, London, St. Catharines, Stratford and Sarnia.

Montreal students protested outside the Soviet Consulate, an imposing, three-storey building located in the last block of a dead-end street, surrounded by a two-metre-high iron fence with a locked gate. Cameras were placed at each corner of the building.[34]

"The vigil outside the consulate continued around the clock for seven days, from December 24, when the verdict was announced," remarked Mark Zarecki, one of the student organizers. "We walked around and around like prisoners in an exercise yard. Gradually the circle grew. By the end of the first day some community leaders joined the vigil. When it became apparent that no one was being arrested, more adults arrived, until hundreds of protesters participated."[35]

"It was magical," recalled CJC's executive vice-president Alan Rose. "There was no generation gap. Adults and students marched silently in single file in the middle of the street filled with fresh snow, slowly treading a circular path, which soon became a glistening circle of ice."[36]

Demonstrations took place globally. The world outcry for clemency for the Leningrad defendants had an effect. On December 31, the Soviets announced that death sentences imposed on Dymshitz and Kuznetsov had been commuted to fifteen years, and the sentences of Mendelevich, Fedorov and Murzhenko had been reduced.

A few days later, on January 3, 1971, seventy-five buses carried people from Toronto and Montreal to the nation's capital to join the Ottawa Jewish community in a rally to protest the Leningrad trial sentences. As thousands of Jews gathered outside the Parliament buildings, CJC leaders met inside with external affairs minister Mitchell Sharp.[37] When their meeting ended, the group led Sharp outside to the front steps. Taking the microphone, he greeted the crowd and remarked, "This demonstration of support is one that will not be unnoticed throughout the world."[38]

Newspapers headlined the stories: "Seven thousand parade in protest," "Jews march on Russian Embassy to protest trials," "Canadian Jewry cries: 'Let my people go!'"[39] Publicity from the Ottawa rally sparked demonstrations in small Ontario communities, which continued for weeks.[40]

Eighteen years later, Ben Kayfetz recalled the outpouring of support. "The news of the death sentences and lengthy prison terms were received with shock and grief in the Canadian Jewish community. No single issue had ever before produced such a sense of unity. The rallies were electrifying. Somehow the Leningrad trials had caught the imagination and indignation of Canadians everywhere."[41]

"The demonstrations worldwide on behalf of the Leningrad prisoners served to solidify public advocacy," Professor Irwin Cotler declared, "not only as a strategy, but as a medium of redress."[42] The world response to the Leningrad trials cast a dramatic light on the plight of Soviet Jewry and led to the support of some of the world's greatest intellectuals. At a rally in Paris, December 30, 1970, French writer and philosopher Jean Paul Sartre proclaimed, "Soviet Jewry has become a claim on the conscience of mankind."[43]

Chapter 4

The Canadian Community Organizes

After the desperate hijack plot by the Riga and Leningrad activists, Nechemiah Levanon felt frustrated that Lishkat Hakesher, the official government office, was unable to take a public stand. He recognized the need for a Soviet Jewry organization in Israel that could raise the level of consciousness of the Israeli public. To this end, in 1971, the Israel Public Council for Soviet Jewry (IPCSJ) was created to give expression to the primacy of Israel in the emigration struggle.[1]

Through this new organization, it became possible for families who were separated from their loved ones to be touched in a way that Lishkat Hakesher was unable to do. Ruth Bar-On, head of the Public Council's information department, was in contact with these families, who, on occasion, were successful in reaching their relatives in the Soviet Union by telephone, or through a letter that managed to arrive uncensored. Bar-On lent support and ensured that reliable information was disseminated to activists worldwide.

With Israel now firmly committed, the time had come to increase the level of world support and to form a mass movement for the redemption of Soviet Jews. The first World Conference on Soviet Jewry held in Brussels, Belgium February 23–25, 1971, brought Jews together from every corner of the world.[2] Of the seven hundred and fifty delegates, fourteen were from Canada.[3] The theme of the conference was *Schlach et ami* (Let my people go).

Through plenary sessions and strategy workshops, the delegates were addressed by former Soviet Jews and leaders with international reputations in the fields of politics, arts and sciences.[4] "The Jewish revival in the Soviet Union arises and draws inspiration from the deepest stirrings of the historic heritage of our people," declared Prime Minister Golda Meir in a message transmitted from Israel to Brussels. "We must ceaselessly demand that every Jew who wishes to come to his historic homeland be permitted to do so."[5]

A major disruption at the conference was the appearance of Rabbi Meir Kahane, the radical leader of the Jewish Defence League (JDL), whose militant tactics were strongly criticized by both the American Jewish establishment and the Israeli government. Kahane's request for admission to the conference had been previously denied due to his terrorist attacks against Soviet diplomats in the United States.[6] On parole pending the sentence of a New York court that had convicted him of disorderly conduct, Kahane had flown to Brussels on the second day of the meeting, barged into the Palais des Congrès and insisted upon addressing the delegates. He was forcibly removed by the Brussels police and expelled from the country.[7]

The expulsion threw the conference into turmoil. Organizers denounced Kahane as an "apostle of violence," claiming that his purpose was to disrupt the proceedings. Not everyone agreed. American film producer Otto Preminger and Israeli politician Menachem Begin argued that Kahane should be given the same rights as anyone else.[8]

The Brussels conference ended with an appeal for world-wide support for Soviet Jewry. The appeal gave solemn expression to ending discrimination against Soviet Jews, to safeguarding their national identity and recognizing their right to emigrate to their historic homeland. It concluded by saying, "We will not rest until the Jews of the Soviet Union are free to choose their own destiny. LET MY PEOPLE GO!"[9]

An increase in emigration soon after the Brussels Conference indicated that the Soviets were sensitive to public opinion. Only 4,235 Jews had left the USSR between 1968 and 1970. In the nine months following the conference, almost three times that number received exit visas.[10]

This prompted Nathan Gaisin, chairman of the Central Region of the CJC, to write to the presidents of Jewish organizations and to the few activists in Montreal, Ottawa and Toronto to form a national

Soviet Jewry committee under the umbrella of the CJC.[11] More than one year elapsed before the committee became a viable entity.

In March 1971, some Toronto university students, led by David Sadowski, Michael Gruda and Mark Clarfield, began to make telephone calls to Soviet Jews in Moscow. They enlisted the support of Russian-born Torontonian Genya Intrator to serve as their translator.[12] This launched a full-time career for Intrator, who became a key player in the Canadian Soviet Jewry movement. "It was only through outside intervention that our family was able to leave Russia in 1934," she remarked. "I knew that it could have been me still trapped there."[13]

Intrator became the translator for the first and subsequent telephone calls to Moscow activist Vladimir Slepak made by "Women for Soviet Jewry," the committee created in Spring 1971 within the Federation of Jewish Women's Organizations.[14] The telephone became the means by which their committee sensitized their constituents to the plight of Soviet Jewry.

Written material from Lishkat Hakesher continued to arrive at the CJC's national office in Montreal. Prior to Passover, one package included the "Matzah of Hope," a special prayer that was introduced in 1971 and recited at seders for many years to come. This prayer reminded Jews in the free world that for Jews in the Soviet Union, the Passover story of Egyptian slavery was a living reality.[15]

In the early 1970s, a "warming trend" best described relations between Canada and the Soviet Union. Anticipating that even better days were to come, Prime Minister Pierre Trudeau announced his plan to visit the Soviet Union in May 1971. Before his trip, two delegations from the CJC met with government officials to put forward their concerns.[16] During the informal talks, both groups were assured that the prime minister intended to raise the issue of Soviet Jewry during his meetings with Soviet officials.

Saul Hayes reiterated CJC's position in a letter to Trudeau, days before his departure. "You know how deeply the Jewish community feels about the position of the Jews in the Soviet Union," he wrote, "and how appreciative it is of your announced intention to discuss the situation with the Soviet leaders. There is every reason to believe that they will listen to you and soften their policy towards Jews."[17]

Trudeau departed for Moscow May 16, the eve of the second set of Leningrad trials for the remaining Jews implicated in the aborted hijack attempt. The trials were to be held in a Moscow courthouse.

During Question Period in the House of Commons the next day, MP Stanley Knowles asked Mitchell Sharp whether the subject of the trials would be discussed by Trudeau during his trip. "Yes," Sharp replied, "almost the last words I had with the prime minister before he left on his aircraft last evening were confirmation that he intended to do so."[18]

The trials ended during Trudeau's visit. The defendants, charged with "conducting ideological sabotage against the USSR," received sentences from one to ten years.[19] Canadian Jewish leaders felt a unique responsibility to speak out, especially since their prime minister was an official guest of the Soviet government.

"Recent information and news reports indicate situation of human rights for Jews in USSR has seriously deteriorated beginning with news of the Leningrad Trial sentences, last week," wrote Hyman Bessin, president of the Zionist Organization of Canada, in a cable to Trudeau in Moscow. "Riga trial of four Jews began Monday. Trial of nine Jews began Wednesday in Kishinev. Trials against Jews now being prepared in Odessa, Kharkov and Tbilisi. All trials are to be secret. Newsmen prevented from communicating with defendants. Would ask you to enquire as to situation and make appropriate representation."[20]

Upon his return, Trudeau announced that a protocol had been signed between the two governments as a gesture on the road to *détente*. The prime minister reported his progress on the subject of Soviet Jewry, "I expressed to Premier Kosygin, the widespread concern in Canada over the alleged refusal of the Soviet government to permit its Jewish citizens to emigrate to Israel or other countries of their choice. I was assured by Mr. Kosygin that these allegations were not well founded and that, in particular, his government had permitted to exit to Israel for many months, a significant number of Soviet Jews."[21]

Saul Hayes believed that Trudeau had not been forceful enough and sent a telegram to the prime minister telling him so. In it, he explained that visas were issued to a few thousand Jews merely to appease Western Jewry and that the harsh sentences imposed at the trials reflected the Soviet attitude toward emigration and served to dissuade other Jews from applying.[22] Trudeau replied, saying that although Kosygin had indicated that the issue of Soviet Jewry was an internal matter, the Canadian government would continue to consider applications for emigration to Canada and would approve them wherever possible.[23]

The Canadian branch of the JDL was made up of students known for their militant stance against anti-Semitic acts. They publicly expressed their feelings about the Soviets' treatment of Jews when the Georgian State Song and Dance Ensemble of the USSR held its opening Canadian performance in Toronto. JDL representatives distributed Soviet Jewry fact sheets to patrons as they entered Maple Leaf Gardens.

The following evening, when the ensemble performed at Place des Arts, the Montreal JDL group was more audacious. Ten members, who had purchased tickets for the performance, took their seats in the second and third balconies of the theatre. When the lights dimmed, the members dropped flyers, condemning the Leningrad sentences, into the audience and dripped red oil onto the stage. They set off smoke bombs and released twenty white rats from tiny bags which had been concealed on their bodies.

Pandemonium broke out. Some members of the audience began shrieking. All action stopped on stage. Security officials were dispatched immediately. Two of the offenders were apprehended while the others managed to escape. "I was jailed for four days," said Mark Zarecki, one of the student organizers, "and was interrogated the whole time. I kept asking for kosher food. The police were confused. They thought I was a Communist and certainly had no understanding what the Soviet Jewry movement was all about."[24] Charged with "endangering Her Majesty's subjects," Zarecki's offense was later changed to "disturbing the peace" and he was fined fifty dollars.

Although most people did not approve of nuisance techniques, some would argue that their tactics produced positive results by pressuring mainstream Jewish organizations into escalating public protests and dramatizing the problem more effectively.[25] After that incident, Montreal's JDL disbanded and most members joined the Student Struggle for Soviet Jewry (SSSJ),[26] which was committed to promote the plight of Soviet Jewry in a more socially acceptable way.

Community events usually slacken in the summertime, but the summer of 1971 marked the beginning of increased Soviet Jewry activity. David Sadowski, Mark Clarfield and two American friends brought the Soviet Jewry issue to thirty Orthodox, Zionist and secular Jewish summer camps throughout eastern Canada and the United States. Their "caravan" brought the Soviet Jewry situation to life for campers, through a combination of songs, film slides, dramatic readings and printed handouts.[27]

In August, a dozen Montreal Jewish women donned black robes and marched outside the Aeroflot office to mark "USSR Day" at Expo's "Man and his World."[28] "I can still feel the jitters now, thinking of how we paraded at the corner of Drummond and Dorchester," recalled MP Sheila Finestone, who was president of the Women's Federation of Allied Jewish Community Services at that time. "There we were, walking back and forth, not quite sure of what to do. I remember feeling aware of our freedom, even though we often didn't realize it. We were all nervous, naive, young mothers, very concerned about what we were doing and at the same time feeling quite proud."[29]

When it was announced, in September 1971, that Soviet premier Alexei Kosygin was planning to visit Canada as a guest of the Canadian government, a confidential meeting took place in Ottawa between The Honourable Mitchell Sharp and Jewish leaders.[31] There, CJC president Monroe Abbey made a forceful presentation for the right of Soviet Jews to their cultural and spiritual identity, as well as their right to emigrate to Israel. He explained that the Jewish community viewed Kosygin's visit as an opportunity to express solidarity with Soviet Jewry.

Sharp informed the group that he was prepared to discuss Jewish concerns with the Soviet leader, but warned that violent acts could weaken the government's position.[31] Subsequent to the meeting, Sharp articulated his concerns in writing: "The extent to which the public and official reception accorded Premier Kosygin next month is positive and friendly will have a distinct bearing on success."[32] Mindful of the warning, Abbey assured the minister that all directives from CJC to its constituents would emphasize restraint. As well, statements released to the media stressed that the Jewish community did not oppose a visit by Kosygin, but rather welcomed the occasion to express Canadian concern for Soviet Jewry.

Kosygin's visit to Canada was heralded by the CJC as a "call to action," and Jews were urged to demonstrate "peaceful militancy."[33] Abbey's letter said, "The lives of our brothers in the Soviet Union must be our first concern. In order not to add to their danger, our efforts must be organized, massive, meaningful and disciplined."[34]

The Soviet premier was scheduled to be in Canada for one week. Since his final itinerary was unavailable, communities planned activities that could be implemented on a day's notice. In major Canadian cities, Jews were alerted through synagogues and Jewish organizations. In smaller communities, Canadian Hadassah-Wizo, the Zionist organization with seventeen thousand female members from coast to coast, urged their constituents to participate in the protests with their families.[35]

Premier Kosygin arrived in Ottawa the morning of October 18. That afternoon, Rabbi W. Gunther Plaut led sixty rabbis, wearing prayer shawls and carrying prayer books, on a march from the Jewish Community Centre to the Soviet Embassy. The three-storey stone structure, with its basement and ground floor windows shuttered, was surrounded by a high iron fence. It resembled a fortress under siege.[36]

"Mr. Kosygin," Rabbi Plaut's voice resounded over a megaphone outside the embassy's iron gate. "We accuse the Soviet government of persecuting Jews, of attempting to stamp out their identity, of fostering anti-Semitism . . . We demand only that you treat the Jews as you treat all other citizens. Give them their cultural identity, give them back their language, give them synagogues that can function, give them schools . . . give them access to their cultural treasures . . . and grant exit visas to the thousands of Jews who have already applied for emigration to Israel."[37]

The rabbis marched from the embassy to Parliament Hill where they held a study and prayer vigil at the Centennial Flame and prayed through the cold, damp night. At 5:00 AM the following day, just as a heavy fog was lifting, a CBC television crew arrived and filmed the rabbis reciting their morning prayers. A few hours later, when Premier Kosygin and Prime Minister Trudeau reached the House of Commons, they saw the rabbis, deep in prayer. One raised a *Shofar* (ram's horn) to his lips. Its wailful sound pierced the crisp fall air.[38] Later, a photograph of the rabbis at the flame, with the Peace Tower, Canada's symbol of democracy, in the background, appeared in major newspapers across the land.[39]

For weeks prior to Kosygin's visit, Jewish organizations, synagogue offices and schools in Ottawa, Toronto and Montreal advertised in the Jewish press that they would close on October 19, to allow for participation in a mass demonstration for Soviet Jewry.[40] One hundred and ten buses carried out-of-town protesters to the nation's capital.

The thousands of men, women and children who made up the freedom march wound through the downtown core to Strathcona Park, one block from the Soviet Embassy. Two hundred volunteers served as monitors, whose job it was to maintain order as the protesters converged on the area surrounding the building. A human barricade of one thousand policemen had cordoned off the street in full view of KGB officers, who were protecting their own territory from behind the iron fence.

The mass of people chanted repeatedly, "One, two, three, four . . . open up the iron door; five, six, seven, eight . . . let our people emigrate." Among the many speakers who paid tribute to the thousands of supporters was Toronto's CJC spokesman, Sydney Harris, who declared, "We must stand together and vow to speak out on behalf of our brothers and sisters until every last Jew in the Soviet Union who desires to be free, is liberated."[41]

When the rally ended, the crowd marched from the embassy to

the Supreme Court of Canada. A light airplane circled the route, trailing a two-metre high banner that read: "LET THEM LIVE AS JEWS OR LET THEM LEAVE."[42]

Jewish protesters dogged every hour of the Soviet premier's eight-day stay as he travelled across the country. In Montreal, demonstrators chanted freedom songs and marched with American actor/singer Theodore Bikel from Kosygin's downtown hotel to the Soviet Consulate. In Vancouver, three thousand members of the Jewish community jammed the courthouse square next to his headquarters at the Hotel Vancouver and a cavalcade of 150 cars carried Edmonton and Calgary Jews to greet Kosygin as he emerged from the Sheritt-Gordon nickel refinery at Fort Saskatchewan, Alberta.[43] Signs urging the Soviets to "Open the Iron Curtain," were held by Winnipeg Jews who demonstrated in front of their council building.

On his last evening in Canada, Kosygin was the guest of the Canadian Manufacturers' Association at a formal dinner at Toronto's Ontario Science Centre. Albert Applebaum and Celia Airst, two JDL supporters, had managed to secure tickets for the event. During Kosygin's speech, calling for better relations between Canada and the USSR, Applebaum interrupted, shouting *"Svoboda, Svoboda"* (Freedom, Freedom). From the lining of her suit jacket, Airst pulled out a small red silk banner bearing a hammer and sickle with the inscription, "Let my people go." Police hustled the pair out of the hall.[44]

Outside the Science Centre, seventeen hundred members of the Metro Toronto police force, bolstered by five hundred Ontario Provincial Police and RCMP officers, were ready for any eventuality. Standing shoulder to shoulder, they formed a double line facing a mass of Ukrainians, Bulgarians, Lithuanians, Latvians, members of the Edmund Burke Society and about one hundred members of the JDL. "We had taken our positions in the small grassy island in front of the Science Centre in full view of the Soviet premier's limousine," said Judy Feld Carr, co-chairman with Albert Applebaum of the JDL group. "As Kosygin drove up to and left the building, we waved signs that read 'Freedom for Soviet Jewry'."[45]

A solid line of police cruisers and a unit on horseback were held in readiness behind the policemen. When the crowd began to pelt the security forces with debris and break through the lines, the mounted police charged forward, causing the demonstration to burst into a frenzied riot.

In an open field across the street and far from the main demonstration, a six-metre-high, electrically illuminated Star of David beckoned six thousand Torontonians to a rally. The gathering, organized by CJC's youth director Steve Ain, threatened to erupt into a riot when JDL members rushed into their midst urging their fellow Jews to join the other ethnic groups under attack by the police. After a brief shoving match with CJC marshals, the militants returned to their previous positions and the peaceful demonstration continued as planned.[46]

Elie Wiesel had been invited to Toronto to address the demonstrators. Standing in the back of an open truck, he declared, "The 'Jews of Silence' are silent no more. Jewish people, be proud. Be proud of your children in Moscow. Be proud of your children in Toronto. Jewish people, you have found your soul again. The process is irrevocable. The process cannot be stopped; it will go on."[47]

Premier Kosygin's Canadian tour was featured on television and radio broadcasts and on the front pages of almost every daily newspaper in the country. The press reported that meetings with political and civic leaders were overshadowed by Jewish protests. Whenever the subject of Soviet Jewry was raised, Kosygin responded by saying, "Much is written in Western countries about Soviet anti-Semitism and persecution, but it is artificial and invented."[48]

Rabbi Plaut assessed the effect of Kosygin's visit in an article in *The Canadian Jewish News*: "Somehow I think the outside world was infected by our spirit. One thing we do know – Mr. Kosygin heard us, or else he would not have devoted so much time refuting our claims. If anything was demonstrated, it was that peaceful action has produced a response. We cannot measure its range. Some day we may."[49]

Chapter 5

A Movement Emerges

There was no word for a Soviet Jew who had been refused a visa to emigrate until the Russian word *otkaznik* was coined in 1971. It was anglicized to *refusenik* by British activist Michael Sherbourne.[1]

Although the media often used the word "dissident" interchangeably with the word "refusenik," the distinction was clear. Refuseniks were Jews who had been refused permission to emigrate to Israel, whereas dissidents wished to democratize the Soviet system. Although many dissidents supported Jewish emigration and many refuseniks supported democratization, there was little overlap between the two movements. It was the centrality of Israel as a Jewish homeland that allowed the Soviet Jewry movement to be a struggle solely for the redemption of Jews.

When a Soviet Jew first applied to emigrate it was not known whether he would receive a visa or be relegated to the rank of refusenik. Those with high academic qualifications were usually refused for one of the following reasons: state security, secrecy, access to classified information.[2] With few exceptions, Soviet scientists, engineers or mathematicians were not in possession of secrets unknown to other industrialized nations. Many Jews only learned that they were in possession of "secrets" when they received their first refusal. When asked what secrets prevented them from emigrating, officials were known to reply, "That is a secret." A popular belief among activists was that educated Jews were denied permission to emigrate because Soviet officials feared a brain-drain, and if they refused visas to prominent Jews, others would be dissuaded from applying.

As a group of people ostracized from society, life in refusal was demoralizing. Even the most prominent academic was forced to accept menial work for fear of imprisonment for "parasitism," a charge brought against anyone unemployed for three months.

Being unable to work in their professions was ruinous to most academics, whose careers depended on keeping abreast of work being done in their field. In Moscow and Leningrad, the cities with the largest and most viable Jewish activist communities, refuseniks retained their professional proficiency through academic seminars that took place in their apartments. Papers were presented by the refuseniks themselves, or by their counterparts who were visiting from abroad.

Cultural seminars were held, clandestinely, in refuseniks' homes. Although the teaching of Jewish history, culture and Hebrew language was not against Soviet law, the authorities treated it as such. Seminars were disrupted on a regular basis and cultural material confiscated.

By the early 1970s, refuseniks could be found in almost every city in the USSR. Some of the more outspoken were arrested on spurious charges, tried in court and sentenced to prison, labour camps or exile in Siberia, for terms ranging from two to fifteen years. They became known as the "Prisoners of Conscience" or "Prisoners of Zion."[3]

Premier Kosygin's visit had been a watershed for Soviet Jewry activity in Canada. It placed the issue on the Jewish agenda, legitimized grass-roots advocacy and united Jews of all ages in a common struggle.

The placing of telephone calls to refuseniks, popular among Toronto student activists, also attracted a group of women at Beth Tzedec Congregation, who called themselves *Pidyon Shevuyim*, a Talmudic reference to the Jew's obligation to "redeem the captives." Some people believed that a phone call from abroad might place the recipient in danger. This theory was refuted by the refuseniks themselves, who were convinced that publicity in the free world guaranteed their safety and greatly improved their chances of receiving a visa.

Placing a telephone call to the Soviet Union was no easy task, since the telephones in most of the refuseniks' apartments had been disconnected. Calls could, however, be received at local post offices.

For the person calling from abroad, the process began three to five days earlier through a "messenger call," initiated by the caller through the overseas operator. The operator then cabled the refusenik as to the time and date of the prospective call. On the pre-arranged day, the recipient would wait inside the Soviet post office to receive the call. Delays that were usually encountered were due to busy circuits and unco-operative Soviet operators. When a call finally did get through, it was frequently disconnected in mid-conversation.

"What else do you need?" Genya Intrator asked of Moscow engineer Victor Polsky during a call placed by Toronto students in February 1972. "What else do we need?" he replied in English. "We need permission to go to Israel. Tell all our friends that we're very grateful for all that they're doing. We hope that their efforts will not be in vain."[4]

Soviet officials thwarted the refuseniks at every turn. Fearing demonstrations during U.S. president Richard Nixon's visit to Moscow in May of 1972, the KGB arrested Vladimir Slepak, Victor Polsky, Yosef Begun, Vladimir Prestin and other leading Jewish activists, along with several Soviet dissidents. They were transported to prisons in outlying towns and released only after Nixon's departure.

The Nixon-Brezhnev talks centred on a new U.S. Trade Bill that would grant most-favoured-nation status (MFN) to non-market economies, with the Soviet Union becoming the major beneficiary. If passed, it would permit Soviet goods to enter the United States at favourable tariff rates and extend to the Soviets substantial long-term credits. Subsidized trade with the USSR was a major part of the American strategy of *détente* championed by President Nixon and Secretary of State Henry Kissinger.

On August 3, 1972, after two-and-a-half years of allowing a slowly increasing flow of Jews to leave the Soviet Union for Israel, the Kremlin imposed a heavy tax on potential emigrants, ostensibly for the cost of their education.[5] The "diploma" tax ranged from 5,400 roubles (US$6,750) for a high school degree to 21,000 roubles (US$25,000) for a Ph.D. These figures represented much more than the average Soviet citizen's annual salary.[6] The introduction of the diploma tax was yet another in a seemingly endless number of strategies of the Soviet leadership to manipulate emigration from the Soviet Union. The tax quashed the glimmer of hope that visas, issued to Jews in 1970 and 1971, had inspired.[7]

Dr. Benjamin Levich, a prominent scientist, released the news at a press conference in Moscow. He described the tax as a form of "twentieth-century slavery."[8] Prime Minister Golda Meir called an emergency session of the Knesset, where she asked all "freedom lovers" to raise their voices in protest: "Let our people emigrate without ransom, without bias, without a price on them, without any discrimination whatsoever."[9]

Soviet Jewry advocates were incensed. At a one-day crisis conference held in London, England, organized by Great Britain's National Council of Soviet Jewry, a resolution was passed demanding that the Soviet government rescind the diploma tax. Following the meeting, protests were organized, and governments made low-key diplomatic representations urging the Soviets to reconsider.

Sydney Harris, who had represented CJC at the conference, appealed to Mitchell Sharp to raise the subject with his Soviet counterpart Andrei Gromyko. "Gromyko informed me that the subject of the diploma tax was an internal matter," said Sharp, reporting on his recent meeting with Gromyko at a Simchat Torah rally in Toronto. "I expected that reply, but I cannot help but think that our representations have not gone unheard."[10]

One American's response to the education tax paved the way for a major change in American policy. He was Senator Henry M. (Scoop) Jackson. Deeply influenced by the brutal Nazi invasion of Norway, his parents' homeland, and profoundly moved by his visit to Buchenwald immediately after the concentration camp was liberated in 1945, Jackson felt a kinship with the Jewish people.[11]

When the education tax was imposed, Jackson consulted with Senators Jacob Javits and Abraham Ribicoff about using legislative means to force the Soviets to rescind the tax, particularly in view of the pending U.S. trade bill.

On September 27, 1972, Jackson first introduced to the Senate his intention to offer an amendment to the Trade Reform Act that would tie U.S. economic benefits to human rights concerns. The heart of his amendment was to deny MFN status to any recipient non-market economy that denied its citizens the right to emigrate or imposed more than nominal taxes or fees on persons who wished to emigrate or as a condition for obtaining an exit visa.[12] The announcement was met with tremendous resistance by Nixon and Kissinger, both of whom favoured quiet diplomacy and insisted that granting MFN status to the Soviets would end the Cold War. They argued that Jackson's amendment would have the opposite effect and, in fact, would endanger Soviet Jews.

Jackson took an unflinching stand. With his aides, Richard Perle and Dorothy Fosdick, he set about drafting the amendment and began to solicit support among members of the Senate and Congress.[13]

The attack against the Soviets for their reviled diploma tax entered the public arena. The American Academic Committee on Soviet Jewry condemned the tax in two full-page advertisements in *The New York Times*. The first was signed by twenty-one Nobel laureates.[14] The second was a letter addressed to Premier Kosygin endorsed by forty-six hundred faculty members from one hundred and twenty North American universities, including thirty-four professors from the University of Toronto. The letter stated: "By imposing unconscionable head taxes on all educated citizens seeking to leave the country, you and your colleagues have transformed the Soviet intelligentsia into a class of indentured servants. And since the decree affects principally Jews who wish to go to Israel, your policy bears the ugly stamp of discrimination."[15]

The American committee inspired the formation of the Canadian Academic Committee for Soviet Jewry, which gained the support of seven Canadian universities. Its first act was to sponsor a petition addressed to the president of the Soviet Academy of Sciences condemning the diploma tax.[16]

On October 4, 1972, Senator Jackson announced in the U.S. Senate, "The one bright light in the hopes of Soviet Jews is the existence of the State of Israel. That Israel should exist is a modern miracle. That the Russian Jews should be denied the right to go is a cruel and inhuman irony. It must be ended." With the support of sixty-five co-sponsors, Jackson submitted his proposed amendment to the Trade Bill on the Senate floor. Viewing the amendment as a powerful expression of American ideals and self-interest, the senator added, "There are times when the depth of our commitment to our deepest values is put to the test, and this is one of those times."[17]

The Israelis could not take a public position in support of Jackson's amendment, but behind the scenes, the response from Jerusalem was unmitigated endorsement. Amos Eiran, counsellor with the embassy of Israel in Washington, had countless meetings with Senator Jackson from the earliest drafting stages. "Although there could never be an official voice of Israel behind American legislation," recalled Jackson's aide Richard Perle, "there was never a moment when Scoop was in doubt that the government of Israel was encouraging the amendment."[18]

In January 1973, Mark Talisman, aide to Congressman Charles Vanik, who had helped draft the amendment, brought the document to Vanik, who introduced it in the House of Representatives. From then on, it was jointly sponsored and became known as the Jackson-Vanik Amendment.

On March 16, 1973, Jackson re-introduced the amendment, with seventy-seven co-sponsors, on the floor of the Senate. Reaction from the Kremlin was almost immediate. Four days later, a spokesman from the Communist party declared that the diploma tax had been suspended.[19] During the seven months that the tax had been invoked, thirty-two thousand Soviet Jews paid the equivalent of between US$1,000 to US$10,000 each for the right to leave the USSR, and a prominent scientist, Dr. Herman Branover, with the help of friends from abroad, paid a ransom equal to US$31,000.[20]

The name Henry M. Jackson had become synonymous with the Soviet Jewry emigration movement. "The right to emigrate is not a Jewish issue, but a humanitarian issue," he told the National Conference on Soviet Jewry leadership meeting on May 8, 1973. Speaking about the progress made for support of the amendment, Jackson said, "In taking this action we are reaffirming the deeply held American conviction that the right to emigrate is fundamental to human liberty. We are, moreover, acting in support of the Universal Declaration of Human Rights, unanimously adopted by the United Nations twenty-five years ago, in which the international community committed itself to uphold the right to free emigration and free return."[21]

The decision to form a national Soviet Jewry committee was finally made at a CJC national executive meeting in Winnipeg in December 1972. It took many more months before a director was hired and the Canadian Committee for Soviet Jewry (CCSJ), headquartered in Canadian Jewish Congress' national offices in Montreal, became a reality.[22]

The CCSJ was formed initially as a tripartite committee comprised of the CJC, B'nai Brith and the Canadian Zionist Federation (CZF), with CJC being responsible for funding.[23] Included under its umbrella were all national Jewish organizations and CJC's regional committees: the Montreal Committee for Soviet Jewry, the Committee for Soviet Jewry, Ontario Region, the Calgary Committee for Soviet Jewry, the Ottawa Committee for Soviet Jewry, the Winnipeg Committee for Soviet Jewry and the Vancouver Committee for Soviet Jewry.[24] The partnership worked together until the late 1970s, when B'nai Brith became dissatisfied with the status quo and embarked upon an independent course of programming. The CCSJ remained as the central Canadian resource for Soviet Jewry and CZF became one of the representative organizations on its committee.

"We must always remember our goal," stated Sydney Harris, the CCSJ's founding chairman, at a meeting September 11, 1973. "The message must get through to Soviet Jewry that we have heard their call and we support them, and the message must get to the Soviet authorities that we will not accept mistreatment of our brethren in the Soviet Union."[25]

Soon after the establishment of the CCSJ, one of their constituent organizations, the National Council of Jewish Women (NCJW), Toronto Section became involved with a refusenik adoption program confined exclusively to Kishinev, in the region of Moldavia.[26] To the eighty thousand Jews of Kishinev, NCJW was a lifeline. Their members elicited the support of Jeanette Goldman, whose fluency in Russian made her an ideal translator for their twice-monthly telephone calls.

Goldman's first refusenik contact was Mark Abramovich, who provided information about the activities of the refusenik communities in the entire Moldavian region. "I was always aware that the Soviets were monitoring my calls," Goldman related, "so whatever I said had to be guarded. I felt a huge responsibility knowing the trust that the refuseniks had placed in us to act upon the valuable information they imparted between our spoken lines."[27]

Throughout the entire Soviet Jewry campaign, NCJW maintained its uniqueness in being the only organization that confined its refusenik adoptions to one region. "Our women were in the trenches," recalled Marsha Slavens, a former chairman of NCJW's World Jewry Committee, "planning Soviet Jewry events for our members and the community, stuffing envelopes, making phone calls, or just writing to our refusenik families. The money for telephone calls came from private donations and from the sale of specially designed Soviet Jewry serviettes. For NCJW, it was a labour of love."[28]

In 1973, Canadian Hadassah-Wizo, another constituent organization of the CCSJ, adopted twenty-eight-year-old Sylva Zalmanson, the only female prisoner of the Leningrad trials, who was into the third year of her ten year prison sentence. Zalmanson's health began to deteriorate after she was put in a punishment cell in Potma Labour Camp for defending another Jewish prisoner from anti-Semitic attacks.

Through Hadassah-Wizo's network of chapters, members were instructed to barrage the Kremlin with letters and cables. A "Committee to Free Sylva Zalmanson" was created under the co-sponsorship of Hadassah and CJC and plans were underway for a national demonstration on her behalf.[29]

Suddenly, a crisis in Israel took the focus off Soviet Jewry. On October 6, 1973, on Yom Kippur, the holiest day in the Jewish calendar, Israel was invaded by Egyptian troops in the south and Syrian troops in the north. This offensive, which became known as the Yom Kippur War, caught most Israelis off guard. Soldiers interrupted their prayers in synagogues, changed into military uniforms and rushed to army bases, where they were sent to various fronts to defend Israel against the onslaught of Arabs, heavily armed with Soviet munitions. Within one week, Israel had driven Egypt's and Syria's forces back, yet the price exacted was horrifying. Twenty-seven hundred Israeli soldiers died.

The Soviet Union's response during the Yom Kippur War was predictable. In an attempt to halt any communication between Soviet Jews and their supporters in the West, all Hebrew and Russian language programs broadcast by Kol Yisroel and the Voice of Israel were jammed and telephone service in refuseniks' apartments was cut off.[30] In what was thought to be a malicious attempt to further debilitate the Jewish state, exit visas were issued to thousands of Soviet Jews, at a time when Israel was least prepared to accept them. Israeli pilots returned from Arab fronts, changed planes, and flew to Vienna to carry Soviet Jews home.

"These are difficult days for the Jewish people," said Prime Minister Golda Meir in a speech broadcast to Jewish communities world-wide. "Israel cannot do it alone." Raising money for Israel became a top priority. Funds were desperately needed for a country at war and burdened, simultaneously, with the cost of absorbing a flood of new immigrants.

"Peace for Israel" and "Freedom for Soviet Jewry" became the themes at all 1973 Simchat Torah rallies. The tension of the times generated a record turnout. At rallies in Montreal, Ottawa, Toronto, Hamilton, Kitchener, St. Catharines, Winnipeg, Calgary, Regina, Saskatoon and Vancouver, speakers condemned Arab aggression and expressed hope for freedom for Soviet Jews.[31]

"The hands that keep the doors locked to Soviet Jews are the same hands that support the aims and send supplies to Israel's enemies," stated J.B. Salsberg, chairman of Toronto's Steering Committee for Soviet Jewry, to thousands of Toronto Jews who gathered in Nathan Phillips Square. "Let us declare our double aspiration: 'Peace for Israel,' 'Let my people go.'"[32]

By the end of 1973, in what was seen as an escalating trend, a total of 34,733 Jews received emigration visas. That was three thousand more than in 1972 and represented the largest exodus since the movement began.

Chapter 6

Eye Witnesses

In January 1971, Montreal community leaders Rabbi Lavy Becker and Boris Levine visited Moscow, Leningrad and Riga to make contact with Jews and to assess the status of Jewish cultural life in the Soviet Union.

When they arrived in Moscow, they went immediately to the synagogue, where they were informed by Rabbi Leib Levin that the Soviet Jewish population had no problems. He spoke highly of Rabbi Isaac Hechtman, the head of Montreal's Jewish Community Council, who solicited funds privately to purchase prayerbooks and religious articles that he sent to Soviet synagogues. The *Gabbi* (sexton) in Leningrad communicated similar information.

The younger Jews whom Becker and Levine met in both cities told another story. They were suspicious of synagogue officials who co-operated with Soviet authorities in order to keep the few remaining synagogues open. They said that Hechtman's books remained in unopened cartons in the synagogues' basement.[1] This led Becker and Levine to support the theory held by many Montrealers that Rabbi Hechtman was welcomed by Soviet government officials on his frequent trips to the USSR because he praised them publicly and refused to acknowledge that there were Jews who wanted to leave.

The two men met Jews in synagogues, in restaurants and on the streets. People approached them guardedly at first and then engaged the foreigners in conversation. "The chance encounters were heartwarming experiences," Becker and Levine stated in their trip report. "You must understand the little nuances of a first contact, a casual question, the beginning of recognition and even the careful certainty in the presence of others. It was a game to some extent. An eminently worthwhile one."[2]

From a booth on the street in Leningrad, they telephoned a Jew whose number they had been given in Montreal. They arranged a rendezvous that consisted of an eighty-minute walk down quiet streets and in a public park. "We asked all kinds of questions and received calm and full, unhesitant answers, interrupted only when someone approached us."[3] This man told them of the existence of underground Hebrew classes, short-wave Jewish radio programs beamed into Moscow from the West and of his family's dream of going to Israel. "We were, in fact, calmed as we were captivated and heartened by this growing group of Jews of 'courage,' not 'silence.' We cannot even estimate how many they are. That they exist at all is remarkable."[4]

Most Jewish Canadians who visited the Soviet Union in the early 1970s travelled with an organized group. Some were among the three thousand who journeyed to Moscow in the fall of 1972 to support Team Canada in the first Canada-Russia hockey series.[5] They brought Hebrew prayer books, Russian-Hebrew dictionaries and religious articles, in anticipation of meeting Jews in the synagogue.[6]

A few individuals made contact with Soviet Jews in their apartments. One of the Toronto travellers, H. Wayne Tanenbaum, briefed by CJC's Ontario Region Soviet Jewry director, Sam Resnick, had divided a number of Jewish books and religious items among many of the hockey players' wives, who willingly packed the articles in their luggage. In Moscow, Tanenbaum made contact with several refuseniks whom he met in public places, and managed to dodge a plainclothesman who followed him to refusenik Dr. Alexander Lerner's apartment.[7]

Montrealers Jack Zittrer and Edward Bronfman spent several evenings visiting Soviet Jews in their apartments, engaging them in lengthy discussions.[8] Bronfman was followed everywhere. He was called to the Canadian Embassy by the ambassador, who instructed him to ask his fellow travellers to stop distributing religious material in the synagogues. Bronfman's notes and film were confiscated before he left the Soviet Union.[9]

The Toronto group related their stories at community meetings when they returned. Robert Kaplan, a federal Liberal candidate present at one of the meetings, emphasized his position, "Political candidates should commit themselves on the Soviet Jewish question and be prepared to appeal directly to the Soviets on behalf of Soviet Jews."[10]

Genya Intrator's trip to the Soviet Union in May 1973 further entrenched her commitment to Soviet Jewry by reinforcing her relationships with Vladimir Slepak, Vladimir Prestin, Victor Polsky and other refuseniks, whom she had come to know through her telephone calls.

A trip sponsored by the Quebec Bar Association in the fall of 1974 was responsible for recruiting several new Canadian activists. After meeting with refuseniks in Moscow and Leningrad, Sylviane Borenstein and Miriam Garvis became actively involved in Soviet Jewry.[11] Similarly, William Miller agreed to head the Quebec lawyers' Soviet Jewry committee that he and fellow travellers, Nahum Gelber and Ted Polisuk, founded after their trip.

It was on the Quebec Bar Association trip that Toronto lawyers Sam Filer and Bert Raphael met for the first time. "As the only tourists present in the Leningrad synagogue that Shabbat morning," Filer recalled, "we were given seats of honour and offered *tallaisim* [prayer shawls] and *siddurim* [prayerbooks]. Looking around, I noticed that not every man was wearing a *tallis* and only a few people had a *siddur*. Then I realized that those we wore had been taken from a padlocked chest. It was a clever propaganda trick. How could there be a shortage of religious articles in the Soviet Union if there were enough to share with foreigners?"[12]

A man, who identified himself as Victor Polsky, asked Filer for a Hebrew prayerbook and accompanied him to his hotel to retrieve it. "Polsky impressed upon us the importance of writing to Soviet officials in Canada and the USSR," Filer stated in his written recollections. "He urged us to conduct public demonstrations, obtain the support of governments and seek legal redress."[13]

The following autumn, Sylviane Borenstein visited the Soviet Union again, this time with the Canadian Bar Association. She and colleague Irving Halperin, along with his wife Grace, accompanied the refusenik Anatoly Sharansky to a forest outside Moscow where hundreds of Jews had gathered to commemorate the festival of Succoth, the Jewish harvest. With them were members of the Israeli weightlifting team, in Moscow for an international competition.[14]

High-spirited Hebrew songs and Israeli dances were interrupted when KGB plainclothesmen appeared from behind the trees. A skirmish ensued as the officials attempted to grab an Israeli flag from the hands of one of the weightlifters. Sharansky whisked the Canadians away, urging them to invite news correspondents to a press conference. "The Moscow-based foreign press are tired of hearing from us," Sharansky told the Canadian lawyers. "It will be much more credible if you call them."[15] The press conference was held in their hotel room and, within an hour, the incident was reported overseas. Radio-journalist Barbara Frum telephoned the Canadians in Moscow for a first-hand report that was broadcast that evening on CBC's "As it Happens."[16]

Chapter 7

International Accountability

In November 1972, representatives of thirty-five countries met in Helsinki, Finland, to establish a Conference on Security and Co-operation in Europe (CSCE).[1] These meetings laid the groundwork for future meetings, which ultimately led to the signing of the Helsinki Final Act. The CSCE was largely a Soviet initiative. It was Leonid Brezhnev's attempt to gain acceptance of the inviolability of Eastern European post-war borders. Western states used the conference as an opportunity to pressure the Kremlin to deal with the issue of human rights.

Three preliminary drafting meetings took place in Geneva, in July and September 1973, and in January 1974. Prior to the meetings, Alan Rose, associate executive director and political liaison for the Canadian Jewish Congress, conferred with American, British and Israeli political experts William Korey, Stephen Roth and Dr. Yoram Dinstein. Rose then informed W.T. Delworth, the head of the Canadian drafting group, that international Jewish leadership viewed the importance of family reunification and the right to emigrate as critical to the CSCE final agreement.[2]

"The July meeting was a conference of foreign ministers," explained Rose. "External affairs minister Mitchell Sharp was very much aware of Canada's responsibility to its Eastern European ethnic population and he forcefully put forward the government's commitment to 'the free flow of men and ideas.' " At the second meeting, Canada pressed strongly for liberalization of Soviet emigration procedures.[3]

Before the third drafting meeting, Saul Hayes wrote to Sharp saying, "We are indeed gratified that Canada has continued to press for co-operation in humanitarian and other fields. We hold firm to the belief that it is critical that there be written into any agreement with the USSR and its allies, a greater flow of information between East and West, co-operation in exchanges in the field of culture and education, the possibility of family joinder and relaxed emigration procedures from the USSR and from the Socialist bloc."[4]

After the third drafting meeting, Alan Rose praised the government's position in an article for the *Congress Bulletin*. "Nowhere is the Canadian government's attitude towards the plight of Soviet Jewry better illustrated than with the CSCE. The position of Canada is strong and unequivocal." In fact, it was Alan Rose who was largely responsible for the Canadian government's posture. In order to gain unanimity on the issue, he shuttled back and forth between Montreal and Ottawa on numerous occasions to confer with Sharp, Claude Wagner and David Lewis – members of all three political parties.[5]

The Helsinki Final Act, or "Helsinki Agreement" as it became known, was signed August 1, 1975. It ushered in a new era of *détente* that was politically and morally binding upon the signatory states. The final document was divided into three Baskets. Basket One strengthened security through guaranteed borders; Basket Two addressed co-operation in the fields of economics, science, technology and the environment; and Basket Three dealt with humanitarian concerns, in particular, religious, cultural and minority rights. As well, it authorized individuals to "know and act upon their rights."[6]

Basket Three had positive implications for Soviet Jews. It stated that "the participating States will deal in a positive and humanitarian spirit with the applications of persons who wish to be reunited with members of their family and to deal with such applications as expeditiously as possible."[7] The participating States could no longer claim that "human rights" was solely an "internal affair."

The Soviet decision to agree to include humanitarian concerns in the final document was a political one. As beneficiaries of Basket One, which legitimized Soviet claims to the Baltic States, they felt compelled to concede to the provisions of Basket Three.

The Helsinki Final Act became a persistent rhetorical mechanism by which countries could exercise their influence. "Review" meetings, devised to implement the provisions of the final document, were scheduled to take place every three years with "Experts" meetings planned for the intervening period.[8]

The World Presidium on Soviet Jewry formed a committee of individuals from Diaspora communities to monitor compliance with the Helsinki accord.[9] Representatives of the committee would meet with their government's delegation prior to each Review and Experts meeting in order to bring them up to date and brief them on Jewish concerns.

The signing of the Helsinki Final Act brought optimism to many Soviet Jews who believed that after arbitrary refusals, emigration restrictions might be eased. Their hopes escalated even higher when, six weeks after the signing, Brezhnev affirmed at an international meeting in Yalta, "The Helsinki declaration is of a binding nature. Our common goal and most important task is to give full effect to these agreements. We assume that all countries represented at the conference will implement the agreements reached."[10]

Changes did not occur. Emigration figures, that had dropped from 34,733 in 1973 to 20,628 in 1974, plunged further to 13,221 in 1975. There was an increase in new refusals. It was no mistake. When Moscow cyberneticist Dr. Alexander Lerner questioned the authorities he was told, "No policy change is planned toward Jews wanting to leave for Israel. There is no need to change it since this policy is already so liberal that there is no room to make it more so."[11]

Some Soviet officials even mocked the agreement. When asked by refuseniks why their applications to emigrate had been denied, they replied cynically, "You have been refused in accordance with the letter and spirit of Helsinki."[12]

Chapter 8

The 35s

When Nechemiah Levanon established the Soviet Jewry department within Lishkat Hakesher in 1955, he had hoped to create in major Western communities a network that would help to implement the policy and action required to liberate Jews from the Soviet Union. By the early 1970s, a broad-based activity on behalf of Soviet Jewry was taking root all over the world.

Information and directives from Levanon's office in Tel Aviv were communicated through Israeli emissaries to national Soviet Jewry organizations abroad, such as the National Council for Soviet Jewry in Great Britain, the National Committee for Soviet Jewry in France, National Conference on Soviet Jewry and the Greater New York Conference for Soviet Jewry in the United States and the Canadian Committee for Soviet Jewry.[1]

These establishment bodies made and implemented their own policies and were supported by their local federations with funds raised through their Combined Jewish Appeal/United Jewish Appeal/ United Israel Appeal campaigns. In each country they served as the source of Soviet Jewry information and lent direction to regional Soviet Jewry committees.[2]

There were, as well, organizations that operated outside the establishment Jewish community. The Student Struggle for Soviet Jewry (SSSJ), for example, had flourished on American and Canadian university campuses since the mid-1960s. What the SSSJ lacked in financial resources, it compensated for in enthusiasm and dedication. Its counterpart in the American adult community was the Union of Councils for Soviet Jews (UCSJ or Union), an advocacy organization created in

1970 by the amalgamation of six community Soviet Jewry grassroots activist groups.[3] The Union ultimately boasted thirty-eight constituent, self-supporting councils. Their activities often provoked vigorous negative reaction from the leadership of the establishment groups who frequently accused them of promoting cases of refuseniks that had not been cleared through Lishkat Hakesher.

Equally threatening to the National Council for Soviet Jewry in Great Britain was "The 35s – Women's Campaign for Soviet Jewry." This autonomous group developed and sustained a continuous, dynamic, activist program on behalf of Soviet Jewry and was funded by generous private individuals in Great Britain. The 35s were the only exclusively female group in the Soviet Jewry movement. Although "35" did not signify the total number of women in each group or their ages, both factors were relevant to their origin.

The 35s were established in 1971 when Yitzhack Rager was the counsellor for Soviet Jewry affairs with the Israeli Embassy in London, England. Raisa Palatnik, an Odessa librarian, had been sentenced on June 24, 1971, to a two-year prison term for possessing "slanderous anti-Soviet material." The material in question was a library of Jewish books and Israeli journals discovered by the KGB during a search of Palatnik's apartment.

Believing that action was needed, Rager approached three highly spirited Jewish women and suggested that they stage a demonstration in honour of Palatnik's thirty-fifth birthday.[4] Grasping the concept of "35," the women informed members of the press that thirty-five women, who were thirty-five years of age, were conducting a silent vigil to mark the thirty-fifth birthday of a Soviet Jewish female prisoner. The women dressed in black and stood outside the Soviet Embassy holding placards pleading for Palatnik's freedom. The following day, Britain's daily newspapers carried the story and photographs of the event.[5]

When Palatnik was released and safe in Israel, she informed the London women that on the day of their demonstration a prison guard told her that an "unnecessary fuss" had been made on her behalf in London.[6] Thoroughly convinced that their cries had been heard behind the Iron Curtain, the women plunged themselves into a dynamic campaign of action. While the group had called themselves "Women's Campaign for Soviet Jewry," the media dubbed them "the 35s," a name by which they became known world-wide.

The hallmark of the London 35s was ingenious demonstrations. Dressed in judicial wigs and gowns, they "convicted" the prosecutors of Kharkov Jew Yuli Brind, imprisoned for two years on charges of "anti-Soviet slander" for speaking out in defence of Israel at a government-sponsored anti-Israel rally.[7] When the women learned that the Soviet regime had forced Moscow refusenik physicist Sergei Gurwitz to clean laboratory floors, they gathered outside the Soviet Embassy, and with long-handled straw brooms, "swept the Soviets off the street." The popularity of the London 35s inspired the birth of several parallel groups in other English cities and within a few years there were a total of nineteen separate 35s' groups in Great Britain.[8]

Yitzhack Rager was transferred to the Soviet Jewry desk at the consulate general for Israel in New York in the fall of 1973.[9] On January 24, 1974, he visited Montreal to speak at a meeting of the Canadian Jewish Congress. That evening Rager told stories about sophisticated, highly educated Soviet Jews who had become pariahs, just because they wanted to study their language, their heritage and emigrate to Israel. He spoke of Alexander Feldman, sentenced to three-and-a-half years in prison on charges of "malicious hooliganism." His crime? – bumping into a woman carrying a cake. "Somewhere on an airplane from Moscow, via Vienna, to Ben Gurion airport," concluded Rager, " is the future prime minister of the state of Israel."[10]

While in Montreal, Rager met with Andrea Cohen Bronfman, a vibrant young woman with a keen interest in Jewish issues, who agreed to sponsor a "Soviet Jewry Write-In" in her home. In March 1974, fifty Jewish women gathered in Bronfman's home to write letters to refuseniks and to meet the charismatic Yitzhack Rager. He captivated his audience with stories about refuseniks and prisoners. "I believe in the power of Jewish women," he announced, as he admitted candidly that his goal was to create in Canada groups of 35s patterned after the British groups. "I have no doubt," said Rager, "that if

Jewish women had demonstrated outside Anthony Eden's office in the 1940s, they would have forced Britain to bomb Auschwitz."[11]

Rager convinced a number of young women who had assembled that day to establish "the 35s" in Montreal.[12] "We didn't know where to begin," Bronfman remarked years later, "but we had our 'name' and we were anxious to get started."[13]

The first demonstration staged by the Montreal 35s was a "freedom seder" on behalf of Sylva Zalmanson, held on the third night of Passover. Fifty women dressed in black stood on the street facing the Soviet Consulate. In front of them was a twenty-foot-long table adorned with candlesticks, bottles of kosher wine and piles of matzah. A blow up photograph of Zalmanson was displayed on either side of the seder table.

Parts of the *haggadah* were read and prayers were chanted in hope for the early release of the only female prisoner of the Leningrad trials. At first, the women were unnerved by eyes peeking out from behind curtains in the darkened building, but then they remembered Rager's words, "In Moscow, Jews can be arrested for staging demonstrations. The worst thing you can catch is a cold!"

This was the first of countless demonstrations organized by the Montreal 35s, all aimed at keeping the issue of the harassment and persecution of Soviet Jews in the public eye. Stan Urman, director of the Montreal Committee for Soviet Jewry, gave considerable support to the group. Knowing that the time had come for the Soviet Jewry issue to gain a higher profile, he provided resource material and helped to direct their activities. Soon, the 35s were the most active Soviet Jewry group in Montreal.

A few months after his visit to Montreal, Rager inspired the birth of the Toronto 35s, and the Ottawa and Winnipeg 35s emerged the following year.[14] The Ottawa group used the Soviet Embassy on Charlotte Street as a focal point for demonstrations, marches and rallies. The Montreal 35s usually demonstrated outside the Soviet Consulate. Since Toronto and Winnipeg had no official Soviet presence, the women held protests in public parks or outside local government buildings.

By the mid-1970s, The 35s – Women's Campaign for Soviet

Jewry was flourishing in Great Britain, Ireland, Scotland, Belgium, Australia, Italy, New Zealand, Canada, the U.S. and Israel.[15] Their activities were geared to educating the public, lending moral support to refuseniks and informing the Soviets that their human rights record was under scrutiny. All groups demonstrated in black and wore large gilt "Prisoner of Zion" medallions in the shape of a Star of David on chains around their necks. The 35s' motto was, "We speak out for those who cannot speak out for themselves."

Hardly a week passed where the women were not involved in some form of visible action to protest the harassment of one or more Soviet Jews. They became proficient in stencilling banners, writing press releases and securing police permits. In each of the four Canadian cities, a small nucleus of women met almost daily to plan demonstrations timed to coincide with Jewish holidays or life cycle events. When a crisis took place, they were on the streets within hours.

Although the core groups of 35s were comprised of Jewish women, they were able to reach out to the general community. "The Montreal 35s could always depend on the Catholic sisters of Notre Dame de Sion," said Montreal 35s member Barbara Stern. "Sister Marie Noelle spoke on behalf of Soviet Jews at meetings and stood with us at demonstrations and mass rallies."[16]

The 35s always tried to find an angle to enable the media to report Soviet Jewry news through local protest. "When Dr. Mikhail Shtern, a Vinnitsa endocrinologist, was sentenced to seven years of prison on false charges of accepting chickens and eggs as bribes from some of his patients," said Ottawa 35s chairman Ruth Berger, "we carried baskets filled with eggs and dead chickens to the embassy gate, to mock the charges."

Newspaper, radio and television coverage, long considered to be the most effective means of influencing the Canadian conscience, was the yardstick by which the 35s measured their success. They learned that the media would not cover every Soviet Jewry event or demonstration. If they wanted press coverage, they had to be where the press was – and reporters always attended the openings of Soviet cultural events.

When the Bolshoi Ballet toured Canada in June 1974, the

Montreal 35s purchased a block of forty seats for opening night. Each seat represented one Soviet Jewish prisoner. Twenty couples arrived at Place des Arts concert hall one hour before the scheduled performance. All were dressed in black formal attire, except for one man, who wore striped prison garb. The "prisoner" led the others in a silent march on the outdoor concourse, while fellow concert-goers looked on.

Ten minutes before the curtain rose, the couples filed into the theatre and took their seats in the orchestra section. The overture began and as the Russian dancers appeared on stage, thirty-nine demonstrators stood at attention and then filed slowly out of the theatre, leaving the prisoner alone in an empty block of seats. The protesters distributed flyers during intermission to explain their actions to the audience.[17]

The next evening, in Toronto, as ballet patrons approached the O'Keefe Centre concert hall, they saw fifty women chained at their shoulders parading back and forth in front of the entrance. One placard read, "I bet they aren't dancing in the gulag."[18] Some people congratulated the group and thanked them for taking a positive stand. Others were hostile. A woman, who had refused to take a handbill, said, "It's a reality that Communists are ruling Russia – but this is culture – it's ballet."[19] The Winnipeg 35s greeted Bolshoi Ballet patrons outside the Centennial Concert Hall wearing striped prison costumes and carrying placards bearing the names of Jewish prisoners.[20]

The Canadian 35s' influence spilled over into smaller communities that could not sustain an ongoing advocacy group, but were able to mobilize women, and some of their husbands, through their affiliation with Hadassah-Wizo. Protesters met the Bolshoi Ballet's plane as it arrived in Halifax and travelled in two buses to Acadia University in Wolfville, Nova Scotia, to demonstrate outside the concert hall where the Bolshoi was performing.[21] Similar protests were staged against the troupe in Regina and Calgary.[22]

On October 25, 1974, some patrons shouted obscenities at the Toronto 35s when they demonstrated in front of Massey Hall prior to the performance by the Kiev Opera and Ballet Company. The women paraded in silence outside the theatre, carrying a set of unbalanced "scales of justice" and signs protesting the impending trial of Moscow physicist Victor Polsky. Polsky had been accused of intentionally hitting a young girl, who had leapt into the path of his car.

A few days later, during a telephone conversation with Genya Intrator, Polsky informed her that the judge had found him guilty. Rather than the usual prison sentence, he had been fined $150. "From the first to the last day of the trial," Polsky affirmed, "I was aware of the help and support of many hundreds of people of all different backgrounds – from housewives to senators. If at the end of the court case, the authorities decided on a light sentence, I see it as a result of these efforts."[23]

Many members of the Jewish community were uncomfortable with demonstrations being staged by their peers. "In those days, respectable Jewish women didn't parade in public, carrying signs," recalled Barbara Glass of the Toronto 35s. "People often wondered how we had the courage to do it. I think the public perception was that it was dangerous."[24]

The full effect of the demonstrations against the Bolshoi and Kiev dance troupes was not known until the following year, when a notice appeared in *The Montreal Star*: "Soviet officials have turned down a proposed Canadian tour by Leningrad's Kirov Ballet because they are concerned about a repetition of certain 'problems' during last year's tour by the Bolshoi and Kiev companies, says Canadian Concerts and Artists' promoter Nicholas Koudriavtzeff." [25]

The issue of patronizing Soviet events had long been a subject of debate. Many Jews argued that they could not support Soviet culture as long as Soviet Jews were being harassed and imprisoned. Others attended performances without qualms. The 35s believed that their presence at Soviet cultural events was acceptable if the purpose was to protest the treatment of Soviet Jews.

When it was advertised that the Beryozka dancers were to perform at Place des Arts in September 1975, the Montreal 35s acquired a block of one hundred seats that they sold to friends. On the night of the performance, most of the ticket-holders, dressed in black formal attire with the large Prisoner of Conscience medallions hanging from their necks, took their places in the concert hall, leaving several women behind to distribute specially designed programs to patrons. The program cover was a replica of the Beryozka poster. Inside, the left page was headlined CAST– a talented company of young dancers, singers and musicians. The right page heading was OUTCASTS, followed by six short paragraphs describing three refuseniks and three prisoners.[26] Murmurings in the audience indicated that the bogus programs had made an impact.

After the first dance number, the protesters rose and filed out of the theatre, leaving one person at the end of each row to prevent the seats being filled at intermission. The demonstration was reported by the CBC and broadcast into the Soviet Union. *La Presse* reported on the event through an article headlined: "Le Beryoska et L'Etoile de David" (The Beryozka and the Star of David). It compared the vacant space in the front section of the orchestra to a gaping hole in one's mouth after a tooth extraction.[27]

Soviet cultural events continued to be "fair game." In 1976, when forty-two masterpieces from Leningrad's Hermitage and State Russian Museum were unveiled to the public in Winnipeg and Montreal, the 35s staged demonstrations at the gala openings – and the Moscow Circus was welcomed to Canada by two "Soviet bears" who led the Winnipeg 35s on a noon-hour march, downtown.[28]

Demonstrations at cultural events could be planned in advance, but most demonstrations were organized on short notice, such as one that came about as the result of a 1975 summer meeting between the Montreal 35s and the Royal Canadian Mounted Police (RCMP). The officers belonged to a special unit that dealt with security at the 1976 Summer Olympics in Montreal and had requested the meeting to determine the group's modus operandi. During their friendly discussion, one officer mentioned that he would be on duty at the formal opening of the Russian Contemporary Art Exhibition that very evening. Previously unaware of the event, the group had little time to plan.

At 6:30 PM, four women, dressed modestly in black, posed as waitresses, to gain early entry to the Expo Museum. They proceeded to the second floor where the exhibition was taking place. An hour later, as the guests began to arrive, Soviet consul Gavruchkin walked right into the four women. When he noticed that one was holding a sealed envelope and a red rose, he whispered to his aide, who quickly approached the officer and informed him that the women were not to make a presentation of any kind.

Gavruchkin cut the ribbon to launch the art exhibition. As champagne was poured, the four circulated among the guests and examined the paintings. After some time the aide informed the RCMP officer that the intruders would have to leave. The 35s drove to the Soviet Consulate and carefully fastened both rose and envelope, containing a letter demanding the release of the Prisoners of Zion, to the iron gate.[29]

Another opportunity for a last-minute demonstration arose in May 1976, after Minsk refusenik Yefim Davidovich, a retired Red Army colonel who had served his country valiantly in World War II, died of a heart attack at the age of fifty-four.[30] As hundreds of refuseniks from across the USSR came to Minsk for Davidovich's funeral, the Montreal 35s staged a mock funeral outside the Soviet Consulate, holding signs that read, "Davidovich died in the USSR: Let him be buried in Israel." The demonstration aroused no media attention, so the organizers decided to repeat it the following day at Dominion Square. The coffin that had been borrowed from Paperman and Sons, Montreal's Jewish funeral director, remained in the back of the author's station-wagon for twenty-four hours. As one might expect, the unusual hearse drew curious stares. George Balcan, the host of a popular local radio show, saw it, and upon learning the details, offered to talk about the second funeral on his program the next morning.

There were fewer-than-usual observers in Dominion Square that day and no press appeared at all. Although demonstrations often produced few results, the 35s were undaunted. As Barbara Stern would say, "When just one refusenik for whom we had struggled was released, it was all worthwhile. It was just like giving birth!"

In the late 1970s, the Canadian 35s popularized the Soviet Jewry issue by wearing and selling silver bracelets engraved with the name of a prisoner. During demonstrations they sported large black buttons with the slogan, "Freedom For Soviet Jews" in bright yellow letters.

When there was no immediate crisis, the Montreal 35s would hold a "luncheon" in downtown Phillips Square on behalf of the prisoners. A large wooden cage kept a few of the women, dressed in striped uniforms, captive beside a three-metre high sign headlined, "Daily Diet in a Soviet Prison Camp." Pieces of cold potato and stale bread were served on trays to passersby, who were invited to sign petitions and postcards of solidarity with Soviet Jews.[31]

Although most of the 35s' activities were planned locally, there were often national programs, and occasionally, an international thrust. The British 35s initiated the "Women's Petition for Human Rights" that was launched in many countries on December 10, 1975, International Human Rights Day. Addressed to the government of the USSR, the petition pleaded the case of Soviet Jewish wives, mothers and children and implored the Soviet government to adopt an attitude consistent with their own laws and with international human rights.

The Canadian group elicited the support of nine national Jewish women's organizations to help obtain Canadian signatures.[32] While special launching ceremonies took place in Toronto and Montreal on December 10,[33] several Toronto and Montreal members joined the Ottawa group on Parliament Hill to secure endorsements from their members of parliament.[34] The women met with former prime minister John Diefenbaker, who stood behind the desk in his small office in the Parliament Buildings and spoke of his long-time support for the Soviet Jewry issue. "Never have I been more hopeless concerning the preservation of freedom than I am now," he remarked. "The USSR is stronger in the world because of our weakness."[35] Although Canada's elder statesman had a policy of not signing petitions, Diefenbaker wrote a note on his personal stationery confirming his support: "To whom it may concern: I have read the 'Canadian Women's Petition for Human Rights' and I entirely endorse it."[36]

MPs Herb Gray and John Roberts convened a press conference to publicly announce the launching of the petition and, following the afternoon session of parliament, the 35s met with their respective MPs to obtain their signatures.

Several members of the Montreal group met with their elected member of parliament – Pierre Elliott Trudeau.[37] As they entered the prime minister's wood-paneled office, he greeted them warmly, passed around a box of chocolates, and said, "Shoot!" They explained that the Helsinki Final Act, signed four months earlier, was being blatantly violated by the Soviet government, as evidenced by the hundreds of refuseniks who continued to be denied permission to join their families in Israel. To illustrate this point, the group presented the case of Anatoly Sharansky, a spokesman for the Moscow refusenik community, who had been denied permission to emigrate and reunite with his wife in Jerusalem.

The prime minister listened carefully and then conceded that Basket Three, which had encompassed the humanitarian aspect of the Helsinki Final Act, had been of great importance to Canada. He said that he was prepared to confront the Soviets on the issue if he had well-documented proof of Soviet non-compliance for a period of six months from the date of the signing. Before leaving Trudeau's office, the group assured him that they would assemble the necessary information.

For the next two months, the Montreal 35s, counselled by Montreal lawyer Aaron Pollack, prepared extensive documentation of Soviet human rights violations and submitted it to the prime minister's office in the form of a brief. A few weeks later, a response came from Klaus Goldschlag, under-secretary of state with the Department of External Affairs. It neither comforted the activists nor advanced the cause.

"While the Canadian government sympathizes with your concerns for those individuals," the letter stated, "it is limited in what it can do on their behalf, particularly with respect to their possible immigration to Israel, as there is no direct Canadian aspect to warrant specific representations by it to the Soviet authorities." On the broader application Goldschlag said, "The Helsinki Final Act is not a 'treaty' and is therefore not legally binding."[38] Brezhnev's declaration, made in Yalta, to adhere to assurances made at the Helsinki signing, had not been noted in Goldschlag's response. Equally disturbing was his disregard for the Final Act's reaffirmation of the principles of the 1948 United Nations' Universal Declaration of Human Rights.

In a letter to Allan J. MacEachen, secretary of state for external affairs, the 35s acknowledged that the Helsinki Final Act was a declaration of intent by the signators who pledged to carry out the letter and spirit of its provisions. "In the years preceding the signing at Helsinki," the letter read, "Canada worked assiduously to expand the humanitarian provisions of the Third Basket. We find it difficult to believe that Canada, of all countries, would retreat into a narrow and legalistic attitude towards such an important international instrument."[39] MacEachen never did respond to the letter.

The lifespan of the Canadian 35s varied in each community. The Ottawa and Winnipeg 35s remained viable forces until the late 1970s. The Toronto 35s maintained its separate identity until the mid-1980s when they merged with the Committee for Soviet Jewry, Ontario Region. The Montreal 35s continued their activity on behalf of the few remaining refuseniks well after the doors of Jewish emigration opened in 1989.

With the mass exodus of Jews into Israel, followed by the demise of the USSR in December 1991, the British 35s changed their direction. They embarked on a program of providing financial assistance to needy Soviet Jews in Israel through a one-on-one adoption of families, a project that is ongoing to this day.

Chapter 9

Some Success

The surprise event of February 1974 was a confrontation at midnight, at Gander International Airport in Newfoundland, between Leonid Brezhnev and ten Jewish men and women from St. John's, 320 kilometres away. A more unlikely spot for a Soviet-Canadian encounter could not have been imagined.[1]

The Soviet leader's plane, en route to Moscow from an official visit in Cuba, stopped in Gander to refuel. The protesters, who represented thirty-five Jewish families in St. John's, had flown through a snowstorm in sub-zero temperatures. When they arrived at the airport armed with signs, "Let My People Go," they were joined by local CBC reporters. The group was confined to an area behind a chain fence, 230 metres from the tarmac, as Brezhnev's Ilyusin 62 jetliner landed and taxied to a stop.

When the Soviet leader disembarked, he was attracted to the commotion near his aircraft. He approached the demonstrators and engaged them in discussion. Dr. Avrum Richler, spokesperson for the group, communicated with Brezhnev through an interpreter. Brezhnev denied Richler's claim that half a million Jews desired to leave the Soviet Union, maintaining that the true figure was thirty-five hundred. Furthermore, when questioned about the failing health of prisoner Sylva Zalmanson, serving the fourth year of her incarceration in Potma Labour Camp, Brezhnev replied, "This woman is an enemy of the State. She committed a criminal act in attempting to hijack an airplane. I am not able to interfere with the course of justice."[2]

The story of the confrontation was broadcast nationally on CBC radio and picked up by international wire services, which might have been why Richler's request for a meeting with Soviet ambassador Yacovlev was granted. A few days later, Newfoundland MP Don Jamieson accompanied Richler and a small delegation from St. John's to the Soviet Embassy in Ottawa. The group had hurriedly obtained four hundred signatures on a petition, demanding Zalmanson's release, that they presented to the ambassador, who politely accepted it.[3]

The case of Sylva Zalmanson had become top priority in Canada. She was the focus of a demonstration held May 1, a national holiday in the Soviet Union, where traditionally, Soviet military hardware was displayed in parades in major cities. That day, the Montreal 35s, joined together at the shoulder by ropes of flowers, marched in single file from Dominion Square to the Soviet Consulate, carrying placards that read, "On this May Day show us your hearts, not your arms" and "May Day means M'aidez for Sylva Zalmanson."[4]

Canadian Hadassah-Wizo members paid tribute to Zalmanson outside the Soviet Embassy in Ottawa, holding banners reading, "If you forget her, the world forgets her."[5] Stale bread, cold potatoes and pieces of dried herring, typical prison food served at Potma Labour Camp, were nibbled by demonstrators under the glare of television cameras.

The campaign to free Sylva Zalmanson included the intervention of Toronto's Charles S. Chaplin, a distributor of international films. In April 1973, during negotiations with Vladimir Kowalsky concerning the distribution of Soviet-made films in Canada, Chaplin tried to make the release of Zalmanson and the family of film producer Boris Gorakoff a condition of his involvement.[6] Kowalsky made no promises.

In March 1974, Chaplin read in the *Hollywood Reporter* that he had been awarded distribution rights for the Soviet film of the Bolshoi Ballet. He immediately mailed the article to Kowalsky with a note reminding him of the request for Zalmanson's and the Gorakoffs' freedom.[7] Three weeks later, Chaplin received word that the Gorakoff family had received visas.

In August 1974, Soviet Jewry activists were rewarded. Sylva Zalmanson was released from prison and granted a visa to Israel, having served four years of a ten year sentence. She was the first of the Leningrad trial prisoners to be freed before her sentence expired.

After spending a few weeks in Israel, Zalmanson began a global tour to gain support for the remaining Leningrad prisoners. "From the beginning we had no illusions," she told audiences. "We would either land up in jail or be shot and killed. Three factors drove us on – our terrible despair, our desire to live in Israel and our youthful hope. We expected an ordinary hijacking trial; instead, much to our surprise and joy, it became a focal point of our struggle. It was only after our trial that Jews were allowed to leave in much greater numbers than in the past. We couldn't have had a better reward."[8]

Across the breadth and depth of the USSR, more and more young people began to identify themselves as Jews. Leonid Feldman of Kishinev had been raised a staunch Communist and was a passionate atheist. His interest in Judaism was ignited at the age of eighteen when he learned that a young man had been imprisoned for owning a book about Judaism. "I was ashamed to think that my country, the most powerful nation in the world, was afraid of one little book," he recalled.[9]

Feldman became more curious about his Jewishness in 1974, when he was advised by a university professor not to apply to the physics institute of his choice because his name was "Feldman." This drove him to seek out members of the Kishinev Jewish community.

One night, in a quiet park, Kishinev activist Mark Abramovich gave Feldman a small, battered book and told him to return it before daybreak. It was a hand-written Russian translation of Leon Uris's *Exodus*. "I read through the night," he recalled, "and I discovered that Jews had been around for three thousand years, that they spoke a language of their own and lived in a country where a Feldman could become prime minister. By morning, I was a Zionist."

Within a short time of applying to emigrate, Leonid Feldman received his refusal in writing, "The Soviet government does not see the necessity of you going to Israel." Feldman joined the ranks of the Kishinev refusenik community.[10]

Emigration figures had peaked in 1973 but were beginning to drop considerably in 1974, due to strained relations between East and West. This resulted from publicity surrounding the proposed Jackson-Vanik Amendment to the 1974 U.S. Trade Bill, as well as a new amendment to the Export-Import Bank Bill.[11]

U.S. president Nixon was planning a visit to Moscow in June 1974. Prior to his arrival, nine refuseniks, along with prostitutes and other "unwanted elements," were rounded up and taken to outlying prisons.[12] Although aware of the arrests, Nixon didn't protest or demand the refuseniks' release. It was thought that he remained silent, hoping for one last chance at an East-West thaw.

Any chance of *détente* between the USSR and the U.S. was rapidly deterioriating because Senator Jackson's amendment was gaining ground in Congress. Secretary of State Henry Kissinger was still opposed to the initiative, but when the amendment was approved in the House of Representatives on December 11, 1973, by a vote of 319 to 80, he and Nixon had little choice but to acquiesce.

The consensus of the refuseniks on the subject of the Jackson-Vanik Amendment was expressed by Moscow refusenik Vladimir Slepak to Canadian writer Barry Conn Hughes who visited the indomitable leader in his apartment in March 1974. "We were somewhat puzzled by Kissinger's speech before the Senate sub-committee," Slepak told Hughes. "Kissinger thinks it could do more harm than good to Soviet Jewry, but to the contrary – we think it will be good for us."[13]

Weeks of correspondence between Jackson and the reticent Kissinger finally resulted in their agreeing to an emigration benchmark of sixty-thousand Jews per year, before the U.S. would waive the Jackson-Vanik Amendment.

The Jackson/Kissinger concession had an immediate effect on the lives of refusenik scientists Victor Polsky and Alexander Voronel. Polsky, who had narrowly escaped a lengthy prison sentence due to world-wide protests on his behalf, and Voronel, founding chairman of Moscow's Scientific Seminar, received permission to leave the following day.

As more and more publicity surrounded the Jackson-Vanik

Montreal, March 8, 1953: Monroe Abbey, vice-president CJC, speaks against "anti-Semitism in Russia and satellite countries" at a protest meeting held at Her Majesty's Theatre. [CJC Archives]

above: Ottawa, January 3, 1971: "Canadian Jewry cries, 'Let my People Go!'" 7,000 Jews from Montreal, Toronto and Ottawa gather on Parliament Hill to protest Leningrad trial sentencings. [CJC Archives]

left: Secretary of State for External Affairs Mitchell Sharp assures protesters, "This demonstration of support is one that will not be unnoticed throughout the world." [CJC Archives]

Ottawa, October 19, 1971: Canadian rabbis conduct vigil at the Centennial flame outside the House of Commons during Soviet premier Alexei Kosygin's visit to Canada. [Rabbi Erwin Schild]

Gander Airport, February 1974: Leonid Brezhnev from behind a wire fence separating him from Jewish protesters from St. John's.

Montreal, June 17, 1974: The Montreal 35s protest harassment of Soviet Jews on the concourse of Place des Arts prior to the performance of the Bolshoi Ballet. [Art Taylor]

Toronto, May 24, 1974: Writer Barry Conn Hughes speaks with Moscow refusenik Vladimir Slepak while Genya Intrator looks on. [*The Canadian Magazine*]

Toronto, October 25, 1974: The Toronto 35s demonstrate against the trial of Moscow refusenik Victor Polsky, outside Massey Hall, prior to the performance of the Kiev Opera and Ballet Company. [David Groskind]

Ottawa, June 9, 1975: (l to r) Alan Raymond, Stan Urman, MLA Harry Blank, Rabbi Howard Joseph, MP John Roberts attempt to deliver packages to the Soviet Embassy for delivery to the forty Soviet Jewish prisoners. [Howard Kay]

Ottawa, December 10, 1975: Former prime minister John Diefenbaker writes note of support for the International 35s' Women's Petition for Human Rights. [Bill Brennan/*Ottawa Citizen*]

Montreal, May 4, 1976: The Montreal 35s stage a mock funeral for retired Red Army colonel Yefim Davidovich, a Minsk refusenik who died before receiving a visa to emigrate to Israel.

Winnipeg, November 2, 1977: "Soviet bears" lead the Winnipeg 35s in a protest march down Portage Avenue to mark the arrival of the Moscow Circus. [Wayne Glowacki/*Winnipeg Free Press*]

Montreal, October 1978: Jewish day school students march on behalf of Soviet Jewry outside the Soviet Consulate.

above: Montreal, October 1979: The Montreal 35s serve a "prisoner's lunch" in Phillips Square. [Howard Kay/*The Canadian Jewish News*]

left: Montreal, November 6, 1977: Avital Sharansky joins a candlelight vigil outside the Soviet Consulate while sixtieth anniversary celebrations marking the Russian Revolution take place inside. [Len Sidaway/*The Gazette*]

Montreal, January 20, 1978: (l to r) Reverend Syd Nelson, Father Barry Jones, Rabbi Sidney Shoham, Reverend John Simms attempt to deliver a bible, a gift for Anatoly Sharansky on his thirtieth birthday, to the Soviet Consulate. [Ellen P. Busby]

Montreal, March 15, 1979: Cathy Maron and Martin Penn put finishing touches to signs for a demonstration to mark the second anniversary of Anatoly Sharansky's arrest. [Tedd Church/*The Gazette*]

December 8, 1978, Moscow: Sixteen-year-old Leonid Brailovsky proudly wears the button, "Bialik for Brailovsky," after learning that Bialik High School in Montreal had adopted him.

December 9, 1978, Moscow: Refusenik Pavel Abramovich utters the word that makes him break into a wide smile – "VI-SA."

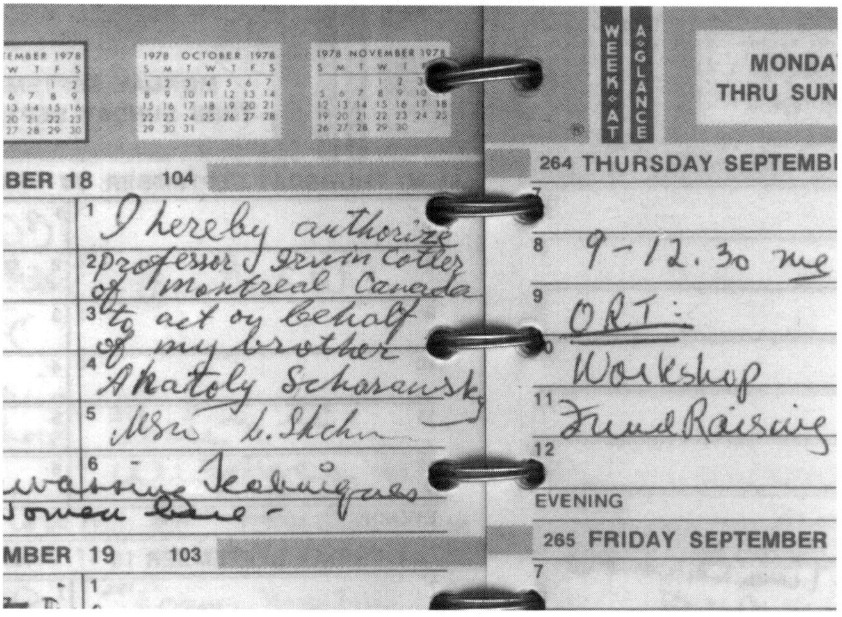

Moscow, December 8, 1978: Note written and signed by Leonid Sharansky in the author's daily diary: "I hereby authorize Professor Irwin Cotler of Montreal, Canada to act on behalf of my brother Anatoly Sharansky."

Amendment, the Soviets were becoming desperate. In the fall of 1974, a KGB official summoned Eduard Kuznetsov, who was serving the fourth year of his fifteen-year sentence, into the prison office. The officer informed him that, if passed, the Amendment would have serious repercussions for the Jews and he urged Kuznetsov to condemn it in writing in return for special personal treatment. Kuznetsov, who had only recently learned of Jackson's initiative through articles in *Pravda*, recognized the trap. He immediately attested to Senator Jackson's greatness and declared unequivocal support for the Amendment.[14]

On December 20, 1974, the Jackson-Vanik Amendment passed both the Senate and the House of Representatives. It was adopted by the U.S. Congress as part of the 1974 Trade Reform Act and signed into law by President Gerald Ford on January 3, 1975.

During the two years that the amendment had been debated, the Soviets issued more than eighty thousand visas. The linkage of trade benefits and emigration was established. Never again would Soviet authorities be able to halt the flow of emigrants without jeopardizing their access to trade credits.[15]

After the congressional enactment, the Kremlin launched a widespread media campaign denouncing the trade agreement, and then began to manipulate the number of visas, causing the numbers to rise and fall with no discernible pattern. They tried to deal with a piece of American legislation they despised, but which wouldn't go away.[16] It appeared that the problem of Soviet Jewry would occupy the world agenda for a very long time.

Riding on the American popularity of "Jackson-Vanik," Moscow refusenik leader Alexander Goldfarb launched his own personal advocacy campaign. The doctoral student in microbiology at the Kurchatov Atomic Institute had received his first refusal in October 1973 on the grounds of "possession of secrets that might affect national security."

In June 1974, he wrote thirty identical letters to his colleagues globally explaining his situation and requesting intervention on his behalf. "Those of you who have visited our laboratory can easily understand the complete absurdity of considering my work on RNA polymerase of E coli and the general research on transcription carried out in the lab to any extent related to warfare and military secrets," he wrote. "Not only have I never participated in any kind of classified research or seen a classified document, but I have never met a person in my department who has. All the results of our laboratory were published in the open press and abroad."[17]

Goldfarb placed all the letters into one large envelope and gave it to Moscow's *New York Times*' bureau chief Hedrick Smith, who agreed to send it out of the Soviet Union in the American diplomatic pouch. The envelope was addressed to Genya Intrator, Goldfarb's telephone contact in Toronto.[18] Upon receipt of the package, Intrator followed Goldfarb's instructions, forwarding the envelope to an American biologist who disseminated the letters to the appropriate parties.

Within weeks, attachés at Soviet embassies and consulates began to receive cables and letters from biologists supporting Goldfarb's application to emigrate. " . . . Dr. Goldfarb's research has been solely concerned with matters of basic research in molecular biology (RNA polymerase in Escherichia coli bacteria)," wrote Professor Max Delbruck, a Nobel laureate at the California Institute of Technology, to the scientific attaché of the Soviet Embassy in Washington. "It seems very far-fetched and illogical that this research would bring him into the possession of secrets that might affect the national security."[19]

Intrator learned of an international genetic conference scheduled to take place in Ansilomar, California, in February 1975. Unable to communicate with Goldfarb directly, she contacted one of his associates in Vienna to have Goldfarb prepare a statement for the conference.

The Soviet Jewry network was tested. A British reporter carried Alexander Goldfarb's written statement out of Moscow and passed it to Michael Sherbourne in London, who then dictated the statement to Intrator in Toronto. She, in turn, transmitted it to Professor Delbruck in California in time to be presented to the international community of scientists at the conference.[20]

Within weeks, there was a positive outcome. In May 1975, Goldfarb was completing his doctoral studies at the Weizmann

Institute in Israel. Alexander Goldfarb's release reinforced the uniqueness of each refusenik case, and the importance of mobilizing the most appropriate advocates.[21]

A new pattern began to develop. Most of the few hundred exit visas issued in the mid-1970s went to new applicants and not to refuseniks, whose actions were closely scrutinized. In protest, on February 24, 1975, a group of Moscow refuseniks staged a demonstration in front of the Lenin Library. They carried banners that read: "Visas, not Prisons." Within minutes, Mark Nashpitz and Boris Tsitlionok were arrested on grounds of "malicious hooliganism," adding two more names to the list of prisoners.

Activists in the free world began to recognize the importance of publicizing individual refusenik cases. One that had gained considerable attention was that of economist Ida Nudel, who for many years had been employed by Moscow's Institute of Planning and Production to assess the standards of hygiene in food shops.

Nudel had been raised in an assimilated family with no Jewish observance. It was the prevalence of anti-Semitism in her workplace and on the streets that prompted her to seek the company of Jewish friends. As she identified more closely with Judaism in the late 1960s, she joined a group of Jews who were studying Hebrew. Ida Nudel applied to emigrate to Israel in 1971, along with her sister Ilana Fridman and her family. The Fridmans received visas immediately, but Nudel was refused on grounds of "secrecy." "The greatest secrets I ever had," she said, "were where the rats and mice built their nests."[22]

Ida Nudel was barely five feet tall, yet she was a giant in her activist stance. Every six months she re-submitted her application. With each refusal she questioned the authorities and courageously withstood verbal abuse and occasional beatings.

Refusing to wallow in her own misfortune, Nudel embarked on a private campaign to ameliorate the situation for the Jewish prisoners. She wrote letters to "her boys" and sent parcels of food, medicine, vitamins, chewing gum and warm clothing – items brought by travellers from abroad. She visited the prisons or labour camps, often delivering the bundles personally.

Ida Nudel became known to the prisoners as a "guardian angel." "Ida's letters often included picture postcards from Israel, as well as Japanese 3-D transparencies," said former prisoner Lasal Kaminsky, "that we gave to prison guards or to other prisoners as barter, in exchange for food."[23] In many cases, her letters were the only source of information they had about their fellow inmates. Between the lines, she managed to include news about those who had left for Israel and of new developments within the refusenik community.

"A person who has not been in prison could not envisage what Ida Nudel means to the prisoners," commented David Chernoglaz, who convalesced at Ida's Moscow apartment after his release from Potma Labour Camp. "Her constant care and attention is the only factor which keeps their morale high. There is no woman on earth whom we value more."[24]

In the spring of 1975, Toronto lawyers Sam Filer and Bert Raphael invited several colleagues to a meeting to discuss the formation of a lawyers' committee to assist Jews in obtaining fair trials under the Soviet constitution and to hold the Soviets accountable to their own laws.[25]

The Canadian Lawyers and Jurists for Soviet Jewry (CLJSJ) was created with Filer as its founding chairman. Its first program was held at the historic Campbell House in Toronto in the presence of forty lawyers and judges.[26] The guest speaker was Victor Polsky, whom Filer and Raphael had met in Moscow. Citing his own example of narrowly escaping a prison sentence after being accused of intentionally hitting a girl with his car, Polsky explained, "There are many, many instances where the Soviets sentence people, not according to law, but according to circumstances."[27] The latest cases were the February arrests of Nashpitz and Tsitlionok. The former refusenik urged the lawyers to fight for the new prisoners' legal rights.

The first letter Raphael wrote on behalf of Soviet Jewry was sent to Ambassador Yacovlev in support of the two young refuseniks. "It is apparent that the nature of the charges against Nashpitz and Tsitlionok have not been disclosed," he wrote. "It has been reported that their trial will take place 'in camera.' The holding of a trial in the manner suggested and the detention of persons without disclosing charges offends the most basic principles of human justice. It is for the purpose of speaking out with respect to such matters that our Committee has been formed."[28]

When Nashpitz and Tsitlionok were sentenced to five years of exile in Siberia, solely for demonstrating for five minutes outside the Lenin Library, the small group of lawyers who formed the committee were incensed and decided to expand their membership. They placed an advertisement in Canadian legal journals and within one year, the names of seven hundred lawyers and fifteen judges from coast to coast were listed on the back of their letterhead.

Arthur Maloney, a criminal lawyer and staunch advocate of civil liberties and human rights, served on the CLJSJ's executive board and retired Supreme Court justice Emmett Hall was named honourary chairman. In 1976, Bert Raphael assumed the chairmanship of the lawyer's committee, a viable entity that held Soviet Jewry programs throughout the year, funded by annual membership dues.

During times of crises, committees were formed for as few as one or two refuseniks. "Friends of the Goldshteins" was created in response to the April 1975 arrests of refusenik physicists Grigory and Isai Goldshtein of Tbilisi, Georgia.[29] In early June, MP Robert Kaplan attempted to call the Goldshtein brothers in Tbilisi from his Ottawa office. The call did not go through. It was hoped that publicity surrounding the foiled telephone call might prevent further incidents.[30] In fact, the Goldshteins lost their jobs and in 1978, Grigory was charged with parasitism and exiled to Siberia for one year.

Jews viewed the Soviet Jewry movement as being driven by the parochial interest of "Jews saving Jews." To non-Jews, the issue was a human rights cause.

The advancement of the movement required the support of individuals with academic or political clout from within the general community. To this end, on June 9, 1975, a "Flight to Freedom" was organized by the Montreal Committee for Soviet Jewry to carry the concept of "symbolic adoption" into the public domain. A chartered plane carried prominent men and women from Montreal to Ottawa to publicly voice their concern for the forty Jewish prisoners.

The group, composed of leaders of the community, arts, sports, government, media, judiciary and clergy, were joined outside the Soviet Embassy by MPs Herb Gray, Tommy C. Douglas, Robert Kaplan and John Roberts. They totalled forty in all.[31] Each person in turn took the megaphone and read the name and biography of the prisoner he or she was adopting. "The best way to employ our freedoms in Canada or throughout the world is to stand up and fight for the freedoms of other people," said Douglas, after announcing his adoption of Josef Mendelevich. "It is still true that eternal vigilance is a duty of liberty."[32]

Dressed in clerical robes, Reverend Father Barry Jones, the director of communications for the Archdiocese of the English Catholic church, described the plight of his adopted prisoner. Moscow electronics engineer Lazar Lubarsky was sentenced to four years hard labour after writing an open letter to a Soviet newspaper declaring his desire to emigrate. "I pledge my commitment to my brother Lazar," affirmed Jones.[33]

Forty wrapped packages containing wool socks, a toothbrush, toothpaste, vitamins, raisins and soap were addressed to each of the prisoners. When the group attempted to deliver the packages to the embassy, a Soviet official refused to accept them. Instead, he invited the four politicians and two clergymen inside to meet with Ambassador Yacovlev. During the forty-five minute meeting, the emissaries spoke about the prisoners' plight.[34] Yacovlev replied that most of the stories circulated in the Canadian press were anti-Soviet propaganda and that questioning a Soviet official constituted an invasion of his country's internal affairs.[35]

John Robertson, who had waited with the others outside the gate, related the experience to his radio audience the next day. He concluded his remarks by saying, "Although during the meeting the ambassador did little more than copy down the names of the prisoners, this recognition of our group was a major breakthrough."[36]

Chapter 10

A Global Gathering

On November 10, 1975, Resolution 3379 denouncing Zionism as a form of racism was passed in the United Nations General Assembly by a vote of seventy-two to thirty-five, with thirty-two abstentions. It was endorsed unequivocally by the Soviet Union. On the day the resolution was adopted, United States ambassador to the UN Daniel Moynihan denounced it as an "obscene act," saying that it undermined the assumption that Israel was a legitimate homeland for the Jewish people.

World Jewish leaders decided that the time had come to convene a second international conference on Soviet Jewry. There was tangible evidence of previous success. In the five years following the first conference in Brussels in 1971, one hundred and fifteen thousand Jews had received permission to emigrate.[1] An announcement was made by the World Presidium on Soviet Jewry[2] and the International Secretariat[3] that the Second World Conference of Jewish Communities on Soviet Jewry was to be held again in Brussels, in February 1976.

Almost immediately, Soviet officials tried to persuade the Belgian government to bar the meeting, but to no avail. They didn't give up. A few days before the scheduled opening, the Soviets held a press conference in Moscow for a group of Jews who had gone to Israel, returned to the USSR, and allegedly testified to the cruelty and discrimination they had encountered there. Instead of discrediting the conference, these theatrics served to legitimize it.

The purpose of the global gathering was not only to promote the plight of Soviet Jews who wished to emigrate, but to enable those who wished to remain in the USSR to live a viable Jewish life. Added to the slogan of Brussels I, "Let my People Go" was the slogan "Let my people know!" Former prime minister Golda Meir was the honourary president and she presided over the three-day event.

The participation of twelve hundred activists, politicians, academics, scientists and students made Brussels II the largest international conference ever held on any Jewish subject. Included among the seventy Canadians present were MPs Robert Kaplan, Serge Joyal and John Roberts.

On opening night, the delegates were seated in the Palais des Congrès, under signposts of their respective countries, when a hush enveloped the massive hall. A group of former Soviet Jews, some of whom had arrived from the Soviet Union only days before, entered the room. Twelve hundred men and women stood at their seats and welcomed them with thunderous applause.[4]

As the delegates remained standing for the singing of *Hatikvah*, a man ran down the centre aisle to the dais, trailing a royal blue flag with a white Star of David in the centre. The "Soviet Jewry freedom flag," designed in refusenik Mark Azbel's Moscow apartment a few weeks earlier, was raised for the first time. Brussels II was declared officially open!

"We greet you from distant Russia," began the opening message to the delegates. "The situation of Soviet Jewry has become drastic today, demanding an equally drastic response. The main task at hand is the unity and strengthening of all efforts aimed at protecting and supporting the mass movement of Jews to Israel, along with a many-sided effort to promote the great national revival of Soviet Jewry. We appeal to you to help us in our cause. If we are fated to give our lives to the cause, then we are ready."[5] One hundred Soviet Jews were signatories to the message. Their names were read aloud, drawing murmurs of recognition from the audience.

The three days were assigned to plenary meetings that could accommodate all the delegates, and to many concurrent workshops and commissions. At the first plenary, elderly Black American civil rights leader Bayard Rustin walked, with the support of a cane, down the long aisle to the stage and in a powerful voice sang the famous spiritual, "Let my People Go!"

Rustin was one of 120 Christian delegates on whose behalf a document entitled "A Call to Christian Conscience" was submitted by Sister Ann Gillen, director of the Chicago-based National Interreligious Task Force on Soviet Jewry. The material had been presented in the names of the Catholic, Protestant and Evangelical participants to Brussels II.

The not unexpected appearance of JDL leader Rabbi Meir Kahane did little to disturb the proceedings on the first afternoon. He was quickly ushered out of the conference hall by security guards and expelled from the country by Belgian police, pursuant to an order dating back to Brussels I. Members of the Presidium held firm to their principles of not accepting Kahane for accreditation, due to his organization's doctrine of intimidation and violence – information that had been relayed to Kahane prior to the conference.

In Brussels, the Canadian 35s met their international counterparts for the first time. Conspicuous in their black attire, the group, numbering thirty women in all, held discussions in corridors and planned strategies with the SSSJ and the UCSJ from the United States, a student group from Germany and the Group of 15 from France.[6]

On the last day of the conference, the 35s gathered outside the Royal Palace with five-year-old Yigal Khnokh, son of Leningrad trial prisoner Leib Khnokh. The young boy presented thirty-five white roses to Her Majesty Queen Fabiola of Belgium.

At the closing plenary session, a declaration was read aloud: "We, representing Jewish communities in every continent, declare to our brethren in the Soviet Union: We are with you in your struggle. We share your faith. We honour your courage. You are not alone! On this historic occasion, we remember the ancient oath of our people: For the sake of Zion, I will not remain silent and for the sake of Jerusalem, I will not hold my peace. As heirs to that tradition, we solemnly declare that for the sake of our brethren in the Soviet Union, we shall not remain silent; nor shall we hold our peace."[7]

A swelling "I do" filled the cavernous chamber of the Palais des Congrès, setting the stage for a masterful concluding speech by Golda Meir. The seventy-year-old grandmother began by asking a rhetorical question. "What is it that anti-Semites can't forgive us . . . what is the greatest of our faults? We refuse to disappear. No matter how strong, brutal or ruthless the powers against us might be, here we are! Millions of bodies have been broken, buried alive and burned to death, but never was anyone able to break the spirit of the Jewish people." Golda Meir concluded her address in a thunderous voice, "If the Russians will not let our brethren be Jews in Russia then let them come to their historic homeland. I guarantee you rulers of Moscow, the Jews of the Soviet Union will be free!"[8]

An exit visa was granted to prominent Moscow refusenik Alexander Luntz the very next day, indicating that the Soviets were sensitive to world pressure.

Emigration figures began to escalate slowly. Following Brussels II, the primacy of Soviet Jewry as an issue for world Jewry was uncontested. The Canadian Committee for Soviet Jewry, chaired by David Satok, hired staff to co-ordinate programming in major Canadian cities and received the largest budget allocation of any CJC committee.[9] The CCSJ was responsible for the formation of two new Soviet Jewry groups: the Committee of Concerned Scientists for Soviet Jewry, modelled after similar committees in Israel, Great Britain and the United States, and the Canadian Parliamentary Group for Soviet Jewry, which paralleled the parliamentary group in Great Britain.

The scientists' committee was headed by University of Toronto physics professor Eric Fawcett, a non-Jew, who became interested in the Soviet Jewry issue after attending a refusenik scientific seminar in Moscow in 1976. "I was struck by the persecution of Jewish scientists in the USSR and the tremendous potential being lost," Fawcett said. "I thought that a scientists' committee could be an extremely effective medium for international understanding."[10] His Jewish colleagues, Calvin Gottlieb, Israel Halperin and Irving Glass, were eager to participate.

MP Robert Kaplan was the natural choice as chairman of the Parliamentary Group for Soviet Jewry for he had played a pivotal role with Soviet Jewry on "the Hill" since travelling with an official government group to the USSR in 1975.[11] Kaplan, however, refused to head the group. He believed that broad-based interest in a Jewish cause was always heightened when it was championed by non-Jews.[12]

John Roberts willingly assumed the chairmanship. He performed his first official function on May 12, 1976, when the Parliamentary Group for Soviet Jewry hosted a reception on Parliament Hill to receive the "Canadian Women's Petition for Human Rights" launched in the House of Commons, five months earlier. Roberts accepted the petition with twenty-five thousand signatures and agreed to deliver it to the Soviet ambassador.[13]

With several official committees in place, interest in the Soviet Jewry issue was heightened, and self-proclaimed activists were becoming confident advocating on behalf of Soviet Jews.

Chapter 11

Soviet Repression – Creative Responses

Kishinev refusenik Leonid Feldman was hoping that Brussels II might be the catalyst to change his destiny, but in May 1976, he received yet another refusal. In protest, Feldman began a hunger strike inside the municipal building where visas were issued. He was arrested and imprisoned on charges of "hooliganism."

When publicity about Feldman's fast reached the West, Kishinev and Politburo officials were deluged with telegrams demanding his release. "On the eleventh day of my hunger strike," Feldman recalled, "I was sitting in rags on the cold stone floor of a Soviet prison with my hair shaven and belly swollen, refusing all food but water, when an official came into my cell and informed me that they had reconsidered my application to emigrate to Israel."[1]

Four months later, Leonid Feldman was enrolled as a student at Hebrew University.

The profile of the Soviet Jewish activist was changing. By the mid-1970s, many of the Soviet Jews who were landing at Ben-Gurion Airport were not Zionists, as the early immigrants had been, but rather used their unique opportunity to "repatriate to their homeland" as a "passport to freedom." They came to Israel to escape Communism and to enjoy the affluence they thought living in a democracy would bring. But life in Israel was often not easy for many of them. In letters they wrote to family and friends in the Soviet Union they complained about the difficulty of learning Hebrew and their inability to find employment in their own professions. As well, they criticized the Israeli government for not making them feel more welcome by assisting them in every possible way.

The negative letters, coupled with anti-Israel propaganda in the Soviet press and the frequent jamming of Kol Yisroel radio, gave birth to the phenomenon of *neshira*, the Hebrew word for "dropping out." This "dropping out" by some Soviet Jews (who became known as *noshrim*), took place at the transit point in Vienna, en route to Israel. There, they were supported by Hebrew Immigrant Aid Services (HIAS) until they received immigration visas and departed for the country of their choice.

By 1974, *neshira* had risen to almost 24 per cent. The next year it reached 50 per cent and by 1976 was still escalating. Fearing that this phenomenon could sabotage the *aliyah* movement, the Israelis sent a number of former Soviet Jews who were well-integrated into Israeli life to Vienna for several months. Their mission was to encourage the *noshrim* to change their minds and persuade them to honour their commitment to emigrate to Israel.

They were successful in very few cases. The emissaries discovered that prospective immigrants had decided upon their destination long before reaching Vienna, and they concluded that in order to discourage *neshira*, information about Israel must be imparted to Soviet Jews while they were still living in the Soviet Union.

In the summer of 1976, Elaine Dubow and I undertook a project aimed at helping to reduce the number of "drop outs." We travelled to Israel to interview Soviet *olim* and recorded their impressions about their new country on tape. In all, we met with fifty-seven new immigrants from thirteen cities of origin in the USSR. They spoke in Russian about the reality of life in Israel and the adjustments they had to make.

Upon our return to Canada, the tapes were translated into English and we discovered that all but two were positive and credible. Arrangements were made with Radio Liberty in New York to broadcast the Russian versions of the tapes into the Soviet Union.[2] As well, many travellers carried copies of the tapes to the Soviet Union and distributed them among the refusenik communities they visited. The feedback was positive and made many Soviet Jews began to think about Israel as their destination.[3]

Some of the English translations became the text of *They Came to*

Stay – the Soviet Jewish Experience in Israel, a booklet published by the United Jewish Appeal in the United States. The following are examples of some of the testimonies:

> "You come to Israel because you have something in your heart, some love and responsibility for your people," said Shimon Jakubovits, a teacher, living in Israel since 1972. "If you have temporary difficulty and hard moments, you will have the strength to overcome them.
>
> Endocrinologist German Shapiro declared, "We are not from another country, we are from another planet. You will never understand sixty years of a corrupt Jewish soul. I feel I am home now.
>
> "Why did I decide to leave Russia?" asked Felix Andriefsky, a violin teacher from Moscow who had arrived in Israel in 1972. "Why didn't I leave earlier?"[4]

The 1976 Summer Olympics took place in Montreal. With three hundred Russians in attendance as athletes or as officials with the Soviet team, there were new opportunities for demonstrations. "Freedom for Soviet Jews," printed boldly in white, on red T-shirts, became the 35s' trademark during the Games. On opening day, a group of local runners wore the signature T-shirts and ran, carrying the symbolic Olympic torch, from the YMHA, through the streets of Montreal to the Soviet Consulate. The message communicated by the T-shirts was clear to all who were present at each event involving Soviet athletes during the Games.

On the final day, July 31, a full-page, fully sponsored advertisement appeared in *The Gazette*. The bold headline over the cases of six refuseniks read: "THE 1980 OLYMPICS WILL BE HELD IN THE SOVIET UNION. 150,000 JEWS WOULD GIVE ANYTHING NOT TO BE THERE."[5]

On October 19, 1976, twelve refuseniks staged a "sit-in" in the lobby of the Supreme Soviet, demanding written explanations for their refusals. In response to their action, dozens of KGB officers herded the group into a bus and drove them to a forest outside of Moscow. Forced to disembark, the refuseniks were attacked and beaten with clubs. Boris Chernobilsky and Josef Ahs were arrested.[6]

The information about the beatings reached Canada early the next morning. By noon, a dozen members of the Montreal 35s, supported by crutches and swathed in blood-stained bandages, stood outside the Soviet Consulate holding placards that read, "USSR, Give VISAS, not BEATINGS!"

The Supreme Soviet incident was the first in a series of protests by Soviet Jewish activists timed to coincide with a three-day meeting of the central committee of the Communist party. The next day, the refuseniks appeared at the Supreme Soviet again, this time demanding that action be taken against the police responsible for the assault.[7] On the third day, Jews marched defiantly through the streets of Moscow with large Stars of David pinned to their coats. Thirty-three of the refuseniks were arrested in the largest roundup since the June 1974 visit of U.S. president Richard Nixon.[8]

In response to the new arrests, thirty-three Montreal students, each bearing the name of one of the arrested refuseniks, led demonstrators from Dominion Square to the Soviet Consulate. There, refusenik Mark Azbel, speaking from Moscow, described the arrests in detail over an amplified speaker system.[9] The next day, all thirty-three activists were released. Two weeks later, the charges against Chernobilsky and Ahs were dropped.

At that time, a group of Moscow refuseniks publicly declared their intention to hold a symposium on Jewish culture and they invited educators from around the world to participate. Their plans were thwarted by Soviet officials who denied entry visas to the invited guests. On December 21, 1976, the day of the scheduled opening of the symposium, all the organizers were placed under house arrest.[10]

On January 22, 1977, Soviet television stations across the country broadcast a government-sponsored film *Traders of Souls*. The anti-Semitic attack portrayed refuseniks as soldiers of Zionism, betraying their homeland in favour of Israel. On the screen were images of smoke and ashes, bombing, devastation and dismembered bodies of murdered children.[11] Refuseniks Vladimir Slepak, Yosef Begun, Yuli Kosharovsky, Anatoly Sharansky and Boris Tsitlionok were singled out as "Western-supported conspirators."[12] There was fear in the refusenik community that this film would fuel the flame of the already ignited official Soviet position of oppression.

At the World Presidium on Soviet Jewry's international conference, held January 1977 in Jerusalem, Western activists discussed increased advocacy and ways to improve the immigrant absorption process in Israel, with the hope of discouraging *neshira*. In a candid meeting with the activists, former prime minister Golda Meir explained that absorption of Soviet Jews in Israel was not the sole cause of *neshira*. Contact between North American or European activists and refuseniks entrenched relationships and increased the likelihood of Soviet Jews choosing other countries.

The problems were immense and no one solution could resolve them. Soviet Jewry activists prepared a list of recommendations that they believed would make Israel more attractive to prospective *olim*.[13]

Early in January 1977, a delegation of Canadian parliamentarians visited Israel. As was customary with visiting dignitaries, they were briefed by Ruth Bar-On of the Israel Public Council for Soviet Jewry and introduced to the relatives of some separated Soviet Jewish families. One of the delegates, Vancouver MP John Fraser, met the mother of physicist Naum Salansky, a refusenik who had been arrested in Vilnius and was soon to be tried on charges of "defaming the USSR."

Upon his return to Canada, Fraser was contacted by the Montreal 35s who asked for his assistance in the Salansky case. "Right from the beginning I was convinced that the more publicity we could get for Salansky the better were our chances of getting someone to do something about it," remarked Fraser. "We had international law on our side. After Helsinki, we had the right to raise the matter at every opportunity."[14]

Fraser wrote to Soviet ambassador Yacovlev on January 31, 1977, asking for a review of Salansky's case.[15] It was important that he proceed quickly, for the trial date was set for February 15. Fraser received no response. On February 11, he raised the issue of Salansky's impending trial during Question Period in the House of Commons and requested official parliamentary intervention. Minister of External Affairs Don Jamieson, responded, saying, "I will make inquiries immediately as to whether we have already made representation. We will do everything within our power to call this matter to the attention of the appropriate Soviet authorities."[16]

Canada was but one country that pressured the Soviets for clemency for Naum Salansky. In what was interpreted as sensitivity to public outcry, on February 14, one day before it was due to start, Salansky's trial was postponed. Six weeks later, he received permission to emigrate.

There was little time to celebrate. News of another arrest in the refusenik community spread quickly. This time it was Yosef Begun, a Moscow refusenik whose background was similar to that of many assimilated Jews. His curiosity about Judaism had been sparked in the late 1960s when he worked as an electronics engineer with an elderly Jewish man who had a strong allegiance to his heritage. When the man saw that in Begun he had an interested pupil, he began to teach him Hebrew. Begun joined a group of Moscow activists and began teaching others what he himself had learned.[17]

When Yosef Begun first applied for a visa to emigrate to Israel in 1971, he lost his job as a senior researcher at the Moscow Institute for Economic Planning. Dismissed from every subsequent job when employers learned of his intention to emigrate, he managed to earn a modest living by teaching Hebrew. According to Soviet law, private tutoring was considered to be socially useful work. Begun attempted to teach the language legally, by reporting all earnings and activities to the appropriate authorities. He even asked to have taxes deducted from his income.

On March 3, 1977, Begun was arrested in his own apartment during a Purim celebration with friends. He was charged with parasitism. While awaiting trial in Matroskaya Tishina prison, he shared a cell with thugs and petty thieves, some of whom implored him to tell them tales about the Bible. Thus began his first series of lectures on Judaism.

One day, as Begun recounted stories about the Jewish holidays, he noticed that one of the listeners, an eighteen-year-old boy, was drawing pictures. "Though simple illustrations, the stories were rendered with feeling and imagination. Most of the drawings were devoted to the Exodus story: baby Moses in his basket, an Egyptian flogging a Jewish slave, and Moses leading the Jews out of Egypt with the pillar of fire leading the way."[18] Privately, the young man revealed his identity to Begun. He was a Jew who had become involved with a gang of homeless teenagers, who were petty thieves. Begun gave him the names of some of his refusenik friends so they might meet when he was released from prison.[19]

With reprisals against the refusenik community occuring on a daily basis, it became a problem for activists to decide upon priority cases. They created innovative programs to attract media attention, with the goal of keeping the spotlight on Soviet Jews.

On March 19,1977, the Canadian 35s joined an international Bar Mitzvah celebration for thirteen-year-old Misha Prestin, son of Moscow refusenik Vladimir Prestin. Young men in synagogues in Ottawa, Montreal, Toronto, and Winnipeg read the Torah portion in Misha's name.[20]

The following week, guests entering the Bayshore Hotel dining room in Vancouver for a private luncheon for the Soviet ambassador to Canada, were handed a menu. Until it was discovered that the two women distributing the menus were not hotel employees, but Soviet Jewry activists, more than half the luncheon guests had received the Jewish "Prisoners of Conscience" daily diet, consisting of one slice of black bread and six ounces of cabbage soup.[21] The women were quickly ushered out.

In an attempt to focus on the case of endocrinologist Mikhail Shtern, then completing his third year of an eight year prison term, Barbara Stern, a stalwart member of the Montreal 35s, and her husband Zalman, invited every Montreal family with the surname "Stern" to their home. The committee of "Concerned Sterns for Shtern" created that evening agreed to work as one family for Dr. Shtern's release.

Before they were able to implement their plans, on March 15, 1977, Shtern was freed; however, the joy of his early release was short-lived. Hours later, it was learned that Anatoly Sharansky, a key refusenik in the Moscow community, had been arrested.

Activists tried to keep the Soviet Jewry issue alive through the media. Some delegates to the CJC plenary assembly in Montreal in May 1977 had been present in Ottawa two years earlier when Father Barry Jones symbolically adopted prisoner Lazar Lubarsky outside the Soviet Embassy. Lubarsky, the fifty-year-old electronics engineer, had been released just months before. As Jones greeted him at the Queen Elizabeth Hotel, he enveloped him with outstretched arms and uttered the same words he had used in June 1975, "My brother Lazar." The photograph of the two men embracing appeared on the front page of *The Gazette* with a caption: "You have no idea what it means to be free!"[22]

Lubarsky was touring North America to secure grassroots and government support for his friend Yosef Begun, whose case was still under investigation. During that time it was announced that Begun's trial would begin on June 1, 1977. Begun's trial was held in a Moscow courtroom and was closed to the public. He was found guilty of parasitism and sentenced to two years in exile in Siberia.

In the fall of 1977, Avital Sharansky visited Montreal to gain support for her husband Anatoly who was under investigation in Lefortovo Prison. Arrangements had been made for a group of clergymen to meet her. "The one thing that attracted me that day," recalled Father Barry Jones, "was the doleful figure of Avital, whose personal situation seemed so desperate."[24]

The Montreal Inter-faith Task Force for Soviet Jewry was created that afternoon, with Jones as its founding chairman.[25] During the struggle for Jewish renaissance in the Soviet Union, the committee functioned with the unequivocal backing of clergymen and Christian lay people from the Anglican, Presbyterian and Roman Catholic churches, who demonstrated on the streets of Montreal and co-sponsored events and programs with Jewish activists.

"Canadian Jewish Congress and the 35s were so well organized," said Father Jones. "They had the information and the organization, so we were able in our own small way to join with them. It was really to show solidarity and support for Soviet Jewry from non-Jewish sources."[26]

December 10, 1977, International Human Rights Day, was uniquely significant for Ned Steinman, the thirteen-year-old son of Montreal activists.[27] On that morning, Ned was called to the Torah as a Bar Mitzvah. His first act as a man was to protest the denial of religious and human freedom for thirteen-year-old Felix Abramovich of Moscow, son of refusenik Pavel Abramovich, who had first applied for a visa to Israel in 1969. "Felix cannot have a bar mitzvah because he's not allowed to be Jewish or be a free human being," said Ned, "so I'm sharing my bar mitzvah with Felix and all the other people in the world who should be free."[28]

In 1977, 16,736 Jews received exit visas – less than half the number who left the USSR during the peak year of 1973. Despite the fact that thousands of Jews were in refusal and that Jewish expression in the Soviet Union was being thwarted at every turn, Levanon's office in Tel Aviv received lists daily of Soviet Jews requesting invitations from Israel.

Soviet Jewry advocacy had become an integral part of Canadian Jewry programming. If Canadian activists had taken a moment to step back to see the road they had travelled, they would have seen tremendous success in bringing together people with various motivations and interests to work toward one goal.

This was unique, for in many countries Soviet Jewry groups were fraught with inter-organizational rivalry. With few exceptions, Canadian activists rose above personality conflicts and focused on achieving freedom for one-quarter of the world's Jewish population.

A contributing factor to the spirit of cooperation among Canadian activists lay in the fact that the Canadian Jewish Congress welcomed members of non-establishment groups – the 35s' and SSSJ, to their Soviet Jewry committees. At the outset, the division of labour was clear. Rallies and programs held on Jewish holidays and commemorative historic events were co-ordinated by the CJC, whereas unconventional demonstrations were staged by the 35s and the students. By the end of 1977, programs were being sponsored jointly. This strengthened the cause and heightened visibility.

Chapter 12

The Helsinki Process

The Soviet Union's disregard for the human rights provisions of the Helsinki Agreement led to the formation of an unofficial " Helsinki Watch" group in Moscow. It was established May 12, 1976, by dissident Yuri Orlov.[1] Eleven people comprised the group - nine dissidents and two refuseniks. The refuseniks were Professor Vitaly Rubin and Anatoly Sharansky.[2] "The Soviet authorities saw in this group, a focus of dissent and opposition to the regime," reported Martin Gilbert. "Sharansky and Rubin saw in it a vehicle for the assertion of the Jewish right of emigration and reunification of families." [3]

Similar monitoring groups were created in other countries. The Canadian government appointed MP Martin O'Connell to chair the Helsinki Parliamentary Committee. In preparation for the Helsinki review meeting in Belgrade, O'Connell asked Martin Penn, national director of CJC's Canadian Committee for Soviet Jewry, to provide him with cases of Soviet human rights' violations.

Since updated material was sorely lacking, Barbara Stern created a three-page questionnaire designed to elicit pertinent information about separated families. It was distributed to families of refuseniks and prisoners in Israel through the Israel Public Council for Soviet Jewry.[4] "For many divided families," recalled Penn, who worked with Stern on the project, "it was the first time that anyone had offered to help."[5]

Within weeks, hundreds of completed questionnaires were returned to Montreal. As well, letters began arriving from many families in Israel, requesting a copy of the questionnaire. New refuseniks' names surfaced.

These questionnaires, many of which required translation, were then collated, edited and typed by Barbara Stern. The end result was a comprehensive, bulky, refusenik list which detailed human rights' violations. The final list for submission to the Canadian delegation to the 1977 Belgrade review meeting included just under thirty cases, based on "security restrictions" or "military service that had exceeded five years."

The Helsinki Review conferences were held in Belgrade in 1977, Madrid in 1980 and Vienna in 1986. Meetings were open-ended, lasting from months to years, until there was unanimity on every issue and a final document was accepted.

Members of non-governmental organizations (NGOs) were permitted to attend the meetings and consult with delegations from Western, neutral and non-aligned missions.[6] "It was next to impossible to meet with delegates of non-friendly countries," recalled Alan Rose, who was present at each review meeting for a period of time. "We had no contact with the Russians until 1980."[7] At the conclusion of each review meeting, the NGOs who monitored compliance for the World Presidium for Soviet Jewry met to evaluate the proceedings and prepare strategies for the next round of talks.[8]

Tom Delworth headed the Canadian delegation at Belgrade. Unlike American delegation leader, Justice Arthur J. Goldberg, who confronted the Soviets directly on their appalling human rights record, Ambassador Delworth raised cases based on principles. The only time that he or any Canadian representative mentioned refuseniks by name was in the corridors, during private conversations with Soviet delegates.[9]

After nine months of bitter wrangling, the Belgrade conference adjourned in a deadlock over the wording of the concluding document. The three-page summary document made no reference to human rights. The Canadian delegation was extremely disappointed. "Our discussions have shown that we have a long, long way to go before we can feel confident that the inherent dignity of the human person and his prerogative to know and act upon his rights are being respected in all places and in all circumstances," remarked Minister of Multiculturalism Norman Cafik in his concluding remarks.[10]

Despite the fact that little progress had made at Belgrade, Western nations were heartened to see that Soviet human rights violations had been raised at a multilateral gathering for the first time. The participating states tacitly accepted the right to criticize the internal practices of other nations.[11]

A few weeks after the conclusion of the Belgrade meeting, Cafik suggested that the government begin to prepare for the second review conference at Madrid. He emphasized that Canadian groups with a special interest in human rights should assist the Helsinki Parliamentary Committee in determining its stance.[12]

In August 1978, it was decided by the CJC leadership that one committee would better serve the needs of Soviet Jews and suggested that the government-appointed Helsinki Parliamentary Committee replace the two-year-old Parliamentary Group for Soviet Jewry. In the months leading up to the Madrid meeting, however, lack of confidence in the Helsinki process and an escalation of harassment of Soviet Jews led to a reversal of CJC's decision. The Parliamentary Group for Soviet Jewry was reactivated in November 1980 under the chairmanship of MP David Smith.

Prior to the opening of the Madrid review meetings in the fall of 1980, a series of hearings were held in Ottawa under the newly appointed Helsinki Parliamentary Committee chairman MP Charles Caccia. CJC was among the groups invited to participate. "Alan Rose and Barbara Stern made regular visits to Ottawa during the hearings," Caccia recalled, "and were responsible for the input, the follow-up and the necessary pressure that developed on behalf of Soviet Jewry. This theme was pressed upon us at every opportunity."[13]

The material that had been prepared for the previous review meeting was unwieldy, so Stern volunteered to collate all the refusenik cases into one document in time for the Madrid meeting. "It took over two months to complete," she recalled. "I typed every word in my house, eleven hours a day."[14]

The finished product was an English and French language publication entitled, "A Study of Jews Refused their Right to Leave the Soviet Union." It contained case histories of six hundred refuseniks and thirty-two Jewish prisoners. Refusals were listed under the categories: "lack of parental consent," "security restrictions," "past military service," "lack of family reunification," "no reason given."[15] The principle of the Helsinki Final Act that had been violated was found at the beginning of each chapter, followed by a comprehensive list of refuseniks.

Stern's second volume, produced in 1981, detailed twelve hundred cases. The third volume, published in 1983, was an addendum to the second. By noting hundreds of individuals who had been refused for more than five years, the books refuted the Soviet claim that the number of refuseniks was limited to a few isolated cases. They also drew attention to the absurdity of some of the refusals, such as that of a sixty-five year-old grandfather, refused because he lacked parental permission.

In addition to being a valuable resource for Soviet Jewry activists, the Canadian books were critical to the Helsinki process. They were systematic, factual and scrupulously credible. "These books were a turning point for people like myself," said Martin Gilbert. "As a result of the first one, I updated my own first Soviet-Jewry book, *The Jews of Russia, their History in Maps and Photographs*."[16]

When the Madrid meetings opened on November 14, 1980, two hundred refuseniks took part in a hunger strike in many cities in the Soviet Union. William Korey, Stephen Roth and Alan Rose of the World Presidium for Soviet Jewry began to lobby allied powers on the very first day.[17] Although the Canadian NGOs[18] who attended the Madrid meeting urged the Canadian delegates to mention prisoners and refuseniks by name, secretary of state for external affairs minister Mark MacGuigan made no reference to specific individuals in his opening address.[18]

Ambassador R. Louis Rogers headed the Canadian delegation. He took six copies of Stern's books, just enough for his six-member group. It was Ambassador Max Kampelman, leader of the American delegation, who assumed responsibility for distributing copies to members of the twenty-eight allied countries and to several of the Eastern-bloc nations.[19]

The Soviets refused to deal with human rights issues despite the fact that the American delegation, at the urging of Kampelman, underlined them at every opportunity. "I remember a tearful exchange on the telephone with the sister of Ida Nudel," Kampelman recalled. "She was a woman whose constant efforts to leave the Soviet Union for Israel were continually rebuffed, leading to her exile . . . It didn't take any effort to persuade me to mention Ida Nudel's name at our meeting."[20]

Ambassador Kampelman encouraged other NATO countries to do the same.[21] His persuasiveness worked. Ambassador Rogers passed refusenik lists to Soviet delegation-head Sergei Kondrashev and most of the NATO nations submitted amendments which strengthened the human rights section of the concluding document.[22]

Instead of lasting six months as anticipated, the Madrid conference dragged on, with breaks, for almost three years. Delays and complications arose over the Soviet invasion of Afghanistan and the death of Soviet leader Brezhnev. Like Belgrade, the Madrid concluding document was a disappointment. Little progress had been made on security and confidence-building or on human rights.[23] Many activists believed that the Helsinki process was in serious jeopardy.

Chapter 13

Arrests and Trials . . . the Circle Widens

By the late 1970s, the Montreal 35s had gained considerable exposure in the adult community and were recognized as initiators of innovative programming. This prompted Arlazar Eliashiv, the principal of the Cote St. Luc branch of United Talmud Torah's Hebrew Day School, to invite me to teach a course on the subject of Soviet Jewry to his sixth-grade students.

By examining their family tree, many students discovered that their roots could be traced to Czarist Russia. They became sensitized to the reality of present-day Soviet Jewry when they compared their lives as Jews with those of their counterparts in the Soviet Union. The class wrote letters to children of refuseniks and designed a six-metre-long freedom mural for Vladimir and Maria Slepak. The mural was unfurled by the class on April 13, 1978, outside the Soviet Consulate, at a demonstration marking the Slepak's eighth year in refusal.[1] Two youngsters were granted entry to the consulate and, once inside, left the mural for delivery to the Slepaks in Moscow.

The six-lesson course became the model for a Soviet Jewry School Kit, produced by CJC and made available to teachers in Jewish schools. Comprised of lesson plans, resource material, maps and visual aids, it enabled the teaching of Russian Jewish history from Czarist times to the present.[2]

Young people were always reliable when it came to Soviet Jewry advocacy. Montreal's Bialik High School's Soviet Jewry committee held a campaign on behalf of Leonid Brailovsky, the teenage son of Victor Brailovsky.[3] During their "Soviet Jewry Week," the entire student body wore yellow "Bialik for Brailovsky" buttons and wrote letters to their adopted refusenik.

On Leonid's seventeenth birthday, four hundred students gathered in the gymnasium for a pre-arranged telephone call to Leonid that never materialized. The thwarted phone call attracted publicity. "Injustice borne alone is a terrifying thing," stated an editorial in *The Gazette* the following day, "but the knowledge that one is not forgotten, that somewhere there are people who care, despite the indifference and even animosity of one's surroundings, can be marvellously sustaining."[4]

Student activity grew more popular. A poster contest with the theme "Soviet Jewry – Freedom" attracted dozens of sixth-grade entries that were judged by prominent local artists. The winning poster was a pen and ink drawing of two bearded prisoners wearing skull caps, set against a scene of Jerusalem. The drawing, reduced in size, became the cover of the Soviet Jewry School Kit and reduced again, for note cards, used as a Soviet Jewry fund-raising project.[5]

On June 1, 1978, International Children's Day, five hundred children from eight Montreal Jewish schools wrote letters, containing hopes and prayers for their school's adopted refusenik child, and left them in a wheelbarrow outside Montreal's Soviet Consulate.[6] The students sang Hebrew songs and read statements in English and French demanding better treatment for Soviet Jews.

As the students returned to their buses, two generations of Moscow refuseniks, who had staged their protests in the safety of six refuseniks' apartments, were removing the banners that they had affixed to their windows or balconies.

The Moscow demonstration had not been without misfortune. In anticipation of the prospective protests, the KGB had surrounded the apartment buildings of Ida Nudel and Vladimir Slepak and prohibited them from leaving to join the others. Frustrated and angry that they had not been able to participate in the refusenik demonstration, the two prominent refuseniks staged their own demonstrations. At 6:00 PM, forty-seven-year-old Nudel walked outside to her balcony and hung a banner that read, "KGB, Give me my Visa." When two plainclothesmen attempted to remove it, she tossed a bucketful of water at them. Slepak and his wife Maria also hung a banner from their balcony railing that spelled out: "Let us go to our son in Israel." The following day, both Ida Nudel and Vladimir Slepak were arrested and charged with "malicious hooliganism." Their trial date was set for June 20, 1978.

"Don't cry my dears," began the letter that Nudel wrote to her family in Israel the night before her trial. "I think it is harder for you than for me because I am living the reality . . . and you are forced to imagine what is happening to me. One has to pay for everything in this world; that is the law. Don't cry; without prison I will not gain freedom."[7]

The judges of The People's Court of the Volgogradsky Region in Moscow barred relatives, friends and foreign news correspondents from entering the courtroom. After four hours of false evidence brought against the pair, the verdict of "guilty" was announced. Both activists were sentenced to four years of internal exile – Slepak, to a Siberian village near the Chinese border, and Nudel, to Krivosheino, a remote village in the Tomsk region of Siberia, six thousand kilometres from Moscow.

Before her sentencing, Ida Nudel addressed the court, "I am standing trial for all the past seven years during which I have learned to walk proudly with my head held high as a human being and as a Jewish woman. Every time I was able to help another victim, my heart filled with an extraordinary feeling unlike any other . . . If the remaining years of my life will be grey and monotonous, these seven years will warm my heart with the knowledge that my life was not without purpose."[8]

Hundreds of cables were sent to Ottawa urging Canadian government leaders to condemn the sentences. The absence of an immediate response prompted the presidents of CJC, CZF and B'nai Brith to co-sign a telegram to The Honourable Don Jamieson. "You may know that the United States government has already condemned the sentences of Slepak and Nudel," it read, "thus we are all the more chagrined that our government has seen fit to remain silent."[9]

The following day, MP Flora MacDonald presented a resolution in the House of Commons condemning the severity of the sentences imposed on Slepak and Nudel. It was passed unanimously.[10]

On the heels of the sentencing of Nudel and Slepak, Yosef Begun, who had been released from Siberian exile, was arrested again, in his own Moscow apartment, in the presence of his wife and son. The housing authorities had refused to grant him permission to re-register in the capital, so he was charged with violating residence regulations. On June 28, ten weeks after he had returned from two years in exile, Yosef Begun was convicted and sentenced to exile for three years in Magadan, a remote Siberian village ten thousand kilometres east of Moscow.[11]

The journey to Magadan dragged on for two torturous months, in an airless, windowless train. Each boxcar was filled with fifteen criminals. Isolated and far from any semblance of modern civilization, Begun was very much alone.

On June 30, 1978, as dusk fell over the old city of Jerusalem, marking the end of the Sabbath, Prime Minister Menachem Begin led thousands of Israeli families to the Western Wall to demonstrate their solidarity with Ida Nudel.[12] At that moment, Nudel was travelling by boxcar on a two-month journey to Krivosheino. Upon arrival, she was placed in a hostel four miles from the centre of the town. She was the only female living among forty male criminals.

Ida Nudel's life became a nightmare. She lived in fear of being attacked by the men, who cursed and drank far into the night. She slept with an axe under her bed and a knife under her pillow. "At worst," she wrote, in a letter to her sister, "I can use it on myself."[13]

A few months after Nudel's arrival in Krivosheino, her friend Evgeny Tsirlin came to visit and brought her an auburn collie. She named the dog "Pizer," a Hebrew word meaning "to scatter or disperse." Her dog helped to separate Ida from the hostile population.[14]

Slepak, Nudel and Begun's trials were followed by the July trial and sentencing of Anatoly Sharansky. The incarceration of Moscow's four leading refuseniks appeared to be part of a Soviet plan to deport dissenters to prison camps before the 1980 Moscow Summer Olympics. U.S. Congresswoman Pat Shroeder wrote to Lord Killanin, president of the IOC, suggesting that they insist that the Soviets refrain from "sanitizing their cities for the next Olympics." [15]

The British 35s had also taken a firm stand. Exactly two years prior to the proposed opening, they launched a petition campaign to remove the 1980 Olympics from Moscow. "If the Olympic Games do take place in Moscow without protest," they wrote in a letter to other activists, "then the free world will have assumed mutual responsibility for crimes perpetrated by the KGB."[16]

The Olympic petition campaign gained the support of the International 35s, the SSSJ, the UCSJ, the Group of 15 and the Israeli organization *Shomer Achi Anochi* (I am my brother's keeper). These groups did not advocate a boycott, but rather supported the removal of the games from Moscow to a site somewhere in the free world. They hoped to obtain one million signatures on the petition and deliver it to the April 1979 meeting of the International Olympic Committee (IOC) in Montevideo, Uruguay.[17] During the promotion of the campaign, activists wore T-shirts printed with a large hammer and sickle, pictured over the words " Olympics Da, Moscow Nyet."

Leaders of the World Presidium of Soviet Jewry resisted the proposal to remove the Olympics from Moscow. They contended that because the Soviets had begun to issue more exit visas, Western Jews should not rock the boat. They also argued that most refuseniks did not support the removal of the Olympic Games.

British activist Michael Sherbourne disagreed. The refuseniks from Moscow, Leningrad, Kiev, Minsk and Tbilisi with whom he spoke on a regular basis endorsed the Olympic petition campaign but were loath to sign a petition for fear of reprisals.[18] "With this Olympic weapon," declared Sherbourne, "we can and we must demand that the Soviets live up to their obligations. We must insist on large-scale emigration, without the nonsense of refusals on spurious grounds . . . and we must demand freedom for all our Prisoners of Conscience. We have a clear goal in front of us. We must move forward with courage and conviction, and we must push on with our removal of the Olympic Games from Moscow."[19]

A letter to the editor by the Montreal 35s, in support of the removal of the games, was published in *The Gazette*.[20] The September

1, 1978 editorial by Ralph Hyman of *The Canadian Jewish News* stated, "Participating nations are certainly aware of the oppressive nature of the Soviet regime – a totalitarian tyranny. It is clear that such a nation cannot be entrusted to foster the kind of congenial atmosphere that is supposed to surround the Olympic Games. To hold them in the vast territorial prison called Russia, besmirches the ideals for which the Olympics stand."[21]

After a resolution to remove the Olympic Games from Moscow was endorsed by the U.S. Senate,[22] Bert Raphael wrote to Don Jamieson, asking the Canadian government to do the same. Jamieson wrote in reply, "It is the government's view that sporting contacts are generally beneficial to Canadians and that although sport can never be wholly divorced from politics, it should not be used as a political instrument."[23] It angered activists to see that the Canadian government would not take an official stand that might make them unpopular with the Soviets.

Although the campaign to remove the games from Moscow was defeated, the irony was that the 1980 Olympics were boycotted by sixty-one countries, of which Canada was one. It had nothing to do with Jews. It was a protest against the Soviet invasion of Afghanistan.

Repressive measures against refuseniks intensified. An unofficial scientific seminar scheduled to be held in Moscow in December 1978 was quashed when the KGB raided Victor Brailovsky's apartment. Scientific material and texts prepared for publication in the underground journal *Jews in the USSR* were confiscated. "Victor pleaded with them to leave an article with mathematical formulae," said his wife Irina, "but they showed no mercy."[24]

Although 28,864 Jews received permission to emigrate in 1978, very few visas went to refuseniks or prisoners. An exception was former prisoner Sender Levinson, who, after having served three years of a six-year prison term on spurious charges of "economic speculation," was released early and was able to join his wife and children in Israel. It is believed that a world-wide cable protest on Levinson's behalf, in which the Toronto section of the National Council of Jewish Women had participated, was responsible for his early release.[25]

In the spring of 1979, a Passover message was received from Leningrad trial prisoner Josef Mendelevich. "We have no bitter herbs to place between the matzah," he wrote, "but we do not need a symbol of our suffering. We have a real suffering here, and that we shall put between the matzah."[26]

It was impossible to second-guess the Soviets. Winston Churchill's 1939 statement about Russia, "I cannot forecast to you the action of Russia. It is a riddle, wrapped in a mystery inside an enigma" was no less applicable forty years later.[27] In May 1979, a Soviet gesture stunned the free world. Leningrad trial prisoners Eduard Kuznetsov and Mark Dymshitz were suddenly released. The two were transported in just twenty-four hours from the darkness of the gulag into a throng of one hundred thousand people, who jammed into the United Nations' Dag Hammarskjold Plaza for "Solidarity Sunday," an annual event planned by the Greater New York Conference on Soviet Jewry.

The crowd broke into tumultuous song as Kuznetsov, bald from his prison haircut, approached the microphone. "Your devotion and energy not only shortened my prison term by two thousand and forty unbearable days," he declared, his voice cracking with emotion, "but also saved my life."[28] When the rally ended, the two former prisoners flew to Israel to rejoin their families.

A few days after the release of Kuznetsov and Dymshitz, five more Leningrad trial prisoners were pardoned by Brezhnev, more than a year before the expiration of their sentences. Boris Penson, Vulf Zalmanson, Hillel Butman, Anatoly Altman and Leib Khnokh arrived together at Ben-Gurion Airport. "Welcome in the name of God," said Israeli prime minister Menachem Begin as he embraced the former prisoners. "We have waited for you for eight and a half years."[29] The release of seven Jewish prisoners indicated a softening of Soviet policy after a year that represented the zenith of a warming trend in East-West relations.

Pressure continued for the release of Ida Nudel. A committee, Israeli Women for Ida Nudel (IWIN, pronounced "I-win") was created in Israel, stimulating the formation of similar committees on her behalf in other countries. The Canadian branch, Women for Ida

Nudel (WIN) was composed of seven women's organizations[30] chaired by Montrealer Ruth Pollack, with MPs Flora MacDonald, Ursula Appoloni and Pauline Jewett serving as honourary chair.[31]

When Flora MacDonald became secretary of state for external affairs in Joe Clark's Conservative government, she reiterated, in a directive to the CJC, Canada's position on Soviet human rights violations. "It is no secret that I use my office to make direct representations to governments in individual cases of denial of rights," she stated. "The most recent is the case of Ida Nudel, whose attempts to emigrate from the Soviet Union have led her to exile in Siberia."[32]

Ida Nudel was adopted by Canadian Hadassah-Wizo whose members, from coast to coast, sent a constant stream of cables and letters to the authorities pressing for her release. They honoured Nudel, in absentia, with their coveted Rebecca Sieff award.[33]

Nudel received thousands of letters sent by supporters from all over the world. Beside her signature on each pink receipt card, prepaid by the sender to whom it was to be returned, she wrote messages in both English and Hebrew, proclaiming her innocence.[34] On one occasion, she wrote her message in Russian on a return card to her sister in Israel. Soviet postal officials read it and subsequently stopped giving the pre-paid cards to her to sign.

From that day on, Nudel refused to accept her international mail. All letters from family, friends and Western supporters were returned, unopened, along with the registration form on which Nudel had written, "Please turn to the Soviet embassy in your country in order to receive information about me. I am refusing my mail as an act of protest."[35]

Nudel was fully aware that her action disrupted the sole opportunity for contact with her family. She explained her position in a letter to Evgeny Tsirlin in Moscow. "I become silent, confident that you will not remain silent. Don't turn to me, but to my tormentors, for information about me, and then my suffering will have meaning and their victory over me will be uneasy and their revenge bitter."[36] Nudel persisted in her protest for one year. When she could bear the silence no longer, she acquiesced, and began to accept her mail once more.

In July 1979, Ida Nudel moved into a log hut that had been purchased and repaired by friends who had come to spend the summer with her. The hut consisted of one large room with a stove. It had an outhouse and water well in a distant courtyard. Tsirlin visited her again that winter. With a home movie camera, he filmed a day in Ida Nudel's life.

The black and white portrayal of Nudel in Krivosheino shows a small black-swathed figure, with a dark shawl covering her head, forcing open the creaky wooden door of her shack and trudging with a water pail across the snowdrifts of the desolate Siberian landscape to get water. "The wind howls like a wolf, springs at her and throws her sideways," wrote Canadian journalist Michele Landsberg, in her column in *The Globe and Mail*. "She is so frail that she has to clutch at a birch tree for an anchor. Then, stoically, she goes on."[37]

The film also shows Nudel, with her dog at her side, hunched over her table, writing letters to the prisoners. In the closing moments, she sits on her small iron cot, turns to the camera and says, "We are idealists . . . but if our suffering will not force every one of you to rush to help us, then it is in vain . . . I so want to believe in my lucky stars. I so want to believe that sometime I will rise up the stairs of an El Al aircraft and my suffering and tears will remain in my memory only and my heart will be full of triumph and victory. And God grant – it will happen soon!"[38]

The film, *Ida Nudel in Exile*, was smuggled out of the Soviet Union, duplicated onto videotape and distributed to Western Jewish communities where it was aired on public television. In Canada, it was seen on "W5," CTV's weekly television news documentary.

Many activists wondered how the Leningrad trial prisoners, heroes from an epic, had remained spiritually intact, despite everything they had lived through and suffered. They wondered how, after years of incarceration, they were able to re-adjust to living with their families.

In August 1979, I conducted interviews with nine of the former prisoners of the Leningrad trials who had begun to build new lives in Israel.[39] Their stories and feelings appeared in *Jewish Voices from the Soviet Gulag*, a booklet dedicated to the eight remaining Prisoners of Zion.

Speaking from his living room on the kibbutz where his wife and daughters had lived during his imprisonment, Hillel Butman remarked, "Prisoners who were well known in the West were treated better than the others. In my eight years in prison, no one ever beat me, whereas many other prisoners were beaten unconscious in their cells."

During his last days in Chistopol Prison, Butman shared a cell with Josef Mendelevich, next to that of Anatoly Sharansky. He recalled the details of his release. "I was removed from my cell in the evening, and taken to another, where I spent the night in isolation. The next morning, I was driven past my old cell. I called out, 'Josef, shalom!' The word, 'shalom, shalom,' rang in my ears as my friends said goodbye. I did not yet know that soon I would be free."

Israel Zalmanson, who had been freed in July 1978, recalled his prison days from his student dormitory at Tel Aviv University. "I knew from information in the Soviet newspapers, which we were able to buy daily, that "Zionist provocation in the West" meant that we were not alone. This gave me the courage to go on."[40]

Anatoly Altman had married within two months of his release and was living on a kibbutz with his wife. "My ideas about Israel were different from reality," he explained. "I thought it was a peaceful country where there would be 'rest of soul' and 'quiet of spirit.' I realize now how many problems there are, but they excite me. I have been sleeping for a long time and now I want to live!"[41]

Eduard Kuznetsov shared an apartment in Rishon LeZion with his wife Sylva Zalmanson, then in her third month of pregnancy. In an emotionally charged moment, I removed the silver Prisoner-of-Conscience bracelet engraved with the name "Eduard Kuznetsov" from my wrist, and placed it on his.

As we munched on pastries, Kuznetsov described the food he had eaten during his nine years of incarceration in a labour camp in Mordovia. "The bread was so mouldy that when squeezed, water would run out. One day, my cell-mates and I pooled our bread and formed letters from it that stuck to the wall. The letters spelled out, 'Give us bread.'"[42]

Kuznetsov turned to me and said, "To survive in a Soviet prison, one has to struggle. Writing was my struggle." He explained how he bribed the guards with chewing gum to get the onion-skin paper required for his writing. Since prisoners were permitted to write only postcards, he tore the thin paper into 8 x 13 cm pieces. Each day he would place a piece of the paper, which fit on a postcard, and with a fine-tipped indelible pen, would record his feelings and daily activity in handwriting so small it could only be read with a magnifying glass.

Kuznetsov frequently swallowed the single sheet of paper rather than be caught writing a daily diary. Every evening, he added the page written that day to the others buried in the earth in his cell. On the day of his release, Kuznetsov dug up his prison diary and swallowed it, page by page. The two hundred pages formed a one-inch thick stack of sheets. Pointing to them, he said, "Each one of these pages has been digested two or three times."[43]

The United Nations' 1979 theme, The International Year of the Child, was modified by Montreal Jewish students who gathered for a demonstration outside the Soviet Consulate wearing T-shirts with the words "International Year of the Soviet Jewish Child."

Toronto's "Day of the Soviet Jewish Child" was launched by Ontario attorney-general Roy McMurtry at a "Kremlin write-in" held at NCJW's council house. Adults and students inserted miniature dolls, symbolizing the Soviet Jewish child, separated from family in Israel, into envelopes with letters addressed to Ambassador Yacovlev.[44]

In November 1979, the CCSJ sponsored a conference in Ottawa entitled: Anti-Semitism in the Soviet Union – the Ongoing Tragedy of Soviet Jewry.[45] Presentations were made by international experts and a panel of radio and newspaper personalities discussed the topic "How to make the media respond."[46]

"Canada reaffirms its commitment to the principles enunciated in the Third Basket of the Helsinki Accord," declared Flora MacDonald to delegates, parliamentarians and former prisoner Boris Penson, at the closing dinner. She read a motion that had been passed in the House of Commons that afternoon: "We call upon the Soviet Union to respect that principle calling for reunification of families and to allow all Soviet-Jewish refuseniks to be reunited with their families in

Israel or elsewhere, and further call upon the Soviet Union to release all Prisoners of Conscience, specifically Anatoly Sharansky and Ida Nudel."[47]

The year 1979 was unique. Some Jewish prisoners were released, and four of the most prominent refuseniks were serving prison sentences. Although most refuseniks received new refusals, 51,320 emigration visas were issued. This figure represented an increase of twenty-two thousand over the previous year. The increase in visas was the result of thawing relations between the two superpowers due to Strategic Arms Limitation Talks (SALT II), between the U.S. and USSR, initiated at the start of the year. Both countries hoped to reach an agreement to limit the number and size of strategic weapons each could deploy.

Then, suddenly, everything changed. In November 1979, the Soviets invaded Afghanistan and the U.S. Senate refused to ratify the SALT II treaty.[48] As anticipated, Soviet Jews were caught in the fallout. It was estimated that by the end of 1980, emigration figures would drop by at least one-half.

Chapter 14

Sharansky's Long Road to Judgment

In March 1975, this message from Moscow reached the free world: "The festival of Passover celebrates the Exodus of our people from the slavery of Egyptian bondage. We earnestly beg you to remember those who at present are bearing aloft the torch of a one-thousand-year-old struggle of our people for freedom; namely those who are fighting for the Exodus of Russian Jewry; for our right to leave a country where we suffer humiliation and persecution; for our right to live with our people in our own land." The message had been dictated over the telephone by Anatoly Sharansky in Moscow to Genya Intrator in Toronto.[1]

Six weeks later, when Montreal 35s' members Elaine Dubow Harris, Barbara Stern and I were in Israel on a Soviet Jewry fact-finding mission, we met Misha Shtiglitz, a commander of an Israeli artillery unit in the Sinai desert. Shtiglitz expressed concern for his brother-in-law in Moscow, whose activities in the Jewish movement made him a prime target for KGB harassment. His name was Anatoly Sharansky.

The next afternoon in the coffee shop of a Jerusalem hotel, we met with Shtiglitz's sister Avital, a beautiful, dark-haired twenty-four-year-old who, in halting Hebrew, spoke with pride of her mathematician and computer specialist husband. She described a man with charisma and confidence, who challenged the regime on a daily basis. "Anatoly has a divine gift," Avital explained. "He is able to appear free in spite of slavery."

Avital had met Anatoly in 1973, after he had received his first refusal. They studied Hebrew together. Anatoly's outspokenness led to frequent arrests on charges of "hooliganism," where he was usually imprisoned for periods of ten to fifteen days. One such arrest took place during President Nixon's visit to Moscow in June 1974. During that time Avital received her visa for Israel. She was informed that it would expire July 5.

Sharansky was released from prison July 4. He and Avital were married that evening in a Jewish ceremony in his parents' home. The next morning Avital and Anatoly parted, clinging to the promise made by a clerk at Moscow's OVIR office who had said, "Your husband will join you in Israel soon. It's a matter of a few months."

By that day in Jerusalem, ten months had passed since Avital's arrival in Israel and there was still no indication that Anatoly would receive his visa. "Your problem is our problem," we assured her that warm May afternoon. As Avital waved a tearful goodbye, we pledged to one another that the Montreal 35s would make Anatoly Sharansky's case a priority.

The Helsinki Final Act, signed on August 1, 1975, brought new hope to the young couple. "They have signed an international agreement," Anatoly wrote to Avital from Moscow, "and it speaks exactly of us, of the reunification of families and free emigration. Soon we will be together in Jerusalem."[2] Instead of a visa, KGB surveillance of Anatoly increased.

The Montreal 35s met their first obstacle in mounting a campaign for Sharansky in November of that year, when Avital and Misha arrived in Montreal on the first stop of a North American tour. Their arrival coincided with the closing dinner of the annual Combined Jewish Appeal campaign.

When the dinner organizers were asked if Avital could speak on behalf of her refusenik husband that evening, they argued that an extra five minutes would disturb the precise schedule and a tearful address might dampen the festivities. As a concession, Avital and Misha were given tickets for the dinner and were introduced from their seats as the wife and brother-in-law of a Moscow refusenik.

The remainder of the time Avital and Misha spent in Canada was more productive. They met with government officials in Ottawa and received media attention in both French and English press. In Avital's words, "In Canada I felt an influx of strength with each new meeting, hoping that someone would think of a new strategy to help drag Anatoly out."[3]

This was the first of many trips that Avital made across the ocean to champion her husband's case. At that time she depended upon Misha as her translator, but was aware that in order to be most effective, she would have to learn English. Within one year, she was able to converse comfortably with any English-speaking person she met.

"They say that the eyes are windows to the soul," remarked Irwin Cotler. "Avital's, then, were the soul of Jewish history. She spoke of Anatoly in a way that made him not only more than an abstraction, but in a way that personalized the struggle in an historical sense."[4]

Avital's special persona drew people to her. Wide-ranging publicity for her heartwrenching story took the form of full-page advertisements in *The Washington Post* and *The New York Times* published on January 20, 1976, the day of the inauguration of President Jimmy Carter. In bold letters above the photographs of Avital and Anatoly were the words: "They were married because they were in love . . . and separated because they were Jewish."

Sharansky's name was virtually unknown in Canada in the fall of 1976 when four hundred students and their teachers from Montreal's Bialik High School gathered in the school gymnasium. The Soviet Jewry program planned for that day coincided with the harvest holiday of Succoth. On stage was a table with a telephone connected to speakers that could amplify a two-way conversation.

Days earlier, "messenger calls" had been made to several refuseniks in Moscow, in anticipation that at least one would come through. Half-way through the Succoth program, the telephone rang. Within seconds, the clear accented voice of a man filled the room.

After conversing with him about the Jewish holiday and reciting a few Hebrew prayers, the student leader said, "Soon we will bc dancing on the streets in Montreal for Simchat Torah." The voice from Moscow replied, "We will be dancing too, not in freedom, but in fear." As the students rose to sing *Hatikvah* no one could have predicted that the man in the telegraph office singing along with them that morning, would soon become the focus of world attention.

Anatoly Sharansky's version of that call was transcribed from the cassette he sent to Avital October 19, 1976, in which he explained that during a period of intense KGB surveillance he had been summoned to the central telegraph office to receive an important call from Montreal. He arrived there with four KGB tails in tow, only to discover that his "caller" was four hundred students from a Jewish high school in Montreal. "The special program ends," he told Avital, "then they say to me, now we are all together, the whole school is listening to you, let's get up Anatoly and we'll sing *Hatikvah*. And I get up . . . and begin quietly to sing *Hatikvah*. All the people in the telegraph office look at me as if I am an idiot. OK, we shall laugh about this sometime."[5]

Sharansky had become a key player in the Moscow refusenik community. His command of English made him an ideal translator for visiting Western politicians and his association with Moscow-based foreign correspondents assured accurate communication with the West. Sharansky spoke out fearlessly for repatriation, not only for Jews, but for Pentecostals and Volga Germans. His contact with the dissident movement and involvement with Moscow's "Helsinki Watch Group" led to preferential attention from the KGB.

When Sharansky, Slepak, Begun and Kosharovsky were named in the January 1977 television documentary, *Traders of Souls*, they filed libel charges against the State television company. KGB surveillance around Sharansky doubled. He told London's Michael Sherbourne over the telephone, "My tail of two has become a box of four."[6]

On March 4, 1977, a letter signed by Sanya Lipavsky, who only then was discovered to be a KGB infiltrator of the Soviet Jewry movement, was published in *Isvestia*. It named four Jews acting in the service of American intelligence and anti-Soviet organizations abroad. Of the four, Mark Ażbel and Vitaly Rubin were living in Israel, the third was sixty-four-year-old Alexander Lerner, and the fourth was Anatoly Sharansky.

Ten days after the publication of Lipavsky's article, Sharansky's "box" was increased to a "cage" of eight.[7] March 15, 1977, as he and two Western journalists left Vladimir Slepak's apartment, Sharansky was seized by four plainclothesmen, thrown into a waiting car and driven away. Still reeling with disbelief, the journalists relayed the information to the West.

That same day, Yuli Orlov and Alexander Ginzburg, two other leaders of the Helsinki monitoring group, were also arrested.

For the next sixteen months, Sharansky was held incommunicado in Moscow's Lefortovo Prison without formal charges. This was in direct contravention of Soviet law that an individual could not be detained without charges for more than nine months. The Soviets conducted the most intensive investigation ever launched against a refusenik. Hundreds of Jews were interrogated from more than twenty Soviet cities, including many people from remote areas of the USSR who had never met Sharansky. Fear was building within the Jewish community. "Today you are a witness, tomorrow, the accused."[8]

The Soviet press reported that Sharansky had served the U.S. Central Intelligence Agency (CIA), making him subject to prosecution under Article 64 of the Criminal Code, which carried a possible death sentence for treason. At a news conference June 13, 1977, President Carter denied the Soviet allegation. "I have inquired deeply within the State Department and within the CIA, as to whether or not Mr. Sharansky has ever had any known relationship in a subversive way, or otherwise with the CIA. The answer is no. We have double-checked this. I have been hesitant to make that public announcement before now, but now I am convinced."[9] The statement appeared to have no effect on the Kremlin leadership.

Knowing that bargaining power was greater before sentencing than after, Western activists embarked on an intensive campaign on Sharansky's behalf. The International Committee for the Release of Anatoly Sharansky was formed under the co-chairmanship of the American politician Father Robert F. Drinan, British parliamentarian John Gorst, and retired Canadian Supreme Court judge, Emmett M. Hall.

As its first undertaking, the committee sponsored a petition addressed to Secretary General Leonid Brezhnev, demanding

Sharansky's immediate release. Through Barbara Stern, the Sharansky committee's Canadian co-ordinator, University of Toronto professors – physicist Eric Fawcett and computer scientist Calvin Gottlieb – obtained the signatures of two thousand computer scientists.[10]

Determined to broaden the base of non-Jewish support, Alan Rose and Barbara Stern met with John Harker, director of International Affairs of the Canadian Labour Congress (CLC), whose long-standing commitment to the "human and trade union rights of all peoples" was known. Sympathetic to the issue, Harker lobbied Soviet officials on behalf of Sharansky and other refuseniks, and he urged the CLC's president Joe Morris to take a firm stand.

Morris wrote to Soviet ambassador Yakovlev in June 1977. He said, "Reports of the serious curtailment of freedom of expression sought by Yuri Orlov, Alexander Ginzburg and Anatoly Sharansky and others, in their attempts to assist the fulfillment of the Helsinki Agreement, caused great concern in the Congress. More recent reports that Jews seeking to give effect to Helsinki by leaving the Soviet Union are being subjected to harassment and vilification, cause us to question your government's interest in human rights."[11]

Shirley Carr, executive vice-president of the CLC, met with Avital Sharansky on one of her North American visits. "Political freedom, human rights and trade union rights are indivisible," Carr assured her, "and the Congress is committed to their defence whenever and wherever they are in jeopardy."[12]

The Sharansky saga carried a unique Canadian connection. Twenty-nine members of Anatoly's family lived in Toronto. This was discovered when Noah Landis, an elderly physician, recognized the name "Sharansky" in the press. "It is a familiar name," he said to his son Herb. "I think he is family."[13] Their suspicion was confirmed when Noah Landis and his cousin Boris Landis wrote to their first cousin Boris Sharansky, Anatoly's father, in Moscow. An energetic correspondence ensued.

"In our dining room on a neat little table rests the photograph of our Tolya and his wife Avital," wrote Boris Sharansky to his Toronto relatives seven months after his son's arrest. "We look at them very frequently and our hearts ache and cry. Oh my Lord, will there ever be an end to this agony?"[14]

This letter sparked action by Noah and Boris Landis's children, Herb Landis and Debby Solomon, who with their spouses, Gloria Landis and Stan Solomon, headed the family campaign and worked indefatigably for the cousin they had never met.[15] They turned to veteran activists Sam Filer and Genya Intrator for assistance. Filer introduced the family to Joe Pomerant, a Toronto lawyer, whom they retained for a brief time. Intrator placed the first telephone call to Sharansky's mother, Ida Milgrom, from the Solomon's home, and for many years, served as the translator for subsequent calls placed by the Toronto Sharansky family. Financing for the telephone calls was raised through a special fund created at Beth Tikvah Synagogue, where the Solomons were members, as well as at Beth Sholom Synagogue.[16]

After holding strategy meetings with Avital in Jerusalem in the summer of 1977, Irwin Cotler invited her to visit Canada. When Avital arrived in Montreal in November, she went directly to a meeting Cotler had arranged at the Faculty Club of McGill University. There she met with Quebec Jurists as well as the Chief Justices of the Superior Court and the Court of Appeal, both of whom were non-Jewish francophones. "Although Avital spoke English haltingly," Cotler recalled, "she had the capacity to convey a message through her pain, on a human level for her husband, and on an historical level for the human rights struggle."[17] A power of attorney giving Cotler a mandate to represent the Sharansky family was drawn up that afternoon, notarized, and signed by Avital.[18]

Avital's visit coincided with the sixtieth anniversary of the Bolshevik revolution, a day of celebration for Soviet nationals. She and Esther Markish were the featured speakers at a rally held for members of the Ottawa Jewish community outside the Soviet Embassy. "Only persistent efforts will ensure that Anatoly Sharansky will not suffer the same fate as my husband," the widow of the slain Yiddish writer Peretz Markish told demonstrators.[19]

That evening, as formally attired guests arrived for an anniversary reception at Montreal's Soviet Consulate, they were greeted by the flickering light of candles held by dozens of Sharansky supporters.[20] Avital stood with them, dwarfed by a three-metre-high photograph of her husband. She held a sign that read, "I am the wife of Anatoly Sharansky."

The Montreal 35s sent a letter with two photographs to Consul General Gavruchkin. One, of Gavruchkin and his wife, had appeared in *The Globe and Mail,* the other of was Avital, standing outside the consulate beside the photograph of her husband. The letter concluded, "We implore you to release Anatoly Sharansky from Lefortovo Prison so that he may be reunited with his wife in their historic homeland, Israel. Then, they too, will stand as you, husband and wife, to spend the remainder of their lives together." A copy of the letter and the two photographs appeared in a local newspaper under the headline, "Tragedy amidst the festivities."[21]

Support for Sharansky was universal. Letters to release Sharansky on humanitarian grounds were sent to Ambassador Yacovlev by the National Council of Women and the Canadian Conference of Catholic Bishops, and Amnesty International adopted him as one of their Prisoners of Conscience.

On December 1, 1977, eight students at York University cabled Prime Minister Pierre Trudeau to intervene on Sharansky's behalf. When there was no immediate response, the students embarked on a hunger strike, pledging to drink only water until he complied.[22] That day, Bert Raphael wrote to the prime minister expressing the support of the lawyers' committee for the student endeavour.[23]

Each day the students sent another telegram to the prime minister and they continued their fast, awaiting his reply. On December 5, MP Herb Gray cabled the fasting students, "You have my support in your efforts to get the Canadian government to raise the case of Anatoly Sharansky with Soviet authorities, urging them to allow him to leave Russia and be reunited with his wife in Israel. I am conveying these views to the prime minister and external affairs minister. I commend you for your courage and commitment."[24]

On December 7, the York University students received a telegram from Trudeau. "I have heard your message of concern for Anatoly Sharansky," he wrote. "Please be assured that the government has been monitoring his case from the beginning . . . and Canadian delegates at Belgrade are pressing for the right of citizens to monitor the implementation of the Helsinki Final Act, the right to emigrate and the reunification of families."[25]

Dissatisfied with the answer, the students cabled their response. "On a moral issue such as this, the prime minister of Canada has a duty and a responsibility to denounce publicly the mistreatment of Soviet Jews and in particular the violation of the human rights of Anatoly Sharansky. We continue our strike and await your reply."[26]

Local newspapers followed the event with great interest. *The Toronto Star* headlined the latest development: "Protestors continue fasting, say PM's message too weak."[27] An article in *The Globe and Mail* reported that Stephen Lewis, Clifford Pilkey, Pierre Berton, the Most Reverend Edward W. Scott, Reverend Msgr. M.P. Lacey and Rabbi W. Gunther Plaut were among twelve prominent Ontarians who urged Trudeau to pressure the Soviets for Sharansky's release.[28]

On December 8, a personal message from MP Robert Kaplan was read to an Ottawa Jewish community gathering, "We should remember how much defenders of freedom owe to people like Sharansky. Without his acts of courage, our cause and the cause of universal human rights would be weaker."[29] Rabbi Don Gerber, chairman of the Ottawa Soviet Jewry committee challenged the government to act. "Quiet diplomacy has become a hallmark of being able to do nothing, under the guise of propriety," he accused. "When will Canadian leaders stop posturing and politicking and start acting like men of principle?"[30] Toronto lawyer Joe Pomerant charged the Canadian government with "immorality, cynicism, indifference and hypocrisy" for its refusal to condemn Soviet persecution of Sharansky.[31]

On December 10, International Human Rights Day, a petition sponsored by the International Committee for the Release of Anatoly Sharansky appeared in newspapers across the country. It was signed by three hundred academics, professionals and politicians.[32] As well, the text of a telegram to Brezhnev, from fifty-seven parliamentarians, was released to the press by Helsinki Parliamentary Committee chairman Martin O'Connell.[33]

When the hunger strike had entered its eleventh day, Norman

Cafik, minister of state for multiculturalism, requested a meeting with the students. "I don't think there is any doubt that we should be speaking up on this matter,"[34] Cafik said. He informed them that the government was supporting the Toronto Sharansky family's decision to sponsor their cousin as an immigrant to Canada. If the Soviets permitted his exit from the Soviet Union, the Canadian government would ensure that all immigration impediments were waived.[35]

The Honourable Don Jamieson delivered this report in the afternoon session of the House of Commons: "I called on the Soviet Ambassador at 1:15 PM this afternoon and made representations to him which reflected the declaration of various members of parliament on all sides. I also assured the ambassador that there were relatives in Canada who were prepared to sponsor Mr. Sharansky and that the Canadian government would issue an order-in-council expediting the entry of Mr. Sharansky into Canada."[36]

The students ended their hunger strike. Although they were aware that Sharansky desired a visa for Israel and not for Canada, the student protest had forced the Canadian government to act.

On December 15, the date Soviet law compelled the authorities to press charges against Sharansky, it was announced that a special resolution had been passed extending the investigative period into Anatoly Sharansky's case by an additional six months. The delay was caused by the Soviets' inability to find anyone to testify to Sharansky's having espionage links in the West. Among the hundreds of refuseniks who were interrogated, not one would admit to the false accusation.[37]

Activists were determined to continue to confront the Soviets on this issue until the date of Sharansky's trial was announced. On January 20, 1978, Sharansky's thirtieth birthday, members of Montreal's Inter-Faith Task Force on Soviet Jewry conducted a prayer service outside the Soviet Consulate.[38] Father Barry Jones, Rabbi Sidney Shoham, Reverend Dr. John Simms and Reverend Sidney Nelson rang the bell on the iron gate in an attempt to deliver a Russian-Hebrew Bible to the Soviet consul general, for safe delivery to the prisoner. There was no response.[39]

After two months with no acknowledgment by the Soviets of the offer of landed immigrant status to Sharansky, CCSJ's chairman Max Shecter led a delegation of activists to Ottawa to meet with MPs Norman Cafik, Herb Gray, John Roberts and Robert Kaplan. Their discussion led to a motion that was passed in the House of Commons February 8, urging the government to renew its offer of Sharansky's sponsorship to Canada.[40]

On March 15, 1978, the first anniversary of Sharansky's arrest, the Canadian 35s held vigils to which their respective communities were invited to participate.[41] In anticipation of Sharansky's trial, CCSJ chairman Shecter wrote to Canadian Jewish leaders to mobilize support. "A Sharansky conviction," he warned them, "will be the signal for a renewed wave of anti-Semitism in the Soviet Union, with the consequent harassment of innocent people; it will reduce to a trickle the number of exit visas."[42]

On July 7, 1978, Sharansky was presented with a document "Charges in the Final Form." It consisted of: Article 64, section A of the Criminal Code – high treason in the form of rendering aid to a foreign state and high treason in the form of espionage; and Article 70 – anti-Soviet agitation and propaganda.

Article 64 – A, "high treason" covered statements that he had signed in support of the Jackson Amendment and meetings with American congressmen and senators; and "espionage" consisted of maintaining lists of refuseniks "under the orders of the CIA," and passing those lists to foreigners. Article 70 covered his work as a member of the Helsinki Watch Group. High treason and espionage carried a maximum penalty of death.

Sharansky's trial began three days later, in a three-storey, brick and stucco courthouse about a mile from the Kremlin. His brother Leonid was the only family member permitted to observe the proceedings. Their mother, Ida Milgrom, stood outside the iron barricades with dissidents, refuseniks, diplomats and hundreds of Western journalists whose entry to the courtroom was blocked by dozens of militiamen.[43]

International news media were intrigued by this event. Anatoly Sharansky had become a symbol of confrontational politics between the Kremlin and the White House, despite President Carter's denial that Sharansky had worked for the CIA. Moscow-based *New York Times* correspondent David K. Shipler wrote, "No political trial in the last decade has contained the array of issues and emotions that the proceedings against Anatoly Sharansky hold for people inside and outside the Soviet Union."[44]

Before and during the trial, cables and letters written by Canadian leaders were sent to Soviet officials and demonstrations were held across the country.[45] Canadian Jewish Congress president Rabbi W. Gunther Plaut addressed a rally of thousands at Queen's Park. "This is not a matter merely for Jews," he declared.

"It is for free people everywhere who care about justice . . . we won't be silenced . . . Not we! Not now! Not ever!"[46] Winnipeg activists staged a twelve-hour protest on the steps of the courthouse. Calgarians held a day-long sit-in beside the statue of the Family of Man.[47] Vancouverites gathered outside city hall and Ottawans demonstrated outside the Soviet Embassy.

Montreal's Soviet Consulate was the site of a round-the-clock vigil that took place for the duration of the trial. Wearing T-shirts with Sharansky's photograph above the words "Freedom for Sharansky," Jews and non-Jews of all ages prayed, sang Hebrew songs and listened to hourly news broadcasts for any information about Sharansky's fate.

Mattresses and sleeping bags were hauled out at midnight, as the vigil continued through the night.[48] Media coverage was constant. A CBC television crew arrived one morning at 5:30 AM to film a dozen men, wearing prayer shawls and phylacteries,[49] as they chanted morning prayers.

In addition to the anticipated Jewish reponse, CLC president Dennis McDermott sent a cable to his counterpart Alexei Shibayev, president of the USSR Central Council of Trade Unions (AUCCTU). In it, he asked Shibayev to urge his government to release Sharansky and to allow all Jews who were prosecuted for expressing their opinions to be permitted to emigrate to the countries of their choice. "Failure to respond positively to the request," the cable stated, "would seriously endanger the spirit of *détente* between the workers of our two countries and could force the CLC executive council to seriously reconsider the decision made by the delegates to our last convention to continue the exchange program between Canadian and Soviet workers."[50]

Shibayev's written reply stated that Jewish activists were sentenced for "anti-state activities" and not for their opinions. This caused the CLC leaders to consider their options.[51]

Sharansky's trial lasted five days. During that time, the prosecution provided reams of written material, much of which accused Sharansky of involvement with Senator Henry Jackson.

On July 14, 1978, the defendant was found guilty of "espionage and of assisting a foreign country in hostile activity against the USSR." He was sentenced to three years' imprisonment and ten years' hard labour in a strict regime camp. The verdict was relayed by a tearful Leonid as he emerged from the Moscow courthouse.[52] He reported that his brother had been calm during the proceedings and, before the sentence was pronounced, had delivered a courageous statement. His mother sobbed uncontrollably in the arms of Andrei Sakharov, who had been at her side throughout the ordeal.

Sakharov, the world's best-known dissident, remarked to reporters outside the courtroom: "Sharansky lived such an open life that it completely precluded any kind of secret activity. He spoke openly against the violation of the right to emigrate and against other violations of human rights. He met openly with foreign correspondents from abroad . . . it was precisely for his boldness and openness, for his consistent humanitarian and honest position that Sharansky has been chosen as the latest victim."[53]

News of the verdict was communicated instantly to the West. "How can one talk of a trial when the outcome is a foregone conclusion?" wrote David Levy, a Moscow-based CBC news correspondent. "Sharansky was framed. The knowledge of Soviet state secrets that he was accused of passing to *Los Angeles Times* correspondent Robert Toth, was no more than that which every educated Soviet citizen possesses."[54]

Both the print and broadcast media made Sharansky's closing

statement public knowledge. It ended with: "For more than two thousand years the Jewish people, my people, have been dispersed. But wherever they are, wherever Jews are found, every year they have repeated, 'Next year in Jerusalem.' Now when I am further than ever from my people, from Avital, facing many arduous years of imprisonment, I say, turning to my Avital: *LeShana Haba'a b'Yerushalayim*. Next year in Jerusalem."[55]

Three days later, in the early evening, four thousand people filled every inch of the street, sidewalks and lawns across from Montreal's Soviet Consulate, to demonstrate their overwhelming feelings of sadness. The program began with a statement from Prime Minister Trudeau, indicating that Sharansky's sentence would have serious implications for *détente*. Speakers from the Montreal Jewish and general community shared their feelings of sorrow. The program concluded with Irwin Cotler's remarks, "The undisguised aim of the Soviet government is to crush both the human rights and Jewish activist movements, and Sharansky is viewed as the heart of the movement."[56]

Hoping to increase pressure on the Soviet government to reverse the judgment against him, Cotler undertook the task of preparing a legal appeal on Sharansky's behalf.[57] The grounds for the appeal were based on breaches of Soviet constitutional, criminal and procedural law. He worked day and night for six weeks. The result was an eight-hundred-page, four-inch-thick document entitled "The Sharansky Case." In addition to citing forty major violations of the Soviet Union's own laws through supporting affidavits and testimony from witnesses, Cotler documented the utter falsity, if not absurdity, of the charges against Sharansky.[58]

On August 30, 1978, the brief was served by a bailiff on Soviet ambassador Yacovlev for conveyance to Procurator General Roman Rudenko. Cotler's covering letter protested the judgment, asked for the right to inspect the decisions in the case, enquired into Sharansky's living conditions and appealed for clemency.

Cotler outlined the details of the appeal brief to reporters at a press conference. "It received global resonance," Cotler remarked, many years later. "This exposure was exactly what we were hoping for – mainly to take the case to the court of public opinion and to mobilize international advocacy."[59]

Cotler was under no illusion that Kremlin officials would acknowledge receipt of the brief or even respond to it. "We had a number of collateral objectives," he stated. "We sought to expose the Soviet Union as a human rights' violator and to expose the violations of what they claimed was their adherence to the Helsinki Final Act. We sought to provide a documentary record of Sharansky's innocence and use the Helsinki Final Act to authenticate that innocence. We sought to use the legal brief to mobilize the support of bar associations, law students and lawyers. Moreover, we wanted to show Sharansky's family and friends that they were not alone."[60]

The CLC acted on its threat. Recognizing that the Soviet trade union movement was standing firm with its government, the CLC severed relations. "I was seen by the Soviets as being a severe obstacle," John Harker recalled. "I was accused of not understanding the nature of the Soviet system because I argued on behalf of refuseniks."[61]

Sharansky had become the most prominent refusenik. The forced separation of a husband from his young bride and his imprisonment on charges of espionage had both personal and political appeal. Support for Sharansky continued long after his sentencing.

On March 15, 1979, the second anniversary of Sharansky's arrest, a symposium, "To know and act upon one's rights," was held in Montreal.[62] Telegrams of support were received from Prime Minister Trudeau and from scientists representing four Canadian universities.[63]

In the spring, a few members of the Jewish Students Network performed *The Trial of Anatoly Sharansky,* based upon Cotler's brief, at York University. The play was a re-enactment of Sharansky's trial in a moot court.

Author Mordecai Richler addressed a Montreal student protest in June. "So long as Sharansky rots in prison," Richler contended, "the least we in Canada can do is ask for an immediate stop to all further cultural and athletic exchanges."[64]

Avital Sharansky had become a skilled activist who won the admiration of everyone who met her. Her father-in-law expressed his feelings about her in a letter to his son in prison. "I'll never forget how shy and vulnerable she seemed when I first met her," wrote Boris Sharansky. "I asked her, 'Why do you speak so softly?' I can see how mistaken I was. How loudly she can speak when it is needed, and with what excitement people everywhere listen to her."[65]

Avital's love and admiration for her husband was obvious. "What sort of man is Anatoly?" was a question often asked of her. "He's just . . . special," she would respond wistfully. "He is very energetic. Very lively. He has a great sense of humour. But most important, he is really free in his soul. It is not as though he wants to be free and fights to be free. He is free. He was born like that."[66]

In the fall of 1979, Avital embarked on an extensive North American tour, armed with copies of her book, *Next Year In Jerusalem*. In this memoir, Avital described the awakening of her Jewishness, her first meeting with Anatoly, his activities as a human rights activist and leader of the Jewish emigration movement, and her personal efforts to have him freed. The launching of her book revived public attention for the man who continued to be seen as the symbol of struggle for Jewish liberation.

Chapter 15

To See for Ourselves

In the late 1970s, British and American Soviet Jewry activists began to travel to the Soviet Union for the sole purpose of meeting with refuseniks. Travel was critical to the growth of the movement. Information could be conveyed to and from refuseniks at a time when the Soviets were cutting telephone lines and jamming radio programs from the West, making communication almost non-existent.

As Canadian activists learned about travel from other countries, the CJC leadership recognized the importance of co-ordinating a similar program in Canada. The travellers carried with them Jewish educational material, clothing, and high-tech items for the refuseniks' personal use and for sale on the black market. The black market supplemented the incomes of many refuseniks who lost prestigious jobs when they applied to leave, forcing them to support their families on meagre salaries from menial work as elevator operators, refrigerator repairmen, book-binders or guards at public buildings.

Travellers' reports were filled with adventure and intrigue. In 1974, Philadelphia activist Connie Smukler left Moscow with a children's board game taped to her body under her clothes. *Route to Freedom, an experience of escape from the Soviet Union* was designed and illustrated by the teenage daughter of Moscow refuseniks. Its many obstacles constantly took the player back to start, epitomizing the reality of life in refusal.[1]

In the summer of 1975, Debbie Shecter, a young woman who attended her first Soviet Jewry rally as a child when Kosygin visited Toronto, travelled with her sister to the Soviet Union. They went to Vladimir Slepak's apartment, where they met with the Slepaks and other leading activists who described the dynamics of the growing Soviet Jewry movement. Their trip set the stage for many years of Soviet Jewry activity by Debbie and her father Max, who served as chairman of the CCSJ from 1977 to 1980.[2]

In June 1978, the lawyer's committee sent Emmett Hall, former Supreme Court justice, Arthur Maloney, ombudsman of the Province of Ontario and Brian Goodman, director of Legal Services and Complaint Policy in Ontario, to Leningrad and Moscow. The purpose of their trip was to assess the treatment of Jews by the Soviet legal system.

The lawyers had hoped for official meetings with the procurator-general and the director of OVIR in both cities. The meetings in Leningrad did not materialize and in Moscow, the junior civil servants with whom they spoke were not qualified to respond to the Canadians' legal queries.

Dr. Benjamin Levich and Dr. Alexander Lerner, members of the prestigious Academy of Sciences, were among the refuseniks the lawyers met. Both scientists had travelled the globe to present papers at international conferences before they applied to emigrate to Israel. After their first refusal, they were ostracized by the Soviet scientific community. "We shall never forget the hospitality these refuseniks extended to us and their indomitable spirit," remarked Hall, upon his return.

As well, Hall submitted a written report on the disparities between theory and practice of the Soviet Criminal Code. In it he wrote, "A nation's legal system, including a constitution which ostensibly is among the most liberal in the world, is being used and abused to the detriment of many Jews living in the Soviet Union."[3] He used, as an example, the incarceration of Slepak and Nudel, whose trials had taken place during the lawyers' visit. The fact that legal experts had travelled 4,800 kilometres to investigate the situation of Soviet Jewry prompted the CBC to devote a segment of the lawyer's trip on the national evening news.[4]

In December 1978, Sharon Wolfe and I travelled to Moscow, Leningrad and Kiev on an organized American tour, which we thought would be a good cover for clandestine activities. When fellow travellers visited tourist attractions, we could meet with Soviet Jews, whose addresses and telephone numbers were coded carefully in our address books.

Packed among our few personal belongings were jeans, dresses, calculators, cosmetics, magazines, books, pharmaceutical and medical supplies, to be given to the refuseniks. The prisoners' needs were different. For them there were soup cubes, vitamins and warm clothing for their personal use, and pens, colourful postcards and chewing gum to give to the guards for extra rations. The travellers also carried two down-filled sleeping bags for Vladimir Slepak and Yosef Begun, who were spending their first winter in Siberia. The supplies were left in the care of several refuseniks who made certain the prisoners received them.

Wolfe and I each wore a heavy necklace which, at close range, was seen to be made up of 180 tiny Stars of David. The necklaces were to be cut and distributed among the refuseniks in each of the cities visited.[5]

Orchestrated intimidation began on the first night in Leningrad when we telephoned Ilya Shastokovsky from the street. A plainclothesman paced back and forth in front of the booth. After an initial meeting, Shastokovsky or at least one other refusenik accompanied us in taxis or on the metro to future meetings. Their presence allayed any fears we had in knowing that we were being followed.

At the door of each refusenik's apartment were slippers of different shapes and sizes for guests to wear after removing their winter boots. Each apartment had bookshelves containing Hebrew texts, Jewish books and a Chanukah menorah. In many apartments, a map of Israel hung on the wall.

Our hosts served tea and cake and as they shared their painful stories, the tears in our eyes met the tears in theirs. They spoke of their children, of how they were ostracized by teachers and peers and robbed of a normal childhood. The life for refusenik children was better understood after viewing the pen and ink drawing of sixteen-year-old Misha Taratuta that hung on the wall of his parents' Leningrad apartment. He called it "a refusenik typewriter." The machine was battered, but the word "Levi's" (the refuseniks' status symbol) was clearly visible. Most of the typewriter's keys were missing or broken. Those that remained spelled the words, "No," "Never," "Not."

Sixty-year-old Kiev refusenik Yitzhack Tsitverblit drew the blinds when we entered his living room. He was afraid to be seen entertaining foreigners. Tsitverblit recounted how, when he was seventeen, he had spent a weekend in the country with some school chums. When he returned home, his entire family was gone, along with most of the Jewish community of Kiev. His eyes welled with tears as he murmured the words "Babi Yar."

Babi Yar was the ravine that became a mass grave for 33,771 Kiev Jews murdered by the Nazis on the weekend of September 29, 1941. In 1976, Tsitverblit recited *Kaddish* (the prayer for the dead) for Jews who had gathered at Babi Yar to commemorate the massacre. In 1977, he was arrested by the KGB on his way to the ceremony. Fearful of a second arrest, the following year he remained at home .

"Babi Yar," answered the Intourist guide when we asked to see the ravine, "is too far away to visit." On our own we discovered that Babi Yar was five minutes from our hotel by car.

Lev Elbert was not intimidated by Kiev authorities. Conversation with him was conducted with the full knowledge of listening devices in his apartment. Looking up to the ceiling, Elbert announced, "My only secret is one the KGB already knows. I want to live in Israel."[6]

During our ten-day stay, Wolfe and I met with more than seventy refuseniks. Each night, in the privacy of our hotel room, we condensed our notes into coded transcripts, burned the original documents and flushed the remnants down the toilet. We communicated with one another on an erasable "magic slate," and spoke only when radio music blared in the background. We were always aware of listening devices in the ceiling.

When we entered Victor Brailovsky's apartment, a scientific seminar was in progress with thirty refuseniks in attendance. The guest lecturer was an American professor, a non-Jew, who had informed the Soviets that his participation in an international scientific meeting in Moscow was conditional on his ability to attend Brailovsky's seminar.[7] "We, in the West, are mirror images of you," we reminded the hosts when their meeting had ended. "The difference between us is that we have a voice. We are here to assure you that we will continue to use our voices to speak out, until each one of you is free."

The refuseniks had been unaware of any Canadian activity on their behalf until Irwin Cotler's appeal brief on behalf of Anatoly Sharansky had arrived through diplomatic channels, only a few weeks earlier. "The sentencing of Sharansky must not be seen as a defeat," they told us. "Massive international advocacy kept the focus on one man and prevented many more refusenik arrests that might have resulted in a full-scale Jewish trial."[8]

Conversations with Victor and Irina Brailovsky focused on various new advocacy strategies. When they accompanied us to the elevator outside their apartment door, we embraced. "Victor," I said, "I'll see you soon." "Where?" he asked. "Yerushalayim," I replied. There was a long pause, then he snapped his fingers and said, "Now that's a good idea. Why haven't I thought of that in the past six and a half years?"

On Saturday, December 9, 1978, Wolfe and I stood with dozens of refuseniks who waited outside Moscow's Choral Synagogue on Archipova Street, as they did each Shabbat afternoon, to meet foreigners. The meeting place was an effective Jewish grapevine. On that frigid, snowy day, the news that Golda Meir had died the day before was passed from person to person.

The sad moments were punctuated with humour. When asked to smile for a photograph, instead of responding with the familiar word "cheese," Pavel Abramovich uttered "VI-SA," which forced him to break into a broad grin.

On the last evening of our visit, mathematician Alexander Ioffe invited many refuseniks to his apartment to meet us. Each one waited patiently to relate his unique story. From them, lists of new refuseniks and lists of Jews requesting invitations from Israel were acquired. Anatoly Sharansky's brother, Leonid, presented a letter from his mother giving Irwin Cotler the power of attorney to represent her son. He wrote and signed an identical message on a page in my day-timer, in case the original note was confiscated.

At the poignant moment when we said goodbye to our friends, I was struck by the fact that had my grandparents not left a small town near Kiev in 1905, it could have been me, waiting for Jewish women to return to Canada to fight for my freedom.

Two months after our return, a letter postmarked "Magadan, Susuman, USSR" arrived from Yosef Begun. The letter began with the words: "Thank you for your warm message." I read between the lines. Begun had received the sleeping bag.

In March 1979, a trip to the USSR by Montreal 35s member Sheila Rosenstein Roth and her husband Stephen was triggered by the knowledge that a Moscow refusenik was named Grigory Rosenshtein. Sheila "adopted" him as her "cousin" and travelled to Moscow to meet him. The Roths were strip-searched on their arrival at Moscow's Sheremetyevo Airport and, during their trip, were conspicuously photographed on the streets.[9]

Most travellers visited activists in large cities. It was equally important to establish contact with Jews in smaller regions where visitors were often the only link to their heritage. In April 1979, CCSJ director Martin Penn visited Soviet Central Asia.[10] He arrived in Alma Ata, the capital of Kazakhstan, on the first night of Passover. Carrying a suitcase filled with kosher food, wine and Passover *haggadahs*, he went immediately to the Weizman family home. The extended family, eighteen in all, was seated at their dining room table. A stack of matzah on a plate was the only reminder that "this night was different than any other."

Penn conducted the first Passover seder that the Weizman family had ever attended. "It was an endless marathon," he recalled. "I read the *haggadah* in Hebrew, one paragraph at a time, then I translated it into English. My travelling companion translated the English into Yiddish, and Weizman translated the Yiddish into Russian." [11] At 2 AM Penn taught the family their first Hebrew lesson, beginning with the basic "*aleph, bet*."[12] The following evening Weizman invited all the refuseniks of Alma Ata to a second seder and the entire process was repeated.

"The exodus of Russian Jews is more important than the exodus from Egypt," said Eliahu Zaks when he met Penn in the synagogue in

Tashkent, Uzbekistan. "In Egypt, Moses went to Pharoah on behalf of the Jewish people," Zaks continued. "In Russia, every Jew has to be his own Moses, and go himself to Pharoah, in order to reach the promised land."[13]

The Bucharian Jews were eager to learn Hebrew, but were fearful of having classes in their flats, which were wired. Penn conducted most of his Hebrew lessons outdoors, in parks. He dictated the words from an elementary text into a cassette recorder that he left behind, to enable his new students to teach others.

In the summer of 1979, Irwin Cotler visited the USSR as a delegate to an international political science conference. Acting under power of attorney for the Sharansky family, he hoped to appeal Anatoly's conviction and thirteen-year sentence. Meetings had been arranged for Cotler with the procurator general of the USSR and the chief justices of the Supreme Court of both the USSR and the Russian republic.[14]

Cyberneticist Dr. Alexander Lerner had been forbidden by Soviet authorities to attend the conference, so he invited Cotler and other delegates to a special seminar in his apartment. His flat was handsomely decorated, reflecting the affluence of better days. Hanging on the walls were oil portraits he had painted of Sharansky, Ida Milgrom and Israel's founding president, Chaim Weizmann.

Ida Milgrom was present as well. She invited Cotler to join her and her husband for their fiftieth wedding anniversary celebration that was to take place the following day at their home in Istra, a small town on the outskirts of Moscow. Cotler obtained permission from Intourist to travel to Istra.

The next morning, he was picked up by car by Leonid Sharansky and Alexander Lerner and his family. On the outskirts of Moscow they were pulled over to the side of the road by officers who took them to a military compound for questioning. "I was the only one interrogated," recalled Cotler. " Dr. Lerner acted as my interpreter. He showed no signs of nervousness, in fact, he radiated a sense of calm and courage, which was remarkable, given his own precarious situation."[15] At first, Cotler demanded that his interrogators contact either the Canadian Embassy, the conference hosts, or *Los Angeles Times* correspondent Dan Fisher, with whom he was planning to dine that evening. The Soviets refused.

During the interrogation, the Soviet officers presented a document for Cotler's signature. The document included his name and passport number. It was an investigative protocol, acknowledging his violation of travel regulations. "It was clearly a contrived interrogation in which I was to sign a confession of judgment," related Cotler. "I refused." The officers asked him to sign a blank piece of paper. He refused. "Whereupon," declared Cotler, "they reintroduced the earlier version of my crime and again asked me to sign. Again, I steadfastly refused. Then I decided to write my accusations of them over their accusations of me, accusing the Soviets of 'illegal arrest,' 'detention,' 'interrogation' and 'false accusation.'"[16]

Cotler insisted that the KGB verify with Intourist that he had been given permission to travel to Istra. The officers instructed Cotler's companions to continue on to Istra, saying that Cotler would rejoin them in a few hours. Lerner insisted upon staying behind, refusing to leave the Canadian alone with his captors.

During the drive back to Moscow with four members of the KGB, Cotler asked Lerner what he thought would happen. The scientist suggested that Cotler might be expelled. Then, breaking into a wide grin, Lerner added, "If that happens, tell them that my family and I want to go with you." With the same light humour, Lerner assured Cotler that he needn't be concerned about missing his meetings scheduled for the following day. "Since everything in my apartment is a matter of public record, I will just sit alone in my living room and say, 'Chief Justice Orlov, Procurator General Rudenko, if Professor Cotler were here, he would have told you the following . . . and I guarantee that there will be a transcript on both their desks in the morning."[17]

Soviet citizens were not permitted to enter hotels, so the two parted on the sidewalk. Lerner looked Cotler in the eye and said, "Remember, whatever happens, don't let them intimidate you." Then he spoke the Hebrew words, "Kol Yisrael arevim ze lazeh — All Jews are responsible for one another."

Cotler was given five minutes in which to pack his bags. He was whisked out of the hotel and into a police car. By passing security and customs, he was driven directly to the tarmac at the Moscow airport and escorted onto a Japanese airliner destined for London. Everything related to the Sharansky case, including a copy of his appeal brief, was confiscated. "I asked an airline official, who had come on board, to call Dan Fisher of the *Los Angeles Times* and tell him that I would not make it for dinner."[18]

Only after the plane took off did Cotler begin to comprehend what had transpired in the previous three hours. He felt ashamed for having caused problems for Lerner and the others. "By the time I arrived in London four hours later, I was deeply upset about what had happened. When I called my wife, Ariella, in Montreal, I told her not to tell anyone." It was too late. Dan Fisher had broken the story to the international media. "That," Cotler said, "was my fifteen minutes of fame." The Canadian high commissioner in London had arranged a press conference at Heathrow airport. "That was clearly a substantive message to the Soviet government of how the Canadian government looked upon my expulsion," noted Cotler. "In fact, minister of external affairs Flora MacDonald lodged a formal protest with the Soviet ambassador."[19]

Weeks later, in Montreal, Cotler received a message from Lerner saying that the expulsion was the best thing that could have happened. "The glimpse of the dark side of the gulag will help the free world to better understand what for refuseniks is a way of life."[20]

Soviet Jewish activists received one refusal after another. They became more desperate for information about their heritage, language and homeland. Books brought by casual travellers no longer satisfied their educational needs. Visits by qualified Jewish educators were necessary in order to advance the movement.

When the Soviet Union invaded Afghanistan in November 1979, the United States cancelled Aeroflot's landing rights. Since Americans weren't travelling to the USSR, Canadian activists felt obliged to pick up the slack.

Although the CJC fully endorsed a travel program, it was important that travellers not be perceived as acting on behalf of the organized Canadian Jewish community. The travel program, co-ordinated by Sharon Wolfe and operated with funds raised through private donations and a sale of treasures and crafts, made it possible for many Jewish scholars to visit the Soviet Union. They became part of an international network of travellers who instilled a sense of *Yiddishkeit* in the souls of Jews who had been deprived of their heritage for more than sixty years.

Travellers were selected for the contribution they might make to the refuseniks and to the movement in Canada.[21] In the spring of 1981, the CJC sent Goldie Hershon and Bracha Tritt to Moscow, Kishinev, Odessa and Minsk. Both women were fluent in Yiddish - a definite advantage in the smaller Jewish communities where no English was spoken. In Kishinev, the activists welcomed the women warmly, reflecting the deep affection they felt for Torontonian Jeanette Goldman, who was their telephone link with the outside world.

"The Jews in Odessa were under constant KGB surveillance and tensions ran very high," recalled Hershon. "One man's suitcase was packed, ready to leave at a moment's notice." The Pevzner family told the women that they had been expecting foreign visitors because a few days in advance of their visit, the telephone in their home had been disconnected.[22]

In Odessa, Tritt, an Israeli-born educator, taught a Hebrew lesson to the eighteen-year-old daughter of refusenik Mark Nepomniashchy, who showed her the Hebrew notes she concealed behind a loose tile in the bathroom.[23] "My greatest moment on the whole trip," she recalled, "occurred in Moscow on the night I addressed forty refuseniks in Hebrew. They were eager for information about Israel and captivated by the stories of my childhood in Israel when I worked with the Irgun."

From 1979 to 1983, Sharon Wolfe sent sixty Montrealers to eleven cities, and briefed and de-briefed hundreds of others who travelled to the USSR on their own.[24] Travellers submitted written reports of each trip that were circulated to briefers in other countries. Similarly, Wolfe received reports from her counterparts as well. One report that came to her attention was that of Toronto law students Rick Orzy and Sheldon Disenhouse, who visited the USSR in the summer of 1979. Their attention to detail prompted Wolfe to recruit them as briefers in Toronto.

"Briefings ease the anxiety of what is, in the best of circumstances, a difficult trip," Disenhouse would explain to travellers at the first of three briefing sessions. The lawyers informed them of their rights according to Soviet law, how to deal with customs at the Moscow airport, methods of internal travel, the mechanics of contacting refuseniks and specific tasks to be undertaken.

Within a short time, the popularity of the travel program necessitated that Disenhouse and Orzy form a briefing team.[25] From 1982 to 1987, more than sixty Torontonians travelled to the USSR annually. Each person was willing to accomplish a mission. The travel program became critical to the sustenance of the movement, filling not only educational needs, but in many cases, bringing life-saving drugs to heart and cancer patients.

In March, 1984, a group of prominent Christians set off on a trip to Moscow, Leningrad and Riga under the auspices of the CJC. The Soviets' refusal of my tourist visa is why Reverend Stanford R. Lucyk assumed the leadership of the group, which included Charlotte Gray, MPP Robert Nixon and Canon Borden Purcell.[26]

The impact of their trip was reflected in the comments they made and in articles they wrote upon their return. "We went as human beings," Lucyk reported to his church congregation, "to look into the eyes of other human beings and to say, as people from half-way around the world, we know. You are not alone!"[27]

Lucyk described climbing a dimly lit staircase in Leningrad, to the flat of a forty-five-year-old refusenik who held a doctorate in mathematics. He had been sentenced to two years of forced labour in Siberia for crimes against the State. "His crime?" asked Lucyk rhetorically. "Organizing seminars on Jewish history and culture in a land in which it is a crime to teach Hebrew."[28] He spoke of meetings with renowned scientists and engineers, dismissed from highly skilled jobs and forced to find work stoking furnaces, repairing refrigerators or operating elevators. "In the Yuri Andropov-Ronald Reagan era of nuclear escalation and renewed cold war, Russian Jews are being held hostage and used as coins of exchange in the international political arena.[29]

Lucyk spoke of a twenty-year-old student who lived a double life. By day at an engineering institute, he played the role of a good Russian. In the evenings, he and four other friends studied Hebrew. "So we went, sometimes tailed, receiving strange and mocking phone calls at all hours in our rooms. We listened to their stories, so that wherever our ounces of influence might count in the courts of this world, the issue might be raised."[30]

Years later, in reflecting upon his 1984 experience, Reverend Lucyk admitted, "My trip to Russia and meeting the refuseniks was one of those life-changing moments for me. The whole Soviet experience sears one's memory and history. I will never be the same."[31]

"Soviet refuseniks fear Cold War talk," was the title of an article Charlotte Gray wrote for *The Toronto Star.* In it, readers learned about Alexander Mariasin of Riga, the former manager of the largest electronics factory in the Soviet Union, who with his wife and daughter had waited for emigration visas for ten years.[32] The Mariasin apartment served as the headquarters for Riga's refusenik community. Listening devices, installed years earlier by a KGB officer who lived in the flat above, were blatantly visible in the ceiling. "I am condemned," Mariasin told the group. " I don't know by whom, I don't know for how long and I don't know for what reason."[33]

Eight years later, Alexander Mariasin spoke about meeting the Canadians. "It was unbelievable. Many Jews from all over the world had visited us in our apartment but never before had Christians come to show their support, particularly leaders of the Church. It was really very touching for outcasts such as us."[34]

In 1985, Montreal Inter-Faith Task Force members Father Barry Jones, Frederick N. Smith, John Hallward and Reverend Alexander Farquhar travelled to the USSR to meet with refuseniks. "It was a rare honour and an extraordinary privilege to meet and talk with such splendid and truly remarkable Soviet Jewish citizens," reported chairman Smith, upon their return. "At the same time, it was disheartening to see the hardships they were forced to endure."[36]

The Soviet Jewry travel program was self-perpetuating. Travellers shared their experiences at public meetings and stimulated others to embark on similar adventures. More importantly, the trips broadened the base of advocates helping Jews in their struggle for liberation.

Chapter 16

The Noose Tightens . . . Activists Respond

> In Moscow, a city with a population of two hundred and fifty thousand Jews, only two synagogues are allowed to remain open; Hebrew theatre, books, magazines and newspapers are forbidden. Kosher food is difficult to find and Jewish education is limited to an underground school . . . a rigid quota system all but bars youngsters from university education . . . the refuseniks must now bear the stigma and torment of living in limbo, waiting out their turn in a purgatory where mere survival becomes no mean victory.[1]

Squeezed into Canadian author Peter Newman's two-week visit to the USSR as a guest lecturer at the Institute of American and Canadian Studies were a few evenings with several refusenik families.[2] "Day by day we are being assassinated psychologically," Vladimir Prestin, a refusenik of ten years standing, told him. "A people can be killed when their heritage is taken away."[3]

Newman's trip took place two months after the Soviet invasion of Afghanistan, when sanctions imposed by the Carter administration had resulted in a Soviet crackdown on internal dissent. Andrei Sakharov was exiled, on January 22, 1980, to the closed city of Gorky and new restrictions were imposed on Jews requesting exit visas. First-degree kinship was made a prerequisite for submitting an application for emigration, meaning that the only invitation from Israel considered bone fide was one issued by a parent or child. Siblings, cousins, aunts and uncles did not qualify.

Canadian activity mounted. The Canadian Lawyers and Jurists for Soviet Jewry convened a forum, "Human Rights in the Soviet Union." Panelists included Dr. Naum Salansky, former refusenik and professor of Aerospace Studies at the University of Toronto, Dr. Robert McKay, director of the Aspen Institute for Humanistic Studies, and Irwin Cotler, professor of law at McGill University. After addressing the issue of human rights violations from their own perspectives, the panelists condemned the new visa law as contravening the basic tenets of the Helsinki Final Act. Letters to that effect were dispatched to Soviet officials.[4]

"How are Soviet Jews different from all other Jews?" asked Rabbi Mordechai Zeitz of Congregation Beth Tikvah, rhetorically, at a community-wide "symbolic third seder" at Montreal's Sheraton Mount Royal Hotel. The rabbi responded, "Others enjoy a connection with their past on which to build a future; Soviet Jews have only memories of the past and bleak hopes for the future." In the shortened *haggadah* reading, the traditional Passover symbols were interpreted in the context of the suffering of Soviet Jews.

Canadian poet Irving Layton read a poem he had dedicated to the Prisoners of Zion, which was inspired by their struggle to retain their Jewishness. He recited, "The lonely opposing martyrs. I kiss your hands, across steppes and barbed wire . . . send you my heartfelt greetings . . . Next Year in Jerusalem!"[5] When the ceremony ended, Layton led one hundred and fifty protesters, holding aloft banners calling for "Freedom for Soviet Jewry," on a torchlight march to the Soviet Consulate. They were accompanied by a van with music blaring: "Go tell it on the mountain . . . Let My People Go."

Once there, the chanting and singing ended and Irwin Cotler launched into a power-charged, emotional speech. Pointing to the yellow brick building behind the iron gate he thundered, "To those who stand behind these bars, J'accuse . . . We accuse you of harassment, of false accusation, of false witness, false imprisonment, brutality and torture." Cotler, whose initiative, drive, magnetism and dedication inspired many Canadians to take action, spoke about the wave of Soviet oppression and the helplessness of the Soviet Jewish community. "All Soviet Jews are the living metaphor for what it means to be a Jew today," he declared, "for what being a Jew has always meant... a people that dwells alone."[6]

In the case of Ida Nudel, Soviet authorities were intransigent. From her place of isolation and exile in Krivosheino she instructed activists through her letters, "Through our suffering, we have been able to push the gates of the USSR just slightly ajar. Through the tiny opening we have made in the Iron Curtain, Jews manage to get out. This is in fact our one solace through our ordeal. But the opening is small and vulnerable, and we implore all of you in the free world to keep a close watch on it and not allow the gates to be slammed shut again."[7]

Nudel's friends in Moscow sent books about gardening to her. She tilled the Siberian soil and began to plant tomatoes, lettuce, carrots, cucumber, potatoes and cabbage. "My garden has kept me alive, literally and spiritually," she wrote to them.[8]

On April 27, 1979, Ida Nudel celebrated her forty-ninth birthday, her first in exile. On that day, the international WIN committee launched a petition urging the Soviets to release Nudel from exile. The Canadian petition was inaugurated in Toronto and Montreal with the support of one hundred women from the business and professional communities and nuns from two convents.[9] When the petition was served on the Soviet embassy eight months later, it held ten thousand Canadian signatures.

The case of Colonel Lev Ovsishcher, a sixty-year-old former commander of a Soviet Air Force squadron in World War II, attracted Canadian attention. In 1972, his application to emigrate to Israel had been denied. As a protest, he returned his seventeen medals to the Soviet government. "It is not that I did not earn these medals," he said, "I earned them with my blood. But I do this action because I am desperate."[10]

When Ovsishcher was stripped of his rank, job and pension, it heightened his resolve to strengthen the Jewish identity of the one hundred and fifty thousand Jews in Minsk. He delivered lectures on "Jewish heroism in the Second World War," and conducted the annual service at the Minsk ghetto monument that memorialized the five thousand Jews who were executed by the Nazis in 1943.

Ovsishcher was adopted by MP John Fraser. "I am an old soldier," the parliamentarian from B.C. explained, "and I was fascinated by the man who had been decorated for bravery and was treated so badly by the country that he had served. I was too young to fight the Nazis. In a way, he fought for me. I was determined to fight for him."[11]

On March 5, 1980, Vancouver activists and the Ovsishcher Committee of Beth Israel Synagogue, crowded into Fraser's riding office to speak with the war veteran by telephone.[12] "Greetings from myself and my fellow brothers in grief," said Ovsishcher through an interpreter. "It is very important that we are not forgotten. The knowledge that we are not alone in this hard time, gives us confidence that we will overcome."[13]

When the KGB prevented Ovsishcher from attending V-Day celebrations marking the thirty-fifth anniversary of the defeat of the Nazis, protests were staged in Vancouver, Calgary and Toronto. The Toronto Committee for Lev Ovsishcher held its first demonstration for Ovsishcher at Toronto's Anshei Minsk Synagogue with two hundred war veterans in attendance.[14]

In May 1980, MP Roland de Corneille,[15] an Anglican priest and former director of B'nai Brith's League for Human Rights, introduced a motion in the House of Commons urging the Soviet government to fulfil its international undertakings and permit Ovsishcher to emigrate to Israel.[16] Fraser brought the case to the attention of Ambassador Yacovlev.[17]

At the Helsinki review meetings that opened in Madrid in November 1980, Vancouver Action for Soviet Jewry (VASJ) chairman Barbara Shumiatcher presented Ovsishcher's case to the Canadian delegation.[18] All pleas by Canadian delegates at Madrid to secure Ovsishcher's freedom were rebuffed by the Soviets.

By 1980, Soviet Jewry advocacy in the West was an extensive and complicated network of Jewish and non-Jewish men, women, students, politicians, clergymen, academics and scientists. What most activists did not know was that Lishkat Hakesher, the Israeli government office that Nechemiah Levanon had been directing for almost twenty-five years, was responsible for coordinating the global Soviet Jewry campaign from behind the scenes. Lishkat Hakesher processed all requests by Soviet Jews for invitations from Israel and had the most comprehensive lists and files.

Its director kept a low public profile. Taciturn and secretive, Nechemiah Levanon handled the enormous task with extraordinary expertise. His name was little known outside the ranks of Soviet Jewry activists. Assisted by his colleague Tzvi Netzer, Levanon issued directives from his small office in Tel Aviv to emissaries in Israeli embassies in Washington, Ottawa, London, Paris and in Israeli consulates in New York, Los Angeles and Sydney.[19]

A man with sharp analytical ability, Levanon was a strong proponent of the two-pronged approach, quiet diplomacy linked with grassroots activism. It was he who, in 1969, convinced Prime Minister Golda Meir that overt protests would assist, not hinder, the Soviet Jewry campaign. This caused her to reverse her stance and make public the letter from the Georgian Jews.[20]

Having once been named a member of the Israeli intelligence by the Soviet international press agency Novosti, Levanon had to be circumspect. He was always aware of his burdensome responsibility and, as such, communicated with Soviet Jewry advocates on a "need-to-know" basis.[21] He deplored the publication of refusenik lists, and for this was criticized by North American activists, particularly members of autonomous organizations. They claimed that he withheld pertinent information and, in so doing, thwarted their activity.

Another controversial issue between many activists and Nechemiah Levanon concerned the issue of *neshira,* the problem that continued to haunt the Israelis. By 1980, 80 per cent of all Soviet Jews who received visas for Israel "dropped out"' in Vienna. After a few days in Vienna, the "drop outs" (*noshrim*) continued on to Ladispoli on the outskirts of Rome, where they lived in caravans and were supported by the Hebrew Immigrant Aid Services (HIAS) until they were able to emigrate to the country of their choice.

Levanon and many Israelis believed that if *neshira* continued to escalate, the Soviets would stop issuing visas for Israel, insisting that the repatriation of Jews to their "homeland" had become a sham. They believed that the solution to terminating *neshira* was to curtail aid to Soviet Jews in Vienna and in Ladispoli by closing the HIAS' offices.

Abba Eban, one of the most eloquent defenders of Zionism, shared this view. He maintained that by choosing America, the Soviet Jews did a great disservice to the Jewish people. "By trading the idea of a homeland for the opportunity of personal gain, the Soviet Jews were in effect trampling on the very dignity and authenticity of the statehood which had served them in their need."[22]

Most Western activists took the position that they couldn't force Jews to go to Israel when they themselves lived in the Diaspora. They were not prepared to ask their own governments to close the doors on Jewish immigration. "Plummeting emigration figures and growing discrimination against Jews in the USSR were bad enough," they said, "without Jews in the West preventing Soviet Jews from going to the country of their choice."[23]

The *neshira* issue was debated in the Jewish press. It was debated at the International 35s conference held in London in March 1980.[24] It was debated one week later at a Soviet Jewry conference in Israel, and once again, in April 1980 at NCSJ's national policy conference in Washington. *Neshira* was a moral issue with no clear-cut solution. It lost its primacy on the Soviet Jewry agenda, however, when the situation in the Soviet Union worsened.

On November 13, 1980, the KGB stormed and searched the Moscow apartment of Victor Brailovsky while a "Sunday scientific seminar" was in progress. They found copies of *Jews in the USSR*, the *samizdat* Jewish cultural journal of which Brailovsky was editor. The officials arrested and charged him with "slandering the Soviet State," an offense that carried a maximum sentence of three years.

Five of Brailovsky's colleagues in Tel Aviv, who had edited the cultural publication prior to emigrating to Israel, issued a statement to the world press.[25] "We, the founders and former editors of *Jews in the USSR* declare herewith full responsibility that this magazine was founded as an organ of self-expression of the two-million-strong Jewish minority in the Soviet Union and because of its very nature, did not, contain any materials of political character."[26]

Physicist and Nobel laureate Dr. Gerhard Herzberg cabled his protest on Brailovsky's behalf to the president of the Soviet Academy of Sciences: "Canadian scientists are absolutely astounded to hear that their Soviet colleague, Victor Brailovsky, has been arrested. At a time when scientific contacts between the Soviet Union and Canada have been strained to the breaking point, the arrest of Brailovsky appears to be a deliberate affront to Canadian scientists by the Soviet authorities."[27]

The disruption of the Moscow seminar prompted North American scientists to host a "Moscow Sunday Scientific Seminar in Exile." It was held in Toronto in January 1981, prior to the opening of a conference of the American Association for the Advancement of Science.[28] There, Herzberg presented a paper on triatomic hydrogen that was followed by a panel discussion moderated by Professor Irwin Glass.[29] The scientists issued strong statements of support for the Moscow seminar which, they contended, was a professional lifeline for their Soviet Jewish colleagues.

Pressure often paid handsome rewards. After serving eleven years in prison and labor camps, Josef Mendelevich, the last of the Leningrad trial prisoners, was released in March 1981. He had suffered starvation in prison and had been subjected to verbal and physical abuse for observing the dietary laws and refusing to work on the Sabbath. Mendelevich's freedom was the result of twenty-three rounds of negotiations between Ambassador Anatoly Dobrynin and World Jewish Congress leaders Edgar Bronfman and Israel Singer. This victory brought hope that economist Ida Nudel might be next.

On April 27, 1981, activists and members of all three provincial parties celebrated Nudel's fiftieth birthday in a committee room of the provincial legislature of Ontario. There they witnessed the presentation of the first "Ida Nudel Humanitarian Award," created to honour a Canadian woman whose achievements on behalf of humanitarian endeavours were recognized nationally.

The award, a silkscreen print by Toronto artist Sharon Binder, was presented to The Honourable Pauline McGibbon, former lieutenant-governor of Ontario, by Jeanette Goldman, chairman of CJC's

Committee for Soviet Jewry, Ontario Region. "McGibbon stands at the forefront of volunteerism and charity," Goldman declared to the assembly. "She identifies with the poor and downtrodden and is deeply concerned with human rights."[30]

Eight weeks later, on June 22, 1981, activists in four Canadian cities planned events to mark the third anniversary of Nudel's conviction and sentencing to Siberian exile. "The indifference of people who take their own rights for granted is the greatest threat facing Ida Nudel and other Prisoners of Conscience around the world," declared Peg Ingram, the chairman of Amnesty International in Winnipeg. Four other prominent women, Olga Fuga, Pearl McGonigal, Beverley Tangrey and Roberta Ellis, each paid tribute to Nudel outside the Manitoba Legislature, in the presence of hundreds of Jews and non-Jews.[31]

Members of Edmonton's Jewish community held a ceremony for the female prisoner on the steps of their city hall and hundreds of women demonstrated in Toronto's Nathan Phillips Square. "Ida Nudel stands as an inspiration not only to her fellow citizens but to all of us," affirmed York University professor of economics Sally Zerker. "We dare not forget her – for to forget Ida Nudel is to encourage the Soviets' efforts to silence the voices of freedom."[32] Ontario MPP Susan Fish implored the women who were huddled under umbrellas in a steady downpour: "Shout with me, so that they hear us all the way to the Kremlin." Raising a clenched fist, the impassioned Fish bellowed, "KGB, Give Ida Nudel her visa!"[33]

"We've got to keep up the pressure to release Ida Nudel. We cannot permit these blatant violations of human rights to go unnoticed or unchallenged," declared MP David Smith. The chairman of the Parliamentary Group addressed MPs and Canadian activists at a luncheon in the House of Commons. "Emigration has decreased to a trickle, but Western governments can't ease off," he added.[34]

Victor Brailovsky had been held incommunicado for six months when, on June 15, 1981, the Soviets announced that his trial would be held two days later.

CCSJ director Martin Penn asked David Smith to propose a

motion in parliament asking Minister of External Affairs Mark MacGuigan to instruct Canadian diplomats in Moscow to seek observer status at Brailovsky's trial. Smith asked Penn to draft the motion that would be presented to the government the following day.

The next morning, an official from the Department of External Affairs contacted Penn in his Montreal office to discuss the response to a motion that was to be presented by David Smith that afternoon. Penn dictated what he felt should be the appropriate Canadian response. "By the time Question Period opened that day," Penn recalled with amusement, "both my question and answer were on the floor in parliament."[35] The motion was passed unanimously.

The two Canadian diplomats who had requested permission to observe Brailovsky's trial were refused admission to the courtroom, along with Western reporters and Brailovsky's friends and supporters.[36] They were all told that there was no space available. It is true that the courtroom was packed, but it was filled with KGB agents who had been transported by bus from other cities to encourage the prosecution and to intimidate the accused.[37]

For two days, testimonies were made by prosecution witnesses, all of whom were unknown to the defendant. Brailovsky refused to be represented by the court-appointed lawyer and conducted his own defense. The verdict, handed down June 19, 1981, was a foregone conclusion. The judge adopted the prosecutor's recommended sentence: "Five years in internal exile with twenty-one months off for time already spent in prison."[38] Victor Brailovsky would spend the next three years in Kazakhstan.

In August and September, the KGB cracked down on refuseniks in major cities across the USSR, resulting in the imprisonment of eleven teachers of Hebrew. The authorities were making emigration almost impossible. Invitations to prospective emigrants from relatives in Israel were rarely delivered, Jews were refused on the basis of insufficient kinship and the processing of visa applications was taking up to two years.

Emigration figures had dropped from 51,320 in 1979 to 21,471 in 1980. Indications were that the 1981 total would be fewer than ten thousand. The hardline policy was a result of strained relations between the White House and the Kremlin.

"A crisis situation exists now for Jews in the Soviet Union and Ottawa should pressure the Soviets to open the gates," stated MP Jim Peterson after attending an emergency conference sponsored by the National Conference on Soviet Jewry in New York. He urged Canadians to join a North American effort to obtain one million signatures on a petition.[39] Two days later, Mark MacGuigan raised the Soviet Jewry issue with his counterpart Andrei Gromyko, during talks at the Soviet UN mission.[40] MacGuigan recalled the encounter, years later. "Gromyko made no comment. He did not respond to my questions, not even to affirm that he had heard me."[41]

The crackdown against refuseniks resulted in an intensification of Soviet Jewry activity across the country.

In May 1981, Toronto's "Solidarity Month for Soviet Jewry" and Montreal's "Unity Week for Soviet Jews" heightened community awareness. Postcard protests on behalf of refuseniks and prisoners became an integral part of meetings of Jewish organizations, schools, synagogues and churches.

Beth Israel Synagogue in Halifax became the site of a weekly Sunday morning "write-in" after community leader Frank Medjuck and Rabbi Daniel Levine returned from a trip to the Soviet Union.[42] Professor Theodore Freidgut, an American exchange fellow at Moscow State University, spoke at the Ottawa Jewish community's annual Soviet Jewry Shabbat.[43] Members of the National Council of Jewish Women in London, Ontario and the CJC's Calgary Committee for Soviet Jewry, began a vociferous campaign for Kharkov refusenik Alexander Paritsky.[44]

In the fall of 1981, Winnipeg 35s chairman Tina Lerner couriered a letter to F.L. Jobin, Lieutenant Governor of Manitoba. In it, she expressed dismay at his agreeing to present a replica of the Canada Cup to a Soviet official.[45] After the event, Jobin responded to Lerner in writing. "I was grateful for your letter because in my presentation remarks, I did state that my being on hand was not an endorsement of Russian policy or practices. Had I not received your letter I probably would have forgotten to make such an observation. Please accept my thanks."[46]

One hundred Vancouver families adopted one hundred refuseniks in their twin city of Odessa, an alliance that was established as a civic endeavour in 1945. A statement to that effect was sent to Ambassador Yacovlev and signed by Mayor Michael Harcourt on behalf of the Vancouver City Council.[47]

The Ontario Region's Soviet Jewry committee was responsible for the emergence of two new government-affiliated, non-partisan committees: the Ontario Legislature Committee for Soviet Jewry[48] (OLCSJ) and the Parliamentary Spouses Committee for Soviet Jewry.

"Our committee was a conduit," remarked MPP David Rotenberg, co-founding chairman, with MPPs Marion Bryden and Jim Breithaupt, of the legislature committee. "We responded to suggestions made by the CJC Soviet Jewry committee or the 35s, and under our official name would send cables or sponsor programs when the need arose."[49]

The spouses group was formed after several parliamentary wives met former Kishinev refusenik Inna Tsukerman in Ottawa.[50] Tsukerman was visiting from Israel to enlist support for her husband Vladimir, who was sentenced to three years in prison for attempting to organize a peaceful demonstration.

The women wrote to spouses of parliamentarians in other provinces to gain support for a petition protesting Vladimir Tsukerman's sentence. Within a few weeks, they had amassed more than two hundred signatures.[51] The spouses committee, under the chairmanship of Penny Collenette, presented refusenik cases to the Soviet ambassador on a regular basis and within a short time their committee became a noted force on Parliament Hill.[52]

Parliamentary committees were updated on Soviet Jewry activity through the monthly newsletter *Pipeline to the USSR*. Compiled by the CJC's Ontario Region Soviet Jewry committee, *Pipeline* provided suggestions for action.[53]

The growing number of refuseniks, increased arrests and a drastic reduction of exit visas prompted Dr. Alexander Lerner to convey a message to Irwin Cotler. When the two had met in the summer of 1979, they devised a code to be used by Lerner if the situation became intolerable. The code words, "Never again," were cabled by Lerner to Cotler.

Acting on the cable, Cotler convened an emergency conference in Ottawa on Human Rights Day. The "Critical Status of Soviet Jewry," co-sponsored by the CCSJ, CZF and B'nai Brith,[54] attracted five hundred delegates who participated in a day-long marathon of plenary meetings and workshops.[55]

Testimonies by the MPs were heartwarming, but of prime importance for the Jewish community was unequivocal support and understanding of the government. Alan McLaine, director of political affairs with the Department of External Affairs, showed great sensitivity to the issue. As he spoke of countless representations made through his department, he shared his frustration with the delegates. "It is a time when you don't know what to do. If you stand on the streets and shout nobody listens, if you use the quiet corridors of diplomacy and negotiate, still nothing happens."

Sara Frankel, the counsellor responsible for Soviet Jewry with the Israeli Consulate in New York, encouraged the government, parliamentarians and activists to carry on. "Canada plays a unique role in the global struggle," she said. "Your political initiatives and demonstrations reach the offices of the Kremlin and serve as a beacon to other countries. You must not give up."[56]

The presence of former prisoner Josef Mendelevich brought hope during a disheartening period for all Soviet Jewry activists. He encouraged them to continue their activity with relentless fervour and declared, "I am here as proof that your efforts are worthwhile." [57]

Chapter 17

Everyone Is Involved

"When the temperatures drop in East-West relations, the locks freeze on Jewish emigration from the Soviet Union."[1] This statement, which appeared in an editorial in *The New York Times* on January 26, 1982, was indicative of a sad and predictable pattern. Jewish emigration from the Soviet Union was on the decline. Only 9,249 Jews had received visas in 1981.

Due to the difficulty in maintaining the momentum of an advocacy campaign when the morale of refuseniks and their Western allies was exceedingly low, it was necessary to recruit new activists to the cause. In February 1982, MP John Roberts was present when a telephone call, placed by Rabbi Harvey Fields and members of Toronto's Holy Blossom Temple resulted in the formation of their Soviet Jewry committee and the adoption of Holy Blossom's first refusenik family.[2] Anatoly and Natasha Vasilevsky of Moscow became part of the "Temple family." Their baby was named during a Shabbat service and, on each Jewish holiday, Rabbi Dow Marmur would draw attention to the family's plight from the pulpit.

"A bond was created through telephone calls placed every two weeks," recalled Marsha Slivka, the committee's first chairman. "I remember the phone call when Natasha Vasilevsky told us that her husband Anatoly was in the hospital...and not a good hospital. All twenty of us, Soviet Jewry committee members and religious school kids, just started crying because we knew 'not a good hospital' meant a mental institution. Those were horrible times."[3]

Holy Blossom's Soviet Jewry committee planned demonstrations, wrote to Soviet officials and lobbied parliamentarians on behalf of their adopted family.[4] They invited temple members to subscribe to a "telegram bank" so that in a crisis, hundreds of telegrams could be dispatched to the appropriate authorities. The monthly bulletin encouraged congregants to write letters or send cables to Soviet authorities on behalf of the Vasilevskys, and to make donations to their Russian Family Fund to help defray the cost of phone calls and packages that the committee mailed to their "family" on a regular basis.[5] The Holy Blossom committee drew up a petition for the Vasilevsky's release and set about obtaining signatures.

Soviet Jewry committees began forming in other Toronto synagogues, creating a new vehicle for the budding bar and bat mitzvah twinning program that had enjoyed great success in many North American cities. Joyce Eklove, who, before moving to Toronto, had helped with twinnings in Montreal, promoted the Toronto bar and bat mitzvah twinnings through synagogue committees and Jewish day and afternoon schools. Within a year, twinnings gained in popularity and took on a life of their own.

Each prospective twin was presented with the name and address of a child of a refusenik, often years before the bar or bat mitzvah was scheduled to take place. Writing letters to the Soviet child helped to form a bond between the two families. "The fact that few children received responses to their letters did not seem to deter them," commented Eklove, "rather, it reinforced the bitter reality of life for Jews in a repressed society."[6] Other Canadian communities integrated bar and bat mitzvah twinnings into their Soviet Jewry programming to help youngsters and adults identify more closely with the Soviet Jewry issue and to boost the morale of refuseniks.[7]

Another educational program that linked East and West involved mailing Hebrew and Jewish contemporary cultural material to refusenik teachers. This filled the void left by the disruption of Jewish cultural seminars and Hebrew classes. Joyce Eklove selected the material, packaged, addressed and registered each parcel. When the parcels were returned unopened, she would re-address them and try again. "Oh, the exhilaration when the occasional pink return card with *todah rabah* (thank you) came back to me," Eklove recalled. "Even the postman would share in the excitement."[8]

Since many packages never reached their destination, the project was ultimately rejected in favour of sending religious educators into the Soviet Union to teach, enhancing the growing religious movement. This educational program, initiated by *Vaad L'Hatzolas Nidchei Yisroel*, an organization based in New York, enjoyed great success.

By the middle of 1982, emigration figures declined to two hundred per month. The emotions of Soviet Jewry activists ran from frustration to despair, but the stalwarts pressed on. The hours spent planning and executing strategies could not be measured, nor could the time spent waiting. In the homes of Torontonians Genya Intrator and Jeanette Goldman, most of the waiting was done near their telephones. These women maintained contact with refusenik families week after week, undeterred by jammed lines and Soviet delaying tactics.

"You know about our protest march, don't you?" asked Kishinev refusenik Gregory Levitt of Jeanette Goldman during one conversation. "We were surrounded by the KGB, photographed and herded into buses. They let me go, but Tsukerman and Lockshin were taken to prison." Goldman pledged to relay the information through the her network and before hanging up, confirmed the next telephone date.[9]

The Soviets appeared deaf to Western pleas. Despite attempts from people all over the world to convince the Soviet authorities to free Ida Nudel from exile, she was released on March 20, 1982, precisely when her sentence ended. One day earlier, a motion had been passed in Parliament "that in light of Ida Nudel's anticipated release from Siberian exile, the House of Commons urge Soviet authorities to make arrangements so that Ida Nudel can be released directly to join her only living relative, her sister, in Israel."[10]

Not only did Soviet officials have no intention of permitting Nudel to emigrate to Israel, they prevented her from returning to her own flat. As a former political prisoner, she was ineligible to register for residency in Moscow. After two months of searching for a place to live, Nudel found two refusenik families in Bendery, Moldavia, who located an apartment for her in their rural town.[11] An official warning was issued to Nudel forbidding her to entertain visitors in her apartment. Far from her network of friends, she might as well have remained in exile.

Support for Nudel's situation was reinforced on April 29, 1982, when the second annual Ida Nudel Humanitarian Award was presented to The Honourable Flora MacDonald during a moving ceremony at the Ontario Legislature.[12] A longtime champion of human rights, MacDonald had raised Nudel's case in the House of Commons on many occasions and was recognized as the most outspoken parliamentarian on her behalf.

Once again, in May 1982, The CCSJ-sponsored "Solidarity Month for Soviet Jewry," sparked programs throughout the Jewish and general community in many cities. Vancouver's May event was a "Cyclathon" that attracted hundreds of Soviet Jewry supporters and cyclists of all ages. Wearing T-shirts that read, "Freedom Ride – 25 miles for Soviet Jewry," they rode the designated route carrying poster-size photographs of prominent refuseniks. The funds pledged by sponsors enabled activists to continue activity on behalf of Vancouver's adopted refusenik families. [13]

Yosef Begun became a victim once more. After completing his second term in exile, he was arrested in November 1982, as he boarded a train in Leningrad en route to Moscow. He had in his possession Hebrew texts and Jewish history books. The charge was "anti-Soviet agitation and propaganda." The arrest was no surprise to Begun, since ten days earlier his Moscow apartment had been searched and much of his Jewish cultural material confiscated. Begun had continued to persevere openly for the right to teach without regard for the consequences. He was an obvious target.[14]

When Begun's wife, Ina, implored the authorities to release her husband, she was warned, "No more noise from abroad." Undeterred by the threat, activity escalated. In Moscow and Leningrad, refuseniks held a day-long hunger strike on Begun's behalf and in the United States, ninety-eight senators signed a petition for his release.[15]

Shortly after Begun's arrest, Soviet Communist party chief

Leonid Brezhnev died. He was replaced by long-time head of the KGB Yuri Andropov. Activsts feared for Begun. The stage was set for a harsh judgment.

Hoping that a cumulative condemnation of the Soviets might result in a reduced sentence, former prisoner Lazar Lubarsky travelled abroad in February 1983, to garner support for his friend Begun, just as he had done for him five years earlier. Lubarsky's meetings in Ottawa resulted in Begun's case being raised in the House of Commons[16] as well as an assurance by John Harker that the CLC would confront the Soviets about Yosef Begun at the forthcoming international labour conference in Geneva.[17]

While under investigation, Begun's personal struggle for human rights was duly recognized. The British House of Commons all-party Soviet Jewry committee named him the recipient of their annual human rights award and along with human rights activists Senator Henry M. Jackson and Madame Simone Weil, Begun was awarded Israel's coveted Jabotinsky Prize.[18]

Yosef Begun was brought to trial October 12, 1983. Refusing the services of a state-appointed lawyer, he conducted his own defence. Begun was convicted of "anti-Soviet incitement" and sentenced to seven years in prison and five years in internal exile. The third-time prisoner expressed appreciation to his supporters in the West through a letter that was read outside the Jewish Agency headquarters in Jerusalem following his trial. "The support of people all over the world helped to raise my spirits. Please keep the letters coming."[19]

The U.S. State Department declared Begun's trial as the "cutting edge of a new wave of repression and officially sanctioned anti-Semitism." Their accusation was substantiated when the "Anti-Zionist Committee," a government-sponsored body that attacked Judaism through anti-Zionism, issued a statement declaring, "Zionism is a form of racism. The mass media in the world, including Zionist propaganda, slanders daily our Soviet Motherland, its history and reality."[20]

The Anti-Zionist Committee was headed by Colonel David Dragunsky, Professor Samuel Zivs and a few other Jews who were willing to make anti-Semitic pronouncements. They professed that the process of re-unification of families was complete, that Jews were no longer interested in emigration and that the few Soviet Jews who still wished to teach Hebrew and Jewish culture were agents of the Israeli secret service.[21] The spurious charges against Zionism were prolific. A news item in *Pravda* on April 1, 1983, stated: "By its very essence, Zionism concentrates in itself extreme nationalistic chauvinism and racial intolerance."[22]

In an attempt to counteract anti-Zionist propaganda, efforts to send educators into the Soviet Union intensified. In 1983, *Vaad L'Hatzolas Nidchei Yisroel* sent an Orthodox rabbi from Toronto to teach Talmud and Torah in three cities. Before his departure he met with CJC briefers and agreed to carry in needed medical supplies.

When in Moscow, the Canadian rabbi met with Ilya Essas, who was recognized as the leader of the religious refusenik group that was intent on recruiting more refuseniks to their ranks. "We haven't become a new people," Essas explained to him, "we've become 'old' in the sense that we are returning to our roots."[23] The rabbi played an integral role in promoting orthodoxy in the Soviet Union. He travelled there frequently and sent other Canadian educators to many Soviet communities to teach. By working with local Soviet Jewry activists, the rabbi broke with the tradition of many of his colleagues who refused to acknowledge the contribution made to Soviet Jewry by secular Jews.

On March 15, 1983, the third World Conference on Soviet Jewry convened in Jerusalem. On the eve of the conference, Yuri Tarnopolsky was arrested in Moscow and another Moscow refusenik, Anatoly Mirkin, committed suicide.[24] Like the previous two meetings held in Brussels in 1971 and 1976, the Jerusalem conference attracted international delegates.[25] Binyanei Ha'ouma, the largest conference hall in Jerusalem, was filled to capacity as Madame Simone Weil, The Honourable Jeane Kirkpatrick, Ambassador Max Kampelman and prominent Israelis addressed the assembly.[26]

British historian Martin Gilbert arrived at the conference having just returned from the USSR. He reported that anti-Semitism had filtered down into the Soviet educational system and that at Moscow's International Book Fair, books of Jewish content had been confiscated from the Association of Jewish Publishers of New York and Israeli book stands.[27]

"The imposition of a new law forbidding the 'pre-paying' of duties on parcels sent to Soviet Jews is making it impossible to mail material goods from the West," Gilbert reported, "and the taxes levied in the USSR are too excessive for most refuseniks. The consensus so strongly expressed to me by many Soviet Jews, was that noise alone, vigilance, protest, alertness, expostulation, would prevent the worst fate for those whom the Soviet state sought to punish as an example."[28]

Canadians made contributions to the designated workshops. Montreal professor René Simard pressed for an escalation of global scientific involvement, MPs David Smith and John Bosley suggested co-ordinated international government action and Penny Collenette recommended the creation of a global network of government spouses.[29]

By the spring of 1983, the Parliamentary Spouses Committee numbered 223 and included the wives of six provincial premiers.[30] The suggestion Collenette had made in Jerusalem bore fruit. On April 29, 1983, leaders of the American "Congressional Wives for Soviet Jewry," Dolores Beilinson, Helen Jackson, Joanne Kemp and Shirley Metzenbaum, joined their Canadian counterparts Penny Collenette, Audrey King, Jane Crosbie, Lucille Desmarais, Carol Regan and Lucille Broadbent for a two-day meeting in Ottawa, to discuss their mutual role in helping to secure freedom for Soviet Jews.

Ofira Navon, wife of Israel's president Yitzhack Navon, sent a messsage to the gathering, "In the name of my country and in the name of those longing to join it, I thank you." Cables were received from the wives of several Canadian provincial premiers and from spouses of political leaders in the United States, West Germany, Australia, New Zealand, Italy and Sweden.[31]

"The purpose of this meeting," announced Collenette to the press in a private room in the House of Commons, "is to issue a challenge to the rest of the political spouses in the Western world to join with us in condemning the Soviet Union's treatment of its Jews." She drew attention to the 95 per cent reduction of emigration visas and the imposition of a law limiting invitations from Israel to first-degree relatives in the Soviet Union.

"The Soviets always hope that we'll just get old and retire," said Helen Jackson, wife of Senator Henry M. Jackson and co-founder of Congressional Wives for Soviet Jewry, "but we are busy making sure that each new Congress stays informed and active on this issue."[32]

After formal meetings with Speaker of the House Madame Jeanne Sauvé and external affairs minister Alan MacEachen, the spouses met at the American Embassy for a reception hosted by Marthe Robinson, wife of the U.S. ambassador. Grassroots activists, parliamentarians and members of the media joined them for dinner in the House of Commons' historic Railway Committee Room.[33] They were addressed by Secretary of State Serge Joyal.

Professor Irwin Cotler provided an update on the movement and praised the spouses, who despite full lives, made the time to speak out for those whose voices were silenced. He concluded his remarks with a reference to British politician Edmund Burke, "The only thing necessary for evil to triumph is for enough good men to do nothing."

The American women agreed to convene a meeting in Washington the following year geared to attract international participation. A joint statement was released to the press, "We, the Soviet Jewry Committees of the Canadian Parliamentary Spouses' Association and the American Congressional Wives deplore the continuing mistreatment of Soviet Jews. In the name of human rights and in accordance with the principles of family re-unification, we demand that Jewish refuseniks be granted their exit visas and that Prisoners of Conscience be released."[34]

Two weeks later, four parliamentary wives were granted a meeting at the Soviet Embassy with Ambassador Alexander Yacovlev, Counsellor Uri Pozdnyakov and their wives.[35] The informal discussion centred on the case of Vladimir Tsukerman who was serving the second year of a three-year prison sentence. Appealing to the Soviet women, Collenette stressed the emotional consequences of a father being separated from his family. Yacovlev agreed to examine Tsukerman's case and expressed an interest in future meetings.[36]

For the first time since the inauguration of the Ida Nudel Humanitarian Award, a personal message from Nudel was read at the presentation ceremony, which took place on May 3, 1983, in a committee room at the Ontario Legislature. "To my dear friends in Canada. Thank you for your support through my long struggle. It was your warmth that gave me the strength to carry on through these long and difficult years. I believe that some day soon we will have success and we will meet in our wonderful Israel."[37]

Members of the Ontario Legislature Committee for Soviet Jewry joined local activists for the presentation of the award to June Callwood, noted author and social activist. In her warm, inimitable manner, Callwood paid tribute to the woman, who, during five years in exile, "took on the whole Kremlin with no power or support from friends." She concluded her remarks by saying: "Ida Nudel's efforts in resisting Soviet authorities show that it does not matter that you are ineffective, it matters only that you try. The real evil is apathy – the willingness to be a passive spectator." [38]

In May 1983, Soviet minister of agriculture Mikhail Gorbachev visited Ottawa. Federal agricultural minister Eugene Whelan hosted a reception for him to which many parliamentarians and their spouses were invited. When Penny Collenette was introduced to the guest of honour, she stated, "I am very upset by your country's treatment of Soviet Jews." Gorbachev was whisked away quickly by his translator, but a few moments later raised his glass to Collenette and smiled. She interpreted the gesture as a willingness to discuss the issue.[39]

Canadian parliamentarians continued to exhibit their support. On May 15, 1983, MP Erik Neilson addressed a CJC leadership conference. "Prime Minister Trudeau is not putting enough pressure on the Soviet Union to let Jews leave that country," he remarked. "I realize we have a parliamentary committee on the plight of Soviet Jews, but the prime minister should be making more frequent statements about anti-Semitism, the infringements of human rights and freedoms in that country."[40]

That summer, Madame Jeanne Sauvé met with Alan Rose and Martin Penn before departing for the USSR with an eight-person parliamentary delegation.[41] She agreed to raise the cases of Pavel Abramovich, Alexander Kushnir, Alexander Lerner, Lev Ovsishcher, Ida Nudel, Anatoly Sharansky and Yosef Begun with Soviet officials.

During their stay in Moscow, the situation of Kiev prisoner Lev Elbert was brought to the delegates' attention by his wife Inna, who had journeyed from Kiev to meet the Canadians. Incarcerated in a labour camp for "draft evasion by a reservist," Elbert was charged with "drug trafficking" when hashish had allegedly been found sewn into the outer lining of his winter jacket. The charge carried a maximum sentence of ten years.[42]

MP Ian Deans urged his colleague MP Don Johnston to raise Elbert's case with a senior member of the Politburo and, upon his return to Ottawa, Deans spoke about Elbert in the House of Commons and encouraged other parliamentarians to write to the Supreme Soviet on his behalf.[43] When the drug charges against Lev Elbert were dropped a few weeks later, it was Deans whom Inna Elbert credited with the success.

"This is a particularly bleak period in political terms," wrote Professor Ben Zion Shapiro in the report of his visit to the USSR in June 1983. "Hourly news broadcasts on radio and television mentioned Israel and the Jews in close juxtaposition to the latest about American obduracy in East-West arms reduction and nuclear freeze discussions. The refuseniks understand that their fate is bound up in the complex state of East-West relations and ask that in the general preoccupation with global issues, the superpowers not forget them."[44]

In Odessa, KGB searches had become routine. Postcards from Israel, Hebrew newspapers, Hebrew audio cassettes and Jewish cultural material were seized from the flats of ten refuseniks.[45] When Yakov Mesh travelled to Moscow to protest the confiscations, he was interrogated by the KGB and told to recant his Zionist views or face army reserve call-up or imprisonment.

Vancouver's Soviet Jewry committee was thwarted in its efforts to maintain contact with their Odessa refuseniks. Telephone lines were disconnected and most letters and parcels, including those sent through the office of Vancouver MP Ian Wadell, were returned with the registration return-receipt cards unsigned. "The Odessa file is not closed," wrote *The Province* columnist Mike Tytherleigh when he learned about the seizures, "but the city's relationship should be ended and Odessa should be told why."[46] Instead of severing the thirty-year-old Odessa connection, Vancouver mayor Michael Harcourt established an "Odessa file for refuseniks" at city hall. He cabled the mayor of Odessa requesting a visa for the Mesh family.[47]

The ongoing crisis for Soviet Jewry compelled MP Jim Peterson, who succeeded David Smith as chairman of the Parliamentary Group for Soviet Jewry, to augment the group's membership. At a luncheon attended by thirty MPs in November 1983, Peterson announced his intention to mount a campaign to make the Canadian Parliamentary Group for Soviet Jewry the largest parliamentary committee on the Hill. "My goal is to create a letterhead which is a living testament of our deep commitment to the issue – an issue that goes beyond partisan politics."[48]

Peterson's initiative was reinforced by luncheon guest British MP Greville Janner, founder of the thirteen-year-old British Parliamentary Committee for the Release of Soviet Jewry. In his remarks to the parliamentarians, Janner said, "Don't underestimate the power of your efforts. Great strides have been made through Western government intervention. At least the Soviet ambassador to Canada agrees to see you. The Soviet ambassador to Great Britain will not meet with us or reply to our letters."[49]

The Canadian Lawyers and Jurists for Soviet Jewry held a seminar in Toronto on December 10, 1983, the thirty-fifth anniversary of the adoption of the United Nations' Declaration of Human Rights. "Dealing with the Soviet Union in the Eighties" drew prominent Canadian speakers and culminated with the presentation of a Human Rights award to MP David Smith.[50]

By that time, Peterson had drafted the constitution for the Parliamentary Group for Soviet Jewry and had sought membership from the entire Senate and House of Commons.[51] At the end of December, the stationery went to press.

The words "Canadian Parliamentary Group for Soviet Jewry/

Groupe de Parliamentaires Canadiens pour les Juifs D'Union Soviétique" were printed in black across a small red Canadian flag. The names of 205 members flanked the page. Peterson had achieved his goal. The Canadian Parliamentary Group for Soviet Jewry was the largest non-partisan committee on Parliament Hill.

The timing couldn't have been better. Emigration had reached a standstill. In 1983, only 1,314 Soviet Jews received visas.

Chapter 18

Emigration Grinds to a Halt

Under Yuri Andropov's leadership, the Soviet policy of curtailing Jewish culture and emigration and of severing contacts with the outside world was reinforced. No Jewish community in the USSR was unaffected. The telephones of refusenik leaders were tapped and frequently disconnected. Radio programming from North America and Israel was jammed. Most letters sent to refuseniks rarely reached their destination. Packages mailed from abroad were subject to excessive duties.

Moshe Abramov, a twenty-eight-year-old refusenik who lived in Samarkand, Uzbekistan, practiced Judaism openly. Soviet officials offered to appoint him chief rabbi of Samarkand if he would publicly renounce his desire to emigrate to Israel. Abramov refused. He was arrested while teaching an unofficial Hebrew class, convicted of "hooliganism" and sentenced to three years in prison.[1]

On January 11, 1984, President Reagan expressed concern over the halt in Jewish emigration in a live policy address broadcast throughout North America and Western Europe.[2] Two days later, in Stockholm, at the Conference on Confidence and Security-Building Measures and Disarmament in Europe, Secretary of State George Shultz focused on the issue of Jewish emigration during discussions with Foreign Minister Andrei Gromyko.[3] *The Washington Post* reported on January 18, 1984, that Israel had been attacked by the Communist party daily *Pravda* in an article that compared the Israeli leadership to that of the Nazis.[4] A spokesperson from the U.S. State Department condemned the anti-Semitic attacks, saying, "The views expressed were so outrageous that we are reluctant to dignify them or even call further attention to them by a response."[5]

A ground swell of activity commenced in the free world when the World Presidium on Soviet Jewry issued directives to inundate Soviet minister of the interior Vitaly V. Fedorchuk with cables demanding freedom for the prisoners and refuseniks.[6]

The Toronto Inter-Faith Council for Soviet Jewry became the newest addition to the complement of Soviet Jewry committees, drawing its executive from the Jewish, Anglican, Roman Catholic and United Church communities.[7] "Many church leaders who were committed to humanitarian concerns were eager to help," recalled Reverend Dr. Stanford Lucyk, the founding chairman. "We fostered Soviet Jewry advocacy by supplying churches with profiles of refuseniks, by asking them to write to encourage the people in Soviet exile and to lobby Soviet authorities on their behalf. Some congregations did that fairly well. As a council we did the same with our government leaders and with Soviet authorities. We exerted whatever moral influence we had in an attempt to elicit the public to act, through meetings, press releases and telegrams."[8]

The Congressional Wives hosted the second International Conference of Parliamentary Spouses for Soviet Jewry in Washington in April 1984. The meeting attracted twenty-two delegates from the United States, Canada, England, Israel and the Netherlands, who met with congressmen and senators and had private briefings with Secretary of State George Shultz and Vice-President George Bush. A resolution was passed and released to the media, calling for the release of all Jewish prisoners, the reunification of separated families and the right to practice religion and culture.[9] The Washington conference set the wheels in motion for a meeting which took place in London, England, the following year.[10]

After only two years in office, Soviet leader Yuri Andropov died. He was replaced by Konstantin Chernenko, a former aide to Brezhnev, under whose regime more than two hundred and sixty thousand Jews had left the USSR. Activists were hopeful that emigration restrictions would be relaxed. Unfortunately for most refuseniks, there was no change.

For Ida Nudel, the highlight of 1984 was Jane Fonda's visit to Bendery. The American actress and human rights activist had met Nudel's sister Ilana Fridman during a trip to Israel with her husband Senator Tom Hayden in 1980. After returning to the United States, Fonda campaigned actively for Nudel's release and kept in constant touch with Fridman by telephone.[11] In the summer of 1983, Fonda refused to attend the Moscow Film Festival unless Nudel was released.

Determined to make some progress, Fonda met with Ambassador Dobrynin in Washington and after months of persistence and with his assistance, managed to secure an appointment, in Moscow, with Rudolf Kuznetsov, chief of the all-union OVIR. Kuznetsov arranged for a permit for Fonda to travel to Bendery, in time for Nudel's fifty-third birthday.

"Such a great country is afraid of such a small woman," Fonda exclaimed when she first embraced Ida Nudel. "We hugged," related Nudel, "and the rest, walking, eating, talking . . . it remains for me till today, a thick haze. I was so excited. I really can't say whether my guest understood my weak English, but I know she saw my situation clearly and understood what I was going through."[12]

A statement in the *Jewish Telegraphic Agency* (JTA) quoted Fonda, "Ida Nudel is a woman whose case has deeply touched my heart. She has risked much to stand up to the Soviet authorities, to practice her faith and to celebrate her Jewish heritage. From her I learned about tenacity and courage, about never giving up."[13]

Nudel's case was championed by Canadian MPs and activists during open hearings held in Ottawa in May 1984. The hearings, entitled "The Status of the Soviet Jewish Community," centred on Jewish emigration, culture and religion relative to Soviet law and international obligations.[14]

Among those called to testify to conditions under the Andropov regime were MPs, Soviet Jewry activists and former refuseniks.[15] It was unanimously agreed by parliamentarians present that day that human rights violations must be raised more vigorously with the Soviets in bilateral discussions and that the Canadian government must speak with a louder voice against repression of rights of Soviet Jews.[16]

The written accounts of the hearings became an official record of Parliament. It was the first time that an ad hoc committee had earned official status on Parliament Hill.

As emigration figures continued to decline, the Soviet Jewry campaign risked becoming a casualty of the "attrition of interest" syndrome. Rabbi Reuven Bulka warned that apathy played right into Soviet hands. "The Russians are not comfortable when their anti-Semitism, their stifling of the fundamental rights of the Jews in Russia occupy world attention," Bulka wrote in *The Ottawa Jewish Bulletin and Review*. "As matters get worse in Russia, instead of increasing the intensity of our protest efforts, we have moved away from involvement. That threatens to make us victims of Soviet strategy."[17]

In the fall of 1984 there was a federal election in Canada. Trudeau's Liberal government was overthrown and the Progressive Conservatives, led by Brian Mulroney, were elected by a large majority. MPs Jim Peterson and David Collenette were defeated, forcing both Peterson and Penny Collenette to step down as chairmen of their respective Soviet Jewry committees. David Kilgour replaced Peterson as chairman of the Parliamentary Soviet Jewry Group and Audrey King, wife of MP Fred King, succeeded Penny Collenette as head of the parliamentary spouses committee.

Kilgour was keen about the Soviet Jewry issue and pledged to expand the committee's membership list.[18] He recruited new Conservative members and invited Sheila Finestone and Nelson Riis to enlist the support of newly elected Liberals and New Democrats.[19]

"Since over a quarter of the Liberal caucus was new," explained Finestone, "it was necessary to educate the prospective committee members about the issue of Soviet Jewry before obtaining their signatures for the new letterhead. It was important too, that the MPs understand the vital role that Canada had played in assuring that human rights were integral to the Helsinki Final Act."[20]

Within months, the membership of the Canadian Parliamentary Group for Soviet Jewry had reached a record number of 273 members. "Unanimity is not something you normally find on Parliament Hill," explained Riis, "or even a willingness by parliamentarians to work together for something with little political gain. The numbers are indicative of the overwhelming commitment of Canadian parliamentarians to the issue."[21]

The appointment of Sharon Wolfe as executive assistant to MP Robert de Cotret, president of the Treasury Board, and her subsequent position as special assistant in the prime minister's office were extremely important for Soviet Jewry. In each capacity, Wolfe counselled parliamentarians on the issue and met with advocacy groups when they visited Ottawa.[22]

In the fall of 1984, the Soviet crackdown on refuseniks intensified. The KGB conducted searches and interrogations in private apartments in Moscow, Leningrad, Riga and Odessa. Jewish books and cultural material were seized and *mezuzahs* were removed from the doorposts of apartments. Alexander Kushnir of Odessa had the Star of David he was wearing torn from his neck.[23]

Seven Hebrew teachers from Moscow, Leningrad, Samarkand, Odessa and Riga were arrested for "malicious hooliganism," "resisting arrest," or "disseminating material defamatory to the Soviet State."[24] Two other Moscow Hebrew teachers, Yuli Edelshtein and Alexander Kholmiansky, became victims of new charges. Edelshtein was accused of "possession of drugs" and Kholmiansky with "possessing a firearm." The incriminating items had been planted in their homes during KGB raids.

On October 20, 1984, forty-two Moscow refuseniks began a rotating hunger strike for the nine teachers of Hebrew. The cable they sent to Secretary General Chernenko stated, "The KGB must think that all of us wishing to emigrate to Israel should now be presented as terrorists, thieves and drug addicts."[25] Within days, more than two hundred refuseniks from ten Soviet cities joined with each person, fasting for three or four days. World attention was drawn to their protest.

The Atlantic Jewish Council intervened on behalf of the Hebrew teachers when Soviet academic Vadim Zhdamovich visited Nova Scotia on a world peace and friendship mission. Shimon Fogel, the council's executive director, telephoned the Soviet official in his hotel room and raised the issue of the arrests. Although Zhdamovich refused to discuss the issue, he did mention that Jews in his country had lost interest in studying their history, language and culture. When questioned about the problem of escalating anti-Semitism, he responded, "anti-Semitism occurs in the Soviet media only because Jews refuse to assimilate into Soviet society."[26]

The arrests, planting of evidence and slander in the media were on the agenda of a two-day national emergency conference convened in Ottawa in November.[27] The purpose of assembling Canadian activists was to rekindle their flagging spirits and to bring the reports and opinions of experts to the table.

Among the experts who reported to the conference was John Harker, director of International Affairs for the Canadian Labour Congress. He informed the delegates that despite the severing of formal relations between the CLC and Soviet Trade Unions in 1978, the two groups did maintain contact. At international meetings, the CLC representatives continued to make representations on behalf of individual refuseniks and prisoners, behind closed doors.

A written response to one such unofficial representation was sent to Harker by an official from Ottawa's Soviet Embassy. It concluded, "The request stated appeared as another confirmation of your refusal to recognize the existence of a society different from your own social and political system."[28] Harker replied, "Soviet Jews are hostages in the game of superpower politics, linking human rights to arms control. I believe that only through respect for human rights will international arms control agreements be reached."[29]

As the forty-two refuseniks continued their rotating hunger strikes, the Israel Public Council for Soviet Jewry invited groups worldwide to conduct a fast on December 10.[30] "The hunger strikes are being staged on the thirty-sixth anniversary of the signing of the Universal Declaration of Human Rights to show solidarity with the Soviet Union's two million Jews and to remind the Soviet leadership that reports of harassment of Jews will resonate throughout the world," said Avraham Harman, IPSCJ chairman.[31]

The morning of December 10, a group of refuseniks in Moscow

delivered a letter to the Supreme Soviet requesting a review of the illegal sentences of the Hebrew teachers, while in Tel Aviv, fasting demonstrators marched from the U.S. Embassy to the Finnish Embassy (the USSR's representative in Israel) to lodge official protests against the arrests. World protests took place that day in front of Soviet embassies and consulates and in public places that would draw both people and media coverage.

In Canada, activists from across the country held day-long fasts to show their support.[32] In the House of Commons, MP Sheila Finestone raised the issue of the nine imprisoned Hebrew teachers. Her statement was followed by a declaration by MP Fred King, "Concerned Canadians across the country fast today, in solidarity with hundreds of Soviet Jews who are now protesting with rotating hunger strikes in a courageous response to the Soviet authorities' latest campaign to destroy Jewish culture."[33]

The Soviet authorities were defiant against the world protests. On that very day, they brought Josef Berenshtein, a teacher of Hebrew in Moscow, to trial. Charged with "resisting the authorities" he was sentenced to four years in labour camp.[34]

By the end of 1984, twenty-four refuseniks were awaiting trial or serving prison terms. Only 896 Jews had received emigration visas. This was Soviet Jewry's darkest hour.

Chapter 19

New Hopes . . . New Recruits

Soviet leader Konstantin Chernenko died in March 1985. He was succeeded by Mikhail Gorbachev, a younger member of the Politburo. Within weeks, it was announced that secretary of state for external affairs Joe Clark was planning a trip to the Soviet Union to meet with the new leadership. CCSJ chairman Barbara Stern contacted Clark, requesting that he address the decrease in emigration, the arrests of Hebrew teachers, the anti-Semitic media campaign and the government-sponsored Anti-Zionist Committee during his official meetings in Moscow.

Regional Soviet Jewry committees asked their constituents and Canadians of influence to write to Clark's office in Ottawa. "It is imperative," read the directives, "that the minister raise the issue of the tragic and deteriorating plight of Soviet Jews, and bring to the attention of the new Soviet leadership the concern of the government of Canada and of the Canadian people."[1] MPP Marion Bryden, co-chairman of the Ontario Legislature committee, wrote, "I am sure you are aware of the persecution of many Soviet Jews, simply because they desire to teach Hebrew and Jewish culture . . . I hope you will take the opportunity offered by your visit to bring some of these matters to the attention of the Soviet authorities."[2]

Clark replied to each letter personally. "My visit to Moscow in the first week of April will provide us with an early opportunity to develop our lines of communication with the new Soviet leadership. My officials and I shall discuss the full range of our bilateral interests, including humanitarian concerns. This of course includes the fundamental rights of Soviet Jews to practice their religion and culture in dignity and emigrate if they wish to do so."[3]

On March 26, three days before Clark's departure, two hundred Canadian students from the North American Jewish Students Network (Network) demonstrated outside the Soviet Embassy in Ottawa.[4] Chairman Naomi Jacobs and student leaders met with Clark and other members of his entourage as a last-minute reminder to raise the Soviet Jewry issue in Moscow. In the House of Commons that afternoon, MPs Kilgour and Attewell spoke about Soviet anti-Semitism and the decline in Jewish emigration and asked Clark to share their concerns with Soviet officials. Clark agreed to do so.[5]

Joe Clark was true to his word. He broached the issue with Andrei Gromyko at every opportunity. When Gromyko indicated that Soviet Jewry was an internal matter, Clark was undaunted.[6] He cited the cases of prisoners Anatoly Sharansky and Andrei Sakharov, plus those of twenty-seven families whose Canadian relatives had sponsored their emigration to Canada.

Clark presented the Soviet foreign minister with a list of one hundred refuseniks. Gromyko perused the list and indicated that many of them had already been authorized to leave.[7] Then Clark informed his host that Canadians would accept warmer relations between their two countries if there was a change in the Soviet attitude toward family reunification and human rights.[8] Gromyko ignored Clark's remarks.

The Soviet bias against Jewish students intensified, as even the most highly qualified were denied entrance to universities. This unwritten policy of most Soviet institutes of higher learning became the focus of the National Council of Jewish Women's annual Soviet Jewry program in May. Hundreds of Torontonians squeezed into the auditorium at "Council House" on Bathurst Street to witness twenty Toronto students accept graduation diplomas in the name of twenty refusenik students and to hear the remarks of Stephen Lewis, then Canadian ambassador to the United Nations.

Naomi Jacobs, one of the "graduating" students, delivered a valedictory address. She articulated cases of several Soviet Jewish students with superior academic achievement whose applications to university were denied, presumably due to their parents' refusenik status.

Lewis responded to Jacob's address with compassion and praised the students for their concern. In expanding on the subtlety by which Westerners must advocate, he said: "It is always a desperately difficult situation to appraise how one balances the public pressure with the private leaning when dealing with a regime with whom confrontation is futile and human beings have to be rescued." Lewis concluded his remarks by declaring: "One day, the refuseniks will be free, but until that day comes, activists must never give up. We must always let the Russians know that we will never forgive and we must always let our people know that we will never forget."[9]

Canadian activists always looked to the Jackson-Vanik Amendment, the piece of American legislation that linked U.S. trade credits with emigration, as a model to encourage the Canadian government to adopt the concept of linkage. Many advocates believed that wheat, Canada's coveted trading commodity with the USSR, should be used as a lever to force the Soviets to change their human rights policies.

Following their visit to the USSR, members of the Montreal Inter-Faith Task Force prepared a strategy paper that they released to Brian Mulroney and Stephen Lewis.[10] The paper proposed linking Canadian-USSR trade agreements to Soviet compliance with the human rights provisions of the Helsinki Final Act.[11]

Mulroney's office replied that the Canadian government did not think that anything was gained by mixing trade with politics. Lewis provided the following explanation: "If I had my druthers, we would indict the USSR noisily at every international opportunity, citing chapter and verse with individual case histories, to document the grotesque disregard for human rights. I'm inclined to believe that if we were to pursue the Russians volubly, wherever possible, we might effect changes without having to resort to economic sanctions. I don't rule out the kind of strategy which you enunciate, I just recognize its enormous complexities."[12]

MP David Kilgour continued to place the Soviet Jewry issue high on the Canadian government agenda. He arranged meetings for activists with Canadian and Soviet officials[13] and lobbied the Soviets at every opportunity.

Kilgour worked with Herb Landis and with Alan Lazerte, director of the Christian Embassy, to promote the production of *Gates of Brass*. The docudrama had been filmed secretly by Christian Embassy devotés Jay and Meridel Rawlings on their third trip to the Soviet Union. *Gates of Brass* premiered in Jerusalem and was shown in forty cities. At each of the single performances in eight Canadian communities, David Kilgour introduced the film and delivered a plea for support for Soviet Jewry.[14]

"*Gates of Brass* is a superb portrayal that heightens the issue of Soviet Jewry for thousands of Canadians," wrote Rabbi Reuven Bulka, co-chairman of Ottawa's Soviet Jewry committee. "Through enactments of oppressive policies of the Soviet regime, remarkably frank statements of refuseniks and historical vignettes, a clear and concise picture of the condition of Soviet Jewry emerges."[15]

The Iron Curtain appeared to be emitting no light, but a slight glimmer came from the Soviet concern for their image abroad. For Jews in the free world, it was easy to celebrate Judaism and the joyous festival of Simchat Torah. For Jews to dance in Moscow with the Torah was a defiant act of courage, of faith and of hope.

In 1985, Canadian Jewry exhibited unparalleled support for Soviet Jewry on Simchat Torah. Months of planning and advertisements, co-sponsored by numerous Jewish organizations, were responsible for bringing the largest crowds ever to Simchat Torah rallies in Toronto, Ottawa, Montreal, Winnipeg and Vancouver. The overwhelming display united Jews and non-Jews in a common cause.[16]

In Amsterdam, hundreds of Dutch citizens from church, government, trade unions and intellectual societies participated in a Simchat Torah demonstration outside the Soviet Embassy. Many Dutch activists joined thousands in Paris the next day to demonstrate their support for Soviet Jewry, prior to talks between Soviet leader Mikhail Gorbachev and French president François Mitterand.[17]

During the Paris meeting, Gorbachev announced that no application for emigration and family reunification would be rejected for "secrecy" considerations after ten years' absence from any position involving state security. "I would be glad to hear of Jews enjoying anywhere such political and other rights as they have in our country," he declared.[18]

Within hours of Gorbachev's statement, Leonid Volvovsky, a Gorky Hebrew teacher and long-time refusenik, was tried and sentenced to three years' imprisonment on charges of "defaming the Soviet state and social system." The evidence used against the forty-three-year-old engineer was the possession of *Exodus*.[19]

On November 19, talks between President Reagan and Secretary General Gorbachev commenced in Geneva. It was the first meeting between leaders of the two superpowers since 1979. Telegrams urging Reagan to raise the issue of Soviet Jewry forcefully with the Soviet leader had flooded the Oval Office.

Although "disarmament" was the underlying issue of the summit meetings, Soviet Jews knew that their futures hung in the balance. As the spotlight focused on the Geneva talks, Soviet Jewry activists staged vigils, prayer gatherings, hunger strikes and demonstrations around the world.[20]

The approach of the U.S. State Department to the Geneva meetings was carefully planned and executed. Knowing that open discussion of the Soviet Jewry issue might embarrass the Soviets and sour the talks, Reagan raised the issue of Jewish emigration and specific refusenik cases with Gorbachev but kept the matter "off the record." His strategy was to "make headway, not headlines."[21]

When the talks concluded, Reagan informed American Jewish leaders that progress had been made. He informed them that during the next summit meeting, scheduled to take place in Washington within the year, public demonstrations would be in order to enable the U.S. administration to present the Soviet Jewry issue as reflective of the wishes of the American public.

No matter how few in number, grassroots advocates could make an impact, even in small cities. David Kaye was a retired businessman and Jewish community leader in Cornwall, an Ontario city with fewer than fifty Jewish families. On December 10, 1985, he staged a fast at the foot of the downtown promenade, where he and his wife encouraged people to write to Ambassador Rodionov to protest the violation of Soviet Jewish rights. "Sure, I'm only one person," said Kaye, "but this is a symbolic protest and large numbers are not required."[22]

By the end of 1985, the Russian words *glasnost* (openness) and *perestroika* (restructuring) described the policy of the new Soviet regime. Although Jewish emigration figures had increased only slightly over the previous year, activists were optimistic and anticipated that change was imminent.[23]

Chapter 20

Accountability is Working

At the Conference on Security and Co-operation in Europe (CSCE), which led to the signing of the Helsinki Final Act on August 1, 1975, three Experts' meetings, each lasting three weeks, were scheduled between the lengthy Review conferences that were to take place in Belgrade in 1977, in Madrid in 1980, and in Vienna in 1986.

The first Experts' meeting dealt with human rights and was held in Ottawa in May 1985. The second meeting, on culture, convened in Budapest in the fall of 1985, and the last meeting, on human contacts, was to take place in Berne in the spring of 1986.

Prior to the Ottawa meeting, CJC representatives were invited to a day of consultations with officials of the Department of External Affairs.[1] Citing extensive case histories and relevant principles of the Helsinki Final Act, Alan Rose demonstrated that the USSR had made no progress in the advancement of human rights since the Helsinki signing. He suggested that "family reunification" and "free and unfettered practice of religion and culture" be raised as fundamental issues at the meetings. "As the host nation," Rose said, "the Ottawa Experts' conference affords Canada an opportunity to take imaginative initiatives to further the CSCE process."[2]

MP David Kilgour and Martin Penn appeared as witnesses at a sub-committee hearing.[3] Kilgour spoke about prisoners Anatoly Sharansky, Yosef Begun and Josef Berenshtein. After presenting an account of the general status of the Soviet Jewish community, Penn submitted a sixty-five page document, "The Position of Soviet Jewry, Human Rights and the Helsinki Accords," which was to be included as an appendix to the days' proceedings.[4]

American, Canadian, British and French members of the World Presidium on Soviet Jewry arrived in Ottawa on the eve of the opening session to impress upon their respective government delegations the importance of stressing Soviet Jewish emigration rights during the meetings.[5] For the first time ever the group was cautiously optimistic. In the two months since Mikhail Gorbachev's ascension to power there had been a slight increase in granting of exit visas.[6]

At the official opening of the Ottawa Experts meeting on May 17, 1985, and in the presence of Soviet Jewry activist leaders and special guest Avital Sharansky, the Canadian external affairs minister welcomed the delegates to Canada for their very important task. "Human rights," Joe Clark told them, "cannot and must not be avoided just because they are sensitive and can sometimes give rise to disagreements between governments."[7]

That day, Avital Sharansky joined hundreds of demonstrators outside the Soviet Embassy for a noon-hour vigil in support of Soviet Jewry that was to be held daily during the three weeks of talks. The vigils served as a gnawing reminder to the Soviets that the world was watching.[8]

The only meetings open to non-governmental officals (NGOs) were the opening and closing sessions. The Soviet delegation insisted that all others be closed to human rights activists, the public and the media. Lay leaders were incensed. "It's wrong and it's counterproductive," said Irwin Cotler, co-chairman of Canada's "Helsinki Watch" group.[9] "If the very people who are monitoring human rights and supplying information to the delegates have no status at the meetings, then who has?"[10] Cotler charged that the decision to exclude NGOs was in itself a breach of the Helsinki Final Act.[11]

Although the Soviet bloc countries managed to keep discussions behind closed doors, the issues of Jewish emigration, attacks on Hebrew teachers, and anti-Semitism in the Soviet media were addressed by Western nations.

In his introductory address, Ambassador Harry R. Jay, the leader of the Canadian delegation said, "It is the hope of the Canadian delegation that our discussions will produce a better understanding of the deep human suffering that is caused by denial of the right to freedom of movement, and that this understanding will lead to a greater respect of this right."[12]

Ambassador Richard Schifter, Washington's chief envoy to the Ottawa meeting, took a more forceful approach. He denounced the Soviets' imprisonment of forty Jewish prisoners and submitted documentation of 177 individual cases.[13] Schifter emphasized that tension between East and West escalated when Soviet authorities oppressed its citizens. The U.S. position was clear. The way to improve East-West relations was to ameliorate the situation for Soviet Jews.

"Moscow is running out of patience with Washington," the Soviets warned Schifter. "Such assaults will seal the fate of the conference."[14] The Soviet delegation continued to deny the legitimacy of Western concerns and deflected most discussions about human rights issues onto the subject of nuclear disarmament.[15]

No conclusion was reached in Ottawa, but the exchange of views contributed significantly to the CSCE process. A statement made at the conclusion of the meeting by Soviet delegation leader Vsevolod Sofinsky indicated that Western states were making some headway. "In the Soviet Union's view," he said, "human rights are a significant element of relations between states."[16]

At the conclusion of the Ottawa meetings, representatives from the CJC and the Parliamentary Group for Soviet Jewry met with officials from external affairs to express their disappointment over Canada's refusal to raise individual cases.[17] They indicated their hope that, unlike the Liberal's policy that had been to advocate only on behalf of Jews who wanted to join relatives in Canada, the new Mulroney government would represent all refuseniks.[18]

"External did agree formally to change their policy and to intervene on behalf of those wanting to emigrate to Israel," said Kilgour. "The problem was that they never really changed their practice. They did work for Sharansky and for Ida Nudel because these cases were stellar."[19]

The Experts' meeting in Budapest in November 1985 was uneventful, but the Berne conference in the spring of 1986 made some progress. For the first time the Canadian delegation cited cases of individual refuseniks and prisoners.[20]

Three months prior to the opening of the third CSCE review meetings in Vienna on November 4, 1986, public hearings were held in Ottawa. Alan Rose, Martin Penn, Barbara Stern and CJC president Dorothy Reitman were invited as witnesses before the Standing Committee on External Affairs and International Trade. The brief submitted by CJC to Canadian delegation head William Bauer included lists of prisoners and refuseniks who had been denied visas for more than ten years.[21]

Months prior to the CSCE review meeting, Irwin Cotler wrote to the foreign ministers of all participating nations asking that they include the case of Ida Nudel on their agenda. In November, Cotler travelled to Vienna to meet with the heads of the Western delegations in order to present Nudel's case.

For the first time since the Helsinki signing, there was cause for optimism. Of the three major review meetings, the Vienna conference had the greatest potential for success. "The Soviets had finally abandoned their philosophy that Soviet Jewry was an 'internal affair,'" remarked Alan Rose. "After all the years of 'nyet, nyet, nyet,' it was now possible to have frank interviews with senior Soviet officials in formal sessions and not only in the corridors."[22]

At the first plenary session, the foreign ministers of each signatory country reiterated the views that their governments had taken at the Helsinki signing eleven years earlier. Joe Clark attacked the Soviets' human rights record and berated them for their continued involvement in Afghanistan. "The West wants action from the Kremlin, not just words," said Clark. "The Soviets must know that they will suffer seriously if they raise expectations excessively and then fail to meet them."[23]

Ambassador Bauer was an excellent choice to lead the Canadian delegation. He was selected for his reputation as an outstanding and outspoken negotiator with the Communists during his postings in Warsaw and Hanoi.[24] Bauer was instrumental in changing the thrust of the Helsinki process by improving the dynamics of lobbying. He recognized the value of NGOs and arranged meetings for them with heads of other delegations.[25]

Bauer rebuked the Soviets for their treatment of former prisoner Ida Nudel and imprisoned Hebrew teachers Yuli Edelshtein, Josef Berenshtein, Vladimir Lifshitz and Alexei Magarik. To retaliate, the Soviet delegation made allegations that Canadians mistreated their native population.

"The new wind which we are told blows from Moscow," Bauer declared during his memorable Human Rights Day speech Decmber 10, 1986, "brings no refreshing change. Indeed, it still blows cold, dumping upon my delegation and others tirades of accusations reminiscent of a period long before the Helsinki Final Act."[26]

Bauer prodded the Soviets to end government-sponsored anti-Semitism, to release Soviet Jewish prisoners and to grant exit visas to long-term refuseniks, specifically those with terminal cancer. His position was firm. If the Soviet Union wanted to discuss disarmament, they would have to change their human rights policies.[27]

Under his direction, the Canadian delegation initiated discussions on national minorities. "We drafted the proposals," explained Bauer, "put them forward, obtained co-sponsors from within the sixteen NATO countries, and then negotiated with the other side. If accepted, each proposal would become a paragraph in the final document." Bauer said that the Canadian delegation was often called the conscience of the West, because it would not compromise on certain issues. "We picked high profile cases, documented by CJC, and used them as emblematics. It was done to embarrass the Soviets and to protect the refuseniks. Our strategy was to make sure that it was more uncomfortable for the Soviets to continue the system than to give it up."[28]

The Vienna meetings lasted for two-and-one-half years with several four-week breaks. By spring 1988, the Canadian delegation was still engaged in bitter disputes with the Soviets. "We would not back down unless we got what we wanted," recalled Bauer, "but we were very careful of what we went for. The field of national minorities and human contacts was our 'baby' and we wouldn't let them bully us."[29]

In an address April 19, 1988, William Bauer stated, "As long as national, cultural and religious minorities are persecuted, forcibly assimilated and denied access to their own roots, then these problems will simply fester like infected wounds and we have no hope of progressing further within the Helsinki process. I think we have to send a signal at the end of this meeting, that we have recognized the importance of the problem and that we have decided to take a humane approach, an enlightened approach, an approach that reflects new thinking and new confidence within the European community. Otherwise people will not understand what we have been doing here for the past two years."[30]

During the course of the Vienna meeting, Soviet foreign minister Eduard Shevardnadze announced that the Soviet Union was inviting the thirty-five CSCE participating states to meet in Moscow in 1991.[31] The Moscow conference was to be the last of the three Experts' meetings on humanitarian issues, collectively called the "Human Dimension." The first was to be held in Paris in June 1989, and the second in Copenhagen in June 1990.

The notion of a human rights forum in Moscow was met with suspicion by governments in the free world. "It is no secret that the Soviet record of compliance with its human rights commitments was a long-time subject of scrutiny and criticism," said Joe Clark at the closing session. "It is also no secret that Canada was one of the last countries to be convinced that such a proposal could ever be considered."[32]

Canada was opposed to the Moscow meeting and stipulated that it would remain so until the Soviet Union first legislated a five-year limit for refusals on grounds of "secrecy," second, permitted NGOs to participate at future CSCE conferences and third, granted visas to the Rabinovich family of Leningrad who were separated from their Winnipeg relatives for eleven years.

After twenty-six months of discussions, the concluding document of the Vienna review of the Helsinki Final Act was signed by the participating states. The date was January 19, 1989, the last day of Ronald Reagan's presidency.

The document created a mechanism whereby any country could

raise human rights issues with any other country at any time. It specified freedom of religion, freedom of movement within and between countries, freedom to receive radio broadcasts, mail and telephone communication and guaranteed the rights of minorities and citizens to monitor the human rights performance of their own governments.[33]

The review process had changed dramatically. What had begun as a forum for thirty-five nations to reduce tensions in Europe culminated in the strengthening of global peace, economic stability and human rights. The USSR had finally acknowledged its obligations in the field of human rights, announced its intention to adopt a new emigration law and begun to withdraw its military forces from Afghanistan.

Jewish prisoners had been released and discrimination against students and harassment of Hebrew teachers had ceased. Jewish emigration figures reached the highest number in nearly a decade.In 1988, 18,965 visas were issued.

Although the concluding document of the Vienna conference clarified and expanded the provisions of all previously signed documents and significant changes had taken place, many Soviet Jewry activists felt betrayed. The repeated Soviet promises to legally regulate the emigration procedure and to guarantee ethnic minority rights to all Soviet Jews had yet to be honoured. They believed that this was essential before a human rights meeting could be convened in Moscow.[34]

In support of this position, the Canadian government established an office for CSCE affairs as an adjunct to the USSR and Eastern Europe bureau of the Department of External Affairs. It was to deal with non-military follow-up activities and to monitor CSCE policy in general. William Bauer served as its ambassador-at-large and Alan Bowker served as co-ordinator.[35]

The Helsinki process turned out to be the largest single factor in changing the USSR's position on human rights. It would later prove to be another important component leading to the demise of Soviet communism.

Chapter 21

From the Gulag to Jerusalem

From the moment that Antoly Sharansky was first arrested on March 15, 1977, his wife Avital dedicated her life to securing his freedom. In December 1979, five months after his sentencing, Avital visited North America. With her unique combination of elegance and passion, she inspired activists wherever she went. Avital returned to Jerusalem in time to attend a rally on January 20 in honour of Anatoly's thirty-second birthday.

On that same day, Sharansky's father suffered a fatal heart attack on a bus in Moscow while on his way to a ceremony marking his son's birthday. Instead of a congratulatory birthday telegram from his parents that day, Sharansky received a message from his mother informing him of his father's death.[1]

Sharansky yearned for his book of Psalms. Small enough to fit into the palm of his hand, the tiny book from Avital, which had been delivered by a tourist just days before his arrest, had been removed from his flat after a KGB search and withheld from him in prison. The book was returned on the day of his father's death. "For forty days I copied the Psalms and read them," Sharansky recalled. "For one thing, it was intense work, which left me no time for sad thoughts and painful recollections. For another, the project helped me study Hebrew."[2]

Soviet law stipulated that a prisoner was permitted visits by a family member twice a year. Every six months, Sharansky's mother Ida Milgrom travelled by train to Chistopol Prison, and later to Perm Labour Camp, to visit her son.[3] These journeys were often made in vain, for visits were frequently cancelled by prison officials for no reason and without explanation. Ida Milgrom saw Anatoly six times in eight years. After each meeting, she reported on his deteriorating health to Avital in Israel, who, in turn, alerted activists in the free world.

In the first few months of Sharansky's incarceration, most of the registered letters Milgrom sent to Chistopol Prison were returned. The few that she received were censored with thick black lines covering most of his writings. Through the sentences that remained, she learned of his severe headaches and eye pain as a result of inadequate nutrition and medical neglect.

On October 10, 1979, and again on November 29, she wrote to the medical authorities in both the USSR and Tartar Republics requesting medical attention for her son.[4] It took four months for a reply from the head of the Ministry of Health. It said, "We would like to notify you that your son, Anatoly Sharansky, was examined by three specialists who came to the conclusion that he is suffering from asthenopia of the eye muscles. He admits improvement in his sight, works and reads while using glasses and has not complained about the medical treatment."[5]

In April 1980, Sharansky was transfered to Perm Labour Camp 35 where he worked as a trainee lathe operator. The job was too strenuous for his feeble physical condition. Western activists sent cables to prison authorities, urging the amelioration of his working conditions.

Tifereth Beth David Jerusalem Synagogue in Montreal held its inaugural "Sharansky Lectureship" that spring. The speaker was Irwin Cotler, who reminded his audience, "If we sometimes feel fatigued in our efforts, let us remember Anatoly Sharansky's words at his trial. After sixteen months of being held incommunicado, without any contact with family or friends, under the threat of imprisonment and death he uttered, 'Next Year in Jerusalem.' That is testimony to the power of Jewish memory, Jewish history, Jewish destiny."[6]

In the fall of 1980, Avital toured European and North American capitals to galvanize support for Sharansky prior to the Helsinki review meetings in Madrid. At the pre-meeting hearings in Ottawa, she was asked, "How does putting pressure on the Soviets help? After all, your husband is still in prison." Avital responded, "Without the pressure, he would be dead."[7] A motion in the House of Commons that day directed the Canadian delegates to the Madrid conference to bring Sharansky's case to the attention of the Soviet delegation. It was passed unanimously.[8]

Avital's presence at the November opening of the Madrid conference provided additional impetus for Western nations to act, but their pleas to the Soviets fell on deaf ears.

At the end of February 1981, the prison authorities confiscated Sharansky's Psalm book. In reply to his protestations, a representative from the Perm region's procurator's office appeared at his cell and said, "It is the duty of the state to guard you in prison from harmful influences, so your religious literature has been confiscated with our consent."[9]

To retaliate, Sharansky declared a work strike. As punishment, he was denied meetings with his family and was placed in isolation in a punishment cell where his daily diet was seriously deficient. One day, his three meals consisted of a tiny amount of fish, soup from sour cabbage with a few potatoes, and oats or barley; on the next, the off-day, he received only one piece of black bread and a glass of hot water, three times a day. To stay within the law, every fifteen days, prison officials permitted him out of the cell for one hour.[10]

The insufficient rations and unbearable cold left Sharansky constantly chilled, dizzy and weak. He had headaches and pains in his eyes and chest, and gums that bled incessantly. Each time they released him for a few days and then insisted that he return to work, Sharansky's response was the same, "Only when you return my Psalm book."

During the period of his work strike Sharansky's mother and Avital received no mail from him and all family visits were cancelled. "My entire struggle for the Psalm book was an attempt to maintain a connection to what was dear to me – Avital, my father, Israel."[11]

The Canadian Lawyers and Jurists for Soviet Jewry held their first annual "Sharansky Lecture" in April 1981 in Toronto. Guest speaker Irwin Cotler made a passionate appeal to the Canadian legal community to send letters and telegrams to the procurator general of the

USSR, urging the delivery of Sharansky's mail and the re-instatement of family visits.

At the end of October 1981, Sharansky was released from the punishment cell. He was taken to a room where a simplified trial was held in the presence of a judge, two witnesses and a prosecutor. A camp official testified that Sharansky had not "started on the path of rehabilitation or repented of his crime, and that his behaviour was a bad influence on the other prisoners."[12] The verdict was delivered within twenty minutes – three years in prison. This sentence concluded his year of struggle for the Psalm book. In the previous twelve months he had spent 186 days in the punishment cell.

On November 4, 1981, Sharansky was transferred again – this time from Perm Labour Camp back to Chistopol Prison where, for the next three years, shutters on the windows of his cell kept the sun from him. His work regime involved weaving netted bags from thick nylon thread. There was a daily quota. A few days after his transfer to Chistopol his Psalm book was returned.

On January 4, 1982, Sharansky was permitted a two-hour visit with his mother and brother. It was their first meeting in eighteen months. Through the glass partition they could see that he was very weak. Sharansky described his struggle for his Psalm book and his days in solitary confinement. They discussed how he would communicate with them. Since prisoners were allowed to write only one letter per month, they agreed that Sharansky would write to Avital one month and to his mother the next.

Two weeks later, Sharansky's thirty-fourth birthday was celebrated by his Toronto family and supporters in the office of Mayor Art Eggleton, where several politicians and community and religious leaders lit candles on a large birthday cake.[13] "Official protest and constant monitoring make it difficult for Soviet officials to act arbitrarily, and often create better conditions," affirmed Eggleton, encouraging supporters to increase the pressure.[14]

In March 1982, the senate of York University in Toronto proposed that an honourary Doctor of Laws degree be conferred upon Anatoly Sharansky at spring convocation. "It was an opportunity to make an important statement as well as to take York University into previously uncharted areas," said Professor Irving Abella, chairman of the honourary degrees committee. "It took a bit of explanation," he added, "to convince Chancellor John Proctor to confer an honourary degree on a Soviet citizen languishing in a KGB penal facility, eight hundred kilometres from Moscow."[15] A formal invitation was issued to Sharansky by York University president H. Ian Macdonald. It was conveyed in the diplomatic pouch to the Canadian Embassy in Moscow and from there to Chistopol Prison.

On June 5, 1982, on the Glendon College campus of York University, Abella spoke briefly about Sharansky and read from a letter written by his mother Ida Milgrom, describing her son's deteriorating condition.[16] The Doctor of Laws degree was accepted on Sharansky's behalf by his lawyer Irwin Cotler.

Correspondence with his loved ones was Sharansky's only escape from his daily routine. The first letter he wrote after the January 1982 visit with his family was confiscated. He was informed by prison officials that there were coded signals in the text.[17] They assured him, however, that his letters would be delivered if he wrote, "I'm alive and well and provided with work. There's no need to worry about me."[18] Sharansky refused. Every two weeks he submitted another letter. Each was confiscated.

Yom Kippur, the holiest day in the Jewish calendar and marked by a twenty-four-hour fast, fell on September 27 that year. On that day, Sharansky declared an open-ended hunger strike announcing that he would consume only water until his letters were delivered. His family received the news with trepidation. "A long fast means inevitable death," his mother told Moscow news correspondents.[19]

After three weeks, Sharansky was force-fed.[20] His mouth was pried open and a tube inserted into his stomach into which liquified food was poured. Every three days, prison guards performed this "life-saving" mission. The response to his hunger strike was a world-wide mobilization of telegram banks, resulting in thousands of cables being dispatched to Chistopol Prison demanding Sharansky's right to receive his mail.

Three weeks into his hunger strike, the Toronto and Montreal 35s staged rallies of protest. On October 19, 1982, Premier David Peterson was among the elected provincial parliamentarians who addressed Sharansky's supporters from the steps of the Ontario Legislature,[21] and in Montreal, the refrain "We are leaving Mother Russia," an original song written about Sharansky by two American activists, was amplified and played repeatedly at noon, for one week, outside the Soviet Consulate.

The 35s' demonstrations forced Ottawa to act. Prime Minister Trudeau asked Geoffrey Pearson, Canada's ambassador to Moscow, to protest Sharansky's treatment to Soviet officials. On November 4, 1982, a motion was passed in Parliament, "That this House urge Soviet authorities to immediately grant Anatoly Sharansky the freedom for which he is so valiantly struggling, thus ending his hunger strike and grave threat to his life."[22] On November 19, a second motion was passed, this time condemning the Soviets for withholding Sharansky's mail.[23]

Sharansky knew that the absence of communication was painful for his family, but he did not give in. "If I surrendered," Sharansky explained, "my ties with home might never be restored... Would Mama and Avital prefer that my letters read like official notices? No, if I gave in, I would lose more than the right to send letters home; I would be losing the spiritual connection with Avital, which had become even stronger since my hunger strike began."[24]

On January 4, 1983, the one-hundredth day of Sharansky's hunger strike, Ida Milgrom and Leonid Sharansky travelled eight hundred kilometres east of Moscow to Chistopol prison for a long-awaited meeting with Sharansky. Soviet officials barred them from seeing him, informing them that the reason for the cancelled visit was because Sharansky refused to resume eating.[25]

Milgrom moved into a hotel near the prison. Each day she would stand at the entrance to Chistopol and demand the right to communicate with her son. Finally, on the one hundred and tenth day of his hunger strike, the authorities permitted an exchange of notes. Sharansky terminated his fast. The family began to receive his letters again.

French Communist party chief Georges Marchais wrote to Soviet leader Yuri Andropov requesting Sharansky's release. This triggered an unusually conciliatory response from the Soviet leader that was published in *L'Humanité,* the French Communist daily. He hinted that Sharansky might earn a reduction in his sentence if Western activists stopped their "noisy campaign" to free him. Most activists agreed that a suspension of pressure would not help. Avital affirmed this saying, "In 1981, I stayed home and said nothing, and nothing happened."[26]

On January 23, 1983, Sharansky's two North American lawyers, Professor Irwin Cotler of McGill University and Professor Alan Dershowitz of Harvard, were invited to testify at a judicial tribunal in San Francisco. Charging that in Sharansky's case, the USSR had broken its own laws, the lawyers presented documentation supporting nineteen violations of Soviet criminal law, eight violations of the Soviet constitution, five errors of fact and twelve Soviet violations of the rights of prisoners. The tribunal adjourned, declaring that additional evidence was required.[27]

Avital Sharansky met with Prime Minister Pierre Trudeau in Ottawa on January 27, 1983, to request that he renew his efforts on her husband's behalf. During Question Period in the House of Commons that afternoon, MP David Smith moved that the Canadian government make representation to Soviet officials calling for Sharansky's release. MP David Orlikow urged Trudeau to appeal directly to Soviet leader Andropov, asking that Sharansky's case be reconsidered on humanitarian grounds.[28]

When Soviet minister of agriculture Mikhail Gorbachev visited Ottawa that May, MP David Smith raised Sharansky's case again. "I think it is important, that while Mr. Gorbachev is in this country, Canadians indicate that the flagrant denials of human rights of Sharansky will not go unnoticed. I call upon Gorbachev to intervene when he returns to Moscow to allow Mr. Sharansky to be released and join his wife, whom he has not seen since the day after they were married, in Israel."[29]

September 1983 marked the half-way point in Sharansky's sentence. Anxious to maintain the pressure, Soviet Jewry advocates, world-wide, deluged the offices of Soviet prison and government officials with telegrams, urging them to release the celebrated prisoner. Cables were sent by members of the International Campaign to Free Yuri Orlov and Anatoly Sharansky, established by University of Toronto mathematician Israel Halperin and Paris scientist Henri Cartan. Their membership included hundreds of distinguished scientists, sixty-nine of whom were Nobel laureates.[30]

"Anatoly is very thin and pale with deep black shadows around his eyes," reported his mother after visiting him in February 1984. It was the first time she had seen him in eighteen months. "Throughout our meeting he had to support his right hand with his left."[31] He said his chest pains felt like "piercing needles." Milgrom appealed for telegrams to be sent, pleading for his immediate hospitalization.[32]

On March 15, 1984, the eighth anniversary of Sharansky's arrest, Canadian activists across the country drew attention to his plight. Demonstrations were staged on the steps of the Vancouver City Hall, outside the Manitoba Legislature and at Toronto's Queen's Park. In the House of Commons, MP Jim Peterson, chairman of the Parliamentary Group for Soviet Jewry, issued a statement urging the Canadian government to appeal to Soviet leader Chernenko to release Sharansky on humanitarian grounds.[33]

Montreal activists conducted a day-long tribute to Sharansky beginning with morning prayer meetings at synagogues and Hebrew Day Schools, followed by a noon-hour ecumenical service at Christ Church Cathedral.[34] An afternoon demonstration was staged by university students outside the Soviet consulate and a special evening event, open to all Soviet Jewry activists, was held at the CJC headquarters.[35]

On July 4, 1984, for the tenth time in ten years, Avital and Anatoly Sharansky celebrated their wedding anniversary apart. During that decade, Avital had brought her husband's case to Presidents Carter and Reagan, Prime Minister Trudeau, Prime Minister Thatcher, President Mitterand and three Italian heads of state.

Avital had become an observant Jew, gaining strength from her religious beliefs and from the vast network of support around the globe. She agonized during the period when there was no written communication from Anatoly and was energized when she began receiving mail again. "When I see his letters, they make me really excited. They make me see how the spirit of a human being can win everything."[36]

By November 1984, there were serious concerns regarding Sharansky's whereabouts. His last letter, saying he was to be transfered from Chistopol Prison, had been received two months earlier. Toronto scientist Israel Halperin sent a cable to Soviet leader Chernenko, "Reliable reports state that Sharansky, in dangerously weakened health, is being transported possibly for thousands of miles in cruel conditions of transport that may kill him . . . if Sharansky disappears or dies, your government will be accused of murder."[37] Through his international committee, Halperin communicated with his colleagues globally to follow suit.

The Toronto Sharansky family formed the "Canadian Committee to save the life of Anatoly Sharansky." Their first project was an ambitious petition campaign spearheaded by Sharansky's cousin Herb Landis, who sent hundreds of petitions across the country, through Jewish organizations, synagogues and churches. During the next few months, the petition sheets were returned, many of them with warm letters of encouragement.[38] When the signatures were tallied, they totalled tens of thousands of names.

The petitions were presented by Avital Sharansky to minister of multiculturalism Gerry Weiner at a rally at Toronto's Beth Tikvah Synagogue, in January 1985.[39] The rally marked the culmination of "Sharansky Freedom Weekend," a three-day event co-ordinated by Sharansky's cousin Stan Solomon and a group of Beth Tikvah supporters to raise funds for Avital to carry on her crusade. Addressing more than one thousand people who had crowded into the social hall, Avital, with her Toronto family at her side, declared confidently to MPs Gerry Weiner and David Kilgour, "I have faith. Not for one minute do I feel this is going to go on forever. Every minute, I feel the next minute will be the time for our separation to be over and we can be together like a normal family. This gives me strength."[40] The weekend included an Oneg Shabbat and three separate parlour meetings held to raise funds for Avital to carry on her crusade.

Anatoly's letters were now being delivered regularly. "And where, I wonder, is my wife observing Shabbat?" he wrote to her, "... In Los Angeles? Or perhaps, with our Canadian relatives? ... As Samson's power was in his hair, so is mine in you, my Avital."[41]

In May 1985, Avital travelled from Israel to Ottawa for the opening session of the CSCE human rights Experts' meeting. She was joined by members of the Toronto Sharansky family and two busloads of supporters from Beth Tikvah Synagogue who demonstrated with her at a vigil outside the Soviet Embassy. During Question Period in the House of Commons, Avital was seated in the speaker's gallery when MP Bill Attewell spoke about her husband. "What was Mr. Sharansky's crime?" Attewell asked, rhetorically. "He simply chose to help organize a group of people who wanted to ensure that Russia abided by the Helsinki Accords, which were signed in 1975. This is not just a struggle to free one more political prisoner, it is a struggle for fundamental human rights."[42]

Four months later, an appeal for the release of Anatoly Sharansky was sent to Secretary General Gorbachev by the International Committee to Free Orlov and Sharansky. The names of supporters filled six pages and included eighty-five Nobel laureates.[43]

In mid-November, Avital and several activists arrived in Geneva for the Reagan-Gorbachev summit meeting. Stan Solomon was there representing the Toronto family.[44] Strict security measures were enforced, giving only authorized persons permission to attend the official meetings. These restrictions were also imposed on the media. Starved for news, they covered every minute of a noon-hour demonstration on behalf of Sharansky.

It began when five young men, draped in prayer shawls, entered Geneva's Aeroflot office. Moshe Ronen, a Toronto law student and the only Canadian in the group, approached the woman behind the counter. He presented his credit card and requested a one-way ticket from Moscow to Tel Aviv for Anatoly Sharansky. The woman replied that it was impossible and that he must leave the office immediately. Former prisoner Josef Mendelevich, another member of the group, quickly taped a poster of Sharansky over a photograph of Lenin hanging on the wall. Within minutes, four men appeared, yanked off the protesters' prayer shawls and pushed the five men into the street.[45] Swiss police were called to the scene. An ABC television cameraman filmed the episode. Within hours, the footage was transmitted by satellite to Israel, Europe and North America.

The demonstrators were taken to a local police station where they were interrogated and forced to spend the night in locked cells. The next morning, the five protesters were escorted by the Geneva police to the airport and put on the first plane to New York.[46]

That afternoon, Avital, dressed in a prisoner's uniform, stood with Stan Solomon and several other supporters at the barricade outside Geneva's Soviet mission. She carried a letter addressed to Raisa Gorbachev that she hoped to present to Nancy Reagan when she arrived for lunch with the Soviet first lady. The letter ended, "Think about me when your husband comes home, or when you are playing with your children. Think about how I cannot be with my husband and how I have no children because of how unjustly my husband has been imprisoned."[47] The police took Avital for questioning before she had an opportunity to execute her plan.

Two months after the Geneva conference, there were indications that Sharansky might be released. He wrote to his family that he was receiving special medical care, was permitted to exercise and was receiving a more nutritious diet. These signals were precursors to amnesty. As activists gathered across Canada on January 20 to mark his thirty-eighth birthday, rumours began to circulate that Sharansky might be freed in an East-West spy swap.

On February 11, 1986, satellite television allowed millions around the world to witness the diminutive Anatoly Sharansky take his first steps into freedom. He crossed Berlin's snowy Glienicke Bridge between East and West Germany wearing oversized trousers, a coat, a fur hat and a broad smile. Sharansky and three Western spies were exchanged for four Eastern spies. The swap was the result of negotiations between the Kremlin and the White House and was masterminded by "spy swap" veteran Wolfgang Vogel, an East German lawyer.[48] The inclusion of Sharansky in an espionage exchange was a Soviet face-saving device not taken seriously by the West.[49] "Tolya is free. Tolya is free," Ida Milgrom shouted at a press conference. "Before my eyes I saw the banners, 'Free Sharansky.' Now they are reversed. 'Sharansky is free!'"[50]

After 3,255 days in the Soviet gulag, 430 spent in isolation in punishment cells, Sharansky was a free man. He met his "bride" in Frankfurt. Seeing Avital for the first time after a twelve-year separation, he looked at her with a sheepish grin and said, "Sorry I'm late."[51] Anatoly and Avital flew together from West Germany to Ben-Gurion Airport where Sharansky was greeted with songs, cheers and tears by an enormous and ecstatic crowd.[52]

"This is a time, when we all speak with one heart," said Prime Minister Shimon Peres, who was the first of a number of Israeli government officials to welcome Sharansky publicly. The masses of tear-stained faces were silent as Natan, having adopted his Hebrew name, spoke to them in Hebrew.

"To all my friends, those in the free world, and to those still waiting to be free: there are no words to adequately express to all of you my utmost thanks for the support you have given to my wife Avital during the many years of the struggle for my freedom. Although the KGB never allowed me the pleasure of receiving your mail, somehow I could sense the constancy and tremendous outpouring on my behalf. I want to let you know how proud I am to have finally reached my homeland, Israel. You, the people of the free world helped me to reach my goal."

Sharansky concluded his remarks, "Our fight must go on... On this happiest day of my life, I am not going to forget those whom I left in the camps, in the prisons, and those who are still in exile, who will continue their struggle for their right to emigrate – for their human rights. Together, we will do it! Shalom."[53]

After conveying his gratitude by telephone to President Reagan, Natan and Avital Sharansky were driven to Jerusalem where Natan was carried to the Western Wall[54] on the shoulders of friends, through a crowd of thousands of cheering Israelis. This was Sharansky's first opportunity to offer a prayer of thanks.

It was evening in Jerusalem, but in Canada the rejoicing continued all day and into the night. "Today is a day of triumph for human rights activists," began MP Sheila Finestone in the House of Commons that afternoon. "Today is a day of celebration as we witness an end to injustice with the release from Russian internment of Anatoly Sharansky. Today is the day that gives hope to all who work from depth of heart and genuine concern on issues of man's humanity towards his fellow man."[55] Tributes to Sharansky were paid by federal members of each of the three political parties, MPs John Turner, Joe Clark and Ed Broadbent, and by the exhilarated chairman of the Parliamentary Group for Soviet Jewry, Bill Attewell.

"Sharansky is a man who has become one less statistic in the ranks of the oppressed," said MPP Don Cousens in the Legislative Assembly of Ontario.[56] His remarks were followed by those of MPPs Bob Rae, Larry Grossman, Robert Nixon and the Premier of Ontario, David Peterson.[57]

"*Le chaim!* To Life," shouted Natan's twenty-nine cousins, who gathered in the Solomon's home that evening to celebrate. Speaking over the clinking glasses of champagne, Debby Solomon exclaimed, "We're ecstatic, absolutely ecstatic."[58]

Newspapers and television news reports carried details of Sharansky's release, his flight to freedom, his first embrace with Avital and the tumultuous welcome in Israel. He was interviewed on "Good Morning America," "Meet the Press" and other network news programs. Anyone who had ever signed a petition, written a letter or joined in a demonstration in support of Anatoly Sharansky felt a personal triumph. As Sharansky shared some intimate details of his release with his television audience, it was clear that his indomitable spirit that had carried him through nine long years of incarceration was resolute to the end. That morning, his guards had confiscated his small book of Psalms, along with other personal possessions. Throwing himself into the snow Sharansky had declared, "not another step until my Psalms are returned to me."

"I wasn't told where they were taking me," Sharansky recalled, "but the sun, like the finger of God, pointed the way. It was a flight to freedom. They had taken away all my belongings, including my prison uniform, which had grown so familiar and comfortable, giving me instead ungainly and clammy civilian clothes. But my little book of Psalms, which was my companion in all the years in the gulag, kept me warm. Through the triumphant Psalms of King David, God was bringing me the joyous news: 'You are free, you have won, you are going to the land of Israel.'"[59]

Moments after Sharansky disembarked from the plane that had carried him to East Berlin, he was ordered to walk "directly" to the group waiting to begin the exchange. In his last act of defiance, Sharansky walked toward his liberators in a "zig-zag" pattern.[60]

Whether it was years of negative media reports or a savvy political decision that led to Sharansky's release may never be known. What is believed, however, is that the world press, the Reagan/Gorbachev talks, Edgar Bronfman's diplomatic tactics, the back-room talents of Wolfgang Vogel, the legal expertise of Irwin Cotler, the indefatigable Avital, a tenacious Ida Milgrom and the efforts of people around the world all contributed to Sharansky's freedom.

To this day, Irwin Cotler does not know who delivered two airline tickets to his doorstep. He and his wife Ariella packed quickly and flew to Israel to meet Avital and Natan after they had spent their first Shabbat together. Cotler sat with the happy couple in the living room of their Jerusalem apartment and presented his "client" with a copy of the appeal-brief that he had prepared eight years earlier. Leafing through it, Sharansky informed Cotler that he had first seen the Canadian lawyer's name in an article in one of the few newspapers he had been permitted to read in Chistopol Prison in 1979. The article had stated, "The spy, Irwin Cotler, masquerading as a lawyer, came to Moscow on an espionage mission on behalf of the spy Anatoly Sharansky." Sharansky smiled at Cotler and said, "Already I liked you!"[61] The article ended, "The spy Irwin Cotler was expelled from Moscow and failed in his espionage mission in the same way the spy Anatoly Sharansky failed in his."[62] The former prisoner broke into a grin. "They were wrong . . . We succeeded in our mission. They failed in theirs." [63]

Barbara Stern embraced the couple in their apartment that same evening. Having spent nine years co-ordinating demonstrations, media campaigns, and countless meetings for Avital in Ottawa and in many other Canadian cities, Stern showed them the 1975 photograph of Avital's brother Misha, standing with three women in the Sinai.[64] Avital turned to Natan and with a warm smile affirmed, "This is how it all began."[65]

Chapter 22

Activity Escalates but No Results

When Mikhail Gorbachev became leader of the Soviet Union in March 1985, Western nations anticipated a more liberal attitude toward Jews. This did not prove to be the case. Soviet anti-Semitism became more widespread and the KGB was employing the same brutal tactics as before.

In January 1986, the U.S. State Department released its annual human rights report which included a section on the Soviet Union.[1] The report proved that the Soviets' human rights performance failed to meet even the most elementary of accepted international standards. Of all the ethnic and religious groups in the USSR, Jews received the most severe treatment, particularly those who wished to practice their religion, study Hebrew or emigrate to Israel.[2]

The facts spoke for themselves. By the end of 1985, twenty-two Jews were serving sentences in prison or labour camps, fifteen thousand Jews had been refused visas and three hundred and fifty thousand had requested an invitation from Israel.

The euphoric celebrations staged in major Canadian cities after Sharansky's release did not mask the reality of thousands of "Sharanskys" left behind. Within days of Sharansky's arrival in Israel, Alexei Magarik, a cellist and one of Moscow's unofficial Hebrew teachers, was arrested on charges of possessing drugs and sentenced to three years in prison. This brought the list of Prisoners of Zion to nineteen.[3]

Many activists believed that the release of Sharansky was a mere public relations ploy. Refusing to revel in the glory of success for too long, Canadians of all ages, professions and disciplines created a critical mass of energy on behalf of long-term refuseniks and prisoners. "Soviet leader Gorbachev is astute," read an editorial in *The Edmonton Journal*. "He must know that his country will have little world sympathy unless it acts decisively on human rights."[4]

The Reverend Bruce McLeod asked readers of his column in *The Toronto Star* to send Passover messages to Yosef Begun. "Letters really make a difference," McLeod wrote, "especially from people who are not Jews. No group in the single human family should be left to cry its pain alone."[5]

Harold Ballard, the owner of Maple Leaf Gardens and the Toronto Maple Leaf hockey team, was quoted in *The Toronto Sun*: "I will tell Alan Eagleson, who's been bringing the Russians to Canada for many years, that I will let them play in the Gardens provided they let a thousand Soviet Jews leave the country."[6]

The Reverend James E. Leland, a clergyman from the rural community of Florenceville, New Brunswick, wrote letters of support to Moscow refusenik Armen Khachturyan.[7]

Genya Intrator wrote about a different refusenik or prisoner each week in "Lifeline Letters," her column for *The Sunday Sun* in Toronto. Included each week were the names and addresses of Soviet officials to whom readers could write.[8]

Toronto and Winnipeg university students demonstrated against the arrest of Moscow refusenik Vladimir Lifshitz, charged with "anti-Soviet slander." His crime was that he had written letters to Western Communist parties and to the government of Israel to plead his own case.[9]

A Freedom Poster Contest was launched in Toronto's Hebrew day schools[10] and students from the Community Hebrew Academy of Toronto celebrated the eighteenth birthday of their adopted refusenik Efim Kelman.[11]

Dr. Mark Keil, chairman of the Soviet Jewry Committee of Edmonton moderated a panel of experts who addressed the community on "Soviet Jewry – Facts, Prospects and Rumours."[12]

Non-stop advocacy in support of Soviet Jewry continued in

Ottawa, January 27, 1980: Nobel laureate Dr. Gerhard Herzberg (left) protests the exile of Nobel laureate Andrei Sakharov. On right is Rabbi Don Gerber, co-chairman of the Ottawa Soviet Jewry committee, which organized the demonstration. [Canapress/*Le Devoir*]

Toronto June 22, 1981: Toronto women gather in Nathan Phillips Square to mark the third anniversary of the sentencing of Ida Nudel. [Colin McConnell/*The Toronto Star*]

Montreal, April 14, 1980: Poet Irving Layton leads a torchlight "freedom march" from downtown Montreal to the Soviet Consulate on the third night of Passover. [Howard Kay/*The Canadian Jewish News*]

Toronto, June 5, 1982: Professor Irving Abella presents an honourary Doctor of Laws degree to Anatoly Sharansky at York University's Glendon College Convocation. Accepting the award on Sharansky's behalf is his lawyer, Irwin Cotler. [CJC Archives]

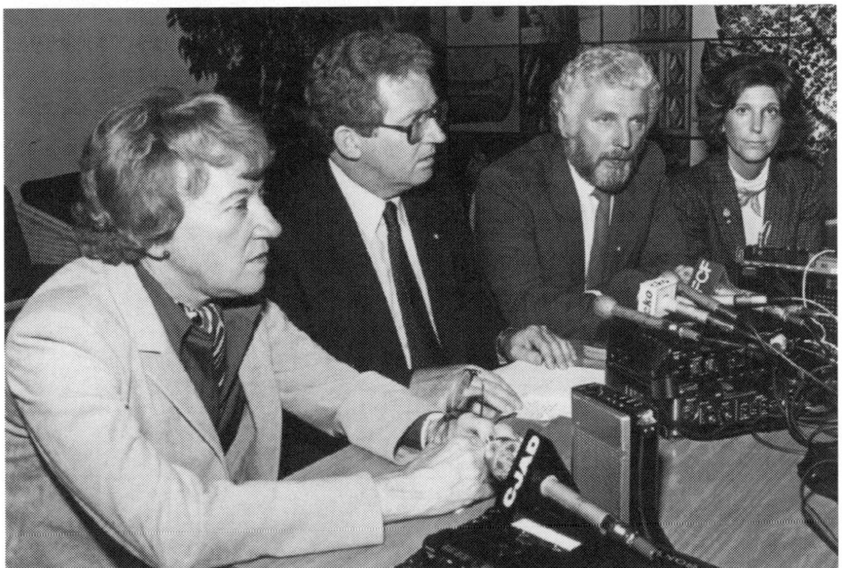

Montreal, September 20, 1982: (l to r) MPs Flora MacDonald, David Smith and Ian Deans report on their trip to the Soviet Union and the attack against Martin Penn and Sharon Wolfe, that left Wolfe (right) with a black eye. [Howard Kay]

Ottawa, April 29, 1983: The Congressional Wives for Soviet Jewry join the Parliamentary Spouses for Soviet Jewry for a two-day meeting in Ottawa (l to r: Joanne Kemp, Jane Crosby, Helen Jackson, Penny Collenette, Lucille Broadbent, Dolores Beilinson, Shirley Metzenbaum, Audrey King).

Toronto, January 12, 1983: Debby and Stan Solomon hear the latest word on the condition of their cousin Anatoly Sharansky during his hunger strike, from Avital Sharansky in Jerusalem. [R. Bull/*The Toronto Star*]

Ottawa, September 15, 1987: Natan Sharansky (centre) receives a standing ovation in the House of Commons. Standing with him in the speakers gallery are (l) Irwin Cotler and (r) MP Bill Attewell. [Canapress]

Vancouver, May 27, 1986: Mimi Estrin addresses Vancouver activist rally on the steps of the courthouse after bus crusaders complete their sixteen day cross-country journey in support of Soviet Jewry. [Ross Cameron/*The Canadian Jewish News*]

Ottawa, October 1986: Soviet foreign minister Eduard Shevardnadze talks to Canadian 35s outside Parliament Buildings before accepting their list of 3,000 long-term refuseniks. [Canapress]

Washington, December 6, 1987: Barbara Stern briefs five hundred Canadians who, along with two hundred thousand Americans, gathered in support of Soviet Jewry in Washington to mark the Reagan/Gorbachev summit. Vladimir Slepak (behind), Bill Attewell, Mort Bessner, Bernard Lang, look on. [Reuters/*The Gazette*]

Toronto, May 1987: MP Barbara McDougall accepts the Ida Nudel Humanitarian Award from Marsha Slavens during a ceremony at the Ontario Legislature. MPP Don Cousens looks on. [Graphic Artists/*Canadian Jewish News*]

Ben-Gurion Airport, October 16, 1987: Upon her arrival in Israel, Ida Nudel embraces actress Jane Fonda, while Nudel's sister Ilana Fridman and Israeli prime minister Yitzhack Shamir look on. [Canapress]

April 16, 1988: Moscow refuseniks demonstrate on Lenin Library steps as militia men move in to break up the protest.

Ben-Gurion Airport, October 18, 1990: Upon arrival on a direct flight from Moscow, this teenager exclaimed, "I start my new life tomorrow with Jewish people. I love you, Israel!" [Ya'acob Katz]

Jerusalem, June 14, 1992: "I'm glad to greet you Mr. Gorbachev, on the same side of the barricade." Natan Sharansky meets the former president of the Soviet Union at a state dinner hosted by Israeli president Chaim Herzog. Herzog and Sharansky's wife, Avital, look on. [Rahamim Israeli]

May 1986, when delegates to the twenty-first plenary assembly of the Canadian Jewish Congress gathered in the parking lot across from the Metro Toronto Convention Centre. A large blowup photograph of Red Square served as the backdrop for CJC leaders Milton Harris, Morton Bessner, Barbara Stern, Ron Appleby and Alan Rose, who each stood with the name of a prisoner – Begun, Edelshtein, Nudel, Lerner or Slepak – affixed to the front of their black robes.[13]

The voices of parliamentarians were heard world-wide after the conclusion of the fifth European Inter-Parliamentary Conference for Soviet Jewry, held in Berne, Switzerland in the spring of 1986. Delegates David Kilgour, Fred King and Lynn MacDonald were present when the resolution was drawn up calling upon the Soviet government "to permit Jews to emigrate, to release Soviet Jewish Prisoners of Conscience and to permit Soviet Jews to pursue religious and cultural activities without harassment."[14]

"If Mr. Gorbachev wants better relations with Canada," Kilgour declared in a press release upon his return to Ottawa, "he should stop the systematic persecution of Jews. It is an obstacle to better bilateral relations."[15]

When Kilgour first assumed the chairmanship of the Parliamentary Group for Soviet Jewry, he presented each new refusenik case to Alan McLaine, head of the East European desk of the Department of External Affairs. "McLaine always responded favourably and with follow-up," Kilgour remarked, "but I felt that soon I would wear out my welcome so I varied the procedure by writing to Soviet officials in Ottawa and the Soviet Union and I encouraged other MPs to do the same."[16]

Initially the parliamentarians received no response to their letters. Suddenly, letters began to arrive from the press office of the Soviet Embassy with explanations for refusals. "Could I please draw to your attention," began one letter from Soviet Secretary V. Bogdanov to David Kilgour, "that the question of anybody's release, Mr. Edelshtein's included, can be decided only upon the basis of legal regulations applied in the USSR, but not on the basis of emotionalism. For this reason, your appeal to release him 'at once' has no legal grounds. You call this person a 'prisoner of conscience,' while in practice he is a criminal."[17]

The case of Ida Nudel had became top priority. The Ida Nudel Humanitarian Award continued to link the former prisoner with Canadian women whose commitment to human rights was exemplary. Sister Mary Jo Leddy had been the 1984 recipient and in 1985, it was author Margaret Atwood.

As Ida Nudel received one refusal after another, her dream of Israel was becoming a recurring nightmare. In February 1986, she wrote to Soviet foreign minister Shevardnadze describing her life since her first refusal fifteen years earlier. She closed, "Dear Minister, all this can be changed by the stroke of a pen, by issuing me an exit visa. My friends will shout some more, but these will be shouts of joy."[18]

Ilana Fridman arrived from Israel to receive accolades heaped on her sister at a "Tribute to Excellence" luncheon in Montreal sponsored by the Canadian Shaare Zedek Hospital Foundation.[19] The Honourable Flora MacDonald referred to Nudel as a "piercing light in the darkness of the Soviet Union" and assured those women gathered in the dining room of the Ritz Carlton Hotel that the Canadian government would continue to make forceful representations to the Soviets until Ida Nudel was free.[20]

Fridman travelled to Toronto to present the 1986 Ida Nudel Humanitarian Award to journalist Michele Landsberg and then continued to Ottawa to meet with Joe Clark.[21] After their meeting, Clark confirmed his assurances to Nudel's sister in writing. "This government's initiatives have placed the Soviet Union very firmly on notice, that Canadian concerns for the plight of Soviet Jewry and the right of individuals such as Ida Nudel to emigrate will not diminish."[22]

From 1971 onwards, thousands gathered each May in Dag Hammarskjold Plaza at the United Nations in New York to mark "Solidarity Sunday for Soviet Jewry." Beginning in 1977, signs pressing for the release of Anatoly Sharansky dominated the surroundings. On May

11, 1986, three hundred thousand people squeezed shoulder to shoulder onto the plaza to welcome their hero as large video screens projected the proceedings to every corner.

Over roars of applause and the strains of *Haveinu Shalom Aleichem*, Israel's ambassador to the United Nations, Benjamin Netanyahu, introduced the man in whose honour everyone had gathered.[23] Sharansky began his remarks, "Every year from this place my wife, Avital, spoke to you, trying to convince you that your efforts were not in vain. The fact that I am speaking to you today is the best proof that she was right."

The crowd cheered as he held up the small book of Psalms that he had refused to surrender to Soviet authorities. "The KGB, my interrogators and my prison guards tried to convince me that I was alone, powerless in their hands. I knew I was never alone. I knew that my wife, my people and all of you were with me. All the resources of a superpower cannot isolate a man who hears the voice of freedom. It was a voice I heard from the very chamber of my soul."[24] Sharansky locked arms with rally organizers and tears flowed with unabashed candour as they sang the Hebrew ballad "*Kol Ha'olam, Gesher Tzar Ma'od*... All the world is a narrow bridge... and the important thing is never to be afraid."[25]

With the release of Sharansky and changes occuring rapidly in the USSR, Soviet officials were eager to present a positive image during Expo '86, the World's Fair, which was to be held in Vancouver. Consul Vinogradov responded favourably to a request for a meeting with Vancouver activists Rita Cohn and Ronnie Tessler. The women presented the Soviet official with the case of Odessa refusenik Valery Pevzner and asked that he use his good offices to expedite Pevzner's release.[26] On another occasion, Soviet consul Alexei Makarov addressed an open meeting organized by the Vancouver committee and publicly accepted the case histories of five refuseniks whose closest family members were residents of Vancouver.[27]

During Expo, numerous events were planned by Vancouver activists Cohn, Tessler and Renee Bellas to keep the issue of Soviet Jewry in public view. They mounted an exhibition of photographs of separated Soviet Jewish families in a storefront near the Expo site, placed blank postcards addressed to refuseniks and prisoners in strategic places in the Soviet pavilion and distributed hundreds of bogus Soviet passports to fairgoers, with the names and photographs of Ida Nudel, Valery Pevzner, Yuli Edelshtein and Yosef Begun. *The Trial of Yuli Edelshtein,* written by local playwright Hilary Nicholls, was performed by amateur actors at the Jewish Community Centre.[28]

Expo '86 gave a group of university students from the Jewish Students' Network the opportunity to take the issue of Soviet Jewry to the people of Canada. In Halifax, on May 11, in bitter cold weather, they chartered a red and gray bus, to which they affixed banners that spelled out "Freedom for Soviet Jews," and set out, with twenty students, for Vancouver. The "Freedom Caravan" picked up other students in many of the fourteen communities along the way.[29] With sleeping bags in tow, the young people camped out in Jewish community centres on their route and ate meals supplied by local parents.

The students were received enthusiastically at each stop as they donned prison costumes, conducted orderly demonstrations and circulated a petition addressed to Mikhail Gorbachev, demanding freedom for long-term refuseniks and prisoners. "One of the Caravan's aims," said co-organizer Leora Silver, "is to show the inconsistencies between the image the Soviets try to present to the world and the realities of life for Jews living in the Soviet Union."[30]

The students joined a local demonstration outside Montreal's Soviet Consulate, they rallied on Parliament Hill with municipal and government officials and carried Soviet Jewry placards on an impromptu walk through the campus of Queen's University in Kingston. They demonstrated outside Queen's Park, at the Manitoba Legislature and on the steps of Edmonton's City Hall.

Sixteen days after they began their fifty-three hundred kilometre, coast-to-coast trek, thirty exhausted but exhilarated students made a triumphal entry into Vancouver to join a large Soviet Jewry rally on the steps of Vancouver's old courthouse building. Their final action took place inside the Soviet pavilion where the petition, with the hundreds of signatures they had gathered en route, was presented to a

Soviet official, after which they inscribed the names of Yosef Begun, Ida Nudel, Vladimir Slepak, Josef Berenshtein and Vladimir Lifshitz in the pavilion's guest book.[31]

In September 1986, it was announced that Soviet foreign minister Eduard Shevardnadze was coming to Ottawa early in October to discuss bilateral relations with Canadian top government officials. Immediately, Joe Clark's office was inundated with letters and telegrams asking him to raise the issue of Jewish emigration with his guest.[32] On the day before Shevadnadze's arrival, the Department of External Affairs announced that the Canadian agenda would include a request for reunification of families in Israel and in Canada.[33]

"On October 2, the plight of Soviet refuseniks hung like a storm cloud over Eduard Shevardnadze wherever he went in Ottawa," wrote Gordon Barthos in *The Toronto Sun*. He was referring to nine members of the Toronto and Montreal 35s who shadowed the Soviet foreign minister during his stay in the nation's capital.[34]

As Shevardnadze and Clark exited the West Block of the Parliament Buildings after their first meeting, they saw the women, dressed in black, holding placards demanding freedom for Soviet Jews. One member of the group was reading names from a list of three thousand refuseniks. Shrugging off security, Shevardnadze approached the group and asked for a copy of the list. He spoke through his interpreter and said to the women, "This is a very good country here – very good people. You can trust me. I won't forget you. If there is a good reason to leave for family reunion, I understand that problem, and I'll look into it personally."[35] With the list in hand, Shevardnadze rejoined Clark, who had been waiting at the limousine that was to take them to a meeting with the prime minister.[36]

The women then walked with MP David Kilgour to the East Block until the meeting between Prime Minister Mulroney and Shevardnadze had concluded. The Soviet official appeared surprised when he emerged from the building to see the same group of women waiting for him. He approached them again and through his interpreter declared, "I took your list. Now you can go home. It's chilly, you'll catch a cold."[37]

As he turned to leave, Shevardnadze was intercepted by Kilgour who presented him with a petition requesting emigration for Soviet Jews and signed by ten thousands Canadians. It was made up of hundreds of pages taped together and rolled like a Torah scroll.

After a private luncheon with several businessmen, Shevardnadze was driven to the governor general's residence for a meeting with Jeanne Sauvé. By now, the women in black were a familiar sight to him. The diplomat smiled and waved to them as his limousine drove through the residence gates.

The Ottawa encounter set a precedent. It was the first time that a senior member of the Politburo had taken a refusenik list from Jewish demonstrators. The story was relayed through international wire services.[38] The changing Soviet attitude set the stage for the bilateral meeting on arms control that was to take place one week later, in Reykjavik, Iceland. There, President Reagan made it clear to President Gorbachev that respect for human rights and individual freedoms would have to be upheld before the United States would enter into arms control agreements with the Soviet Union.

Soviet Jewry activists knew that they couldn't be nearly as effective lobbying Soviet officials without the help of the Canadian government. Joe Clark's commitment to Soviet Jewry did not go unnoticed. On November 13, 1986, at a luncheon attended by Toronto lawyers and activists, Bert Raphael, chairman of the Canadian Lawyers and Jurists for Soviet Jewry, presented Clark with a Human Rights Award.

When David Kilgour stepped down as head of the Parliamentary Group for Soviet Jewry at the end of 1986, he was replaced by MP Bill Attewell. Within days of the new appointment, a Soviet delegation visited Canada. One of its members was Victor Afanasyev, editor-in-chief of *Pravda*, the official Communist party newspaper. During their meeting with a group of MPs, Attewell raised the issue of human rights and presented the Soviet delegation with Jewish emigration figures. There was a brief altercation and a few angry words were spoken by the Soviets.[39]

The episode, written up by Afanasyev, was included in an article entitled "Eleven Days on the Other Side of the West," which appeared in *Pravda* on January 19, 1987. "It cannot be said that all went smoothly during our visit to Canada," Afanasyev wrote. "A round-table discussion involving twenty Canadian parliamentarians was held one day. A good half of the deputies were diehard anticommunists... the Jewish question was discussed particularly keenly. Bill Attewell, chairman of the Canadian Parliamentary Group for the Defense of the Rights of Soviet Jews and a member of parliament, delivered a paper on 'violations of Jewish rights in the USSR' in a threatening and downright accusatory tone." The article concluded, "The paper was stuffed with a whole mass of fables about the position of our citizens of Jewish nationality and wild fabrications that I cannot bring myself to write about. It later emerged that this gentleman had never been to the Soviet Union, never met a single Soviet citizen of Jewish nationality or received one complaint about a rights violation."[40]

On December 10, 1986, there was Soviet Jewry activity across the country. B'nai Brith's program involved fifteen mayors representing municipalities in Quebec, Ontario, Manitoba and Alberta. Each mayor offered honourary citizenship to one refusenik at a ceremony held in his respective office.[41]

Montreal churches, corporations, department stores, banks and hotels displayed large blue streamers symbolizing human rights for Soviet Jews on the entrances to their buildings.[42] Three Vancouver residents presented the cases of their refusenik relatives at a local press conference.[43] Outside the Ontario Legislature, 123 Torontonians dedicated one long-stemmed rose to a refusenik whose visa had been denied for ten years or more. The 123 roses were then couriered to Ambassador Rodionov in Ottawa.[44]

On December 16, 1986, the telephone rang in the apartment of Andrei Sakharov, who was serving his seventh year of exile in the closed city of Gorky. On the other end of the line was Mikhail Gorbachev, calling to inform the celebrated dissident that he was free.

Sakharov returned to his Moscow apartment pursued by reporters questioning him about issues dealing with the Soviet regime. He was reluctant to predict the future. "Soviet policy, is still inconsistent," he said. "One day dissident Anatoli Marchenko is tormented and allowed to die in prison, and the next day Andrei Sakharov is set free."[45] The Nobel laureate was cautiously optimistic about the prospect of a better life for Soviet Jews. "I really do not like making forecasts," he declared, "but I think that the new leadership of our country is interested in economic progress and the elimination of negative aspects, and an essential condition of achieving this is openness in society. This includes freedom of movement inside the country, freedom of emigration and return, freedom of thought, freedom to distribute information and religious freedom."[46]

Activists were becoming impatient. Only 914 Jews received exit visas in 1986.

Chapter 23

Parliamentary Trips to the USSR

For parliamentarians to advocate effectively on behalf of Soviet Jewry it was necessary for them to understand the reality of life for Jews in the Soviet Union. The CCSJ began to invite MPs to travel there under the auspices of the CJC. Separate trips were arranged for representatives of all three political parties in 1982, 1984, 1985 and 1987. These were financed by private contributions to a "travel fund" headed by Milton Harris and Edward Bronfman, who solicited private support from friends and community leaders.

Prior to each trip, the Department of External Affairs attempted to arrange meetings for the travellers with Soviet officials, but succeeded with only the first and last trips, when there was a warming trend between East and West. This proved the direct correlation between the status of multilateral relations and the reception afforded Canadian dignitaries.

The first parliamentary trip took place September 1982 during David Smith's tenure as chairman of the Parliamentary Group for Soviet Jewry. The delegation was led by Martin Penn and Sharon Wolfe. It included MPs Flora MacDonald, Ian Deans and David Smith and Smith's wife, Heather.[1]

The group was received by officials of the Supreme Soviet, the Foreign Ministry and the Institute of American and Canadian Studies. "The Soviets tried to suggest that there were only a small number of Jews who wanted to leave and that 'refusals' were given to those who had access to State secrets," reported Smith.[2] "They listened to us but remained inscrutable."[3] When the Canadians tried to discuss Jewish emigration, the Soviets raised the subjects of nuclear disarmament and world peace. The officials refused to arrange for MacDonald to meet with Ida Nudel, the woman in whose name she had been honoured the previous spring. Even Canadian ambassador Jeffrey Pearson's request to allow Nudel to travel from Bendery to meet MacDonald was rejected.

Dr. Alexander Lerner acted as the delegation's unofficial host in Moscow. "His risks were considerable," remarked Ian Deans. "He accompanied us from place to place and was even called in by the KGB and warned not to see us again. Not intimidated by the threat, he continued as before."[4]

The travellers were unaware of any surveillance while in Moscow. Their experience in Leningrad, however, was quite different. They arrived in early morning on the overnight train from Moscow and then separated for a few hours. Penn and Wolfe went together by Metro to Ilya Shastokovsky's flat. He drove them to Aba Taratuta's apartment, located on the outskirts of the city. As they entered the foyer of the apartment building, they were attacked and robbed by three assailants.

A punch in the jaw laid Shastokovsky flat on the ground. Wolfe was hit in the face. Her glasses were knocked off and her purse and camera snatched. One man grabbed Penn's briefcase, pushed him to the floor and stepped on his face. The attackers fled, leaving the three victims shaken.

Shastokovsky drove Penn and Wolfe to their hotel where they located their travelling companions and reported the incident to the police. They were not seriously injured, but both received bruises and Wolfe had a black eye. They doubted that the attack was a random mugging. Their doubts were confirmed when the policewoman who conducted the investigation, documented each carefully worded answer concerning the purpose of their visit. When furnished with a description of the assailants, she recorded nothing. The shock of the incident abated and the group continued with their plans to meet refuseniks that evening. A certain levity eased the tension when it was realized that among personal briefing notes in Penn's stolen briefcase was a large piece of vacuum-packed Kosher smoked meat.[5]

Since there was no official Canadian presence in Leningrad, the group was debriefed the following morning by officials at the U.S. Consulate.[6] They were led through the bowels of the building into a large room where air-conditioners blasted loudly. In the centre was a free-standing transparent room, impervious to listening devices. Inside, Penn and Wolfe recounted the mugging incident of the previous day to U.S. consular officials.[7] That afternoon, the U.S. consul-general accompanied the Canadians on a train to Helsinki where they were scheduled to board their plane to Montreal. Although he claimed to be carrying the U.S. diplomatic pouch on a routine trip to Helsinki, the Canadians suspected that because of the incident the previous day, the American official chose to escort the group safely out of the country.[8]

Newspaper reporters and photographers, who greeted the travellers when they arrived at Mirabel airport, were quick to publish reports of the attack. Photographs of Wolfe's badly swollen face and black eye appeared in *The Montreal Star*. An article in *The New York Times* portrayed the incident as a Soviet attempt to further isolate the refusenik community by inhibiting tourists from making contact with them.[9]

"We didn't expect that one trip would work miracles," said Flora MacDonald during a press conference in Ottawa. "What was important, though, was the human contact we made. It showed the refuseniks that there are opinion-makers in the Western world who really care."[10]

When Jim Peterson assumed chairmanship of the Canadian Parliamentary Group for Soviet Jewry in December 1983, he announced his intention to lead an official trip to the Soviet Union the following spring. Only 1,314 visas had been issued in 1983, the lowest number since the emigration movement began. Peterson was interested in seeing the conditions for Soviet Jewry first hand.

Soviet counsellor Alexandrov paid Peterson a visit in his office and suggested that the timing for a parliamentary trip was "not appropriate." The MP responded, "If you can assure me that the people we are going to visit will receive emigration visas then I'll postpone the trip."[11] Since no such assurance was made, Peterson continued with his plans.

In January 1984, Peterson delivered to the Soviet Embassy a petition with thirty-eight hundred signatures on behalf of the Vasilevsky family.[12] The following day, embassy officials notified Peterson that his trip was not considered "official" and no dignitaries would meet with them in the USSR.[13]

Peterson's delegation included Lynn MacDonald, Fred King, King's wife Audrey and CJC representatives Alan Rose and Barbara Stern. Their visas arrived at Montreal's Mirabel Airport only moments before they were to board their flight to Moscow – an omen of what was to follow.

The Canadian contingent was harassed from their arrival at Sheremetyevo Airport. They were forced to submit to a two-hour search of their baggage conducted in full view of Canadian ambassador Peter Roberts who had come to greet them. KGB agents followed the Canadians outside their hotel, on the street and on the subway, and on one occasion when they reached the top of the stairs of a busy metro station, they were observed by men speaking into walkie-talkies.[14]

Telephone calls made to refuseniks from telephone booths in the street were often disconnected in mid-sentence, but only after the time and place of meeting was established. When the group arrived at the pre-arranged spot, there were usually several plainclothesmen there to greet them.

Outside Elena Dubianskaya's apartment building, the parliamentary contingent found twenty KGB agents guarding the entrance. "We were afraid of endangering the refuseniks," Stern said, "so we circled the block to find a telephone and called to inform Elena of the situation. Moments later, she and Mark Nashpitz, who had recently been released from prison, made their way through the human barricade, threw their arms around us and led us into her apartment."[15]

The group was shadowed everywhere. "When we arrived at the synagogue on Shabbat morning" Peterson recalled, "we were embraced warmly by the Jews there. Suddenly they stopped talking to us, aware that the KGB had entered."[16] There were other anxious moments. One evening in Moscow, two agents followed them to

Alexander Ioffe's apartment. Suddenly all the street-lights went out. As they approached the apartment complex, three burly men were standing alongside an ambulance backed up to the door of the building. The refuseniks inside assured them that it was an attempt to terrorize people who were coming to their meeting. "Our refusenik friends had learned to live under this pressure," remarked Peterson.[17]

The intimidation occurred in Leningrad as well. On several occasions after evening visits with refuseniks, the group was met on darkened streets by KGB officers, easily identified by their long black leather coats and plaid scarves.

During their eight-day visit to the USSR, the group met with more than seventy Soviet Jews who were eager for the opportunity to share their stories. They thanked them effusively for coming to see them at a time when so many others were afraid to do so.

"Jews who want to emigrate to Israel are being used as pawns in the Cold War," declared Peterson at a news conference in Ottawa upon his return.[18] He explained that the Soviet campaign to link the Jewish issue to East-West politics was an attempt to force the U.S. government to modify its policies on nuclear disarmament. "Disarmament is possible," added King, "only in an atmosphere of accelerating trust, which the Russians can bring about by respecting their own signatures on international agreements."[19]

In April 1985, MPs David Kilgour, Sheila Finestone and Nelson Riis were accompanied to Moscow and Leningrad by CJC president Milton Harris and his wife Ethel. The MPs, who travelled on diplomatic passports, carried suitcases filled with Jewish cultural material and medication for the refuseniks. Not one of their bags was opened.

The group did not experience the oppressive surveillance encountered by others on the previous two trips, nor did they receive the measure of hospitality they had anticipated, considering that the CSCE human rights Experts conference was scheduled to take place in Ottawa the following month.[20] Official meetings that had been requested had not been confirmed before their departure. When

Canadian embassy officials tried to arrange on-the-spot meetings for them, all requests were rejected.

"The only meeting that the Soviets were willing to organize was with the anti-Zionist committee," recalled Harris, "but the refuseniks with whom we spoke about it were adamantly opposed, so we refused. The feeling was unanimous in our group, not to do anything that was against the refuseniks' sensibilities."[21]

Kilgour explained their official position during a press conference held in his Moscow hotel room. "We are profoundly concerned with the public statements coming from the anti-Zionist committee, which we believe to be anti-Semitic and only pretending to be concerned about Jews in the Soviet Union. Meeting the 'anti-Zionists' would be analagous to informing Russians visiting Canada that the only people they could meet were the Ku Klux Klan."[22]

It was a time of political change. No one knew how the fate of Soviet Jews would be affected by new leader Mikhail Gorbachev. "It's difficult to say just what the Soviet government will do," Moscow mathematician Naum Meiman told them. "Above all, judge Gorbachev by his deeds, not his words."[23]

The group visited Boris Begun, who was on the forty-fifth day of a hunger strike precipitated by the refusal of camp officials to allow letters from his father Yosef Begun to be delivered to his family. "I had never seen anyone on a hunger strike before," recalled Nelson Riis. "I remember walking through the door of his little apartment and thinking there was actually a smell of death in the place. I then began to understand the personal tragedy, the human suffering and the sense of hopelessness and despair. But that spark, that determination, that commitment was still there and it inspired me even more."[24]

They met Ida Milgrom after her return from a fifteen hundred kilometre trip to Perm Labour Camp to visit Sharansky, and Inna Berenshtein, whose husband Josef was left partially blind after being attacked by fellow prison inmates wielding broken bottles. Berenshtein was denied hospitalization by prison authorities who claimed that his wounds were self-inflicted. Riis, himself a former Sunday school teacher, was outraged. "Imagine, Berenshtein was imprisoned for teaching religious studies – for what I used to do."[25]

"Anti-Semitism is now the one single official ideology in Russia." These words of Leningrad refusenik Roald Zelichonok rang true when the Canadians saw a poster, hanging in public view, depicting an Israeli walking arm in arm with Hitler over the bodies of Arab children.

"I can finally put a human face to human rights," stated Sheila Finestone at a press conference in Ottawa upon their return. Finestone's involvement with Soviet Jewry dated back to 1971, when she co-ordinated the first women's demonstration outside the Aeroflot office in Montreal. "After our trip to the Soviet Union, I had a strong sense that on the Conservative side we could count on David Kilgour to carry the message," Finestone said. "That was very comforting to me as a Jewish Member of Parliament."[26]

In May 1987, MPs Bill Attewell, Howard McCurdy and Lucie Pepin visited the USSR with Jeanette Goldman. *Glasnost* had presented new opportunities. A press conference was held for Ida Nudel at the Canadian Embassy in Moscow in the presence of the parliamentarians, senior diplomats and members of the foreign press. As the petite woman spoke about her life, it was clear that after sixteen years of waiting, her spirits had reached a low ebb. Her most recent visa application had been rejected just two months earlier.[27]

The Canadians met with Soviet government officials and members of the Soviet press. Vadim Zagladin, a Central Committee member responsible for emigration matters, admitted to the MPs that twenty thousand Jews had been refused permission to leave the country. Until then, officials had acknowledged the existence of only four thousand refuseniks.

When *Pravda* editor Victor Afanasyev entered the room for a meeting with the Canadian delegation, he recognized Attewell. Recalling their unpleasant exchange in Ottawa, the Soviet muttered to an aide in Russian, "Here comes the defender of the Jews." He was obviously unaware that his remarks had been understood by Goldman. After perfunctory greetings, Afanasyev removed a list from a file and read aloud the names of many Jews who were holding prominent jobs in the Soviet Union. This, he told them, proved that Soviet officials did not discriminate against Jews.[28]

Bill Attewell and Jeanette Goldman were the only members of the group who received travel visas for Kishinev. They were greeted at the airport by former prisoners Osip Lokshin and Simon Shnirman, who presented flowers to Goldman whose voice they had heard over the telephone for many years. Before *glasnost*, refuseniks would never have met with foreigners in public.

The manager of the hotel in Kishinev invited Goldman to speak to a local television crew about her travels in the Soviet Union. Unaware of the trap, she agreed. Instantly, the reporter denounced her on camera as a foreigner who assisted criminals. He exposed, on camera, some unflattering articles written about Goldman in the Kishinev press.[29]

The delegation received mixed messages during their one-week stay. In their candid discussions with Soviet government officials, the words *glasnost* and *perestroika* peppered their talks as well as assurances that emigration policies were changing. However, the fact that thousands of Jews were still being held as political hostages convinced them that the changes were merely superficial and that the mechanism of Soviet oppression remained firmly in place.

Chapter 24

A Matter of Life or Death

Dr. Gerald Batist, a Montreal Jewish doctor specializing in cancer research treatment, travelled to the Soviet Union in the spring of 1986. He was given the telephone numbers of Rima Braave and Tanya Bogomolny, two Moscow refuseniks who had cancer. As well, Batist planned to contact Dr. Yosef Irlin. Irlin, a refusenik who worked in experimental oncology and had not been permitted to conduct research since he first applied to emigrate in 1979.[1]

Batist's casual meetings with these three refuseniks confirmed his suspicion that cancer treatment in the Soviet Union was far below Western standards. In addition, he learned that Soviet cancer patients were forced to accept the physician assigned to their case and could not seek a second opinion or choose alternate treatment.

When Batist returned to Montreal, he communicated with his colleagues in Canada, the United States and Europe, requesting that they appeal to the appropriate Soviet authorities for Dr. Irlin's release. The oncologist's case was raised at a medical conference in Budapest and within a few months, Irlin received permission to emigrate. This gesture indicated to Batist that the Soviets were interested in co-operating with the West on cancer research.[2]

Dr. Batist maintained contact with Rima Braave and Tanya Bogomolny. He soon gained new names – Benjamin Charny and Inna Meiman of Moscow, and Lea Mariasin of Riga all of whom were refuseniks who had been diagnosed with terminal cancer.

The diagnoses of all the cancer patients brought to Batist's attention were varied. Braave had ovarian cancer, Bogomolny had breast cancer, Charny was suffering with a malignant melanoma, Meiman had sarcoma of the spine and Mariasin had multiple melanomas. Each refusenik had been refused a temporary visa for treatment in the West.

Hoping to draw attention to their desperate plight, the cancer patients organized a press conference on June 12, 1986, in Charny's apartment, to which Moscow-based foreign correspondents were invited.[3] The letter they read that day was addressed to Mikhail Gorbachev:

> We are cancer patients living in the Soviet Union. We have all been told that there is no hope for us and that further treatment will be useless. We are aware of new experimental procedures being used in other countries and these treatments have been offered to us by doctors in a number of countries throughout the world. We feel that we have a right to live. But if our diseases are fatal, then we surely have the right to seek alternative treatment wherever it is available, especially since our Soviet doctors cannot provide it. Beyond this, it should be the right of dying persons to spend their remaining time with loved ones. We therefore request the right to be reunited with our families outside the Soviet Union.[4]

Inspired by the courage of the cancer patients, Dr. Batist contacted the Charny, Braave, Bogomolny and Mariasin families in the West and discovered that they were all eager to work to free their afflicted relatives. He formed the International Cancer Patients Solidarity Committee and, like the Moscow group, used press conferences to publicize their cases.

Dr. Phil Gold, an oncologist and chairman of the Department of Medicine at Montreal General Hospital, assisted Batist in organizing a North American press conference for June 26, 1986. Members of the media gathered in a conference room at Montreal General Hospital where they were addressed by Gold, Batist, Tanya Bogomolny's sister, Ben Charny's brother and Sheila Kussner, a cancer survivor and founder of the Hope and Cope program at Jewish General Hospital in Montreal.

Kussner spoke of the cruelty of the Soviet government in refusing to permit cancer patients to emigrate. "It not only denies them hope," she said, "but it adds unbearably to their stress. There's no room for cold-war politics where cancer is concerned."[5]

During the next three months, six press conferences were held in other cities. The second took place July 11 at Beth Israel Hospital in New York City where New Jersey senator Frank R. Lautenberg was a participant. "These patients are fighting for their lives," he told reporters. "For them, a visa may spell the difference between life and death."[6] Lautenberg enlisted the support of fifty-six senators, each of whom signed a letter to Gorbachev underlining the urgency of the cancer patients' situations.

With each press conference, Dr. Batist learned more about publicity and the media. "I understood the value of talking in emotional and personal terms. I learned about packaging," Batist explained to Peter Gzowski, the host of CBC radio's "Morningside." "At the beginning we would tell lengthy stories and run home to watch the news to find that only a few sentences had been selected. We studied all the press clippings. We learned that the media liked concise facts and that they always focused on the emotions of the separated Western families. We learned of the importance of having at least one family member present at each press conference."[7]

On July 22, 1986, in a boardroom of the Medical Science Building at the University of Toronto, a group of experts spoke of the medical and psychological effects on patients being treated for cancer who were separated from their loved ones.[8] In the presence of local television and newspaper reporters, members of the Charny, Bogomolny, Braave and Mariasin families each told stories of their terminally ill relatives, men and women who were denied the comfort and support of their families when they needed it most.[9]

Batist further emphasized that every cancer patient must endure the dual stress of illness and the possibility of death and that each should have the right to seek treatment wherever it is available and to live in a supportive family environment. "As a doctor," Batist said, "I am an advocate of my patients' well-being. As such, I say most emphatically that these patients are suffering unduly and that the treatment of their disease is being compromised by their emotional stress. This will impact on both the quality and length of their lives."[10] Articles that appeared in Toronto and Montreal newspapers focused on the human aspect and declared that, for most of the patients, time was running out.[11]

Encouraged by telephone conversations with the patients themselves, Batist forged ahead. The fourth press conference was held August 26 at the New England Medical Center in Boston. The chiefs of oncology of all six major teaching hospitals in Boston[12] were present. Their special appeal to President Reagan emphasized that human survival transcended politics and urged that he press the Soviets to allow the cancer patients to emigrate to the West for medical treatment. The appeal was made one day after the United States and the Soviet Union had signed an agreement for joint cooperation in cancer research.[13] "We physicians are in no way questioning the quality of medical care in the Soviet Union," said Dr. Robert Schwartz, Chief of the Hematology and Oncology department at the New England Medical Center. "We are not making a political statement to the President. We are making a humanitarian appeal. Every cancer patient needs familial support in his personal struggle and all patients should have the right to a second opinion."[14]

CBS television news commentator Dan Rather reported the event on the evening news. He highlighted the emotional agony experienced by the families in the West and described their feelings of helplessness.

On September 11, a telephone call was placed to four Moscow cancer patients from a U.S. Senate hearing room in Washington.[15] Senators, medical doctors and members of the press were present as Tanya Bogomolny expressed her frustration at not being able to receive adequate medical treatment. In the room in Washington was her elderly father, who pleaded, "If there is a God, my daughter should be with me."[16]

Reports of the press conference were broadcast into the USSR by Voice of America, the BBC and Radio Canada. The following morning, the refusenik cancer patients were asked to report to local clinics for medical examinations. Three weeks later, Tanya Bogomolny received permission to leave the Soviet Union.[17]

"As an oncologist," Dr. Batist explained during the press conference in Ottawa on October 14, "I deal with people dying of cancer all the time. But I was trained to distinguish between what can and cannot be fixed. What frustrates me in this situation is to see the fixable not done."[18] Members of Parliament and representatives of the Canadian Cancer Society voiced their support for the refusenik cancer patients.[19]

In November 1986, Batist attended the Helsinki review meetings in Vienna in the company of Ben Charny's brother, Rima Braave's mother and Tanya Bogomolny, who had already begun treatment for her cancer in the United States. Batist brought them to meet with Canadian external affairs minister Joe Clark and Ambassador Bill Bauer, and U.S. Secretary of State George Shultz, Senator Alfonse D'Amato and Ambassador Warren Zimmerman. Each agreed to raise the subject of the cancer patients with the Soviet delegation.

In Vienna, Batist introduced himself to some of the Soviet delegates and passed a letter, through them, to Mikhail Gorbachev. The press credentials that Batist had acquired for himself and the patients' families allowed entry into an international news conference where Leon Charny pleaded the case of his brother Benjamin. In tears, Rima Braave's mother held a poster of her daughter with the words: "Please let my daughter die in my arms."[20]

Two weeks after the Vienna meetings began, Rima Braave was granted permission to emigrate. The thirty-two-year-old woman's arrival in the West, on December 19, 1986, produced great excitement. U.S. Senator Gary Hart, who had petitioned for her release, flew with her from Moscow to Vienna where they were met by Senator D'Amato, and both accompanied her to Rochester, New York. There, Braave's mother greeted her with a crowd of supporters.

For most of the refusenik cancer patients, permission to leave the USSR came too late. Six months after Rima Braave, was reunited with her family she died of advanced ovarian cancer. Inna Meiman, who was granted a temporary medical visa in January 1987 for treatment of the malignant tumour on her neck, died without the comfort of family at Georgetown University Medical Center, three weeks after her arrival in Washington.[21] Her husband Naum, a retired mathematics professor, had not been permitted to accompany her because the medical research he had conducted thirty years earlier made him a security risk.[22]

On February 6, 1987, Lea Mariasin, her husband Alexander and daughter Faina arrived in Toronto, where they were met by Lea's sister Mara Katz and her family. Although the Mariasins had battled for freedom for fifteen years, Lea's deteriorating illness dampened the family's happiness.

"You can't possibly understand," Alexander Mariasin told reporters at a news conference held at the Toronto General Hospital. "You are in a brilliant hospital here. The people who remain there can't receive help like you can. I became Lea's doctor for the last five years. I read medical books and directed her treatment," he said weeping. "You can't imagine."[23]

Attempts to save Lea's life were futile. The cancer had spread to her bone marrow and she died six months after arriving in Canada.

Another cancer patient, Leningrad refusenik Yuri Shpeizman, who suffered from a heart condition and lymphosarcoma, died of a heart attack in Vienna just hours before realizing his dream of living in Israel. "The tragic story of Yuri Shpeizman," remarked Batist, "underlines the fact that these people are critically ill and there is an urgency involved in allowing them to leave."[24]

Gerald Batist capitalized on the Soviet Union's need for American co-operation in the field of cancer research and urged Senator Edward Kennedy, who had taken a special interest in the Charny case, to apply pressure on the U.S. Senate.

On March 23, 1987, Kennedy spearheaded a campaign to obtain unanimous consent from one hundred senators to press Gorbachev to release patients with serious medical conditions. A letter addressed to the Soviet leader was signed by every member of the Senate. It documented recent deaths of cancer patients as a reminder of the need for immediate attention and named eight patients whose situations were desperate.[25] "The American people would view swift and positive action on these cases as a significant step towards improved Soviet-American relations," the letter read. "We hope that you will involve yourself personally in this matter."[26] Many senators showed their support for the issue by wearing "Freedom for Charny" buttons in the Senate.[27] Timing was critical. The Soviets were anxious to renew a joint U.S.-Soviet agreement for exchange in the field of cancer research.

Batist was invited by Congressman Henry Waxman to testify at a House of Representatives subcommittee hearing on "Health" to be held April 7, 1987. "If the Soviets cannot come forward on the easy task of resolving the emotional anguish of the separated families," he declared at the hearing, "then how sincere can they be in fully participating in a joint program in the hope of finding a future cure for cancer?"[28] Ben Charny informed them by telephone from Moscow, "I have sent many letters to the authorities with no response. I am deeply touched by your concern. The best medicine for me is an exit visa."[29]

As one cancer patient after another received an emigration visa, Charny received only refusals. His medical situation was worsening. Large tumours were visible on his neck and he was suffering from a severe heart condition, exacerbated by stress. It was impossible to understand why Benjamin Charny was refused permission to leave the USSR. Perhaps it was due to medium-level Soviet bureaucracy. Unquestionably, the denial of a visa for Charny went against the Gorbachev image. "As the human rights problems of the world go," wrote *New York Times* journalist Anthony Lewis, "the Charny case is of modest dimensions. It can set no great precedents, shake no institutions. So far as one can tell, the only stakes are the human longings of one family."[30]

On April 27, 1987, Ben Charny was informed not to apply again until 1995. "Nineteen hundred and ninety-five is clearly a date that, without adequate medical treatment, Ben Charny will not live to see," said Batist. "It is important to recognize that although some patients have been released, the authorities are making it clear that they will not be manipulated."[31]

Batist believed that the Soviets delayed granting visas to the cancer patients because they feared unfavourable comparisons between their medical techniques and more advanced North American methods. "As a result," Batist said, "they wait until there is little hope of recovery. Medically, it is absolutely outrageous and inhumane that these people should have even a moment of their lives compromised because of a political decision."[32]

In the summer of 1987, Charny's wife and daughter staged a hunger strike in Moscow while his brother fasted outside the Soviet Embassy in Washington. The international media coverage resulted in an exit visa for his daughter Anna and her husband. The couple emigrated to Boston with their baby daughter on September 18, 1987, and from there, Anna continued her crusade to save her father's life. That fall, she raised Ben Charny's case at conferences and meetings in many North American cities, causing a spontaneous campaign on his behalf.[33]

In desperation, Benjamin Charny's family turned to Armand Hammer, the American industrialist whose business dealings with the Soviets were well known. Hammer, who had arranged the release of Moscow refusenik David Goldfarb in 1986, agreed to champion Charny's case. He negotiated with his Soviet contacts, flew to Moscow and returned on October 21, 1988, in his private jet with Charny aboard. Waiting with the family on the tarmac at Logan Airport in Boston were Senator Edward Kennedy and Gerald Batist. Benjamin Charny's treatment at the New England Medical Center commenced immediately. He was one of the lucky ones.

The ultimate success of the International Cancer Patients' Solidarity Committee lay in the initiative of one Canadian who was able to cut through the encumbrances of East-West politics. The censure of the world medical community forced the Soviets to concede on a humanitarian issue which they knew would further their national interests.

Chapter 25

The Iron Gates Begin to Part

Gorbachev's policies of economic reform, openness and limited democratization were accompanied by an administrative decree that was implemented on January 1, 1987. Known as the "new law," it outlined rules for obtaining emigration visas.

This decree stated that the classification of "secrecy" could be lifted after five years. This brought hope to long-term refuseniks. It also limited eligibility for emigration to those with "blood relatives of the first-degree" living abroad. This brought despair to many others. Ninety per cent of the four hundred thousand Jews who had indicated their desire to leave would not qualify.[1]

The law also specified that all applications for emigration must include a notarized waiver from family members left behind, absolving the potential emigré of his or her financial responsibility for them. Since family members rarely signed the waiver, a new type of refusenik emerged. Dubbed the "poor relative," this person was not even able to apply.

For Ida Nudel, the news was heartening. Sixteen years had passed since she had worked in her profession. Legally, she could no longer be refused on grounds of secrecy. Furthermore, she had a sister living in Israel.

Nudel was featured in the January 1987 issue of *Orah*, the magazine of Canadian Hadassah-Wizo. "These actions mean everything," she told Hadassah members who called her in Bendery from their national convention. "Public demonstrations by world Jewry provide refuseniks with a primary means of protection from more drastic Soviet action."[2]

Moscow mathematician Alexander Ioffe decided to challenge the new emigration law. Refused repeatedly for reasons of secrecy since 1976, Ioffe commenced a hunger strike when his son Dimitry applied with his wife and young daughter and received his first refusal. The young couple was refused on the grounds that they had "no close family members abroad."

Ioffe cabled Mikhail Gorbachev. "This refusal is ridiculous. My wife and I have been trying to leave the USSR for over ten years and have been consistently refused. How could our son possibly have close family members abroad?"[3] Gorbachev did not respond. "A hunger strike," declared the older Ioffe, "is the only means I have now at my disposal."[4]

Ioffe had endeared himself to many Canadian activists who had visited him in Moscow and who now supported his decision to fast. During a cross-country conference call, regional Soviet Jewry chairmen agreed to maintain continuous telephone contact with Ioffe during his hunger strike and elicit the support of Canadian academics.[5]

The cross-Canada calls came to Ioffe in rapid sucession on January 11, 1987, the first day of his fast. "I am deeply touched by all of your support," he told them. "I hope with all my heart that we shall succeed. Today has been Canada Day. There have been so many calls."[6] Canadian support was further exemplified when Mary Mosser, a counsellor with the Canadian Embassy in Moscow, visited Ioffe in his apartment on January 14. She found him physically fit and in reasonable spirits.[7]

The heads of the mathematics departments of fourteen Canadian universities sent cables to Soviet officials and to the chairman of the Soviet Academy of Sciences.[8] Petitions addressed to Gorbachev were circulated in the science departments on each campus. "Through this difficult period," said Ioffe in an interview broadcast live on the CBC science program, "Quirks and Quarks," "it is the encouragement of all my friends abroad that is sustaining me."[9]

Canadian requests for a visa to Israel for Ioffe's son flooded the Kremlin's offices. Nobel laureate Gerhard Herzberg joined the campaign. "When is the Soviet government going to learn that the whole stalemate in arms control hinges on a change in the observance of human rights in the Soviet Union?" asked Herzberg in a statement to the press. "I call on them to learn and to give the Ioffe family the right to leave."[10]

By the third week of his hunger strike, Ioffe was suffering severe headaches but he continued his fast, surviving on hot water alone. "My only demand is that my son and his family be allowed to go to Israel," reiterated Ioffe. "There is no law or morality behind the refusal to give them such a possibility."[11] Nineteen days after he began his hunger strike, the chief secretary of the Academy of Sciences, Georgyi Scriavin, telephoned the mathematician and informed him that Dimitry and his family would receive their visas. Eight months later, Alexander Ioffe, his wife and daughter were given permission to leave and the family was reunited in Israel.[12]

Hunger strikes were considered to be the last resort for most refuseniks. They were effective only if publicity was generated in the West. Former prisoner Lev Elbert and his wife Inna had been waiting for exit visas for eleven years. When they began a hunger strike in Kiev, members of B'nai Brith's Wilson Heights Lodge staged a rotating hunger strike in Toronto.[13] Parallel hunger strikes took place in many other countries. The Elberts ended their fast only after they were assured that their file would be reviewed by the Supreme Soviet.

The changes occurring in major Soviet cities found their way to Chistopol Prison. Newspapers were made available to inmate Yosef Begun and officials from the procurator general's office came to meet with him on a regular basis. "I was told that the Soviet government would release me if I agreed to sign a statement saying that once freed, I would not repeat my crime of becoming involved with anti-Soviet activity," recalled Begun. "I refused, insisting that my activity had never been anti-Soviet."[14]

The prisoners were released from Chistopol one at a time. Begun was one of the few who remained. He was continually asked to request a pardon. He refused, vowing that the only statement he would make was that if released, he would continue to work to establish rights for a national culture for Soviet Jews.

On February 20, 1987, after having served four-and-one-half years of a thirteen-year sentence, including two hundred days in isolation, Yosef Begun was released. He was the only Jew who had served three separate terms in the Soviet gulag. As his train pulled into Kazan Station in Moscow, Begun was greeted by a crowd of friends singing Hebrew songs. They pressed flowers into his arms and hoisted him onto their shoulders, dancing joyfully on the platform.[15] "It is my dream to be with my people in Israel," Begun affirmed, "and I will continue to fight for Jewish cultural identity in the Soviet Union as I have for sixteen years, until such time that the right to emigrate will be mine."[16]

Begun's release from prison was cause for optimism, until he applied to register as a Hebrew teacher. His application was rejected. "Refuseniks are still treated as traitors," reported Begun in a telephone call to Israel, "and due to the new emigration law, the problems have multiplied. There is 'openness' for other cultures, but not for Jews."[17]

The new emigration restrictions that prohibited "poor relatives" from applying for emigration visas were met with protests in the West. Vigils were held in Vancouver, Victoria, Edmonton, Calgary, Saskatoon, Winnipeg, London, Toronto and Montreal. "Tonight, Jews in Canada are linked hand in hand to show support for Soviet Jewry," said Stephen Granovsky, a student organizer of the Winnipeg gathering that had brought people of all ages to the Jewish Community Centre. Students from Joseph Wolinsky Collegiate, Winnipeg's Jewish high school, dressed as prisoners and held candles in the darkened auditorium.[18]

The guest speaker was Moshe Ronen, a Toronto lawyer and longtime student activist, who had recently returned from the Soviet Union. "In order to talk to a friend who comes to visit," Ronen told them, "you have go outside to a park and hope that somebody from the KGB is not waiting for you there. We were stopped on several occasions, right on the street, and warned: 'no more visits.'" He spoke of a man, a "poor relative," whose former wife, whom he had not seen in ten years, had refused to sign the financial waiver. This action alone removed any possibility for him to emigrate. "I hope the West can see through Moscow's public relations as fig leaves to cover naked oppression,"[19] said Ronen.

On March 8, International Women's Day, a newly formed refusenik group, Jewish Women Against Refusal (JEWAR), staged a three-day hunger strike in private apartments. JEWAR was made up of seventy women from Moscow, Leningrad, Kiev, Odessa, Kishinev, Riga and Minsk. Through their collective action, the women hoped to convince Western governments that thousands of Soviet Jews were still waiting for exit visas.

"More than ten years have passed since we first applied to emigrate," began the JEWAR women's message. "Since that time we have been ousted from the social and communal life of society into the murky waters of an anti-Israel and anti-Zionist propaganda campaign. Almost all of us and our husbands are deprived of the right to work in our professional fields. We have suffered from acts of harassment yet we have never violated law and order. Our efforts to raise our children and educate them in the spirit of Jewish national traditions have been utterly defeated. Have we no right to reunify with our own people? Please save us and our children."[20]

The pressure continued. Judith Bloom, educational co-ordinator of CJC's Committee for Soviet Jewry, Ontario Region, along with Roz Lewis and director Ben Prossin, accompanied fourteen junior high school students from Toronto's Hebrew day schools on a train bound for Ottawa. The students brought with them bags filled with eight thousand letters addressed to Ambassador Rodionov. The letters pleaded for the release of the JEWAR refuseniks and their children.

At the House of Commons, MP Bill Attewell met with the students and accompanied them to a meeting with Prime Minister Brian Mulroney. From there they went to the Soviet Embassy, where they fully expected to leave their bags of letters outside the gate. The delegation was surprised to be invited inside to meet with the ambassador and First Secretary Choupin. The Soviet officials listened to the students' plea for the long-term refuseniks, accepted their letters and posed with them for photographs.[21] The fact that an open and frank dialogue had taken place was an indication of change.

In April, a delegation of Jewish leaders, led by National Conference on Soviet Jewry chairman Morris Abram and World Jewish Congress president Edgar Bronfman, travelled to Moscow to raise the cases of long-standing refuseniks with Soviet officials.[22] The Soviets agreed to review the list of eleven thousand Jews who had been denied emigration for five years or more and spoke openly about the possibility of resuming diplomatic relations with Israel.[23] Konstantin Karchev, the minister of religious affairs, assured the leaders that more synagogues would be opened, that Jewish books would be imported and that emigration would increase.

Although Abrams and Bronfman were optimistic, most activists remained skeptical, believing that Kremlin officials were appeasing Western leaders in anticipation of the superpower summit to be held in Moscow in June. After a few months passed, the skeptics were proven correct. Although the emigration figures had escalated slightly, the obstacles for applying to leave had yet to be removed.[24]

Refuseniks were beginning to feel confident that they could move about without fear of reprisal. This made it possible for many to accept an invitation to participate in a Passover seder at the American Embassy.[25] The presence at the seder table of Secretary of State George Shultz, who had flown to Moscow for the event, affirmed the U.S. government's commitment to freedom of Jewish observance in the Soviet Union. That evening, the traditional Passover refrain "Next year in Jerusalem" was adapted by the refuseniks to, "This year in Jerusalem."

There were other visible changes. Jews from across the Soviet Union stood in line for hours at an Israeli booth at the Moscow Book Fair, waiting for the opportunity to buy Jewish books and to view videotapes of Israel. Another change was not a positive one. It was the emergence of Pamyat, an ultra-nationalistic, chauvinistic organization whose anti-Semitic invective was reminiscent of Czarist days. Pamyat held public anti-Semitic meetings unimpeded by the State, which caused profound concern among the Jewish population.[26] The same *glasnost* that had eased some constraints and provided new opportunities for dialogue also allowed reactionary organizations to flourish.

The Soviet Jewry movement continued to attract new advocates. Canadian industrialist and real estate developer Albert Reichmann visited Moscow in the spring of 1987. During talks with high-level Soviet officials about prospective business deals, Reichmann, an orthodox Jew, made clear his intention to meet with members of the Soviet Jewish religious community. He was taken to refuseniks' apartments by a driver from the Canadian Embassy.

Reichmann's continued association with the observant refusenik community contributed to the growth of orthodoxy among Soviet Jews. He played a leading role in the establishment of the first legal academy of Talmudic and Jewish studies and was instrumental in securing the release of the Rais family of Vilnius, who had been waiting for visas since 1972.[27]

CJC president Dorothy Reitman, her husband Cyril, MP David Berger and his wife Monica, and Edward Bronfman visited with refuseniks of long-standing on their trip to Moscow and Leningrad in August 1987. They found their meeting with Dr. Lerner in his Moscow apartment to be an extraordinary experience. In his late seventies, Lerner was indeed growing old in the Soviet Jewry movement, yet his optimism and hope that he would be repatriated to his homeland and reunited with his daughter never left him.

A trip to the Soviet Union by Professor Henry H. Weinberg inspired him to appeal to me, as co-chairman of the Committee for Soviet Jewry, Ontario Region, to co-ordinate a campaign for Yuli Edelshtein. Edelshtein, the young Hebrew teacher who had been arrested on charges of alleged possession of drugs, had sustained serious injuries in a labour camp accident. When I asked Selma Edelstone, experienced in humanitarian causes, if she and her husband Gordon would help their "cousin" Yuli, she responded, "We have no cousin in Russia, but come over and we'll talk about it."

"Edelsteins for Edelshtein" was created that evening. Every

Edelstone, Edelstein, Edelshteyn, Edelshtein and Edelson family in Toronto was invited to Selma and Gordon Edelstone's home for a "family" meeting. Fifteen members of the "Edelstein clan" met, most for the first time, and pledged to work for their adopted cousin. Each new relative sent telegrams to Soviet officials demanding Yuli's release. They also appealed to their MPs to lobby on his behalf. Concerned about Yuli's health in Siberia, the Canadian cousins purchased a down-filled parka and sent it to him with a Toronto traveller.[28]

A CBC cameraman and a reporter came to the second family gathering to film a story about the Edelshtein connection for the local news. Four months later, the crew returned to record a celebration party on the day of Yuli's release from prison.[29] The Toronto "Edelshtein family" sent cables of appreciation to Soviet officials with one last request – a visa to Israel for Yuli Edelshtein.[30]

Ten months after they first heard about Yuli, the former prisoner was welcomed to the Edelstone home by the whole "family." "So many relatives all at once," Yuli joked. "A call came and you answered it. Some people don't believe that activities like this can be of any help. Without this movement of ordinary people, without public demonstrations, we wouldn't have had a chance."[31]

In the fall of 1987, after lobbying for four years for the release of the Vasilevsky family, members of Holy Blossom Temple in Toronto felt the euphoria of victory. Anatoly and Natasha Vasilevsky received their visas. A few months later, the couple visited Toronto and Anatoly spoke from the pulpit one Shabbat morning. Choked with emotion, he affirmed, "I believe that one temple in Canada kept my family safe."[32]

The Vasilevskys' freedom inspired Holy Blossom Temple to adopt the Klotz family of Moscow, and when they received visas, the committee adopted another. A total of twelve refusenik families were adopted by this temple during a ten-year period.[33] A handful of members kept abreast of their families' needs through direct telephone calls or through contact with activists in other countries.[34]

Holy Blossom Temple developed its own travel program to the Soviet Union, subsidized by their Russian Family Fund.[35] Their senior rabbi, Dow Marmur, was highly supportive of the program and encouraged the assistant and associate rabbis to participate. "The four trips we took were important to the success of our adoption program," said Marsha Slivka, who led each, "because that is where our refuseniks and our twins came from. We would return from a trip and call a synagogue president or committee chairman and say, "We've just met the most wonderful family. You must help them."[36]

Eleven Toronto synagogues focused on refusenik adoptions.[37] Their Soviet Jewry committees formed a "synagogue support group" as a sub-committee of the Ontario Region's committee, that Slivka chaired. It was after a trip to the Soviet Union by Rabbi Harvey Meirovich of Beth Sholom Synagogue and Cantor Eliezer Kirshblum of Adath Israel, that the Ontario Rabbi's Council for Soviet Jewry was formed, with Meirovich as chairman. Its task was to validate and promote new activity among the already existing committees in many of the synagogues and to sensitize non-participating rabbis.

By then, Adopt-a-Family programs were in place in many Canadian communities and ideas were often shared. Congregation Beth Tikvah in Dollard des Ormeaux, Quebec, designated a chair on their *bima* that remained empty for their adopted refusenik, Vladimir Shakhnovsky, until he was freed. At Adath Israel in Toronto, attention was drawn to an antique chair that also remained empty, until Lev Furman of Leningrad received his visa, visited Toronto and sat in "his chair."[38]

Ida Nudel's requests for a visa continued to be denied. On her fifty-sixth birthday, MPPs and Soviet Jewry activists crammed into a large committee room at Queen's Park in Toronto for the presentation of the seventh Ida Nudel Humanitarian Award – this time, to MP Barbara McDougall.[39] Many people who were present that afternoon had witnessed each of the previous six award ceremonies. They agonized over the fact that the woman in whose name the award had been created was still a hostage of the Soviet government.

Nudel had sent a message to the gathering through Jeanette Goldman, who had spoken with her from Bendery a few days earlier. "I was forty when I first applied for an exit visa. Will I ever again celebrate a birthday with my family?"[40]

After a few brief remarks by the three Legislature Committee for Soviet Jewry co-chairmen,[41] Marsha Slavens, co-chairman of the Ontario Region's committee, described McDougall as "devoted, determined and compassionate" for her commitment to Soviet Jewry, specifically, her endeavours on behalf of two Kishinev refuseniks.

McDougall responded to the honour saying, "After meeting Leonid Vainshtein's and Mark Polansky's wives in Jerusalem, I was struck by how wearing it is to live in limbo, not knowing whether your family would ever be a family in the normal sense again. There is a sense of death about that kind of long separation because the capacity to rebuild one's family once it is reunited is diminished enormously."[42] Paying tribute to the long-time supporters of Soviet Jewry, she said, "It's not what we give to Soviet Jews by helping, it's really what they give to us by their courage, warmth, spirit and their hope. It is we who are in their debt."[43]

On May 5, 1987, the Lester B. Pearson Building in Ottawa was the venue for a Soviet Jewry symposium. Delegates from nine Canadian cities[44] gathered to discuss policy and strategy in the light of changes in the USSR. Historian Martin Gilbert presented a report on the current state of the refusenik community and other speakers provided accounts of Soviet intransigence in long-term refusenik cases.[45] Delegates were urged to increase pressure until the Soviet government's deeds paralleled their words.

Changes were becoming visible. The Soviet Union's first step toward re-establishing diplomatic ties with Israel began in the summer of 1987 when a Soviet consular delegation leased space in a high-rise apartment building in Tel Aviv. In September, former prisoners Yosef Begun, Victor Brailovsky, Vladimir Lifshitz, Lev Elbert and long-term refuseniks Aba Taratuta and Vladimir Prestin all received exit visas.

Within days, Alexei Magarik, the last prisoner to be sentenced, was released after having served only half of his term, and twenty members of the poor relatives group were told by OVIR to submit applications for exit visas, despite the fact that they lacked financial waivers.[46]

"It's a gift to George Shultz on the eve of the preliminary pre-summit meeting in Washington with Shevardnadze," said the less-fortunate Vladimir Slepak, on the phone from Moscow to Tel Aviv. The remaining core of veteran refuseniks hoped that their turn would come after the summit talks, scheduled to take place at the end of the year in Washington.

"Beware of these gestures" was the warning to Canadian audiences and government leaders by Natan Sharansky during his whirlwind visit to Montreal, Ottawa and Toronto in September 1987, timed to coincide with Shevardnadze's pre-summit meetings with Shultz in Washington. "Gorbachev is aware that the Soviet economy is urgently in need of reform. Major changes will occur if the West is firm in its demands of linking human rights to arms limitations."[47]

Canadian activists had waited for seven months to greet Sharansky. "You are a symbol of hope for all others," said Barbara Stern, introducing the former prisoner to the thousands who packed Shaar Hashomayim Synagogue in Montreal, "and we shall not let down our efforts on their behalf."[48] When describing his experiences, Sharansky remarked, "Day after day the officials tried to convince me that the world had changed, that I had to compromise. In order to cope with my fear I convinced myself that between me and the KGB there was a war – but between me and Jews there was no war."[49]

Sharansky was the inaugural speaker at the Natan Sharansky Lectureship in Human Rights at McGill University Law School and guest of honour at a luncheon attended by judges, lawyers, professors and former prime minister Pierre Trudeau. The event marked the tenth anniversary of Avital Sharansky's address to the same gathering.

In Ottawa, Sharansky met with political leaders of all three parties and greeted a capacity crowd at Beth Shalom Synagogue.[50] When Parliament convened that afternoon, Speaker of the House, John Fraser, paid tribute to the man whose name had been mentioned countless times in those chambers.

The moment was electric. Eyes were drawn upward to the speakers gallery where Sharansky sat with several of his supporters, and, as if on cue, the members of the House of Commons rose to their feet to deliver a five-minute ovation for the man who had come to the nation's capital to express his thanks.[51]

That evening, Massey Hall in Toronto was filled to overflowing.[52] As Sharansky walked onto the stage, the audience rose and delivered a resounding chorus of *Haveinu Shalom Alecheim*. "How sweet and fitting it is when we can come together in unity," said Irwin Cotler in his opening remarks. "You can feel it here this evening, the moral power of solidarity in a just cause, inspired by the courage and commitment of Natan Sharansky, a true hero of our time, at a time when there are so few heroes."[53] The Doctor of Laws degree, conferred upon Sharansky in absentia five years earlier, was presented by Harry Arthurs, president of York University.

The introduction of the celebrated prisoner that evening briefly traced the history of Toronto's involvement with him and concluded, "Natan Sharansky, we were with you in prison, in labour camps, in isolation cells. We were with you when your only companions were hunger and frost. For nine years you were never alone. We hope that you can feel the ocean of love that envelops you this evening."[54]

Sharansky approached the microphone to more cheers and applause. He spoke of his years in captivity and of how he was fortified by the knowledge of non-stop activity on his behalf. The audience was charmed by his humour, warmth and infectious smile. "You have proven with your protests," he told them, "that an army of students and housewives is much stronger than the KGB."

Sharansky reminded the audience that the Soviets' human rights record was much worse under Gorbachev than under Brezhnev. Only eight thousand Jews would receive visas by the end of 1987, compared to more than fifty-one thousand in 1979. "Don't be blinded by Gorbachev's dazzle," he cautioned them. "The gap between perception and reality has never been greater."[55]

Sharansky encouraged supporters to carry on. "Our voices must still be heard. We must insist upon observance by the Soviet Union of its human rights undertakings, including the unrestricted option of emigration for every Soviet Jew. We cannot waste this golden opportunity. Every Jew in Canada has the chance to play a part in this historic struggle. Let us prove that the fate of Soviet Jews is in our hands."[56]

Natan Sharansky was living proof of the words spoken by Irwin Cotler so often during Sharansky's captivity, "The struggle for human rights will ultimately prevail over those who attempt to repress them."[57]

On October 2, Ida Nudel travelled to Moscow to meet friends who were still trying to restore her residency permit there. Each trip from Bendery was fraught with anxiety, for on several occasions she had been forcibly ejected from the bus by KGB officials. When she reached the apartment of her friend Judith Ratner she was told, "A call has just come from Bendery with the news. You have a visa!"

Nudel telephoned Rudolf Kuznetsov at OVIR. "You have a visa," he assured her, "return to Moldavia immediately." She called her sister in Israel, "Ilana, I have a visa. I just found out five minutes ago from Kuznetsov. I believe it's for real. I have a visa!"[58]

Less than two weeks later, Ida Nudel stepped into the private Boeing 727 jetliner of Armand Hammer. The U.S. industrialist was becoming a veteran in arranging the release of prominent refuseniks. Three weeks earlier, when Eduard Shevardnadze had asked him to fly to Afghanistan to assist in settling the armed conflict there, Hammer had agreed. "But you must give me Ida Nudel in return," he explained. Shevardnadze responded, "I promise."[59]

Four hours after the plane took off, the pilot announced, "In five minutes we will arrive at Ben-Gurion Airport. The crew and I congratulate Ida Nudel on her return to her homeland." Hammer and his wife cracked opened a bottle of champagne and together with Nudel toasted the start of her new life.[60]

When the plane landed, Ilana Fridman stepped inside for an emotional reunion with the sister she had not seen in sixteen years. "Those years seem to have flown by in a minute," remarked Nudel, "and at the same time to have crawled like an eternity."[61] She descended the steps of the jetliner into blinding floodlights and throngs of people. At her side was her collie, Pizer, who had been her companion during her exile. She embraced her long-time friend Anatoly Sharansky. They hugged one another and wept in wordless disbelief. Nudel and Sharansky had planned strategies together in

Moscow many years before. Each had paid a tremendous price for freedom. At last they were both home, in Israel.

Encircled by her family, Israeli leaders and a jubilant Jane Fonda, Ida Nudel expressed her feelings that were broadcast by satellite to networks across the world. "A few hours ago, I was almost a slave in Moscow. Now I am a free woman in my own country. It is the moment of my life. I am home in the soul of the Jewish people."[62]

Suddenly, a telephone was handed to her on the tarmac. It was George Shultz calling from Washington. He had met Nudel on one of his frequent trips to Moscow and had worked diligently to help secure her release. "I'm home, I'm home," she told him. "Thank you, for this moment of my life."[63]

A few days later, a gathering was held in Nudel's honour at Binyanei Ha'ouma in Jerusalem where three thousand new immigrants had come to extend their welcome. Nudel took her place at the microphone and, over waves of resounding applause, responded to their warm welcome in English.

"*Olim Hadashim* (new immigrants),"[64] she began, "all of us share the same experience – to be cut off from one society and to establish ourselves in another. It has been a long road for many Soviet Jews from Russia to Israel. Many died on their way. Sharansky went through nightmares. My life also wasn't easy. But not for one moment in sixteen years did I ever reject the idea of going to Israel, despite all I went through. I congratulate all of us. We succeeded, we won! For me, this has been a personal victory which I owe to my family and to the thousands of Jews and Christians who stood behind me, supporting my resistance."

She spoke of the many difficulties facing immigrants in a new country and appealed to her audience to have patience. "If you have problems, don't write bad letters to friends," she told them. "Come to me, I'll help you."[65]

Chapter 26

The Reality of Glasnost

At the National Conference on Soviet Jewry leadership assembly held in Washington in October 1987, a group of Canadian activists joined their American peers to assess the changing situation in the USSR. They were there, as well, to discuss strategies for the upcoming East-West summit meetings, the date of which had yet to be announced.[1]

Of particular interest to the delegates were assurances made by Frank Carlucci, assistant to the president for National Security Affairs and Ambassador Rozanne Ridgeway, assistant secretary of state for European affairs. "This administration is committed to freedom of religion," declared Carlucci, "and our obligation to the movement of Soviet Jews becomes undiminished." Ridgeway, who was to accompany George Shultz to Moscow the following week for pre-summit talks with Shevardnadze, announced, "Shultz goes off to Moscow next week with human rights the equal of arms control." Three hundred delegates rose at their seats and responded with sustained applause.[2]

On October 15, in what was thought of as a pre-summit manoeuvre, the Soviets announced the release of Vladimir Slepak. His square-cut beard was now totally grey, one indication that sixteen years had passed, yet his eyes danced with youthful elation as he and his wife arrived at Ben-Gurion Airport. "It is not for nothing that the Jews are called the most optimistic people in the world," he announced to political leaders, reporters and loved ones who had gathered to meet him. "I have waited two thousand years for this moment."[3]

Within days of Slepak's arrival, a celebration in honour of his sixtieth birthday was held at President Chaim Herzog's residence. Slepak was surrounded by family and lifelong friends, and the peaceful look on his face suggested that memories and reality had merged into one.

Herzog paid tribute to Slepak as the father of the Soviet Jewry movement and presented a gift from the State of Israel in appreciation of his steadfast leadership in the Moscow refusenik community for seventeen years. In the midst of the festivities, the telephone rang. On the line was Alexander Lerner calling to extend his congratulations from Moscow. The call was a gnawing reminder that the struggle was not yet over.

On October 30, 1987, an announcement was made from the White House that U.S. President Ronald Reagan and Soviet Premier Mikhail Gorbachev would meet in Washington, December 7, 1987, to sign a treaty to eliminate the superpowers' arsenal of intermediate range nuclear weapons.

A coalition of every Jewish organization in the United States had been standing by for months, waiting to mobilize thousands of people for a mass demonstration in Washington. The date for the protest was set for the day before the Reagan/Gorbachev meetings. Canadian activists printed flyers appealing to their supporters, "Take the day off on Sunday, December 6 and come to Washington." Planes were chartered and demonstrators enlisted.

On the morning of December 6, Moscow activists took part in a hunger strike in Smolensky Square. Two dozen refuseniks were taken into police custody before they could reach the site and the few who did arrive were attacked by plainclothesmen. Peter Arnett, Cable News Network's Moscow bureau chief, who was filming the incident with his crewmen, was taken into custody and detained for two hours.[4]

In Tel Aviv, Israel, thousands attended a rally in a sports' stadium to hear President Chaim Herzog, Prime Minister Yitzhack Shamir and Foreign Minister Shimon Peres each express their hope that at last the Jews of the Soviet Union would be able to come home. The voice of veteran refusenik Yuli Kosharovky was carried by telephone from Moscow and amplified for all to hear. "In the era of *glasnost*," he declared, "we can see not only a great gap between the promises and our reality, but signs of a return to the previous situation."[5]

Five hundred Canadians from Montreal, Ottawa, Toronto, Winnipeg and Vancouver flew to Washington for the day.[6] At a pre-rally meeting held in a hotel, they were welcomed by Allan Gotlieb, Canada's ambassador to the United States. After messages from Canada's three political leaders were read aloud, Vladimir Slepak entered the room to a round of thunderous applause. His very presence represented the culmination of years of struggle by many men and women in that room, who had come to Washington to share a precious moment.

Bearing placards that read like a road map of the United States and Canada, supporters marched down Constitution Avenue to Capitol Hill until two hundred thousand people were assembled on the ellipse south of the White House. The Canadians were distinguishable by their white wool tuques, imprinted with a red maple leaf and the word "Canada."[7]

It was a day of cheers and tears as MP Bill Attewell, Nobel laureate Elie Wiesel and Vice-President George Bush, along with other American dignitaries, delivered messages of hope for a positive result of the summit meeting. NCSJ president Morris Abram read a statement by President Reagan, emphasizing that "refuseniks" would be the "unseen guests" at his side during his talks with Gorbachev. During the two-hour rally, most eyes were on Ida Nudel, Yuli Edelshtein, Vladimir Slepak and Anatoly Sharansky, all former Prisoners of Zion, who collectively were the symbol of consummate victory.

The East-West summit that began the following morning provided an important opportunity for constructive dialogue. It concluded with the signing of a treaty to eliminate medium-range nuclear missiles and an announcement by Gorbachev of a timetable for the withdrawal of Soviet troops from Afghanistan. No statements were made on the subject of human rights. Although 1987 had seen the list of prisoners reduced to zero, and many prominent refuseniks beginning new lives in Israel, the 8,155 Jews that had emigrated that year, represented only 15 per cent of the 1979 emigration figure, and was a mere fraction of the total number of Jews who sought to leave. There were gestures and promises, but no results.

On January 20, 1988, it was Yosef Begun descended the gangway from an El Al airplane at Ben-Gurion Airport into the gaze of hundreds of friends, political leaders and journalists who gathered around him in joyous welcome. Immediately, a burly, bearded Israeli soldier, carrying a machine gun stepped forward and embraced the former prisoner. Begun appeared embarrassed and confused. "Yosef, don't you recognize me?" the young man asked. "We were in prison together in Matroskaya Tishina." It triggered an instant memory. He was the artist who had illustrated Begun's first lectures on Jewish history in 1977. The young man had taken Begun's advice. After serving his brief prison sentence, he visited Begun's friends in Moscow, joined the activist movement and applied for a visa to emigrate.[8]

In February 1987, Professor Irwin Cotler was one of nineteen members of the International Helsinki Federation for Human Rights to attend meetings in Moscow. During the course of the meetings, Cotler and a few other delegates met with Soviet justice minister Boris Kravtsov, who assured them that abuses in the emigration process had ended. The information that Cotler gleaned during visits with the refuseniks disputed this claim.

"The situation in the USSR is full of contradictions," reported Cotler upon his return to Canada. "The Soviets have put the refuseniks in the centre of a pincers movement, requiring notarized permission from a first-degree relative abroad on one hand, and consent from members of the family in the USSR on the other. If they don't catch you with that, then they catch you with the 'state secrets' nonsense."[9] Declaring that *glasnost* was nothing but a "charm offensive," Cotler announced the establishment of *Interamicus*, an international consortium of lawyers who were prepared to fight for the legal rights of Soviet Jews. Their caseload consisted of three hundred families, all of whom had been refused exit visas for a minimum of five years.

"We wish to seek official affiliation of our group with *Interamicus*," were the introductory words of a letter to Cotler written by Yuli Kosharovsky in Moscow. A radio engineer by profession, Kosharovsky had endured seventeen years of refusals for reasons of "state secrecy" in a job he had left in 1968. "As your affiliate in the USSR, we would undertake to provide you with information on the issues of legal and human rights within the Soviet Union, especially where emigration, family reunification, culture and religious and national rights are concerned."[10]

On March 6, International Women's Day, the JEWAR group gathered in apartments in nine Soviet cities to conduct their second annual three-day hunger strike.[11] A Canadian "telephone marathon of support" was organized for the refusenik women's group that had grown to 120 members.[12]

"Thank you for all the encouragement you have shown us during our hunger strike," said Judith Lurie to members of Toronto's Inter-Faith Council for Soviet Jewry on the third and final day. "We all hope that world-wide recognition will create the kind of pressure needed to secure our release."[13]

Two days later Yuli and Inna Kosharovsky embarked on a private hunger strike to mark their seventeenth year in refusal. They pleaded with Western politicians to support them. "We have wasted our adult lives in a fruitless struggle with a heartless bureaucratic machine," said Kosharovsky, in a world-wide appeal.[14]

The signatures of two hundred members of the Canadian Parliamentary Group for Soviet Jewry filled a petition to Gorbachev, urging that Kosharovsky's situation be reviewed.[15] The Kosharovskys ended their fast a few days later, after being notified that their case was "in the process of examination."[16]

The Toronto Jewish Women's Federation (JWF), the umbrella organization representing twenty-thousand Jewish women from more than fifty volunteer groups, was presented with the case of refusenik Elena Keis of Leningrad.

Keis's saga had begun in 1974 when her sister Anna Rosnovsky, a gifted violinist, was forbidden to take her three-hundred-year-old violin with her when she emigrated to Israel. Their mother, Meita Leikina, arranged for a Yugoslavian musician to enter the Soviet Union with a worthless violin, swap it for Anna's, take the cherished instrument out of the country and send it to Anna in Israel. Leikina wrote to her daughter in Tel Aviv saying that the violin was on its way. The letter was intercepted by the KGB. Leikina was arrested, charged with trafficking in contraband, brought to trial and sentenced to prison.

After a year in isolation, Leikina was sent to a penal institution for the mentally ill and given mind-altering drugs that caused irreversible brain damage. After her release in 1978, she received permission to emigrate to Israel. She was too ill to be cared for by her daughter and was placed in a nursing home in Israel.

Elena Keis and her husband Giorgi Kuna had waited until five years had expired from their previous engineering jobs before applying for a visa. During that time, Giorgi drove a truck to support the family and Elena studied and taught Hebrew. Their first application was made in 1980 and was refused on grounds of secrecy. They reapplied every six months and received one refusal after another. Elena's communication with her sister Anna, who was a principal violinist with the Israel Philharmonic Orchestra, was through letters and infrequent telephone calls.

The Toronto Jewish Women's Federation announced their adoption of Elena Keis in their spring 1988 news bulletin *In Touch*, a supplement to *The Canadian Jewish News* that reached thousands of Jewish households in Toronto.[17] JWF's campaign to secure freedom for Elena Keis began with an international petition appeal to Eduard Shevardnadze. It was followed by a meeting with Ambassador Rodionov in Ottawa, where a delegation of women made a personal plea for Keis's release.[18]

Changes in Soviet policy made it possible for all denominations of Judaism to flourish in the USSR. Visitors from abroad came to teach the traditions of liberal Judaism to members of *Hineini,* the founding congregation of the reform movement. Although Hineini was first established in Moscow under the leadership of Zinovy Kogan, sister congregations were emerging in many Soviet cities.

Rabbi Richard Hirsch, director of the World Union of Progressive Judaism in Jerusalem, led a group of North American Reform Jewish leaders to the Soviet Union to assist Hineini's fledgling leadership.

Among them was Rabbi Jordan Pearlson, spiritual leader of Temple Sinai in Toronto, who was accompanied by Temple Sinai's president Austin Beutel and his wife, Nani, chairman of Temple Sinai's Soviet Jewry committee.

That times had changed was undisputed, especially for the Beutels whose first trip to the Soviet Union had taken place during the 1972 Canada-USSR hockey games. "Then, we couldn't even talk with Soviet Jews," recalled Nani Beutel, "but this time, many refuseniks joined our group at our Moscow hotel for a traditional Shabbat dinner."[19]

The easing of restrictions in issuing travel visas to Western activists allowed plans for a CJC-sponsored mission to the USSR, in April 1988, to move forward. The participants were Irving Abella, professor of history at York University, Robert Fulford, journalist and former editor of *Saturday Night,* Conservative MP John Oostrom, and The Reverend John Erb, spiritual leader of St. Michael and All Angels Church and chairman of the Toronto Inter-Faith Council for Soviet Jewry. I was planning to lead the delegation, but lost hope of doing so when my visa was denied six weeks before the scheduled departure date. It was the intervention by officials from the Department of External Affairs, that caused the Soviets to reverse their decision.[20]

Upon arrival at Moscow's Sheremetyevo airport we were greeted by Mary Mosser of the Canadian Embassy, who informed us that she had arranged a meeting with Konstantin Karchev, the Soviet chairman of religious affairs. "The bureaucrat Karchev was not only generous with his time," explained Robert Fulford to Ambassador and Mrs. Vernon Turner during lunch at the Canadian Embassy two days later, "but also with his rhetoric, jargon, pretensions and several other things that normally go under extremely impolite names. While Karchev sprayed the room with those two great iconic power words of the Gorbachev era, *glasnost* and *perestroika*, fifty refuseniks, who were demonstrating peacefully outside the Central Committee headquarters, were arrested and held for six hours with no food or toilet facilities."[21]

The old generation of Sharanskys, Nudels, Beguns and Slepaks had been replaced by new heroes of the Soviet Jewry movement – Kosharovsky, Cherniak, Kislik, Uspensky, Lurie, Keis, Elbert, Rais. "These new refusenik leaders are as passionate, as idealistic, as courageous, as dedicated as those who came before them," remarked Irving Abella, "and they have the added advantage of having learned at the feet of their masters."[22]

The resurgence of Jewish life in the USSR was viewed differently by the Jews who wanted to leave and those who wanted to stay. The refuseniks, led by Yuli Kosharovsky, believed that in order to enjoy a full Jewish life there was no choice but to emigrate. Ethnographer Mikhail Chlenov, who headed the Jewish cultural group, believed that if Jews were able express their Jewish identity within the USSR, they would have no reason to leave.

The two men displayed their differences openly. Kosharovsky argued, "A Jew will never feel comfortable in the Soviet Union. *Aliyah* is the only answer." Chlenov vowed, "I will fight for cultural rights for Jews. One day, there will be a strong Jewish Diaspora right here."

Our small group joined three hundred Moscow Jews on a strip of muddy road outside the Jewish cemetery to pay tribute to the memory of the victims of the Holocaust. Buses filled with KGB plainsclothesmen were parked forty-five metres away. Some of the officers photographed and videotaped the proceedings, while others patrolled the area. Large blocks of granite served as a dais for leaders to deliver speeches about the Holocaust.

The only English-language address was made by Irving Abella, whose remarks were translated into Russian by Mikhail Chlenov, sentence by sentence. "As we stand here this afternoon, we remember many things," Abella began. "We remember an entire generation lost to us. We remember the children who never knew laughter or joy. We remember the remarkable talents destroyed by the Nazis, a vibrant culture snuffed out. We remember the dynamic Jewish communities of Europe, forever destroyed . . . But let us remember something else. Let us remember the indifference of the Western world which made the Holocaust possible. The Nazis planned and carried out the murder of six million Jews, but the killings, the gassings were allowed to take place because of the apathy of the world's democracies."[23] The Moscow Jews nodded their heads. Between the lines Abella had articulated Western Jewry's steadfast commitment to the liberation of Soviet Jewry.

While I accompanied John Oostrom and Yuli Kosharovsky to the Canadian Embassy for a meeting with the Ambassador, the other three joined Judith Lurie for a demonstration at the Lenin Library. At 6:00 PM, fifteen refuseniks emerged from the subway station. Some wore large yellow Stars of David pinned to their chests and others held small Israeli flags. Lurie wore a home-made banner over her jacket. The demonstrators climbed the steps of the library before about a dozen bystanders. Within minutes the Jews were surrounded by burly men, shoved down the stairs and loaded into two waiting buses. As the buses moved off into traffic, Irving Abella called out, "*Glasnost.*" A plainclothesman standing beside him responded with "*Glasnost* Soviet style."

"*Glasnost* Soviet style" followed us to the railroad station as we boarded car number 18 for an overnight train ride to Leningrad. A stranger appeared, looking for "Mr. Otello." We pleaded ignorance. The name "Otello" was close enough to "Abella" for us to realize that the Holocaust speech at the Jewish cemetery had been noted by the authorities.

There were lighter moments. In Leningrad, we joined a celebration at Lev Furman's flat. After fourteen years of refusals, harassments and threats of arrest, Furman had finally received a visa. He was leaving for Israel the next morning with his aged father, his wife Marina and their baby daughter, whose name, Aliyah, was symbolic of her parents' longing for Israel. "Aliyah, has had her last bath in Leningrad," said Marina. "Her next bath will be in the Mediterranean Sea."

Glasnost had not benefitted Elena Keis, whose applications to emigrate to Israel were still denied on grounds of secrecy. The petite, dynamic woman, given to laughter and warm hospitality, welcomed us into her living room filled with her refusenik friends. Every person's story was different, yet each had a common thread – application, refusal, loss of job, harassments, more applications, more refusals, frustration, despair.

Elena related her painful history that began with the violin and continued with the ongoing agony of being separated from her family. The latest blow was that her seventeen-year-old son Andrei, despite his superior academic achievement, had not been accepted into university. This meant he was likely to be drafted into the navy on his eighteenth birthday. After serving two years, Andrei would be considered a security risk for another seven, making the family ineligible for emigration for at least another nine years.

"Elena writes beautiful poetry," said one of her friends. "She writes about our feelings – about what it's like to be a refusenik." After some coercion, Elena left the room and returned with a thin brown book. Leafing through the pages in Russian, her friend showed us poems about refusal, family separation and Elena's dream of living in Israel. Turning to her I said: "Elena, this book is going to get you out!"

Elena wrote an English introduction for her poetry and John Oostrom undertook to see that the little brown book left the Soviet Union in the Canadian diplomatic pouch.[24]

Before World War II, Vilna, Poland burgeoned with a rich Jewish culture. In 1988, the word "Getto" on an ancient wall in Vilnius was the only reminder of days past. Although the few thousand members of the Vilnius Jewish community were isolated, the refuseniks were becoming observant, influenced by their leaders Carmella and Vladimir Rais.

For most of their sixteen years in refusal, entry to the Rais's apartment was barred to visitors by the KGB, who were stationed in the flat below. Even during our visit, all conversations took place in whispered tones.[25] Carmella's paintings covered the walls of their small apartment. They were dramatic expressions of who she was and where she wanted to be. One depicted twelve people seated at an oval table on which rested a pair of candlesticks, a twisted bread and a goblet of wine. The Shabbat table seemed to move from the bright red pyramids in the bottom right corner of the painting toward ancient golden walls in the distance, as if fleeing Egyptian bondage to Jerusalem.

"*Glasnost* is nothing more than a deodorized dictatorship," declared Irving Abella at a press conference held at the Ontario Legislature upon our return. "It is a vastly successful public relations ploy that has managed to replace the refuseniks' struggle for human rights as the focus of media attention. *Glasnost* has left the plight of the religious and cultural refuseniks, the former prisoners, the poor relatives and the two women's groups in the background."[26] Abella implored Westerners to continue to lobby, protest and create innovative programs to further expose the plight of Soviet Jews.[27]

On the heels of the CJC-sponsored trip, Genya Intrator led fifteen members of Beth Tzedec Congregation in Toronto to Moscow, Leningrad and Kiev, where they made contact with refusenik leadership in each city and expressed their concerns to Soviet officials about long-term refuseniks and poor relatives.[28] Upon their return to Canada, the Beth Tzedec Soviet Jewry Committee prepared and submitted a brief to Joe Clark, with recommendations for action by the Canadian government.[29]

Refuseniks pinned their hopes on the Reagan-Gorbachev summit meeting, scheduled to take place in Moscow on May 29. In a letter sent in April 1988, Judith Lurie said, "Now that the summit talks are approaching, the refuseniks want to press upon the Soviet authorities and make them grant us exit visas. We are going to demonstrations but the authorities detain us, take us to police stations, and fine us. They don't imprison people for demonstrations now, but it can be changed at any moment. The situation is very unstable, so our mood is low."[30]

During five days of high-level talks, JEWAR members conducted a hunger strike. Six of the women were invited to meet President Reagan at the U.S. ambassador's residence. He assured them that his administration would continue to press for unimpeded emigration.[31] Richard Schifter, the assistant secretary of state for human rights and humanitarian affairs, who had accompanied the president to Moscow, presented the cases of many refuseniks to the Soviet authorities and was informed that twenty-eight families would soon be receiving exit visas.[32]

Schifter remained optimistic. Changes were occurring almost

daily. The first kosher restaurant opened in Moscow, an official Hebrew course was approved in Baku and a Jewish library was established in a private apartment in Leningrad. Some refuseniks had even been given tourist visas to travel abroad.

The possibility of receiving a tourist visa motivated Judith Lurie to visit her mother in Israel that summer. Before her three-week visa had expired, she left Israel for Washington to present her own case to American politicians.

Shirley Hanick, chairman of Holy Blossom Temple's Soviet Jewry committee, who had been advocating on Lurie's behalf for many years, accompanied her to the U.S. capital. "We met with senators, congressmen and congressional wives," recalled Shirley, "and all of them were touched by Judith's sincerity. They were struck particularly by the fact that within days, she would return to her husband in Moscow and resume her refusenik status."[33]

Efforts to sensitize the public to the reality of *glasnost* never ceased. In July 1988, an exhibition of photographic images entitled, "Survival of the Spirit – Jewish lives in the Soviet Union," began its North American tour at the Ontario Legislature. The photographs and texts were the work of Houston photographer Janice Rubin and *Toronto Star* journalist Nomi Morris, who had visited the Soviet Union in 1986.[34]

The opening of the exhibition coincided with JWF's launching of Elena Keis's poetry. The English version of *Believe me, Sister* appeared in a slender brown booklet from which Judge Rosalie Abella read aloud a poem, about the poet's agony of separation from her mother, to the MPPs and supporters who crowded into the reception room.[35]

For Elena Keis, time was running out. JWF sponsored a telegram blitz to persuade Leningrad officials to release her family before September 9, the day when Andrei would be drafted into military service.

Toronto social activist and journalist June Callwood responded to a call for help by writing about Keis in her weekly column in *The Globe and Mail.* "As Soviet leader Mikhail Gorbachev astounds the world with his government's tentative steps toward a more open society," Callwood wrote, "a desperate, frightened Elena Keis, forty-six years old, is waiting in her apartment for *glasnost* to reach her door."[36] The article ended with a plea to readers to express their concerns to Soviet authorities.

Ontario trade minister Monte Kwinter met Keis in Leningrad when he was examining joint-venture business opportunities with the Soviet Union. He told the Soviets, "It's very difficult if you're going to be requiring help from us, and we find you have the kind of oppression that keeps Elena Keis from reuniting with her family."[37]

There was global support for the Keis family, as well. After Michael Sherbourne's translations of Elena's poetry were published by the Long Island Committee for Soviet Jewry, Elena met with world-renowned violinist Isaac Stern. During that summer, Zubin Mehta, conductor of the Israel Philharmonic Orchestra, visited Keis in Leningrad. A dramatic plan came about as the result of their meeting.

The plan bore fruit on October 9, 1988. It was a warm evening when international film stars Gregory Peck and Yves Montand welcomed four thousand Israeli dignitaries and people from around the world to the base of Masada for a spectacular concert to mark the fortieth anniversary of Israel's statehood. As lasers illuminated the majestic fortress in the middle of the Judean desert, Gustav Mahler's second symphony was performed by the Israel Philharmonic Orchestra under the baton of Zubin Mehta.

When the last note of the musical masterpiece resonated beneath the midnight sky and the applause had subsided, Mehta stepped forward carrying a telephone. All eyes were on him as he put the receiver to his ear and shouted into the mouthpiece, "Hello Lena, this is Zubin." Immediately, a dark-haired female member of the orchestra stood up. She placed her violin on her chair, approached centre stage and took the receiver from Mehta. Placing it to her ear, she began to speak in Russian, with fiery passion, to the person on the other end of the line.

The conversation between Anna Rosnovsky at Masada and her sister Elena Keis in Leningrad was amplified for all to hear. At first, Elena spoke in Russian to Anna, and then, in English to the audience. She expressed her appreciation for the opportunity to participate in the celebration of Israel's fortieth anniversary and concluded, "You can be sure that we will continue our struggle for our repatriation, for our right to be Jews, for our desire to live at home. You must be sure that we won't stop until our dream comes true... You know my story. It is the story of many refuseniks. Don't forget us. Wait for me, my sister... I'll come."[38]

Indeed, she did. Within two weeks, Elena Keis received her visa.

In November 1988, a black limousine flying the Canadian flag wound its way through Moscow streets past the Israeli Consulate at 56 Bolshaya Ordinka. On the sidewalk outside the temporary premises, were hundreds of Jews waiting patiently for their turn to initiate the emigration process.

Inside the limousine were Brian Mulroney, Joe Clark and Albert Reichmann, who were in Moscow to investigate the possibility of Canadian-Soviet joint-venture projects. Their afternoon sojourn was to the Steinsaltz Yeshiva, the newly created academy of Talmudic and Jewish studies established by Israeli Rabbi Adin Steinsaltz in co-operation with the Soviet Academy of Sciences.

The Canadians met with thirty refuseniks who were studying under the tutelage of Israeli faculty members. "You've had difficult times, we know that," Mulroney said to the group who were crammed into a tiny room at the Jewish school, "but we have discussed your situation with President Gorbachev and other leaders and all of them have given us an assurance of better days to come."[39]

The better days were reflected in the emigration figures that reached 18,965 in 1988. The total was more than double that of the previous year.[40] Activists had been accustomed to fighting the Soviets. They weren't certain how to behave now that the enemy was becoming friendly.

Discussions about this issue took place when the International Council of the World Conference on Soviet Jewry gathered in Jerusalem in December 1988. There, Nechemiah Levanon, recognized globally as the first person to have identified the need for an organized Soviet Jewry campaign, addressed the delegates, "When the

Soviet Union is behaving as if it recognizes the right of the Jews of the USSR to emigrate to Israel, when the harassment of Jewish activists trying to teach and study Hebrew and to develop Jewish cultural activity has stopped, when the regime is hastening to develop some kind of Jewish activity on its own initiative and under its sponsorship and supervision, we are obligated to weigh carefully what we will demand from the present regime and what we will do in the face of new opportunities."[41]

Nechemiah Levanon reminded the activists that all was far from ideal. Radio transmissions to the USSR from the BBC, Radio Liberty, Voice of America and the CBC were received unimpeded, but Voice of Israel continued to be jammed. Soviet artists and entertainment ensembles from the USSR had performed in Israel, but to date, Israeli troupes had not been invited to perform in the Soviet Union.

"Do not disarm," was Levanon's warning. "There is still more to do. He concluded by reminding his audience that a new Soviet Union would present unique opportunities for Western participation, open to be discovered. "Our movement was based, all these years, on the marvellous triangle: Israel – World Jewry – Soviet Jewry. This is the partnership which must now act with energy, enterprise and inspiration."[42]

Chapter 27

Operation Exodus

On January 20, 1989, George Bush was inaugurated as president of the United States. Within days he telephoned Mikhail Gorbachev and promised no "foot dragging" in the improvement of U.S.-Soviet relations.[1] No one could have predicted just how rapid the improvement would be.

The year 1989 was to be one of dramatic change in the Soviet Union. As internal politics flared with the election of Boris Yeltsin to the Soviet Parliament and the Baltic republics struggled for independence, Jewish heritage and culture flourished. Among the many new organizations receiving official sanction and support were the Jewish Cultural Association in Moscow, the Soviet-Israel Friendship Society in the Baltic republics and a Union of Hebrew Teachers.[2]

"Without question, Gorbachev is the man who is putting this change into effect," said MPP Monte Kwinter, speaking at a Toronto luncheon organized by the lawyer's committee. "His policies of *glasnost, perestroika* and *demokratsia* are truly revolutionizing Soviet society."[3]

The atmosphere of the new USSR was evident at the four-week CSCE Human Dimension Experts meeting in Paris in January, where most discussions centred on minority and nationality rights. Moscow refusenik Alexander Shmukler and cultural activists Mikhail Chlenov and Roman Spektor received travel visas, enabling them to attend the meeting as NGOs.

On February 12, 1989, the Solomon Mikhoels Cultural Centre opened in Moscow. Named for the Jewish actor murdered in Stalin's 1948 purges, the centre represented the most important breakthrough in Jewish culture in the Soviet Union in fifty years. It was as the result of months of negotiations by Isi Leibler, president of the Executive Council of Australian Jewry and vice-president of the World Jewish Congress.[4]

Guests from all around the world came to celebrate. A message from Prime Minister Yitzhack Shamir was delivered by Arye Levin, head of Israel's diplomatic delegation to Moscow, which operated out of the Dutch embassy. The message read: "The revival of the culture of the Jewish people, its literature, its art and the Hebrew language is a sign of positive change in the Soviet Union which will bring a new level of understanding between our two countries."[5]

Leibler, Elie Wiesel, Edgar Bronfman and five foreign ambassadors to the USSR addressed the five hundred Soviet Jews and Jewish leaders from other countries who attended the opening event.[6] Canada was represented by Senator Nathan Nurgitz of Winnipeg and CJC's executive director Jack Silverstone.

Silverstone was cautiously optimistic and reminded Canadians that the issue of long-term refuseniks still remained. "Although the numbers have been greatly reduced, three hundred families have been waiting more than five years to receive exit visas."[7]

It was important to use the upcoming 1991 human rights conference in Moscow as leverage. "The present situation in the Soviet Union will only continue to improve if it remains a major concern of Western governments," said Barbara Stern. "We have always guided ourselves by the requests of Soviet Jews themselves. They have said, if there is a lessening of support on their behalf, the present promise will never become a reality."[8]

The case of Moscow refuseniks Judith and Emmanuel Lurie resounded globally as their Toronto campaign became an international affair. Shirley Hanick contacted the Luries' supporters in Canada, the United States, Australia and Europe and co-ordinated a cable blitz for January 25.[9] Although Yuri Rechetov's office in the Soviet Foreign Ministry was bombarded with telegrams, the Soviets did not respond. The Lurie's time had not yet come.[10]

International Women's Day in the Soviet Union was again

marked by a hunger strike, this time staged by forty members of JEWAR. Four children aged twelve to sixteen had joined their mothers in the fast. "For us this is a rather sad moment," said Inna Uspensky during a telephone conversation with Toronto activists calling from the office of Metro Toronto Chairman Alan Tonks. "It shows that life in refusal is so unbearable that even the children have decided to express themselves." [11]

"The Soviet Jewry movement is over! All the Jews who want to leave, have left." These sentiments were echoed by many establishment leaders who believed that Soviet Jewry advocates should retire. "Is It All Over But The Shouting?" was the title of a forum at the twenty-second plenary assembly of the CJC featuring panelists Isi Leibler, Shmuel Shenhar, Alan McLaine, Irwin Cotler and Yuli Kosharovsky. Shenhar, the consul assigned to the Soviet Jewry desk at the Israeli Consulate in New York, explained, "Although emigration figures have increased substantially to more than four thousand per month and thousands of Soviet Jews are receiving tourist visas to visit Israel, as of April 30, 1989, there are still twenty-eight hundred refuseniks who have been waiting to emigrate for more than two years."[12]

McLaine expressed the official Canadian government position. "The challenge today is the uncertain direction in which the Soviet Union is moving. Let's listen carefully to what Gorbachev says and hold him to his word."[13]

In the sixteen months since Irwin Cotler and Yuli Kosharovsky had met in Moscow to discuss *Interamicus,* major changes had occurred. "Jews are witnessing a revolution in Soviet government policy regarding the emigration of Soviet Jews and refuseniks," Cotler said. " The future of Soviet Jewry is not only what the Soviet Union does, but what we do." "Is it all over but the shouting?" As long as the Soviets said "no" to the Luries, Schvartsmans, Rais, Uspenskys and many others, Western activists also replied "No!"

The continuing struggle was reinforced at the International Foundation for the Survival and Development of Humanity conference in Moscow, attended by lawyers, law professors and human rights activists from ten countries. CLJSJ chairman Bert Raphael and his colleagues Stan Raphael, Rick Orzy, Irwin Cotler and Irwin Fefergrad were delegates.

"We were bombarded with personal requests for help by refuseniks who came to meet the lawyers," said Raphael, who accepted sixty cases on behalf of the CLJSJ. "Despite *glasnost* and *perestroika*, the USSR is a bureaucratic mess. There are still line-ups for basic items in Soviet stores and food and consumer goods are of the poorest quality."[14]

Glasnost was a mixed blessing. Although it brought some freedoms to Soviet citizens, the poor economy and a resurgence of nationalism among many ethnic groups had triggered virulent anti-Semitism. Extremist voices became louder, causing panic among the Jewish population.

"Anti-Semitism," said Grigory Kanovich, a Jewish author from Vilnius who had been recently elected to the Soviet Congress of People's Deputies in Lithuania, "grows like grass in the Soviet Union – very quietly. There aren't any earthquakes, but underneath the ground you can feel the tremors." Kanovich's article, entitled "A Jewish Daisy" appeared in a Lithuanian newspaper. ". . . Should we leave the Soviet Union? Is it possible to stay when both secretly and openly there is being built a nuclear arsenal of hatred of our people, when we are shamelessly slandered on the pages of influential newspapers and magazines? Is it possible to stay when thunderbolts of intolerance and enmity flash threateningly above our heads, when around us the atmosphere is increasingly one of suspicion and mistrust? To go? To stay? To go? To stay? . . ."[15]

Kanovich submitted a petition addressed to the Chamber of Deputies of the Supreme Soviet and signed by two hundred deputies. It warned of the dangers of anti-Semitism and suggested how it could be prevented. Gorbachev did not respond. Kanovich was forced to admit, "The answer to our sorrows, to our danger, to our legitimate complaint is state-imposed silence."[16]

The movement still had its combination of dynamic highs and lows,

lows and highs. Just when the Lurie family was about to be featured on a telephone hook-up between Moscow and Holy Blossom Temple, Soviet Jewry committee chairman Shirley Hanick heard the news. After ten years of waiting, the Luries had received visas!

One more family was out, and still another suffered. The attempt by Winnipeg's Alla Wolfson to obtain freedom for her sister Lilia Rabinovich in Leningrad appeared futile. As a last resort, Rabinovich embarked on a hunger strike, prompting Winnipeg's Soviet Jewry activists to co-ordinate parallel hunger strikes across Canada. National media coverage prompted Joe Clark to intervene. Shortly thereafter, Wolfson was reunited with her sister after fourteen years of separation.[17]

On June 13, 1989, the board of governors of the National Conference on Soviet Jewry[18] agreed to support a temporary waiver of the Jackson-Vanik Amendment. The piece of American legislation, limiting trade credits to the USSR, had forced the Soviets to change their policies.

"The decision to support the waiver is not without reservations," declared NCSJ's executive director Martin Wenick, speaking at Toronto's Adath Israel Synagogue.[19] "It is based on Soviet assurances of a sustained level of emigration, strict limits on the restriction of 'state secrets,' a resolution of the problems of 'poor relatives' and progress on the cases of long-term refuseniks." Wenick assured the audience that the situation would be closely monitored by the U.S. government and the NCSJ.[20]

On October 1, 1989, the United States administration announced its plans to close the transit facilities in Vienna and in Ladispoli, outside Rome, ending the problem of "caravans" of Jews waiting for more than one year for entry visas to other countries. The phenomenon of *neshira* had come to an end. Soviet Jews wishing to emigrate to the United States or elsewhere could apply directly in Moscow at the embassy of their choice. As well, the United States imposed a quota of thirty-thousand Soviet refugees annually. A quota was good news for Israel, whose future and security was dependent on immigration and whose doors were open to all Jews. Many Soviet Jews would choose Israel rather than remain in the USSR.

As emigration from the Soviet Union began to increase, activists in the West began winding down their activity. The Montreal Inter-Faith Task Force for Soviet Jewry began to evaluate its efforts. "Twelve years ago when this task force was formed," Father Barry A. Jones wrote in a letter to his associates, "we never dared to dream that many Jewish families seeking emigration from the Soviet Union would be permitted to leave. Fifteen hundred Soviet Jewish tourists are now arriving in Israel each month... and this year, emigration has exceeded the record for the decade. In view of the positive changes in the Soviet Union, our advisory board has decided to suspend activities. Should the need arise again to 'man the barricades, we will respond to the call with the same concern as we did twelve years ago."[21]

On the eve of Simchat Torah, two hundred members of Ottawa's Jewish community marched outside the Soviet Embassy. "It's difficult to imagine coming here and being grateful for progress," said Rabbi Reuven Bulka, "but this is truly a new era for Soviet Jews – to think of what has happened now is nothing short of a miracle."[22] Rally participants sang Israeli songs and held signs reading, "Let's keep the doors open." Bulka exchanged greetings with embassy guards and invited them to join the marchers for hot drinks.[23]

Change became a reality when the Jewish Agency for Israel (JAFI), the recipient of philanthropic funds raised by Diaspora communities worldwide, established a "Unit for the USSR and Eastern Europe." In the fall of 1989, they sent Yosef Tropiansky, JAFI's first emissary, to Lithuania to open a Jewish school in the Soviet Union.[24]

November 1989 marked the first time that a Soviet official addressed the annual National Conference on Soviet Jewry meetings in Washington. Yuri Rechetov assured the delegates that their aspirations for Jewish culture and free emigration in the USSR were being fulfilled.[25]

On December 18, 1989, the first official Jewish gathering since the Bolshevik Revolution was held in Moscow. The purpose of the four-day meeting of the "Congress of Jewish Organizations and Communities of the USSR" was to seek a common platform and an umbrella organization for the 150 autonomous Jewish groups in the Soviet Union.

More than four hundred Soviet Jews from 123 Soviet communities and observers from Israel, the United States, Canada, Australia, the Netherlands, France and Britain attended the conference.[26] Canada was represented by CJC's Alan Rose and the Ontario region Soviet Jewry Committee's co-chair, The Honourable Mr. Justice Ted Matlow. Former prisoners Vladimir Slepak and Yosef Begun represented the "Soviet Jewry Zionist Forum," Israel's newest organization.[27] As the delegates entered the meeting, they were assaulted by members of the anti-Semitic Pamyat who shouted obscenities and held placards that read, "Jews Out" and "Down with Communism and Zionism."[28]

The four days were replete with discussions on how to encourage Jews who wanted to emigrate while protecting those who wished to build a Jewish renaissance in the USSR. Delegates addressed the problem of growing anti-Semitism and the American quota on Jewish emigration. "Without a background in democracy, they argued and debated each issue," reported Matlow. "Some threatened to walk out if their views could not prevail."[29]

The conference ended with the creation of the Confederation of Jewish Organizations and Communities in the USSR, known as the "Vaad," with a nine-member presidium.[30] The Vaad's co-chairmen, Mikhail Chlenov, Samuel Zilberg and Yosef Zissels, announced their affiliation with the World Jewish Congress. WJC's director Israel Singer welcomed them into the WJC family and declared: "Our meetings are pluralistic and anarchic, like yours. We have resources but we don't have dreams. We have come here to ask you to dream for us."[31]

In the evening of October 26, 1989, El Al flight 008 from Budapest arrived at Ben-Gurion Airport. It carried 205 Jews from various cities of origin in the Soviet Union who had departed from Moscow, on an Aeroflot flight, early that morning. The new *olim* walked from the aircraft through blinding lights into the arms of Israelis of all ages.

Waving miniature Israeli flags, the welcoming throng presented the newcomers with roses and chocolates and sang over and over, "Haveinu Shalom Alecheim."

As the *olim* were led to chairs set up on the tarmac, all eyes turned to a large dais in front of a backdrop that read, "Exodus '89 - Welcome to Israel." After words of official welcome by Jewish Agency officials, the *olim* proceeded to the terminal building where documents were processed and luggage retrieved.

Before leaving the airport, the new immigrants received an Israeli passport and money to finance their first few months in Israel. Some were sent to an absorption centre and others departed in the company of relatives or friends, soon to receive their own apartments. Within a few days all the *olim* would begin the process of learning a new language and adjusting to the customs of their new country.

After living for seventy years under a regime of enforced atheism that systematically suppressed Jewish identity, the hopes and dreams for Soviet Jewry were fulfilled. What had begun as a trickle in the early 1970s had become an exodus of historic proportions. The Jewish exiles from Russia were returning home. The El Al flight that brought 205 Soviet Jews to Israel on October 26, 1989, was the first of "Operation Exodus."

Epilogue

The opening of the gates of emigration from the Soviet Union marked the final chapter of the Soviet Jewry advocacy movement. It marked, as well, the first chapter of an electrifying period of Jewish history. In 1990, 186,815 Jews emigrated from the Soviet Union, with the majority going to Israel. Overnight, Diaspora Jewry re-directed its energies from "raising voices" to "raising funds" to finance the operation of bringing vast numbers to Israel and to assist in the staggering cost of integrating them into Israeli society.

"Operation Exodus" fund-raising campaigns were conducted around the world. The $90 million raised by Canadian Jewry during the initial three-year period was channeled by the United Israel Appeal of Canada through Keren Hayesod in Jerusalem to the Jewish Agency for Israel.

Diplomatic relations between Israel and the Soviet Union allowed for official Israeli organizations to begin operating in the USSR – The Joint Distribution Committee (JDC), to send in educators and educational material, the Jewish Agency for Israel, to strengthen Jewish identity and foster *aliyah* and Lishkat Hakesher, to process emigration papers and implement the "Law of Return."[1]

Diaspora Jewry also had the opportunity, along with Israelis, to participate in the revitalization of Jewish culture in the Soviet Union. The *Chabad Lubovitch*, the Union of Orthodox Jewish Congregations, United Synagogue of Conservative Judaism and the World Union for Progressive Judaism (Reform), each sent educators to assist fledgling religious movements.

Investigative trips to Samarkand, Uzbekistan, by Canadians – Judge Ted Matlow and Alan Rose in December 1989, Rabbi Martin Cohen in July 1990, and Cantor Benjamin Maissner in October 1990, confirmed that the Jewish community of fifteen thousand was in need of qualified educators.[2] This gave birth, in the summer of 1991, to a CJC-sponsored Jewish heritage program, when Roma Bross of Montreal and Josef Schechtman of Beersheva taught Hebrew and Jewish culture to both Ashkenazi and Bucharian Jewish communities in Samarkand.[3]

History unfolded rapidly. In September 1991, the CSCE Human Dimension meeting held in Moscow concluded with a document condemning racism, xenophobia and anti-Semitism. Aeroflot and El Al began to operate direct flights between the Moscow and Tel Aviv. The adoption of an emigration law granting every Soviet citizen the right to leave and enter the USSR prompted the United States to waive the Jackson-Vanik Amendment.[4] The Soviet Communist party was abolished, giving way to the creation of the Commonwealth of Independent States. At the end of December 1991, Mikhail Gorbachev resigned as president of the USSR and the flag atop the Kremlin was lowered for the last time. Communism in the Soviet Union had ceased to exist.[5]

The following three years were characterized by economic instability and political turmoil caused by opponents of free market reform. Despite the fact that Jewish culture and religion were able to flourish with the full co-operation of the authorities, the future of a strong and viable Jewish community in the former Soviet Union was in question. Increasing anti-Semitism in Russia and the Ukraine, the rapid progression of Islamic fundamentalism, the rise of nationalism, and ethnic rivalry escalating into full-scale wars in the Caucasus and southern regions is why six to eight thousand Jews per month left for the Jewish state.[6]

Operating out of thirty-one offices, and headed by Baruch Gur, JAFI promotes *aliyah* through ongoing educational and cultural programs and works through four levels of government to prepare documentation and facilitate the safe transfer of Jews to Israel.[7] The total number of Soviet Jews who emigrated to Israel from the time

"Operation Exodus" began in October 1989 until the end of December 1994 is 542,959.[8] It is expected that another five to eight hundred thousand will leave the former Soviet Union within the next five years.

The largest *aliyah* movement in the history of the Jewish people was made possible by men and women who embodied the living spirit of the symbol of freedom. Collectively, they spent hundreds of years in prison and thousands of years in refusal. These Soviet Jews were courageous enough to protest openly when it was so much safer to remain silent.

This is what they are doing:

Ruth Bar-On heads the Israel Public Council for Soviet Jewry which conducts educational programs for new immigrants, provides financial and employment assistance to scientists and intervenes on behalf of former Soviet Jews in crisis.

Yosef Begun is editor and publisher of *Yerushalaim*, a Russian-language magazine about Israel that is distributed to former Soviet Jews living in the Diaspora, the CIS and Israel.

Victor Brailovsky teaches mathematics at Tel Aviv University.

Yuli Edelshtein is chairman of Olami, an organization that conducts educational programs for new immigrants. He is a vice-president of the Zionist Forum.

Lev Elbert is an engineer with Israel's electrical company. He is responsible for the construction of gas turbine power stations in the southern part of Israel. He works as a volunteer for the Israel Public Council for Soviet Jewry.

Leonid Feldman, a former refusenik from Kishinev, was ordained a Conservative rabbi at the Jewish Theological Seminary in New York. He is the spiritual leader of Temple Emanu-El in Palm Beach, Florida.

Alexander Ioffe is a professor of mathematics at the Technion in Haifa.

Elena Keis lives on a settlement in the West Bank. She has recorded her story in the book *Caged*.

Yuli Kosharovsky is chairman of Tekol Ltd., a company involved with technological projects in Israel. He is a vice-president of the Zionist Forum.

Anat Kuznetsov, the daughter of Sylva Zalmanson and Eduard Kuznetsov, wrote the Israeli hit tune, "Kama Tov Shebatem" ("How good it is that you have come").

Eduard Kuznetsov, sentenced to death in the Leningrad trials, is the editor of *Vesty*, a Russian-language newspaper in Israel.

Dr. Alexander Lerner, now in his eighties, is a professor of applied mathematics at the Weizmann Institute of Science and is working to develop an artificial heart.[10]

Nechemiah Levanon has retired to Kfar Blum. The eighty-year-old "godfather of the Soviet Jewry movement" recently completed his memoirs.

Ida Nudel lives in Carmel Yosef, a suburb of Tel Aviv, where she cultivates a vegetable and herb garden. She works with under-privileged immigrants and is founder of Em l'Em (Mother to Mother), an organization that provides assistance to single-parent immigrant mothers.

Raisa Palatnik, the Odessa librarian for whom "the 35s" was created, works at a library in Jerusalem.

Avital Sharansky lives in Jerusalem with her husband Natan. She is the dedicated parent of their daughters, Rachel and Chana.

Natan Sharansky is an associate editor for *The Jerusalem Report*, Israel's weekly English news magazine. He chairs the Zionist Forum, an organization that serves as an intermediary with government ministries and provides guidance and financial assistance to new immigrants.

Yasha Kazakov, remembered as the first Jew to have fought his way out of the Soviet Union, has changed his name to Yasha Kedmi. In 1969, he clashed with officials of Lishkat Hakesher over the issue of public advocacy for Soviet Jewry. Still responsible for the fate of the Jews, Lishkat Hakesher is the Israeli government department that serves as the liaison to the former Soviet Union. Yasha Kedmi is now its director. Soviet Jewry has come full circle

Jewish Emigration from the Soviet Union

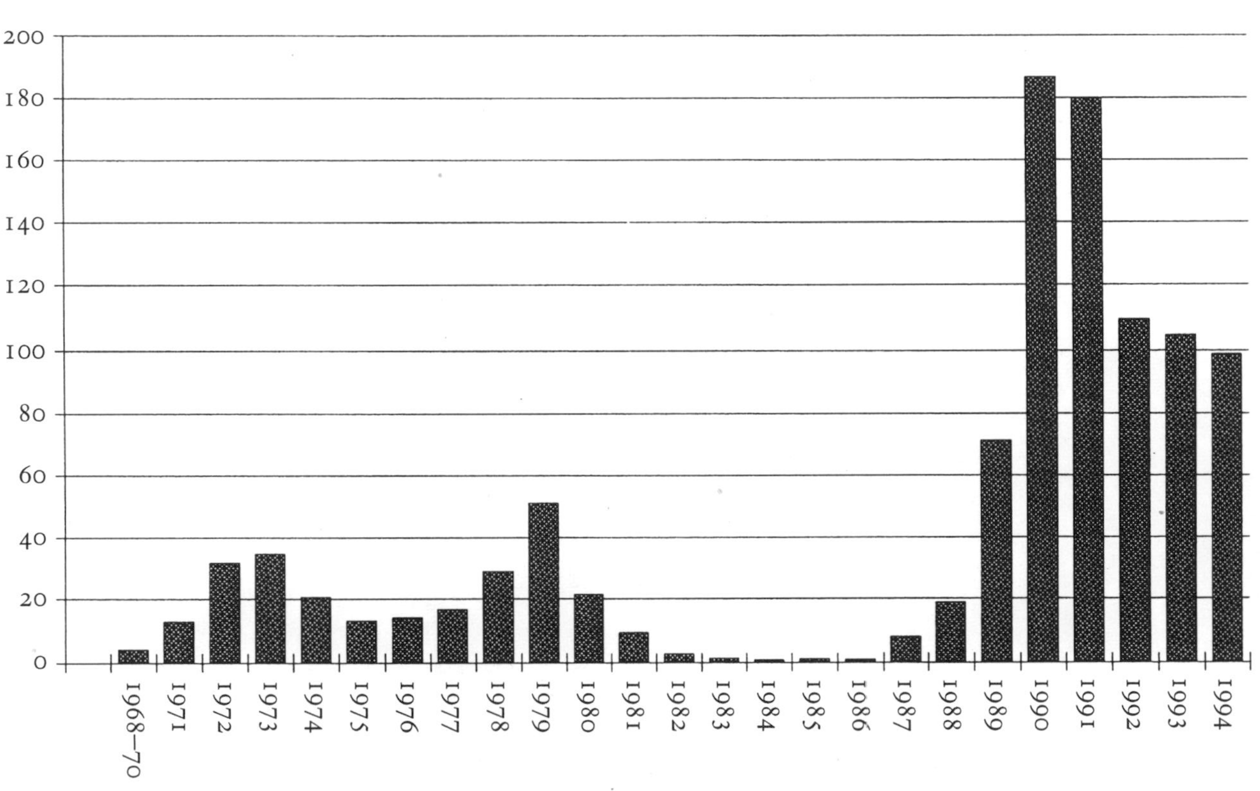

Emigrants (in thousands)

Notes

NOTES, CHAPTER I

1 Keren Hayesod, the Israeli-based organization that receives money raised by United Jewish Appeal campaigns in every country but the United States and channels it to the Jewish Agency for Israel.

2 Personal recollections, Wendy Eisen.

3 Martin Gilbert, *The Jews of Russia: their history in maps and photographs* (Cambridge: The Burlington Press, 1976), p. 3.

4 Emmanuel Litvinoff, "70 Years of Soviet Jewry," *Insight Soviet Jews* (London: Contemporary Jewish Library Ltd., 1987).

5 Proposed by Czar Alexander III's chief advisor Konstantin Pobedonostsev. Abba Eban, *Heritage – Civilization and the Jews* (New York: Summit Books, 1984), p. 248.

6 Martin Gilbert, *The Jews of Russia*, p. 27.

7 Ben-Gurion, Prime Minister 1949–53; 1955–1963; Weitzmann, President, 1949–1952; Shazar, President 1963–1973; Sharett, Prime Minister, 1954–55; Eshkol, Prime Minister 1963–1969.

8 Henry H. Weinberg, "Soviet Jewry: Faith and Defiance," *Midstream* (August/September), 1987.

9 August Shtern, editor, *The USSR vs Dr. Mikhail Stern* (New York: Urizen Books, 1977), p. 266.

10 Abba Eban, *Heritage – Civilization and the Jews*, p. 248.

11 *Jewish Literacy*, p. 247.

12 Beilis was accused of murdering a twelve-year old Christian boy and using his blood for the baking of matzoh at Passover. The intervention of Russian intellectuals led eventually to Beilis' acquittal.

13 H. M. Caiserman, Annual Report, CJC, March 1920, CJC Archives. *In solemn protest against massacres of Jews in Eastern Europe, many thousands of Jewish people made pilgrimages through the streets of Montreal yesterday. The city has never witnessed a more touching spectacle than this mourning procession, which was but one of several conducted in America.* "Protest and reproach," *The Montreal Daily Star* (November 26, 1919).

14 Rebecca Rass and Morris Brafman, *From Moscow to Jerusalem* (New York: Sheingold Publishers Inc., 1976), p. 231.

15 *Jewish Literacy*, p. 472.

16 Karl Marx, *The Oxford Dictionary of Quotations*, Third Edition (Oxford: Oxford University Press), p. 333.

17 Louis Lazare and Dr. S. Gold were co-chairmen of the Birobidjan campaign that

took place April 4–19, 1937. *Jewish Chronicle,* April 1937. Alan Raymond interview with the author, February 26, 1992.

18 Lionel Kochan, editor, *The Jews in Soviet Russia since 1917* (Oxford: Oxford University Press 1970), p. 34. On August 26, 1951, Belgrade radio reported that Birobidjan had been abolished as an autonomous region by order of the Soviet government and incorporated into the province of Khabarovsk. *The American Jewish Yearbook* (New York, 1952.)

19 Emmanuel Litvinoff, *Insight Soviet Jews* (November, 1987).

20 Martin Gilbert, *The Jews of Hope* (New York: Penguin Books, 1984), p. 55.

21 Egypt, Syria, Jordan, Lebanon, Iraq and Saudi Arabia.

22 *Jewish Literacy*, p. 297.

23 Ibid.

24 Golda Meir was born Golda Myerson in Kiev. She was raised in Milwaukee, Wisconsin, and emigrated as a young adult to Palestine. Meir was Israeli prime minister from 1969 to 1974.

25 Golda Meir, *My Life* (New York: G.P. Putnam, 1975), p. 250.

26 Allan Bullock, *Hitler and Stalin, Parallel Lives* (Toronto: McClelland and Stewart, 1991), p. 956.

27 *American Jewish Yearbook, 1952,* p. 3.

28 B.G. Kayfetz, "Anniversary of Shame," *The Canadian Jewish News* (August 1972).

29 *Encyclopaedia Judaica,* Vol. 15 (Jerusalem: Keter Publishing House, 1972), p. 327.

30 *Canadian Jewish Chronicle* (March 6, 1953), p. 1.

31 *Jewish Daily Eagle* (March 5, 1953), p. 4.

32 CJC, Inter-Office Information, March 9, 1953.

Notes, Chapter 2

1 Nechemiah Levanon interview with the author, December 25, 1991.

2 Ibid.

3 Avigur, who had served as a leader with the Haganah (founded in 1920 to protect Jewish lives against Arab attacks) before the creation of the State, joined the Mossad in 1948. He directed "Aliyah Bet," the operation of smuggling the remnants of European Jewry who had survived World War II into Palestine.

4 Meir Rosenne served with the Israeli Embassy in Paris and Emmanuel Litvinoff served in London. Shaul Avigur served with the consulate general for Israel in New York.

5 In 1956, Levanon was replaced in Tel Aviv by Benjamin Eliav, a former member of the Irgun (a militant group formed in Israel to respond to Arab terrorism). In 1959, Eliav was appointed consul general in New York.

6 J.B. Salsberg interview with the author, August 25, 1989.

7 Ibid.

8 Ibid.

9 Saul Hayes, QC, was executive director of the CJC, from 1942–1975.

10 Ambassador Meir Rosenne interview with the author, July 10, 1989.

11 Ibid.

12 Rabbi Stuart E. Rosenberg, *The Real Jewish World* (Toronto: Clarke Irwin, 1984), p. 289.

13 "Fear Hangs over every Jew," Dr. Stuart E. Rosenberg, *The Toronto Star* (April 11, 1961).

14 *The Real Jewish World,* p. 297.

15 Ibid.
16 Ibid, p. 296.
17 Ibid.
18 Ibid.
19 Ibid.
20 Dr. Stuart E. Rosenberg, *The Toronto Star* (April 10, 1961).
21 *The Real Jewish World*, p. 299.
22 Speech delivered by The Rt. Hon. John G. Diefenbaker for the Canadian Association for Labor Israel, supporters of the Social Democratic Labor movement in Israel, April 4, 1962. The Rt. Hon. John G. Diefenbaker Centre, Saskatoon, Saskatchewan, Speech series, Vol. 81, no. 1081.
23 Ambassador Meir Rosenne interview with the author, July 10, 1989.
24 *The Real Jewish World*, p. 304.
25 Editorial, *The Telegram* (October 29, 1963).
26 Martin Gilbert, *The Jews of Russia*, op. cit., p. 59.
27 Letter to The Hon. Paul Martin from Michael Garber, December 13, 1963.
28 He raised the issue of Soviet Jewry whenever he met with Soviet premier Alexei Kosygin or Soviet foreign minister Andrei Gromyko. Paul Martin telephone interview with the author, August 1989.
29 Decter wrote articles about Soviet Jewry in the 1950s that were published in *The New Leader.* An article by Decter, "The Status of Jews in the Soviet Union," appeared in the January 1963 issue of *Foreign Affairs*, Glenn Richter interview with the author, January 8, 1995.
30 Senator Herbert H. Lehman, Justice William O. Douglas, Rev. Martin Luther King, Bishop James A. Pike, Walter Reuther, Norman Thomas and Robert Penn Warren.
31 *The Real Jewish World*, p. 304.
32 "Gov't appealing to Reds – Martin," *The Ottawa Citizen* (January 9, 1964).
33 The January 9, 1964 article described Jews as parasites who circumvent the law and grow rich at the expense of material goods in short supply. Letter to Soviet counsellor A.Y. Popov from Dr. Stuart Rosenberg, March 15, 1964, CJC Archives.
34 "Russia – refusal to permit entry of Passover bread," House of Commons Debates, March 24, 1964, p. 1397.
35 Sam Lewin represented the CJC at the meeting.
36 The AJCSJ was under the auspices of the National Jewish Communal Relations Action Committee (NJCRAC). In September 1971, the AJCSJ was re-named the National Conference on Soviet Jewry.
37 "Russian anti-Semitism deplored in Resolution," *The Gazette* (December 8, 1964).
38 Irwin Cotler interview with the author, April 12, 1989.
39 A national gathering held alternately between Montreal and Toronto every three years to discuss the Jewish agenda.
40 The Washington office covered Soviet Jewry activity from the mid-west to the west coast, until 1975, when an office was established in Los Angeles. At the height of the Soviet Jewry campaign there were a total of nine Israeli offices dealing with advocacy for Soviet Jewry. (New York, Washington, Los Angeles in North America; Mexico and Argentina in Latin America; London, Paris, Rome and Stockholm in Europe) Interview with Consul Oded Eran, Israel Consulate, New York, January, 1993.
41 Remarks by Nechemiah Levanon on the occasion of the twentieth anniversary of the NCSJ, October 21, 1991, *Newsbreak*, January 10, 1991.
42 Soviet Jewry Resolutions of the Fourteenth Plenary Session of Canadian Jewish Congress, 1965, CJC Archives.

43 The resolution was introduced by B'nai Brith leader Max Shecter, "Canadian Jewry Must Speak Out," *The Canadian Jewish Chronicle* (June 3, 1966), personal files of Rabbi Stuart Rosenberg, National Archives of Canada, Ottawa.

44 *The Real Jewish World*, p. 310.

45 Report from Canadian Jewish Congress Leadership Congress, May 1966, CJC Archives.

46 Elie Wiesel, *The Jews of Silence: A Personal Report on Soviet Jewry* (New York: Holt Reinhart and Winston, 1966), p. 69.

47 Elie Wiesel, "The Sun Rises for Soviet Jews," *The New York Times* (February 26, 1989).

48 *The Jews of Silence*, p. 103.

49 Rabbi Stuart E. Rosenberg interview with the author, July 25, 1989.

Notes, Chapter 3

1 A Study of Jews Refused their Right to Leave the Soviet Union," Volume 2, Part 1, compiled by Barbara Stern for the CJC, December 1981, CJC Archives.

2 Rass and Brafman, p. 9.

3 Ibid.

4 Leonard Schroeter, *The Last Exodus* (New York: Universe Books, 1974), p.46.

5 Rass and Brafman, p.9.

6 Leon Uris at a dinner in honour of Connie and Joe Smukler of Philadelphia, in support of Israel Bonds, November 1990, personal recollections Wendy Eisen.

7 Letter signed by Charles A. Kent, Chairman, Committee of Concern for Soviet Jewry, October 2, 1967, CJC Archives 31–F6, Vol. 82.

8 The protest march was sponsored by Canadian Jewish youth groups.

9 When there were no relatives in Israel, Lishkat Hakesher found "other ways."

10 *From Moscow to Jerusalem*, op. cit., p. 105.

11 Ibid, p. 9.

12 Ibid, p. 111.

13 Zvi Raviv interview with the author, October 16, 1994.

14 *From Moscow to Jerusalem*, p. 115.

15 Ibid, p. 116.

16 Zvi Raviv interview.

17 *The New York Times* (November 11, 1969), p.3.

18 Ben Kayfetz, *Toronto Jewish Reporter* (April 1970), p. 8.

19 *From Moscow to Jerusalem*, p. 159.

20 Sponsored by the "American Jewish Conference on Soviet Jewry" and the "Conference on the Status of Jews," *Encyclopaedia Judaica*, p. 505.

21 Among the American signatories were Canadians Maxwell Cohen, dean of McGill University Law School and Lewis S. Feuer, professor of sociology at the University of Toronto.

22 Edward Kuznetsov, *Prison Diaries* (New York: Stein and Day Publishers, 1975), p. 7.

23 *From Moscow to Jerusalem*, p. 170.

24 Telford Taylor, *Courts of Terror, Soviet Criminal Justice and Jewish Emigration* (New York: Alfred A. Knopf, 1976), p. 8.

25 *Prison Diaries*, p. 7.

26 *From Moscow to Jerusalem*, p. 203.

27 *Prison Diaries*, p. 11.

28 "Defendants Sing 'Am Israel Chai' and Recite Prayer in Court," JTA, JDL and

Soviet Jewry, Spring 1971. The "Sh'ma" expresses Judaism's belief in monotheism. Rabbi Joseph Telushkin, *Jewish Literacy* (New York: William Morrow and Company Inc., 1991), p. 667.

29 *Prison Diaries,* p. 8.

30 Josef Mendelevich and Uri Fedorov were sentenced to 15 years, Alexei Murzhenko, Leib Khnokh, Anatoly Altman received 14, 13, and 12 years respectively; Boris Penson and Sylva Zalmanson received 10 years; Israel Zalmanson 8, and Mendel Bodnya, who had fully confessed to his deeds, received a light sentence of 4 years.

31 *From Moscow to Jerusalem,* p. 207.

32 "Canada joins world protests," *The Canadian Jewish News* (January 1, 1971), p. 6.

33 Excerpts of speech delivered by Rabbi W. Gunther Plaut on December 30, 1970 at Nathan Phillips Square, Toronto, TJC/CJC, Ontario Region Archives, 1970–155A.

34 Ontario Street, later re-named Avenue du Musée.

35 Mark Zarecki interview with the author, August 2, 1990.

36 As a student in England in the 1950s, Rose helped to organize demonstrations against the Soviets' "cosmopolitan" campaign. Alan Rose interview with the author, August 2, 1990.

37 Sydney Harris, Perry Meyer, Alan Rose, Monroe Abbey, Hy Hochberg, Ben Kayfetz.

38 Activities Report #13, Sydney Harris, QC, Chairman CJC Central Region (January 5,1971).

39 *The Montreal Star* (January 4, 1971); *The Ottawa Journal* (January 4, 1971); CJC *Bulletin,* Vol. 27. No.1 (January, 1971).

40 A rally was held in Hamilton with Mayor Victor Copps and MP Lincoln Alexander as special guests. Jews from Brantford, Guelph, Galt, Preston and Waterloo gathered in solidarity in Kitchener. Alan Rose was featured as guest speaker. *Kitchener Record* (January 1971); *The Suburban* (January 6, 1971), p. 1.

41 Ben Kayfetz, former director CJC, Ontario Region, interview with the author, July, 19, 1989.

42 Irwin Cotler interview with the author, October 31, 1990.

43 Rally in Paris, France, December 30, 1970, CJC Archives.

NOTES, CHAPTER 4

1 Zalman Abramov was founding chairman, Abe Harman, president and David Prital, director.

2 "Brussels 1" was an international effort, convened by the North American, Latin American, European and Israeli Conferences on Soviet Jewry together with the World Jewish Congress, the Jewish Agency and B'nai Brith International Council.

3 Canadian delegates to Brussels included: Clara Balinsky, Hyman Bessin, Meyer Bick, Henry Blatt, Frank Dimant, Philip Givens, Sydney Harris, QC, Rabbi Joseph Kelman, Rabbi David Monson, Professor Perry Meyer, Alan Rose, J.B. Salsberg, Blanche Wiesenthal, Samuel Zacks.

4 Dr. Mendel Gordin and Vitaly Svetchinsky from Moscow, Grisha Feigin from Riga, Kraina Shur from Leningrad and Ella Tamshajn from Kovno; David Ben-Gurion and Menachem Begin from Israel; Saul Bellow, Dr. Albert Sabin, Abraham Shlonsky, Paddie Chayefsky, Elie Wiesel, Arthur Goldberg and Otto Preminger from the United States; memorandum from Clara Balinsky, Public Affairs Chairman, Canadian Hadassah-Wizo, March 9, 1971, National Archives of Canada, Ottawa.

5 "Let Soviet Jews Go," *The Canadian Jewish News* (March 5, 1971,) p. 1.

6 They harassed Soviet diplomats stationed in the United States by shouting, "Russian Go Home," and carried signs reading, "This is a Soviet Swine who oppresses Russian Jews." On November 25, 1971, a pipe bomb explosion rocked the building housing the New York offices of Aeroflot, the Soviet airline and Intourist, the Soviet tourist agency. On January 8, 1971, a bomb exploded at a Soviet embassy annex in Washington. The JDL claimed responsibility for the action. JDL and Soviet Jewry, *An International Newspaper* (Spring 1971), personal files of Judy Feld Carr.

7 "Stormy session in Brussels ends with plea to aid Soviet Jews," *The Jerusalem Post* (March 2, 1971).

8 "World Conference on Soviet Jewry," *The Canadian Jewish News* (March 5, 1971), p. 6.

9 Brussels Conference Appeal, 1971, CJC Archives.

10 Jewish Emigration from the USSR Statistics, The Committee for Soviet Jewry, Ontario Region, CJC Archives 1990.

11 Letter to Frank Dimant, director FZO, from Nathan Gaisin, Chairman, Central Region, CJC September 7, 1971, CJC Archives.

12 David Sadowski interview with the author, June 19, 1989.

13 Genya Intrator interview with the author, February 9, 1990.

14 FJWO was chaired by Gerda Frieberg. Intrator took over the chairmanship of Women for Soviet Jewry from founding co-chairpersons Myra Sadowski and Harriet Cooper.

15 The Matzah of Hope, distributed by CJC, March 1971, CJC Archives.

16 Alan Rose, Perry Meyer, Hy Hochberg, Monroe Abbey, Ben Kayfetz met with Mitchell Sharp May 7, 1971; Alan Rose, Perry Meyer, Murray Spiegal, Harry Wolfson, Monroe Abbey, David Sadowski, Saul Hayes met with Pierre Trudeau's parliamentary secretary, Barney Danson, May 11, 1971, CJC Archives.

17 Letter to The Rt. Hon. Pierre Elliott Trudeau from Saul Hayes, May 10, 1971, CJC Archives.

18 House of Commons Debates, Vol. 115, 3rd Session, 28th Parliament, May 17, 1971.

19 Butman, 10 years; Mikhail Korenblit, 7 years; Kaminsky and Yagman, 5 years; Mogilever, 4 years; Dreizner, Boguslavsky, Lev Korenblit, 3 years; Shtilbans, 1 year. Leonard Schroeter, *The Last Exodus,* p. 206.

20 Cable from Hyman Bessin to Pierre Elliott Trudeau, May 26, 1971, CJC Archives.

21 House of Commons Debates, Vol. 115, Number 141, 3rd Session, 28th Parliament, May 28, 1971.

22 Telegram to The Rt. Hon. Pierre Elliott Trudeau from Saul Hayes, June 8, 1971, CJC Archives.

23 Letter to Saul Hayes from The Rt. Hon. Pierre Elliott Trudeau, June 30, 1971, CJC Archives.

24 Mark Zarecki interview with the author, August 2, 1990.

25 Ronald Rubin, "The New Style of Soviet and Other Jews," as quoted by Mindy Skapinker, *Canadian Jewish Involvement with Soviet Jewry, 1970–1990:* The Toronto Case Study, PhD thesis, 1993, p. 50.

26 The Canadian SSSJ was led by Abie Ingber.

27 David Sadowski interview with the author, July 7, 1989.

28 Congress Bulletin, (September 9, 1971). p. 1, CJC Archives.

29 Sheila Finestone, MP, the daughter of former CJC president Monroe Abbey, interview with the author, May 29, 1990.

30 The meeting took place September 17, 1971. The group led by CJC president Monroe Abbey included Sydney Harris QC, Hy Hochberg, Leon Kronitz, Hyman

Bessin, Judge Harold Lande, Professor Perry Meyer, Alan Rose, Murray Spiegel. Aide Memoire, CJC, September 1971, CJC Archives.

31 Ibid.

32 Letter to Monroe Abbey from The Hon. Mitchell Sharp, September 24, 1971, CJC Archives.

33 "Simchat Torah rallies to launch protest," *Congress Bulletin* (September, 1971), CJC Archives.

34 *The Canadian Jewish News* (October 1st, 1971), p. 4.

35 Following the establishment of Canadian Hadassah's Public Affairs Department in 1970, Soviet Jewry seminars were held in many cities. Hadassah-Wizo bulletin, "Public Affairs Across the Country," Public Affairs Department, Hadassah-Wizo Organization of Canada, Convention 1972, p. 1. Personal files of Cecile Shore.

36 Steve Hendler, "5,000 Jews expected in protest," *The Montreal Star* (October 19, 1971), p. 1.

37 Ibid.

38 The ram's horn trumpet is used by Jews in religious ceremonies and as ancient battle-signal, *The Concise Oxford Dictionary* (Oxford: Oxford University Press), 1982.

39 John Gray, "Kosygin target of peaceful protests," *The Montreal Star* (October 19, 1971), p. 1.

40 "SHUTDOWN: The National Office and Montreal Office of the Hadassah-Wizo Organization of Canada will remain closed ALL DAY, Tuesday, October 19. For Hadassh-Wizo members to join in the Soviet Jewry Protest March to Ottawa, Tuesday, October 19th, 1971. Mrs. Hyman Wisenthal, National President; Mrs. Sam Rabinovitch, Montreal President. "Public Affairs Across the Country," personal files of Cecile Shore. "When Kosygin comes to Canada, PROTEST FOR SOVIET JEWS – Leave your businesses, your homes, come to OTTAWA, October 19, 1971, *SSSJ Newsletter,* Montreal, p. 14–16.

41 Among the speakers were Ottawa community leaders Abe Palmer and Rabbi Simon Eckstein. The main address was delivered by Rabbi W. Gunther Plaut; Sydney Harris spoke for CJC; Clara Balinsky for the Canadian Zionist Federation; Boris Moroz for the Montreal Committee for Soviet Jewry and David Sadowski for the Student Council for Soviet Jews, *CJC Bulletin,* ibid, p. 2, CJC Archives.

44 Ibid.

45 *The Canadian Jewish News* (October 29, 1971), p. 1.

46 "JDL members interrupt Premier's call for better relations," *The Globe and Mail* (October 26, 1971), p. 1.

47 Judy Feld Carr interview with the author, November 20, 1993.

48 "Police ride horses into Kosygin's pickets," *Toronto Star* (October 29, 1971). Soviet Jewry activity began to flourish in Toronto, the core members of the Toronto JDL abandoned their activity and became involved with Syrian Jewry. Dr. Ronald Feld became the first chairman and after his death, his widow, Judy Feld Carr, assumed the chairmanship.

49 Elie Wiesel, *The Canadian Jewish News* (October 29, 1971), p. 1.

50 *The Globe and Mail* (October 21, 1971), p. 1.

51 Rabbi W. Gunther Plaut, *The Canadian Jewish News* (October 29, 1971), p. 5.

NOTES CHAPTER 5

1 By 1973, Sherbourne was making as many as four or five telephone calls in one evening, to cities all over the Soviet Union. Personal recollections of Michael Sherbourne, July, 1992.

2 *Outlook,* NCSJ, no. 10 (March, 1974), p.4, National Archives of Canada, Ottawa, MG 28V 133,Vol. 32.

3 "Several non-Jews, among them Alexei Murchenko and Yuri Federov who had been involved in the Leningrad airplane incident, were also given the designation of 'Prisoner of Zion'," Alan M. Dershowitz, *Chutzpah* (Boston: Little, Brown and Co. 1991), p. 252.

4 Jerry Pearl and Mark S. Anshan, "Russian Jews urge more phone calls," *The Canadian Jewish News* (February 25, 1972), p. 8, CJC Archives.

5 *Outlook,* National Conference on Soviet Jewry, No. 1 (September 22, 1972).

6 It was suggested that the Soviets levied the tax to prevent a brain-drain and to secure hard currency, obtained if Western Jewish communities agreed to pay the exhorbitant ransom. "Soviet Jewry fees – The Ransom of Jews," MCSJ, CJC Archives.

7 Remarks by Richard Perle at a dinner honouring Max Kampelman in Washington, November 8, 1987. Personal files of Helen Jackson.

8 "Soviet Jewry fees – The Ransom of Jews."

9 "Knesset calls on world to protest Russian tax," *The Canadian Jewish News* (September 1, 1972), p. 1.

10 From a speech delivered by Mitchell Sharp, October 1, 1972, in Nathan Phillips Square, Toronto, TJC/CJC Archives, 13/4.

11 Robert G. Kaufman, *Principled Internationalist: The Foreign Policy and Human Rights Legacy of Senator Henry M. Jackson* Article submitted to the International Commemorative Conference on the occasion of the twentieth anniversary of the Jackson-Vanik Amendment, Jerusalem, January 1995.

12 *The Jackson-Vanik Amendment, Changing the World through Congressional Action,* Committee to Commemorate Senator Henry M. Jackson and the Struggle for Human Rights, Article submitted to International Commemorative Conference on the occasion of the twentieth anniversary of the Jackson-Vanik Amendment, Jerusalem, January 1995.

13 Richard Perle interview with the author, January 7, 1995.

14 "Twenty-one Nobel laureates urge the repeal of the Soviet Head Tax," *The New York Times* (October 1, 1972), National Archives, Ottawa, MG 28, file 1, Vol.32.

15 Academic Committee on Soviet Jewry, Chairman, Hans J. Morgenthau, Secretary, Harris Schoenberg, *The New York Times* (October 31, 1972).

16 Cochaired by Professors Irwin Corter and Murray Freedman. Carleton University, McGill University, Queen's University, University of British Columbia, University of Toronto, University of Western Ontario, York University. The petition appeared in *The Globe and Mail,* December 10, 1972.

17 Excerpted remarks by Senator Henry M. Jackson on the Senate floor, October 4, 1972, personal files of Richard Perle.

18 Richard Perle at the International Commemorative Conference on the occasion of the twentieth anniversary of the Jackson-Vanik Amendment, January 9, 1995.

19 "Forty-four given permits as diploma tax reported lifted," *The Canadian Jewish News* (March 30, 1973), p. 1.

20 "Scientist paid $31,000 to get out of Russia," *The Toronto Star* (February 10, 1973).

21 Senator Henry M. Jackson at a meeting with NCSJ leadership, May 8, 1973, CJC Archives, 1973, 14/11.

22 McGill University professor Harold Waller was named chairman, pro tem. The directors of the CCSJ were: David Sadowski, 1973–1974; David Shanoff, 1975; Sam Resnick, 1976–1977; Martin Penn, 1978–1988; Carole Moscovitch, 1988–1989.

23 B'nai Brith was a volunteer service organization with 20,000 Canadian members.

The Canadian Zionist Federation was an organization devoted to the advancement of Zionism.

24 In 1972, five Canadian cities had regional committees: Montreal Committee for Soviet Jewry, chaired by Lee Gertsman; Winnipeg Committee for Soviet Jewry, chaired by Elodee Portigal and Lois Nathanson; Vancouver Committee for Soviet Jewry, chaired by Betty Nitkin; Ottawa Committee for Soviet Jewry, chaired by Rabbi Ben Friedberg; and the Toronto Steering Committee for Soviet Jewry, chaired by J.B. Salsberg. The Toronto Steering Committee encompassed the following ad hoc committees: Women for Soviet Jewry, chaired by Genya Intrator; Student Council for Soviet Jews, chaired by Fern Faust; Canadian Academic Committee for Soviet Jewry, chaired by Irwin Cotler and Dr. Murray Freedman; Canadian Friends of Soviet Jewry, chaired by H. Wayne Tanenbaum. Minutes of the Canadian Committee for Soviet Jewry meeting held at Shaarei Shomayim Synagogue, Toronto, September 11, 1973, p. 2, CJC Archives, 1973–4, No. 26.

25 Ibid.

26 The Moldavian region included the communities of Bendery, Tiraspol and Byeltzy.

27 Jeanette Goldman was chairman of NCJW's World Jewry Committee until 1980 and chairman of the Committee for Soviet Jewry, Ontario Region, 1980–1985. Jeanette Goldman interview with the author. August 30, 1989.

28 Marsha Slavens interview with the author, August 8, 1989.

29 Executive director of Canadian Hadassah-Wizo, Lily Frank and Montreal member Heather Drazner were co-chairmen of the Sylva Zalmanson Committee, Minutes of the Canadian Committee for Soviet Jewry, September 11, 1973.

30 Joseph Telushkin and Richard Stone, "Soviet Jewry learns of the War," *The Times of Israel* (January, 1974).

31 Members of the non-Jewish community who spoke at the rallies were – Toronto: David Smith, Dr. B. Robert Bater, Rev. Canon Arthur Brown, Rev. John Meagher; Montreal: Rev. Roland de Corneille; Hamilton: MP John Munro, Father John Sherlock, Rev. Rex Dolan; St. Catharines: MPP R.M. Johnston, The Hon. Robert Welch, MP; Winnipeg: MP James Richardson MP, Premier Ed Schreyer, Canon James Brown.

32 "Simchat Torah rally brings record attendance in demonstration for Israel and Soviet Jewry," *The Canadian Jewish News* (October 26, 1973), p. 9.

NOTES, CHAPTER 6

1 Report of trip to the USSR, Rabbi Lavy Becker and Boris Levine, January 15–25, 1971, CJC Archives.

2 Ibid.

3 Ibid.

4 Ibid.

5 Members of the Montreal contingent were Nani and Austin Beutel, Sheila and Jack Zittrer and Edward Bronfman. Torontonians included H. Wayne Tanenbaum, Larry and Carole Grossman, Susan and Sheldon Taerk.

6 Sheila Zittrer interview with the author, January, 1993.

7 H. Wayne Tanenbaum interview with the author, February 2, 1992.

8 Sheila Zittrer interview.

9 Edward Bronfman interview with the author, March, 1991.

10 "Group wants to make Soviet Jewish question a federal election issue," *The Globe and Mail,* (October 7, 1972), p. 5.

11 The Montreal women received names and addresses of refuseniks from CJC's Quebec region's Soviet Jewry director, Stan Urman. Interview with Sylviane Borenstein, November 24, 1991; Garvis became chairman of the Montreal Committee for Soviet Jewry and later, chairman of the Helsinki Watch committee for the CJC.
12 Sam Filer written recollections for the author, August 1990.
13 Ibid.
14 Sylviane Borenstein interview with the author, November 24, 1991.
15 Irving Halperin interview with the author, December 13, 1992.
16 Ibid.

Notes, Chapter 7

1 The CSCE was comprised of Canada, the United States, and thirty-three European countries, including the USSR.
2 Canadian Committee for Soviet Jewry Report, p. 4, (September 6, 1973), CJC Archives.
3 Alan Rose interview with the author, August 2, 1990.
4 Letter to Mitchell Sharp from Saul Hayes, December 1973, CJC Archives.
5 Minister of external affairs Liberal Mitchell Sharp, Conservative spokesman for foreign affairs Claude Wagner, and the leader of the New Democratic Party David Lewis, "Pre-Plenary Report," *Congress Bulletin,* February/March, 1974, CJC Archives.
6 "Helsinki: a noble but naive try," John Gellner, *The Globe and Mail* (August 1, 1985).
7 CSCE documentation, p. 1, CJC Archives, 1/3, p.3.
8 CSCE documentation, p. 3, CJC Archives 1/3, p.3.
9 Chaired by Britain's Stephen Roth. Canada was represented by Alan Rose.
10 Post-Helsinki documentation, CJC Archives, 21/10.
11 Ibid.
12 Avital Sharansky, *Next Year in Jerusalem* (T.J. Hunt Ltd., 1980), p. 79.

Notes, Chapter 8

1 In Great Britain, the National Council for Soviet Jewry was chaired by June Jacobs. In the United States, the National Conference on Soviet Jewry (NCSJ), founded as the American Jewish Conference on Soviet Jewry, was established in 1971 with Jerry Goodman as director from 1971 to 1988. Other directors were: Myrna Shinbaum from1988 to1992 and Mark Levin from 1992 to the present. The NCSJ was the major Soviet Jewry information centre in North America with offices in Washington and New York. Jerry Goodman interview with the author, July 25, 1989.

The Greater New York Conference for Soviet Jewry (GNYCSJ) had membership organizations in Manhattan, Brooklyn, the Bronx, Queens and Staten Island. In addition to ongoing advocacy, the GNYCSJ co-ordinated "Solidarity Sunday" in New York City, a demonstration held each May, where thousands came to show their support of Soviet Jewry. The GNYCSJ was directed by Malcolm Hoenlein from 1970 to 1976, Margy-Ruth Davis from 1976 to 1980 and Zeesy Schnur from 1980 to 1992 and Susan Green from 1993 to the present. In 1981 it became the Greater New York Coalition for Soviet Jews. Susan Green interview with the author, January 8, 1995.

The Canadian Committee for Soviet Jewry was the central address for Soviet Jewry in Canada and operated out of the CJC national offices in Montreal. Its directors were: David Sadowski from 1971 to 1974; David Shanoff 1975; Sam Resnick from 1976 to 1977; Martin Penn from 1978 to 1979; Carole Moscovitch from 1988 to 1989. Martin Penn interview with the author, August 1, 1990.

2 By the mid-1970s, the CJC regional committees were: Montreal Committee for Soviet Jewry; Ottawa Committee for Soviet Jewry; Committee for Soviet Jewry, Ontario Region (formerly The Toronto Steering Committee); Winnipeg Committee for Soviet Jewry; Calgary Committee for Soviet Jewry, Edmonton Committee for Soviet Jewry, Vancouver Action for Soviet Jewry (formerly Vancouver Committee for Soviet Jewry).

3 Presidents of the UCSJ included: Louis Rosenblum, Harold Light, Si Frumkin, Inez Weissman, Stuart Wurtman, Irene Manekovsky, Robert Gordon, Lynn Singer, Morley Shapiro and Pamela Braun Cohen.

4 Joan Dale, Doreen Gainsford and Barbara Oberman. Yitzhack Rager interview with the author, January 8, 1995.

5 Among the early members of the London 35s were: Joan Dale, Doreen Gainsford, Barbara Oberman, Gloria Green, Myra Janner, Rochelle Duke, Rita Eker. Doreen Gainsford was the founding chairman until she emigrated to Israel in the late 1970s. She was succeeded by Rita Eker and Margaret Rigal. Rita Eker interview with the author, March 19, 1989.

6 Ibid.

7 Leonard Schroeter, *The Last Exodus,* p. 262.

8 Rita Eker interview.

9 Rager succeeded Yehoshua Pratt in 1973 and remained with the consulate general for Israel in New York until 1976, when he was succeeded by Chaim Ber.

10 Personal recollections of the author.

11 Interview with Yitzhack Rager, June 20, 1990.

12 Among the founding members of the Montreal 35s were: Andrea Cohen Bronfman, Ellen Cohen, Elisabeth Dalfen, Wendy Litwack Eisen, Elaine Dubow Harris, Carrie Naimer Lehman, Angela Lipper, Dani Pollack, Marion Schauber, Gita Shapiro, Joy Schreiber, Barbara Stern, Greta Tarshis. Chairmen: Wendy Litwack Eisen, 1974–1981; Barbara Stern 1981–1992.

13 Andrea Bronfman interview with the author July 18, 1989.

14 Carol Reiter and Barbara Glass were co-chairmen of the Toronto group. Among the founding members were: Ruth Gilad, Jeanette Goldman, Genya Intrator, Linda Paton, Marilyn Raphael, Gella Rothstein, Dodie Rudson, Hilary Schneiweiss, Marilyn Siegel, Theresa Swern.

Simone Goldberg was the founding chairman of the Ottawa 35s, succeeded by Ruth Berger in 1976. In 1978, the Ottawa 35s joined forces with the Ottawa Committee for Soviet Jewry under the umbrella of the Ottawa Vaad. Co-Chairmen were: Ruth Berger and Rabbi Don Gerber 1978–1980; Ruth Berger and Rabbi Basil Herring, 1980–1984; Dr. Walter Handelman and Rabbi Reuven Bulka, 1984–1988; Sonny Tavel and Rabbi Reuven Bulka, 1988–1992. Ruth Berger interview with the author, August 2, 1989.

Barbara Glass and Carol Reiter helped to establish the "Winnipeg 35s." They included: Tina Lerner, chairman, Fran Ballon, Joyce Basman, Doris Bass, Karen Behar, Barbara Davidoff, Nella Eskin, Ettie Frank, Gail Garland, Rochelle Kantorowich, Janey Jacobson, Jo-Ann Katz, Judy Lichtman, Jeanne Pauls, Evelyn Schaefer, Emily Shane, Freda Steel, Elaine Stitz, Group of 35 Flyer, September 1976, Manitoba Archives.

15 Los Angeles had the only 35s group in the US.
16 Barbara Stern interview with the author, March 6, 1989.
17 The flyer concluded, "Today 40 Soviet Jews rot in prison because of this desire. It is in their name that we have purchased 40 tickets. To show our solidarity with them those seats will remain empty during the performance." Personal files of Wendy Eisen.
18 "Bolshoi is the target," *The Canadian Jewish News* (June 28, 1974).
19 Barbara Glass interview with the author, June 1, 1990.
20 "Ballet meets protest," *The Tribune* (July 13, 1974), p. 3.
21 The Halifax demonstration was organized by Frank Medjuck and Peter Stone, Frank Medjuck, written recollections sent to the author, November 25, 1992.
22 The demonstrators in Halifax, Regina and Calgary were members of Hadassah-Wizo, "Public Affairs Across Canada," Public Affairs Department, Hadassah-Wizo Organization of Canada, January 1974–January 1976, personal files of Cecile Shore, London, Ontario, Soviet Jewry Chairman of the Public Affairs Department of Hadassah-Wizo.
23 Ibid.
24 Barbara Glass, interview with the author, June 1, 1990.
25 "Soviets Turn down Ballet Tour," *The Montreal Star* (May 8, 1975).
26 Refuseniks: Anatoly Sharansky, Alexander Lerner, Uri Podriachik; Prisoners: Boris Penson, Dr. Mikhail Shtern, Israel Zalmanson; *Beryozka Program*, personal files of Wendy Eisen.
27 "Le Berioska et L'Etoile de David," *La Presse* (September 3, 1975) CJC Archives.
28 "Pickets at an exhibition," *The Gazette* (October 7, 1976); "Soviet hypocrisy protested," *The Montreal Star* (October 7, 1976); "Soviet art opening picketed," *Winnipeg Free Press* (August 12, 1976); Report of the Winnipeg 35s, 1977, CJC Archives.
29 Personal recollections of Wendy Eisen.
30 "Who will be next: Dissident's death blamed on KGB," *The Montreal Star* (April 26, 1976).
31 "Group of 35 protests treatment of Soviet Jews," *The Suburban* (October 25, 1979).
32 Canadian 35s, Canadian Hadassah-Wizo, National Council of Jewish Women, Na'amat Pioneer Women, Emunah Women, Canadian Women's Ort, B'nai Brith Women of Canada, Women's League for Conservative Judaism, Jewish Women's Federation.
33 The Toronto ceremony took place at City Hall and was attended by Mayor David Crombie and many Toronto aldermen. Department of the City Clerk, City Hall, Toronto, Ontario, January 22, 1976, CJC Archives, 21/10.Montreal's launching was chaired by City Councillor Nick Auf der Maur. Professor John Humphrey, president of Amnesty International addressed the assembly followed by a signing ceremony involving forty prominent Montreal women. *Report of the Montreal 35s – 1975*, personal files of Wendy Eisen.
34 MPs Robert Kaplan, Bud Drury, Hugh Faulkner, John Roberts, Gordon Fairweather and former prime minister John Diefenbaker; CCSJ Press Release, "Canadian Parliamentarians endorse the cause of Human Rights for Soviet Jewry," December 12, 1975, CJC Archives, C 14/6.
35 "New Campaign to free oppressed Soviet Jews," *The Ottawa Journal* (December 12, 1975).
36 Letter of endorsement from The Rt. Hon. John G. Diefenbaker, PC, QC, MP, former Prime Minister of Canada, (1958–1963), personal files of Wendy Eisen.
37 Sylviane Borenstein, Wendy Liwack Eisen, Elaine Dubow Harris, Martin Penn.

38 Letter to Elaine Dubow, c/o Group of 35, from Klaus Goldschlag, Under-Secretary of State for External Affairs, March 8, 1976, CJC Archives, 21/10.

39 Letter to The Hon. Allan J. MacEachen from Elaine Dubow, March 30, 1976, CJC Archives, 21/10.

NOTES, CHAPTER 9

1 Ben Kayfetz, "Brezhnev defends policy in encounter at airport," *The Canadian Jewish News* (February 8, 1974), p. 1.

2 Ibid.

3 Ibid.

4 "M'aidez" is colloquial French for "Help me," press release, Group of 35, Contacts: Angela Lipper and Ellen Cohen, CJC Archives, Vol.1/ No. 3.

5 Speakers included, Rabbi Benjamin Friedberg, spiritual leader of Ottawa's Agudath Israel and chairman of the Ottawa Committee for Soviet Jewry; J.B. Salsberg, Chairman, Toronto's Committee for Soviet Jewry; Genya Intrator, Chairman, Women for Soviet Jewry.

6 Letter to Charles S. Chaplin from Herbert S. Levy, Executive Vice-President of B'nai Brith, April 25, 1973, B'nai Brith files 1973, National Archives of Canada, Ottawa.

7 Charles Chaplin was one of the Canadian Soviet Jewry movement's unsung heros. On each of his five visits to the Soviet Union between 1975 and 1985 to negotiate the distribution of other Soviet films, he made "freedom for at least one refusenik" a condition of all contracts. Chaplin claims responsibility for the release of Sylva Zalmanson, the Gorakoff family of Moscow, the Lifshitz family of Tashkent, Inna Rutenberg of Moscow and lastly, in 1989, the Rabinovich family of Leningrad. Charles Chaplin interview with the author, July 28, 1989.

8 "Silva drops by to say thanks," *The Montreal Star* (November 12, 1974), p. F1; "Suicidal skyjack plot a plea to be set free," *The Gazette* (November 12, 1974).

9 Rabbi Leonid Feldman interview with the author, January 2, 1994.

10 Ibid.

11 Victor Brailovsky, Alexander Voronel, Mark Azbel, Mikhail Agorsky, Alexander Luntz, Dimitry Katz, Grigory Rosenstein, Vitaly Rubin, Anatoly Sharansky.

12 Barry Conn Hughes, "Next Year in Jerusalem? A surreptitious visit with some Soviet Jews who want out," *The Canadian Magazine* (June 8, 1974), p. 3–4. The weekly newsmagazine was distributed in thirteen Canadian newspapers coast to coast.

13 Personal remarks by Eduard Kuznetsov at the International Commemorative Conference on the occasion of the twentieth anniversary of the Jackson-Vanik Amendment, Jerusalem, January 9, 1995.

14 Richard Perle, "The Scoop on Sen. Jackson: He doomed an Evil Empire," *Forward* (January 6, 1995).

15 Ibid.

16 Biography of Alexander Goldfarb, CCSJ flyer, October 1975, CJC Archives.

17 Genya Intrator interview with the author, February 9, 1990.

18 Letter to the Scientific Attaché of the Embassy of the USSR in Washington, D.C., from Max Delbruck, Professor of Biology, California Institute of Technology, Pasadena, California, August 30, 1974, personal files of Genya Intrator.

19 Statement dated: Moscow February 10, 1975, to the International Conference on

Genetic Engineering, Ansilomar, California, Feb. 24–27, 1975, personal files of Genya Intrator.

20 Armand Hammer, *Hammer, an autobiography* (New York: G.P. Putnam's Sons, 1987), p. 35.

21 "Give me a Visa," *Portrait of Ida Nudel,* National Conference on Soviet Jewry, 1975, p. 2.

22 Statement by Lasal Kaminsky, prisoner, 1970–1975, *Our Ida Nudel, Testimonies of Former Prisoners and Refuseniks,* published by Israeli Women for Ida Nudel, Tel Aviv, 1980, p. 58.

23 Statement by David Chernoglaz, prisoner, 1971–1974, ibid, p. 1.

24 Present at the inaugural meeting were: Ron Cowitz, Sam Filer, Ralph Lean, Syd Moscoe, Bert Raphael, Moishe Reiter; Memorandum of meeting ad hoc committee of Lawyers for Soviet Jewry held October 29, 1974, personal files of Bert Raphael.

25 Among those in attendance were: The Hon. Mr. Justice Lieff, The Hon. Mr. Justice Lerner, The Hon. Justice B. Barry Shapiro.

26 "Law specialists meet to support Soviet Jews," *The Toronto Star* (April 29, 1975).

27 Letter from Bert Raphael to Ambassador Alexander Yacovlev, March 11, 1975, personal files of Bert Raphael.

28 Phyllis Pollack and Ruth Pollack chaired the Goldshtein committee for the MCSJ. "More Jews arrested," *The Suburban* (April 23, 1975).

29 The Montreal Committee for Soviet Jewry was chaired by Beverly Bronfman and directed by Stan Urman. Report to Executive Committee of the CCSJ, December 9, 1975.

30 Among the notables were: Gita Caiserman-Roth and Stanley Lewis, artists; Charlie Phillips, Canadian Labour Congress; Alan Raymond, historian; Dr. John E. Robbins, Amnesty International; Archdeacon Roy Playfair; Louise Garoux-Dubois, poetess; Steve Ferrughelli, Montreal Alouette Star Fullback; Judge Alain Montpetit; Dusty Vineberg-Solomon, journalist; John Robertson, radio personality; Professor Warren Harvey, McGill University; Rabbi Howard Joseph; Rabbi Sidney Shoham; Father Barry Jones, Archdiocese of Montreal; Quebec MLA Harry Blank; *The Canadian Jewish News* (June 20, 1975) and CJC Bulletin (June 1975).

31 Ibid.

32 Barbara Stern interview with the author, March 6, 1989.

33 *The Canadian Jewish News* (June 20, 1975).

34 Minutes of the CJC Executive Committee meeting, June 17th, 1975, CJC Archives.

35 John Robertson, CFCF Radio, Montreal, June 10, 1975.

Notes, Chapter 10

1 5,630 Jews had been granted permission to emigrate from 1967 to 1971. William W. Orbach, *The American Movement to Aid Soviet Jews*, p. 159.

2 World Presidium: Joseph Almogi, David Blumberg, Arye Dulzin, Gregorio Faigon, Lord Fisher of Camden, Avraham Harman, Claude Kelman, Philip M. Klutznick, Stanley H. Lowell, Rabbi Israel Miller, Nehemias Resnizki, Rabbi Alexander M. Schindler, David Suskind, Alexander Voronel; Brussels II program, personal files of Wendy Eisen.

3 International Secretariat: S. Zalman Abramov, Charlotte Jacobson, Claude Kelman, David Susskind, Albert D. Chernin, Eugene Gold, Jerry Goodman, Yehuda Hellman, Raya Jaglom, Greville Janner, Abraham Karlikow, Pierre Kaufmann, Joseph L. Klarman, Moshe Krona, Shneour Levenberg, Zvi Netzer, Sergio

Nudelstejer, Victor Polsky, Moshe Rivlin, Alan Rose (Canada's representative), Stephen Roth, Mark Turkow. Brussels II program, personal files of Wendy Eisen.

4 Irma Cherniak, Mordechai and Mira Pritzker had just arrived from Vienna. Report on Brussels II, Dr. William Korey, Director, B'nai Brith International Council. February 27, 1976, CJC Archives, Montreal.

5 "Brussels Conference II – an impressionistic report," Lewis D. Cole, Chairman, National Jewish Community Relations Advisory Council, USA.

6 The German students had challenged the international postal system and had won. International postal regulations stated that countries are required to pay triple the amount of the total postage cost of "registered mail" if registered letters are not delivered. The German students collected large sums of money from the Soviets for undelivered mail sent to refuseniks.

7 The "Group of 15," led by David Selikowitz in Paris, dealt with fifteen cases at a time.

8 Declaration of the Second World Conference of Jewish Communities on Soviet Jewry, personal files of Wendy Eisen.

9 Taped recording of Golda Meir in Brussels, 1976, personal files of Wendy Eisen.

10 David Satok interview with the author, July 9, 1990.

11 Fawcett attended three Scientific Seminars in Moscow refuseniks apartments – in 1976, 1977 and 1978. Professor Eric Fawcett interview with the author, March 25, 1992.

12 The Parliamentary delegation in the spring of 1975 included: Senators: the Hon. Ray Perrault, the Hon. William C. Petten. the Hon. Rhéal Bélisle; MPs Walter D. Baker, G.W. Baldwin, Florian Coté, André Fortin, Dr. Gaston Isabelle, Robert Kaplan, Stanley Knowles, Steve Paproski, Walter Smith. Personal files of Robert Kaplan.

13 Robert Kaplan interview with the author, July 5, 1990.

14 Report of the Montreal 35s, 1976, personal files of Wendy Eisen.

Notes, Chapter 11

1 Rabbi Leonid Feldman interview with the author, January 2, 1994.

2 Radio Liberty is a privately incorporated radio station, financed by the Congress of the United States. During the Cold War it reached millions of listeners in the Soviet Union in Russian and in many other languages. Its sister station, Radio-Free Europe, reached audiences in the Communist-dominated countries of Eastern Europe. The broadcast of the Russian tapes was made possible by Dr. Gene Sosin, then a senior executive in Radio Liberty's New York bureau. Dr. Gene Sosin's notes to the author, December 28, 1992.

3 Fifty-seven tapes were translated into English. They were distributed to Canadian travellers by the Montreal 35s and to Americans by the NCSJ.

4 Wendy Litwack Eisen and Elaine Dubow Harris, *They Came to Stay: the Soviet Jewish experience in Israel,* United Jewish Appeal Inc., USA, 1977.

5 The advertisement was sponsored by the "35s"– Montreal Women's Campaign for Soviet Jewry, The Student Struggle for Soviet Jewry, Montreal Committee for Soviet Jewry, Canadian Committee for Soviet Jewry. *The Gazette* (July 31, 1976), p. 11.

6 The Toronto Star (October 20, 1976).

7 "Jews stage sit-in at Supreme Soviet in rare protest," *The Gazette* (October 25, 1976).

8 "Soviet police arrest 33 Jews as party begins top-level meet," *The Gazette* (October 26, 1976).

9 Annual report of the Montreal Group of 35, submitted by Wendy Litwack Eisen, 1976–1977, personal files of Wendy Eisen.

10 Canadian Committee for Soviet Jewry, Information bulletin on Soviet Jewry, Vol. 3, Issue 4, April 1977, p. 2.

11 "Underground teacher," *The Jerusalem Post,* International Edition (October 16–22, 1983).

12 Martin Gilbert, *Sharansky – Hero of Our Time* (New York: Elisabeth Sifton Books, Viking Penguin Inc., 1986), p. 160.

13 Among the recommendations were that planes with new immigrants land during the day, instead of in the middle of the night; that Israelis be at the airport to welcome them; that Israeli officials permit the new olim to choose where they want to live, instead of forcing them to go to an absorption centre, often in a remote area of the country.

14 The Hon. John Fraser interview with the author, April 11, 1991.

15 Letter to His Excellency Alexander Yacovlev from MP John Fraser, January 31, 1977, CJC Archives, Vancouver.

16 MP John Fraser request for representations to Soviet Union to release Nahum Salansky, House of Commons Debates, 2nd Session, 30th Parliament, Vol. III, February 11, 1977, p. 2967.

17 Ruth Beloff Begun, "He's only just Begun – Yosef Begun: Portrait of a hero as a free man," Lifestyles (February, 1992).

18 Ruth Beloff Begun, "Unguessed routes to Jewish routes," *The Jerusalem Post* (April 5, 1993).

19 Ibid.

20 Report of the Montreal 35s, 1978, CJC Archives.

21 The luncheon was hosted by the Borad of Trade. Vancouver Soviet Jewry Committee, 1977, CJC, Vancouver.

22 John Fitzgerald, "Freed Soviet prisoner meets the reverend who got him out," *The Gazette* (May 13, 1977).

23 Interview with the Toronto rabbi, January 9, 1992.

24 Father Barry Jones interview with the author, August 1, 1990.

25 Founding members of the Committee were Father Barry Jones, Rev. Sid Nelson, Reverend John Simms, Reverend John Watson. Subsequent chairmen were: Rev. Sid Nelson, Fred Smith, Rev. Alec Farquhar. Frances Sheppard was the unofficial Secretary; John Hallward became active in the early 1980s and promoted Soviet Jewry through the Roman Catholic Church. Fred Smith succeeded Father Barry Jones as chairman from 1984 to 1988.

26 Father Barry Jones interview.

27 Carolyn Steinman was chairman of the Montreal Committee for Soviet Jewry, 1980–1982.

28 "Ned shares Bar Mitzvah with 'oppressed' Soviet," *The Gazette* (December 10, 1977), p. 10.

29 Ibid.

30 *The Bulletin* (December 15, 1977), CJC Archives, Vancouver.

NOTES, CHAPTER 12

1 Yuri Orlov and Alexander Ginzburg were not Jewish, but were sympathetic to the Jewish cause.
2 Vitaly Rubin received a visa in 1977. He was killed a few years later in an automobile accident in Israel.
3 Martin Gilbert, "A birthday behind bars," The Jerusalem Post International Edition (January 22–28, 1984).
4 Barbara Stern interview with the author, October 14, 1990.
5 Rabbi Martin Penn, interview with the author, August 1, 1990.
6 Switzerland, Sweden, Finland and Yugoslavia.
7 Alan Rose interview with the author, August 2, 1990.
8 William Korey from the US, Stephen Roth from the UK and Alan Rose from Canada.
9 Barbara Stern interview.
10 Closing Canadian statement by The Hon. Norm Cafik, representative of the Secretary of State for External Affairs to the Belgrade meeting of the CSCE, March 9, 1978, CJC Archives.
11 Rabbi A. James Rudin, " Did the Belgrade Conference make a difference?" *Christianity Today* (August 18, 1978), p. 21.
12 House of Commons debates, May 31, 1978, p. 5929.
13 Charles Caccia, MP, interview with the author, March 7, 1991.
14 Barbara Stern interview.
15 Ibid.
16 Letter to Wendy Eisen from Martin Gilbert, June 20, 1992.
17 NCSJ, Press Release, November 21, 1980, National Archives, Ottawa, MG 2BV 133, vol. 32, file 2.
18 Alan Rose, Barbara Stern, Bert Raphael, Irwin Cotler
19 Barbara Stern interview.
20 Max M. Kampelman, *Entering New Worlds* (New York: HarperCollins, New York, 1991), p. 278.
21 Barbara Stern interview.
22 R.Louis Rogers interview with the author, March 11, 1992.
23 William Bauer interview with the author, August 13, 1991.

NOTES, CHAPTER 13

1 The students joined a demonstration on April 13, 1978. Standing among the group of 35 was radiologist Dr. Michael Mindel, representing thirty radiologists from nine Montreal hospitals. Mindel attempted to deliver a letter of support for their colleague Maria Slepak.
2 Written by Wendy Litwack Eisen, Educational Coordinator, Montreal Committee for Soviet Jewry, edited by Martin Penn, printed and distributed by CJC, 1978.
3 The Bialik High School's Soviet Jewry Committee was chaired by Jane Respitz.
4 "Côte St. Luc students wait in vain for phone call to Soviet 'refusenik,'" *The Gazette* (December 21,1978).
5 The winning poster was drawn by Alain Lancry of Ecole Maimonides.
6 "Jewish kids plead for Soviet kin," The Montreal Star (June 2, 1978).

7 *Ida Nudel, A Hand in Darkness:* The autobiography of a refusenik (New York: Warner Books Inc., 1990), p. 159.

8 Our Ida Nudel, p.5.

9 Bert Raphael, chairman of the CLJSJ and Dennis McDermott, president of the Canadian Labour Congress sent letters to the prime minister, asking that he protest the sentences imposed on Vladimir Slepak and Ida Nudel, June 22, 1978, CJC Archives. Telegram to the Hon. Don Jamieson signed by Max Shecter, Chairman, CCSJ; Rabbi Gunther Plaut, President, CJC; Phil Givens, President, CZF; Hy Lampert, President, B'nai Brith of Canada; June 22, 1978, CJC Archives.

10 Letter to Alan Rose from the Hon. Don Jamieson, August 8, 1989, CJC Archives.

11 "The Hebrew Language on Trial," The Public Committee for Yosef Begun, Israel Public Council for Soviet Jewry, 1983.

12 *The Jerusalem Post* (June 30, 1978), personal files of Wendy Eisen.

13 Olivia Ward, "Ida Nudel: The determined dissident," *The Toronto Star* (November, 1986).

14 *A Hand in the Darkness,* p. 193.

15 Letter to Lord Michael Morris Killanin, President, International Olympic Committee, Lausanne, Switzerland, from US Congresswoman Patricia Shroeder, June 21, 1979, personal files of Wendy Eisen.

16 Letter from Rita Eker, Chairman London 35s to Wendy Litwack Eisen, Chairman Montreal 35s, July 1978. Personal files of Wendy Eisen.

17 "Petition to remove the 1980 Olympics from Moscow," CJC Archives, 7/13.

18 Moscow: M. Kremen, A. Lerner, L. Ulanovsky, G. Rozenstein, V. Brailovsky, A. Stolar, V. Yelistratov; Leningrad: A. Taratuta; Kiev: V. Kislik; Minsk: L. Ovsishcher; Vilnius: E. Finkelstein; Tbilisi: I. Goldshtein, ibid.

19 Statement from Michael Sherbourne to a meeting of the Union of Councils for Soviet Jewry in Washington, September 23, 1978, personal files of Wendy Eisen.

20 It read in part: "The spirit of freedom and open competition engendered by the Olympic Games should be consistent with the policies and practices of its host country." "Can Olympic spirit thrive in USSR?" Letter to the editor by Wendy Litwack Eisen, Chairman, Group of 35, Women's Campaign for Soviet Jewry, *The Gazette* (August 4, 1978).

21 "Misusing the Olympics," Editorial, *The Canadian Jewish News* (September 1, 1978), p. 4.

22 "Alert," Union of Councils for Soviet Jewry, Volume 2, No. 45, September 18, 1978.

23 Letter to Bert Raphael from The Hon. Don Jamieson, September 29, 1978.

24 David K. Shipler, "Soviet police said to raid homes of dissident Jews in three cities," *The New York Times* (December 23, 1978).

25 Marsha Slavens interview with the author, August 8, 1989.

26 NCSJ Newsbreak, March, 1979.

27 "I cannot forecast to you the action of Russia. It is a riddle, wrapped in a mystery inside an enigma but perhaps there is a key. That is Russian national interest." Winston Churchill, National Broadcast, September 25, 1939, Martin Gilbert, *Churchill: Finest Hour,* Vol. 6., p. 50.

28 Remarks by Eduard Kuznetsov at "Solidarity Sunday for Soviet Jewry," April 29, 1979, National Interreligious Task Force on Soviet Jewry, National Archives of Canada, Ottawa.

29 "Aborted hijacking ends in tearful Israeli reunion," *The Gazette* (April 30, 1979), p.8.

30 IWIN was created in February, 1979. The seven organizationa included were: National Council of Jewish Women, Mizrachi Women's Organization of Canada,

Canadian Hadassah-Wizo; Emunah Women, Pioneer Women-Na'amat, Women's Federation, Allied Jewish Community Services, Montreal; Women's Canadian ORT; B'nai Brith of Canada. Anna Spivack was the Ontario coordinator of WIN.

31 After being appointed Secretary of State for External Affairs in May 1979, MacDonald was suceeded by MP Diane Stratus. Letter to Ruth Pollack, National Coordinator WIN Committee, from Alan P. McLaine, Director Europe Division, Department of External Affairs, December 28, 1979, CJC Archives, 25/3.
32 As reported in letters to the editors of leading Canadian newspapers, from Ruth Pollack, December 10, 1979, CJC Archives.
33 May 1979, Canadian Hadassah-Wizo, Soviet Jewry report of 1979. Personal files of Cecile Shore.
34 *A Hand in Darkness,* p. 190.
35 Ibid.
36 Excerpts of the text of a letter sent to her sister via Evgeny Tsirlin in Moscow, dated September 22, 1978, ibid, p. 191.
37 Michele Landsberg, *The Globe and Mail* (June 18, 1981).
38 "Ida Nudel's Long White Night," *The Jerusalem Post* (June 17, 1986).
39 Anatoly Altman, Hillel Butman, Mark Dymshitz, Leib Khnokh, Eduard Kuznetsov, Anatoly Malkin, Boris Penson, Israel Zalmanson, Vulf Zalmanson.
40 Wendy Liwack Eisen, *Jewish Voices from the Soviet Gulag* (Jerusalem: UIA/Keren Hayesod, 1979).
41 Anatoly Altman interview with the author, August, 1979.
42 Ibid.
43 Eduard Kuznetsov interview with the author, August 1979.
44 Members of synagogues, religious schools and seven Jewish organizations participated in the program chaired by Judith Bloom. It was sponsored jointly by the World Jewry Committee of the NCJW and the CJC Committee for Soviet Jewry. Judith Bloom interview with the author, June 10, 1992. "Launch Kremlin Write-in," *Canadian Jewish News* (September 6, 1979).
45 "Meet the Press," moderator: Sid Margolese, Standard Broadcasting System; Panelists: Patrick Best, *The Ottawa Citizen;* Al Makay, CJOH News, Ottawa; Charles Lazarus, journalist, *Canadian Jewish News.* "Speakers, workshops on Soviet Jews examine Soviet human rights 'games'" *Canadian Jewish News* (November 29, 1979), p. 3. Irwin Cotler analyzed the phenomena of Jews "dropping out" in Vienna. Dr. William Korey, director of International Policy Research for B'nai Brith, USA, paid tribute to former Leningrad prisoner Boris Penson.
46 Speakers included: World Zionist Organization chairman Charlotte Jacobson; delegate to the UN's Human Rights Commission Walter Tarnopolsky; NCSJ Director Jerry Goodman; Professor Emil Fackenheim, Alan Rose and Professor Irwin Cotler.
47 House of Commons Debates, November 26, 1979, Motion by MP Duncan M. Beattie, seconded by MPs Herb Gray and Pauline Jewett.
48 Michael R. Beschloss and Strobe Talbott, *At the Highest Levels* (Great Britain: Little, Brown and Company Ltd.), p.113.

NOTES, CHAPTER 14

1 Passover statement dictated by Anatoly Sharansky from Moscow to Genya Intrator, March 1975, personal files of Wendy Eisen.
2 Martin Gilbert, "A birthday behind bars," *The Jerusalem Post,* International Edition (January 22–28, 1984).

3 Ibid, p. 73.
4 Irwin Cotler interview with the author, October 31, 1990.
5 *Next Year in Jerusalem*, p. 49.
6 Martin Gilbert, *Sharansky, Hero of Our Time* (New York: Elisabeth Sifton Books, Viking Penguin Inc., 1986), p. 165.
7 Ibid p. 179.
8 Interview with Avital Sharansky, *The Suburban* (November 16, 1977), p. A–24.
9 Alan M. Dershowitz, *The Best Defense*, p. 267.
10 Barbara Stern interview with the author, March 1989.
11 Letter to Ambassador Alexander Yakovlev from Joe Morris, President, Canadian Labour Congress, June 30, 1977, personal files of John Harker.
12 Information bulletin, Canadian Labour Congress, November 14, 1977. These initial stirrings of discontent culminated in the CLC severing relations with the Soviet Union, an action that lasted from 1978 to 1986. John Harker interview with the author, April 11, 1991.
13 Herb and Gloria Landis and Debby and Stan Solomon interview with the author, August 14, 1990.
14 Letter to Noah and Boris Landis from Boris Sharansky, October 24, 1977, personal files of Herb Landis.
15 Herb Landis' and Debby Solomon's grandfather and Sharansky's grandfather were brothers.
16 Rabbi Feder of Beth Tikvah Synagogue and Rabbi Monson of Beth Sholom Synagogue promoted the Sharansky telephone fund at every opportunity. As well, there was an "angel," David Leikin, a Toronto insurance agent, who asked the purchaser of each insurance policy he sold to make a donation to the Sharansky telephone fund. Genya Intrator interview with the author, August 17, 1990.
17 Ibid.
18 Drawn up and notarized by the late Danny Metarlin, notary of the Province of Quebec.
19 Minutes of a planning meeting of the Canadian Committee for Soviet Jewry held in Ottawa, November 7, 1977, p.4, CJC National Archives, 2/3.
20 The demonstration was co-sponsored by the Montreal 35s, the Montreal Committee for Soviet Jewry and the Montreal Inter-faith Task Force for Soviet Jewry.
21 *The Suburban* (November 16, 1977).
22 Among the fasting students were: Shelley Brooker, Danny Eisen, David Gotfrid, Penny Mepen, Raizel Robinson, Ralph Rubenstein.
23 Letter to The Rt. Hon. Pierre Elliott Trudeau from Bert Raphael, Chairman, Canadian Lawyers and Jurists for Soviet Jewry, December 1, 1977, personal files of Bert Raphael.
24 Telegram to "Fasting students," c/o Lou Garber, Central Square, Ross Building, York University, Toronto. December 5, 1977.
25 Telegram to: "York University Students on Hunger Strike," from Pierre Elliott Trudeau, Prime Minister of Canada, Prime Minister's Office, Ottawa, December 7, 1977, CJC Archives, 22/11.
26 Excerpt of telegram sent on December 7, 1977 to The Rt. Hon. Prime Minister Pierre Elliott Trudeau by students on Hunger Strike at York University, CJC Archives, 22/11.
27 *The Toronto Star* (December 8, 1977).
28 "PM urged to plead for Soviet in prison," *The Globe and Mail* (December 12, 1977).

29 Telegram from MP Robert Kaplan to the Ottawa Community Assembly, December 8, 1977, CJC Archives, 22/11.

30 "Rabbi lashes out at politicians," *The Journal* (December 10, 1977).

31 "Lawyer blasts Gov't silence on Sharansky," *The Journal* (December 9, 1977).

32 A Petition to Chairman Leonid I. Brezhnev: "Is Human Rights a Crime?" sponsored by the International Committee for the Release of Anatoly Sharansky, *The Montreal Star* (December 10, 1977).

33 It read: "*We do not wish to interfere in internal affairs, but we believe that human rights denied to Anatoly Sharansky are of universal and international concern.*" "MPs protest imprisonment of Soviet's Shcharansky," *The Toronto Star* (December 10, 1977).

34 Cafik assured the students that should the USSR refused to grant the request to release its prisoner, the Canadian government was prepared to take further action. *The Ottawa Citizen* (December 10, 1977), p. 12.

35 Present at the meeting with Cafik were members of the Sharansky family, Max Shecter, Joe Pomerant, MPs Robert Kaplan and Aideen Nicholson, several York University students, Sam Resnick and Ruth Rayman, ANATOLY SHARANSKY, The Canadian Connection, prepared by Sam Resnick, February 6, 1978, p. 2., CJC Archives, 22/16.

36 House of Commons Debates, December 12, 1977, p. 1763. "Hunger strike over, Cafik offers support," *The Globe and Mail* (December 12, 1977).

37 Among the refuseniks interrogated were well-known activists Yosef Ahs, Yakov Gordin, Lev Roitburd, Boris Tsitlonok, Benjamin Fein, Lev Ulanovsky, Dina Beilina, Victor Brailovsky, Martin Gilbert, "A Birthday behind bars," *Jerusalem Post,* International edition (January 22–28, 1984).

38 Rev. Canon Kenneth Cleater, Rev. Father Barry A. Jones, Rev. Sydney Nelson, Rabbi Sidney Shoham and Rev. Dr. John Simms.

39 The inscription read: "*Anatoly Sharansky, on your 30th birthday, with hope, concern and affection,*" Press Release, Montreal 35s, Jan. 20, 1978, CJC Archives 22/16.

40 House of Commons Debates, February 8, 1978, p. 2651, CJC Archives, 22/22.

41 The Winnipeg 35s sponsored a public rally opposite the Joseph Wolinsky Collegiate, where students were holding a twenty-four hour fast. The Winnipeg Group of 35 flyer, "Rally for Sharansky set for March 15th," March 9, 1978, Manitoba Archives.

42 Letter to Canadian community leaders from Max Shecter, Chairman CCSJ, March 15, 1978, personal files of Max Shecter.

43 "The Sharansky Trial," *Time Magazine* (July 24, 1978), p. 20.

44 David K. Shipler, "Portent of Soviet Dissident's Trial," *The New York Times* (July 10, 1978).

45 They included: a letter co-signed by Presidents of CJC, B'nai Brith, Hadassah-Wizo, Canadian Zionist Federation, CJC Archives, 22/23; letters from the International Committee for the Release of Anatoly Sharansky, (ICRAS) Lord Reading Society of Quebec (an association of Jewish lawyers and jurists in Quebec) and seventy professors from the University of Sherbrooke, CJC Archives, 22/14.

46 Dick Beddoes, "What results for rhetoric?" *The Globe and Mail* (July 13, 1978), p. 8.

47 *Winnipeg Free Press* (July 11, 1978), p. 1., CJC Archives, 22/7.

48 Across the road from the Soviet Consulate, housed in a small building, was the Desola Club, a private Jewish club that provided kosher meals and bathroom facilities for Soviet Jewry demonstrators during Sharansky's trial and on many other occasions.

49 Small leather box containing Hebrew texts on vellum, worn by Jews at morning weekday prayer to remind them to keep the law, *The Concise Oxford Dictionary,* Oxford University Press, 7th edition, 1982.

50 Cable from Dennis McDermott, President CLC to Mr. A. Shibayev, President AUCCTU, July 12, 1978, personal files of John Harker.
51 John Harker interview with the author, April 11, 1991.
52 "The Moscow Trials," *Newsweek* (July 28, 1978), p. 20.
53 As reported in the bulletin, "International Campaign – Orlov and Sharansky," May-June 1984.
54 David Levy, "Tolya will have a powerful tale to tell," reprinted in *The Canadian Jewish News* (February 27, 1986), p. 9.
55 Closing words at Sharansky's trial, recorded by his brother Leonid, *The New York Times* (July 15, 1978).
56 Speakers included: Miriam Garvis, Chairman MCSJ, Cantor Solomon Gisser, Rabbi Mark Golub, Professor Irwin Cotler, Alan Rose, Nick Auf der Maur, Father Barry Jones and Martin Penn. Update on Sharansky, MCSJ, July 1978, CJC Archives, 22/2.
57 "Sharansky appeal launched," *The Gazette* (August 31, 1978), p. 1.
58 Testimonies included those of American correspondent, Robert Toth, Professor Richard Pipes and Igor Melchuk. Included in the forty violations were: denial of due process of law at the time of arrest, infringement of the right to privacy, illegal search and seizure procedure, unlawful pre-trial detention, the denial of the right to a defense counsel of his own choice, and the denial of the right to a fair trial. The Law and the Soviet Union, Memorandum to CCLJSJ from Bert Raphael, November 13, 1978, personal files of Bert Raphael.
59 Irwin Cotler interview with the author, October 31, 1990.
60 Ibid.
61 John Harker interview with the author, April 11, 1991. Harker left the CLC in 1986 when relations with the Soviet Trade Union were just being restored as a result of the improving situation with Jewish emigration in the light of *glasnost* and *perestroika*.
62 Panelists included John Simmonds, executive secretary of the CLC, Paul Chapin, director of Eastern European Affairs at the Department of External Affairs, Irwin Cotler and Avital Sharansky. City Councillor Nick Auf Der Maur acted as moderator.
63 Telegram addressed to Professor Irwin Cotler and Mrs. Avital Sharansky from Pierre Elliott Trudeau, Prime Minister of Canada, March 19, 1977, CJC Archives, 22/25. Prof. Irving Glass, Aerospace and Engineering, University of Toronto; Dr. Robert Bell, Principal McGill University; Dr. Eric Fawcett, Department of Physics, University of Toronto; Prof. Larkin Kerwin, Department of Physics, Laval University; Prof. Gerhard Herzberg, Chancellor of Carleton University, "Soviet dissidents must be remembered," *The Gazette* (March 19, 1979), Editorial page.
64 "Author Richler joins in Sharansky protest," *The Canadian Jewish News* (June 1979).
65 Natan Sharansky, *Fear No Evil* (New York: Random House, 1988), p. 268.
66 "Avital's ordeal," *The Jerusalem Post Magazine* (March 2, 1979), p. 5.

Notes, Chapter 15

1 The game was designed by Shoshana Ramm, the sixteen-year-old daughter of Dmitri. It was produced by the U.S. Board of Jewish Education and made available to English speaking Soviet Jewry groups.
2 Debbie Shecter interview with the author, July 8, 1991.

3 "To Russia with Love," Canadian Bar Association, December 1978, p. 15, personal files of Bert Raphael.
4 Sam Filer's written recollections sent to the author, July 1991.
5 The necklace was crafted by Philadelphia activist Bobbie Morgenstern.
6 Personal recollections of Wendy Eisen.
7 They were briefed by Dorothy Hirsch of the U.S. Committee for Concerned Scientists.
8 Personal recollections of Wendy Eisen.
9 Sheila Roth interview with the author, September 8, 1992.
10 Alma Ata, Tashkent, Frunze, Buchara, Samarkand.
11 Martin Penn interview with the author, November 27, 1991.
12 The first two letters of the Hebrew alphabet.
13 Martin Penn interview.
14 "Canada will make formal protest over Soviets' expulsion of Cotler," *The Gazette* (August 21, 1979).
15 Irwin Cotler interview with the author, October 31, 1990.
16 Ibid.
17 Ibid.
18 Ibid.
19 Ibid.
20 Ibid.
21 Sharon Wolfe and Martin Penn interview with the author, August 1, 1990.
22 Goldie Hershon interview with the author, August 2, 1990.
23 Bracha Tritt interview with the author, November 24, 1991.
24 The Irgun, the Israeli underground, was established in the late 1930s by members of the revisonist movement led by Jabotinsky. From 1942 to 1948, these activists, under the leadership of Menachem Begin, fought the British to repeal their mandate and establish an independent Jewish State in Israel.
25 Anna Gonshor took over the Montreal travel program in 1983.
26 The briefing team included Joyce Eklove, Marsha Slivka and Sarah Samuels.
27 Charlotte Gray, Ottawa journalist; Robert Nixon, Member of the Ontario Legislature; Canon Borden Purcell, Ontario Human Rights Commission chairman; Rev. Stanford R. Lucyk, Minister, Timothy Eaton Memorial Church.
28 "A Report from Russia," sermon by the Reverend Stanford R. Lucyk, Timothy Eaton Memorial Church, Toronto, March 18, 1984.
29 Ibid.
30 "Reagan presidency bad news for Jews in Russia," *Kingston Whig-Standard* (October 15, 1984).
31 Ibid.
32 Reverend Stanford Lucyk interview with the author, July 25, 1990.
33 Charlotte Gray, "Soviet refuseniks fear Cold War talk," *The Toronto Star* (April 15, 1984).
34 "The Mariasins: Family of outcasts," ibid.
35 Alexander Mariasin interview with the author, Toronto, July 16, 1992.
36 Letter to Edward Bronfman from Frederick N. Smith, May 31, 1985, personal files of F. N. Smith.

Notes, Chapter 16

1 Peter C. Newman, "Dateline: Soviet Union, The 'Dead Souls' of Moscow," *Maclean's* (January 21, 1980), p. 5.
2 Peter Newman interview with the author, January 29, 1992.
3 "Dateline: Soviet Union, The 'Dead Souls' of Moscow" ibid.
4 "Urges more lawyers to act for human rights," *The Canadian Jewish News* (April 10, 1980), p. 10. Bert Raphael, *Chairman's 1980 report* May 28, 1980, personal files of Bert Raphael.
5 "Seder, March to Consulate, tribute to Soviet Jewry," *The Canadian Jewish News* (April 17, 1980), p. 1.
6 Ibid.
7 "Ida Nudel, the determined dissident," *The Toronto Star*.
8 Letty Cottin Pogrebin, "A Communist Plot," *Ms.* (October, 1988).
9 They included: Joan Macklin, President, Business and Professional Women's Club of Montreal; Ruth Hinkley, President, National Council of Women of Canada; Marguerite B. Eudes of the Conseil des Arts; Madelaine Herbert of the Association des Infirmieres du Quebec and Claire Lalonde of the Federations des Femmes du Quebec. Sister Marie-Noelle and Sister Margaret Roberts collected the signatures of all the nuns from Centre Mi-Ca-El and the Sacred Heart Convent. "One hundred well-known women lend support to Ida Nudel," *The Canadian Jewish News* (May 30, 1979).
10 "Free Col. Lev Ovsishcher," as related by Ilya Goldin, former Minsk activist, distributed by the Toronto Committee for Lev Ovsishcher, 1980, personal files of MPP Reverend Roland de Corneille.
11 The Hon. John Fraser, Speaker of the House of Commons, interview with the author, April 11, 1991.
12 Present at the call were Fraser, Calgary alderman Nomi Whalen, Barbara Shumiatcher, members of the Vancouver Action Committee for Soviet Jewry and members of Congregation Beth Israel's "Ovsishcher Committee," Mr. and Mrs. Mickey James, Betty Nitkin, Lorne Cristall, Joel Bellas.
13 " 'It is very difficult now," – John Fraser calls Ovsishcher," *The Bulletin* (March 13, 1980), CJC Archives, Pacific Region.
14 The committee, chaired by Joel Hirsch, was an outgrowth of Friends of Pioneering Israel. Included in the program was the colour guard of the Toronto post of the Jewish War Veterans of Canada and the Temple Sinai Choir.
15 Rev. Roland de Corneille served as director of B'nai Brith's League for Human Rights from 1971 to 1979, when he was elected to Parliament. Roland de Corneille interview with the author, July 4, 1991.
16 Standing Order 43, May 20, moved by MP Roland de Corneille, and seconded by MP Bill Kempling: "MPs urge Soviets to extend rights," *The Gazette* (May 21, 1980).
17 Letter to the Hon. Mark MacGuigan, MP, Secretary of State for External Affairs, from MP John Fraser, August 5, 1980, personal files of Roland de Corneille.
18 Letter to Roland de Corneille from MP Jesse Flis, December 4, 1980, personal files of Roland de Corneille.
19 Nechemiah Levanon, "Special focus on 'Special Office,' "*Alert,* The Union of Councils for Soviet Jews, Vol. IV, No. 18, March 18, 1980.
20 Nechemiah Levanon interview with the author, December 25, 1991.
21 Ibid.
22 Abba Eban, "The Soviet Dropout Issue," *Congress Monthly*, Volume 43, Washington,

D.C., 1976, as found in *Canadian Jewish Involvement with Soviet Jewry, 1970–1990, The Toronto Case Study,* the 1993 PhD dissertation of Mindy Avrich-Skapinker.

23 NCSJ Policy Statement, submitted for approval to the 1980 Policy Conference, April 15, 1980, Washington, D.C., CJC Archives, 15/13.

24 Participants at the conference included members of the British, Swiss, French, Belgian, Canadian 35s, SSSJ, UCSJ and Comité de Quinze.

25 Professor Alexander Voronel, Professor Mark Azbel, Vladimir Lazaris, Dr. R. Nudelman, E. Sotnikova.

26 "Former editors of unofficial journal speak out for Victor Brailovsky," National Conference on Soviet Jewry, Press Service, November 21, 1980.

27 Text of telegram in the body of a letter to the editor of the Ottawa *Citizen*, "Scientist silenced," *The Citizen* (December 17, 1980).

28 Canadian Committee of Scientists and Scholars (CCSS) Press Release, personal files of Irwin Cotler, CJC Archives.

29 Panelists included: Professor Eric Fawcett, Department of Physics, University of Toronto; Dr. Naum Salansky, formerly of Vilnius, USSR, Institute of Aerospace Studies; Dr. Jeremy Stone, Director of the Federation of American Scientists.

30 *The Canadian Jewish News*, May 7, 1981.

31 Olga Fuga, regional director of the Canadian Council of Christians and Jews; Deputy Mayor Pearl McGonigal; Dr. Beverley Tangrey, Professor of Economics at University of Manitoba; and Roberta Ellis of the Manitoba Action Committee on the Status of Women, "Rally for Ida Nudel," *The Jewish Post* (June 25, 1981), CJC Archives, Winnipeg.

32 Address by Professor Sally Zerker to Ida Nudel Rally, June 22, 1981, personal files of Sally Zerker.

33 "Rally held for dissident," *Toronto Sun* (June 23, 1981).

34 "MPs pledge pressure over Soviet dissidents," *The Toronto Star* (June 23, 1981), p. A15.

35 Martin Penn interview with the author, August 1, 1990.

36 Motion under S.O. 43, House of Commons Debates, Human Rights, p. 10,634, June 16, 1981.

37 Bert Raphael, letter to the editor, *The Globe and Mail* (June 18, 1981).

38 Robert Gillette (Los Angeles Times), "Strange ways of Soviet Justice," *The Toronto Star* (June 24, 1981).

39 "Canadians must help Soviet Jews: Toronto MP," *The Toronto Star* (September 22, 1981).

40 "Gromyko ignores question by MacGuigan over Jews," *The Globe and Mail* (September 30, 1981).

41 The Hon. Justice Mark MacGuigan interview with the author, April 11, 1991.

42 Frank Medjuck's written recollections for the author, November 25, 1992.

43 Ottawa's Soviet Jewry Shabbat was held in a different synagogue annually. A guest speaker dramatized the dynamics of Soviet Jewry from the pulpit. Report of the Ottawa Soviet Jewry Committee, 1981, Ruth Berger and Rabbi Dr. Basil Herring co-chairmen, CJC Archives, Ottawa.

44 Soviet Jewry activity in Calgary was generated through Hadassah-Wizo and Young Judea until 1979 when the Calgary Committee for Soviet Jewry was created and chaired by Rena Cohen. "Fight for human rights," *The Calgary Herald* (December 12, 1981), CJC Archives, Calgary. "City group forms to help Paritskys, Soviet outcasts," *The Calgary Jewish Star* (November 6–19, 1981), CJC Archives, Calgary. Calgary efforts were co-ordinated by Shira Waldman of NCJW, Karen Behar and Gila Lesky of the House of Jacob sisterhood, and Rena Cohen, chairman of the Calgary Committee for Soviet Jewry Chairman, CJC.

In the early days in London, Ontario, Simchat Torah rallies and Soviet Jewry letter-writing programs were coordinated through Hadassah-Wizo and the NCJW. In 1979, Dr. Harold Mersky established a committee to spearhead a petition campaign at the University of Western Ontario on behalf of Alexander Paritsky.

45 Letter to The Hon. F.L. Jobin, Lt.-Gov. of Manitoba from The Winnipeg 35s (Shelley Feuer, Gail Garland, Joanne Katz, Tina Lerner, Gwen Satran, Evelyn Schaefer, Emily Shane), October 2, 1981, personal files of Tina Lerner.

46 Letter to the Winnipeg 35s from Bud Jobin, December 9, 1981, personal files of Tina Lerner.

47 Barbara Shumiatcher, Chairman of the Vancouver Action for Soviet Jewry 1978–1982, interview with the author, November 1990.

48 The man behind the scenes in setting up the Legislature Committee was Mordechai Ben Dat, researcher for MPP Jim Breithaupt and policy research analyst for the leader of the opposition.

49 David Rotenberg interview with the author, July 27, 1990.

50 Penny Collenette, Lucille Broadbent, Jane Crosbie, Lucille Desmarais, Audrey King and Carol Regan.

51 One hundred signatures from federal spouses and 125 from provincial spouses, including the wives of premiers – Cathy Davis, Ontario; Anne Blakeney, Saskatchewan; Adele Pawley, Manitoba; Anna Lee, Prince Edward Island; Marina Peckford, Newfoundland; Audrey Bennett, British Columbia, "Spouses of MPs petition for release of Soviet Jew," *The Globe and Mail* (December 1981).

52 Penny Collenette interview with the author, August 2, 1990.

53 *Pipeline* was produced by the Ontario Region Committee for Soviet Jewry of CJC, Jeanette Goldman, chairman 1981–1986 and Sam Resnick, director, 1971–1987, TJC/CJC archives.

54 The conference was co-chaired by Barbara Stern and Ruth Leroy.

55 Among the Plenary speakers were: Barbara Stern, Irwin Cotler, MPs David Smith, Jim Peterson, David Orlikow, John Fraser, Serge Joyal; Israeli guests were Sara Frankel, Josef Mendelevich. The workshops included "education," "travel," and "media."

56 Remarks by Sara Frankel, personal notes of Wendy Eisen, December 10, 1981.

57 Report of the Montreal Committee for Soviet Jewry, CJC Archives, June 1981.

Notes, Chapter 17

1 "Still The Prisonhouse of Peoples," *The New York Times* (January 26, 1982).

2 The telephone call was initiated by members of Holy Blossom Temple's Israel-Diaspora committee: Valerie Sloman, Barbara Stupp, Joan Kerbel and Rabbi Jim Prosnit. Also present at the call were Harvey Fields and MP John Roberts with Genya Intrator serving as translator.

3 Marsha Slivka interview with the author, May 29, 1991.

4 Letter from David Smith, MP, Chairman of the Parliamentary Group on Soviet Jewry, to Marsha Slivka January 4, 1983.

5 "The Postman doesn't come too often to the Vasilevskys," *Holy Blossom Temple Bulletin* (March 25, 1983), personal files of Marsha Slivka.

6 From 1983 to 1986, there were more than two hundred twinnings in Toronto annually. Most rabbis enthusiastically endorsed the program and presented a certificate to each child as a lasting reminder of the special event. Temple Sinai, Beth David, Beth Avraham Yosef (Toronto), and Beth Tikvah relied on the co-ordination

of Eklove's twinning committee, a sub-committee of the Ontario Region's Soviet Jewry Committee. Holy Blossom Temple's twinning program was co-ordinated by Marsha Slivka and Beth Tzedec Synagogue's by Genya Intrator.

A bar or bat mitzvah twinning took place at Beth Tikvah almost every week. Rabbi Marcus felt this to be an integral part of Beth Tikvah's educational program. Joyce Eklove interview with the author, June 30, 1990.

7 In 1983, Adam Brett, son of Naida Rubin, director of Soviet Jewry programming through the community relations office of CJC in Winnipeg, twinned his Bar Mitzvah with Carmi Elbert, son of Lev Elbert in Kiev.

8 Ibid.

9 Aviva Layton, "To Russia with love," *Today Magazine, The Toronto Star* (May 15, 1982).

10 Raised by The Hon. Flora MacDonald, "Human Rights," House of Commons Debates, March 19, 1982, p. 15,617, personal files of Roland de Corneille.

11 Moisey Lieberman and Viacheslav Royak.

12 The event was sponsored by the OLCSJ and CJC's Ontario Region Soviet Jewry Committee. Speakers included: MPPs Jim Breithaupt, David Rotenberg and Marion Bryden, and Ontario Region Soviet Jewry chairman, Jeanette Goldman. "MacDonald receives award," *The Canadian Jewish News* (May 13, 1982).

13 The "Freedom Ride" Cyclathon was co-sponsored by Canadian Jewish Students Network, Vancouver Action for Soviet Jewry (Pacific branch, Canadian Committee for Soviet Jewry) and B'nai Brith Hillel, prior to the event remarks were made by Wilf Sternin, former Soviet Jew; Barbara Schumiatcher, VASJ chairman; Melanie Rosenbaum and Stacey Berlow of Network "Vancouver cycles for Soviet Jewry," *The Bulletin* (May 27, 1982).

14 On October 20, a five-hour search of the apartment led to the seizure of Hebrew teaching cassettes, a tape recorder, a typewriter, 112 books and pamphlets on Jewish themes. Martin Gilbert, "Underground teacher," *The Jerusalem Post,* International Edition (October 16–22, 1983).

15 Ibid.

16 House of Commons Debates, 1st Session, 32nd Parliament (February 22, 1983), p. 23,091.

17 Shirley Carr was to represent the CLC in Geneva. "ILO to include Begun case on Geneva agenda," *The Canadian Jewish News* (March 3, 1983), p. 10.

18 The $100,000 award was shared with U.S. Senator Henry Jackson and France's Mme. Simone Weil. Upon his arrival in Israel in January 1988, a cheque for $33,000, Begun's share of the prize, was presented to him by Israeli prime minister Shamir. Yosef Begun interview with the author, October 8, 1992.

19 "Begun wants people to write to him," *The Jerusalem Post* (October 27, 1983).

20 "Soviet anti-Semitism flares up," *Business Week* (May 30, 1983).

21 Report, Committee for Soviet Jewry, Ottawa Region, April 1985, CJC Archives.

22 The *Pravda* article was exposed in Canada by Christian supporters Jay and Meridel Rawlings. Notes on visit to the Soviet Union – Jay, Meridel and Chris Rawlings, March 27–April 6, 1983, personal files of Wendy Eisen.

23 The anonymous rabbi, interview with the author, January, 1992.

24 Report of Jeanette Goldman, Committee for Soviet Jewry, Ontario Region, March 1983, personal files of Wendy Eisen.

25 There were forty-two Canadians present.

26 Madame Simone Weil of France, former president of the European Parliament; the Hon. Jeane Kirkpatrick, U.S. ambassador to the United Nations; and Ambassador Max Kampelman, American CSCE delegation-head in Madrid Israeli speakers

included Dr. Gideon Hausner, Professor Yoram Dinstein, Arye Dulzin, Josef Mendelevich, President Yitzhack Navon and Prime Minister Menachem Begin. Telegrams of support were sent by Presidents Reagan and Mitterand and Prime Ministers Thatcher, Trudeau and Hawke.

27 A new popular game in Soviet schools was "Concentration Camp," where Jewish children were forced to take numbers, and then were locked into cupboards while the Soviet children stood chiding them.

28 "Soviet Jewish life 'worst in decade,'" (as reported in the *Baltimore Sun*), *Winnipeg Free Press* (March 17, 1983).

29 Report of Jeanette Goldman.

30 Audrey Bennett, B.C.; Jeanne Lougheed, Alberta; Adele Pawley, Manitoba; Patsy Lee, P.E.I.; Marina Peckford, Newfoundland; Kathy Davis, Ontario.

31 Hazel Hawke, wife of Australian prime minister; Thea Muldoon, wife of New Zealand's prime minister; Veronika Carstens, wife of the president of West Germany; Lily Schreyer, wife of the governor general of Canada. "Political wives join to aid Soviet Jews," *The Ottawa Citizen* (April 29, 1983), p.42.

32 Press release from the Parliamentary Spouses Association, May 4, 1983, personal files of Penny Collenette.

33 Present were Kathy Davis, wife of Ontario Premier Bill Davis, Arlene Perly Rae, wife of Ontario NDP leader Bob Rae, Maureen McTeer, wife of Progressive Conservative leader Joe Clark and Maurice Sauvé, husband of Madame Jeanne Sauvé.

34 Join statement issued by the Parliamentary Spouses for Soviet Jewry and the American Congressional Wives for Soviet Jewry, May 5, 1983, personal files of Penny Collenette.

35 Penny Collenette, Lucille Desmarais, Lucille Broadbent and Audrey King. The meeting was arranged by Alan McLaine, head of the Department of External Affairs Eastern European Desk. Alan McLaine, interview with the author, August 2, 1989.

36 "MPs' wives plead for Soviet Jews," *The Toronto Star* (May 14, 1983), p. A3.

37 Remarks of Ida Nudel in Bendery, as spoken to Jeanette Goldman, April 24, 1983.

38 "Callwood overwhelmed by top award," *The Toronto Star* (May 4, 1983), p. A16.

39 Interview with Penny Collenette, August 2, 1989.

40 "Push Moscow to let Jews leave, PM told," *The Toronto Star* (May 16, 1983), p. 10.

41 The delegation included: Madame Jeanne Sauvé, her husband, Maurice; The Hon. and Mrs. Yvon Pinard, president of the Privy Council; The Hon. and Mrs. Donald Johnston, Minister of State for Economic and Regional Development; Mr. Doug Lewis, House Leader of the Official Opposition; Mr. Ian Deans, House Leader New Democratic Party. Memo from Alan Rose to the National Officers of CJC, August 1, 1983.

42 "False Soviet charges 'just the beginning,' " Esther Nobleman, Chairman, Canadian Committee for Soviet Jewry, Pacific Region, *Jewish Western Bulletin*, Vancouver, B.C. (December 15, 1983).

43 House of Commons Debates, Human Rights, "Plight of Ina and Lev Elbert," September 19, 1983.

44 "Report on a Visit to the Soviet Union," Bunny and Ben Zion Shapiro, June 19–July 2, 1983.

45 "Repression stepped up in Odessa," *Jewish Western Bulletin* (June 30, 1983), CJC Archives, Vancouver.

46 "Say goodbye to Soviet sister city," *The Province* (September 23, 1983).

47 Written report by Esther Nobleman, November 27, 1989. Esther Nobleman assumed the chairmanship from Barbara Shumiatcher in 1983 and worked with

Rita Cohn, Ronnie Tessler and CJC executive director, Mark Silverberg. It was geographically appropriate for Vancouver activists to communicate with West coast communities through the Union of Councils for Soviet Jewry in Seattle and the Bay Area in San Francisco.

48 "British MP: Keep up the pressure," *The Canadian Jewish News* (December 3, 1983).

49 Ibid.

50 Speakers included Leslie C. Green, Professor of Law at the University of Alberta, MP Ian Deans and Deirdre McLoughlin, a Catholic leader who had visited the USSR. The conference was held at Beth Tikvah Synagogue, Ontario Region for Soviet Jewry Report, 1983.

51 The constitution stated: "*The goal of the Parliamentary Group for Soviet Jewry is to work on behalf of Soviet Jews, to monitor their status, to press for their release and their religious freedom, to work for the release of those refused exit visas and those Jews imprisoned for exercising their rights.*" Copy of the constitution of the All-Party Parliamentary Group on Soviet Jewry: Memo to Canadian Senators and Members of Parliament from MP David Kilgour, November 30, 1984, personal files of David Kilgour.

NOTES, CHAPTER 18

1 "President Reagan expresses concern for Soviet Jewry," *Newsbriefs*, NCSJ, 1984.

2 *Newsbriefs.*

3 William Korey, "Soviet Jews' Anxiety," *The New York Times* (January 14, 1984).

4 "Pravda Sharply Assails Israel, Zionism," *The Washington Post* (January 18, 1984).

5 Ibid.

6 Ibid.

7 Rev. Stanford Lucyk, chairman; Rabbi Dow Marmur, Rabbi Erwin Shields, Rabbi Benjamin Friedberg, Rev. Bruce McLeod, Rev. Elizabeth Kilgour, Sister Mary Jo Leddy, Rev. John Erb, Canon Borden Purcell, Rev. John Hilborn, Rev. Ron Scott, Rev. Robert Trimble, Rev. Tim Grew. Fred Smith, formerly of Montreal, joined the committee in 1988. The lay members were Professor Irving Abella and Wendy Eisen.

8 Remarks by the Rev. Dr. Stanford Lucyk, May 23, 1992, CJC Plenary.

9 "Pressure on Soviets will Continue," *The Canadian Jewish News* (April 12, 1984).

10 At the third and final meeting, parliamentary spouses were represented from the United States, Canada, Britain, the Netherlands, France and Israel. Representing Canada in London were: Chairman Audrey King, Janet Crosbie, Donna Wenman, Janet Foster, Lucille Broadbent, Doreen Doody, Penny Collenette. Goldie Hershon accompanied the group as the CCSJ representative.

11 Fonda delivered speeches about Nudel, wrote to American politicians and Soviet officials and ran in four ten-kilometre races on behalf of Soviet Jewry.

12 *A Hand in Darkness*, p. 287–8.

13 "Fonda meets with Nudel," JTA, *Daily News Bulletin* (May 2, 1984).

14 The hearings were coordinated by Sharon Wolfe and Martin Penn and sponsored by the Parliamentary Group for Soviet Jewry.

15 MPs Jim Peterson, John Fraser, Roland Comtois, Ian Deans co-chaired the hearings. Witnesses included: MPs Lynn McDonald, Fred King, Flora MacDonald; Canadian Soviet Jewry experts: Barbara Stern, Jeanette Goldman, Martin Penn, Alan Rose, Professor Irwin Cotler; Alexander Slepak, son of refusenik Vladimir Slepak, Lev Utevsky, former refusenik and Isaac Paritsky, brother of prisoner Alexander Paritsky. "Soviets use Jews as bartering tools, MPs told" *The Toronto Star* (May 15, 1984).

16 "Canada must become more forthright in its human rights policy." House of Commons debates, May 15, 1984, p. 3,732 "The matter of Soviet human rights violations must be raised more vigorously in bilateral discussions with the Soviets," MP Lynn McDonald, House of Commons Debates, May 16, 1984, p. 3,773. MP David Orlikow urged the prime minister to speak with a louder voice against repression of rights of Soviet Jews, House of Commons Debates, May 22, 1984, p. 3,924.

17 Rabbi Reuven P. Bulka, "Are we caught napping?" *The Ottawa Jewish Bulletin & Review* (October 5, 1984).

18 Sharon Wolfe interview with the author, August 1, 1990.

19 They were assisted by MPs Robert Kaplan, Ian McDonald and Howard McCurdie. David Kilgour interview with the author, August 2, 1989.

20 Sheila Finestone interview with the author, May 29, 1990. (Sheila Finestone's personal commitment to the issue of Soviet Jewry dated back to her days as president of Women's Federation of Allied Jewish Community Services in Montreal. Almost fifteen years later, in her new capacity as an elected Member of Parliament, she was recruiting fellow Parliamentarians for support for the same issue.)

21 Nelson Riis interview with the author, March 7, 1990.

22 Ibid.

23 A protest campaign to inundate UN Secretary General Perez de Cuellar with postcards condemning the Odessa searches, undertaken by the Inter-religious Task Force for Soviet Jewry in the United States, was spearheaded in Canada by Herb Landis. He enlisted the support of MP Roland de Corneille, Rev. Hilchey, Archdeacon of the Anglican Church in Canada and Alan Lazerte, head of the Canadian friends of the International Christian Embassy in Jerusalem. Ten thousand cards were mailed from Canada. Reports reached the West that the confiscated items had been returned. Herb Landis interview with the author, August 28, 1990.

24 Moshe Abramov (Samarkand); Josef Berenshtein (Moscow); Yacov Gorodetsky (Leningrad); Yacov Levin, Yacov Mesh, Mark Niepomnishchy (Odessa); Zachar Zunshain (Riga).

25 Soviet Jewry update, CCSJ, November, 1984.

26 "Soviet guest of honour fails to make appearance," *The Chronicle-Herald* (November 3, 1984).

27 Among the MPs attending the November 21 meeting were opposition leader John Turner, justice critic Robert Kaplan and newly-appointed Parliamentary Group chairman David Kilgour. Speakers included: sovietologist Dr. Alan Pollack; international affairs director of the Canadian Labour Congress, John Harker; Consul of Israel to New York, Yeshayahu Barzel; University of Toronto sociologist, Dr. William Michaelson; Nicolas Etheridge, member of the Canadian delegation to the CSCE Experts Meeting on Human Rights; MP David Kilgour, Father Barry Jones, Rabbi Reuven Bulka.

28 Letter to John Harker from Soviet counsellor Fomitchev, as quoted in a report by John Harker at the National Meeting of the CCSJ, November 21, 1984, p. 7, personal files of John Harker.

29 Ibid.

30 "Declare December 10, 1984 Fast Day," Memorandum from the CCSJ to Canadian Soviet Jewry Committees, Ottawa.

31 "World protests to spotlight plight of Soviet Jews," *The Globe and Mail* (December 11, 1984).

32 Montrealers gathered outside the Soviet Consulate. Torontonians fasted at Queen's

Park. Speakers were MPPs, Marion Bryden, Robert Nixon, David Rotenberg. An all-party resolution condemning the arrests and imprisonment of the Hebrew teachers was passed inside the Legislative Assembly. "The House condemns suppression of Jewish culture and urges the Soviet Union to drop charges and release those unjustly imprisoned and allow them to continue in the pursuit of learning." Moved by The Hon. Mr. Wells, seconded by Mr. Nixon and Mr. Martel, Orders of the Day, Legislative Assembly of Ontario, December 10, 1984, p. 47.

33 Forty copies of the resolution, each signed by a member of the legislature, were mailed to the Soviet ambassador in Ottawa. "Human Rights – Plight of Hebrew Teachers in USSR," House of Commons Debates, December 10, 1984, p. 1,050.

34 Yacov Levin sentenced to three years; Josef Berenshtein, four years; Yuli Edelshtein, three years; Alexander Kholmiansky, eighteen months; Mark Nepomniashchy, three years, "The Soviet Campaign against Hebrew teachers," NCSJ, April 1985.

NOTES, CHAPTER 19

1 Letter to the Quebec Region Executive of Canadian Jewish Congress from Goldie Hershon, Chairman, Montreal Committee for Soviet Jewry, February 26, 1985, CJC Archives.

2 Letter to The Hon. Joe Clark, from Marion Bryden, MPP, March 6, 1985, personal files of Wendy Eisen. "The preservation of Human Rights must at all times be a major concern of the Canadian government with respect to our relations with the Soviet Union. I would request that you advise me, at the earliest opportunity, of the steps that your government is taking to ease the plight of Soviet Jewry." Letter to The Rt. Hon. JoeClark from Jean Chrétien, March 7, 1985, CJC Archives, 24/5.

3 Letter to W. Bernard Herman from The Rt. Hon. Joe Clark, March 29, 1985, personal files of Wendy Eisen.

4 "Students protest Soviet treatment of Jews," *The Citizen,* Ottawa (March 27, 1985), p. A3.

5 House of Commons Debates, "Anti-Semitism – USSR treatment of Jews," March 26, 1985, p. 3370.

6 "Clark raises issue on Soviet visit – Gromyko spurns human rights appeal," *The Globe and Mail* (April 4, 1985), p. 1.

7 Ibid.

8 In response to a question by MP Alex Kindy, House of Commons Debates, "USSR – Minister's discussions on reunification of families," April 23, 1985, p. 4,024.

9 *The Canadian Jewish News* (June 2, 1985).

10 Father Barry Jones, Alex Farquhar, John Hallward, Fredrick N. Smith, "A Special visit to the USSR," *The Cathedral Newsletter* , John Hallward, summer 1985, personal files of F.N. Smith.

11 Letter to Stephen Lewis, Canadian Ambassador and Permanent Representative to the United Nations, from Father Barry Jones, June 14, 1985.

12 Letter to Father Barry Jones from Stephen Lewis, September 4, 1985, personal files of Father Barry Jones.

13 Letter to Dr. Henry Kolatasz, Department of External Affairs, Eastern European Division, from David Kilgour, requesting a meeting with the Montreal Inter-faith travellers, October 7, 1985, personal files of David Kilgour. Letter to the Rt. Hon Joe Clark from David Kilgour, MP, August 2, 1985, CJC Archives 23/5.

14 Single performances took place in concert halls in Ottawa, Montreal, Toronto, Winnipeg, Edmonton, Red Deer, Vancouver, Victoria October 22 – November 6,

1985. Letter to Mr. Barry Bowater from David Kilgour, October 3, 1985, personal files of David Kilgour.

15 Publicity promotion for *Gates of Brass,* Ottawa Committee for Soviet Jewry, April 1985.

16 Messages were received from Brian Mulroney, John Turner, Ed Broadbent and read at each Simchat Torah rally. Mulroney wrote: "*We continue to be concerned with reports of religious and cultural oppression of Soviet Jews together with the drastic decline in the number of Jews allowed to emigrate.*" "Greetings from the Prime Minister of Canada," October, 1985, CJC Archives. The Toronto Simchat Torah Rally, held on October 6, was sponsored by the "Coalition for Soviet Jewry," comprised of fifty-five Jewish organizations, schools, youth groups and synagogues. A full-page advertisement appeared in *The Canadian Jewish News* listing more than one thousand supporters. Men, women and children, led by twelve rabbis carrying Torahs, marched from the Jewish Community Centre to Earl Bales Park. "Soviet Jews need West's help 1,500 at rally in Metro told," *The Toronto Star* (October 7, 1985); Ottawa's Simchat Torah Rally took place on October 6 outside the Soviet Embassy, with MP Sheila Finestone as guest speaker, press release, Jewish Community Council of Ottawa, CJC Ottawa; A full-page advertisement, with photographs and biographies of two refuseniks and four prisoners, appeared in *The Gazette* promoting Montreal's Simchat Torah Rally. On October 13, more than one thousand protesters gathered in the rain in Dominion Square and marched to the Soviet Consulate; The Winnipeg community gathered outside the City Hall on October 6. Mayor Bill Norrie and MLA Marty Dolin addressed the crowd; Mayor Michael Harcourt was the keynote speaker at Vancouver's Simchat Torah rally on October 6, 1985, outside City Hall. Simchat Torah Rallies – 1985, CCSJ CJC Archives.

17 Reported by Rabbi Awraham Soetondorp of the Hague, special guest at an Ontario Region Soviet Jewry meeting held November 7, 1985 at the Ontario Legislature, personal files of Wendy Eisen.

18 Spoken by Mikhail Gorbachev, General Secretary of the Communist Party of the Soviet Union, October, 1985, reprinted from NCSJ Newsletter, CCSJ, CJC Archives.

19 "Gorky Hebrew teacher sentenced to three years imprisonment," *Jewish Telegraphic Agency* (October 28, 1985).

20 A "day of prayers for peace and human rights" took place from sunrise to sunset at the peace monument in Toronto's Nathan Phillips Square." Morning prayer services were followed by a rotating silent vigil until noon, when academics, artists, media personalities and politicians delivered short messages or prayers. Jewish Students Network and Hillel students focused on the prisoners during the afternoon. The vigil concluded with evening prayer services at sundown. Committee for Soviet Jewry, Ontario Region, CJC.

21 Report of the NCSJ Convention, Washington, D.C., Rick Orzy, December 8–10, 1985, personal files of Wendy Eisen.

22 "Protests treatment of Jews," [*Cornwall*] *Standard Freeholder,* Cornwall (December 10, 1985).

23 One thousand one hundred and forty Jews received visas in 1985.

Notes, Chapter 20

1 Letter to Milton Harris, President Canadian Jewish Congress, from R. Harry Jay, head of the Delegation of Canada to the CSCE Experts' Meeting on Human Rights, January 18, 1985, CJC Archives.

2 Presentation by Alan Rose to the Department of External Affairs Consultation on Madrid, Ottawa Experts' Meeting on Human Rights, February 26, 1985, CJC Archives, 1985.

3 Members of the sub-committee on "Human Rights in Eastern Europe" were: MPs David Orlikow, David Kilgour, Andrew Witer and Reginald Stackhouse who presided.

4 Minutes of Proceedings and Evidence of the Sub-committee on Human Rights in Eastern Europe of the Standing Committee on External Affairs and National Defence. May 1, 1985, CJC Archives 24/5.

5 Britain: Stephen Roth, Arieh Handler; Canada: Alan Rose; United States: Kenneth Bialkin, Israel Singer, Howard Friedman, Jacqueline Levine; France: Claude Kelman; Australia: Isi Liebler; Sweden: Jan-Eric Levy; Israel: Zalman Abramov "Helsinki Accords meeting - Soviet Jews on agenda," *The Canadian Jewish News* (May 16, 1985), p. 2.

6 One hundred and sixty-two Jews emigrated in April. "Changes seen in attitude towards Soviet Jews," *The Canadian Jewish News* (May 23, 1985), p. 3.

7 "Soviet Jewry and Soviet Credibility," Dr. Mark Keil, Professor of Chemistry, University of Alberta, *Jewish Star* (June 13-27, 1985), CJC Archives.

8 Toronto's Beth Tikvah Congregation filled two "freedom buses" with supporters and travelled to Ottawa to meet with government officials on the day that Avital Sharansky was there to press for Anatoly's release. The vigil was co-ordinated by the Ottawa Soviet Jewry Committee co-chaired by Walter Hendelman and Rabbi Bulka." Message to USSR: The World is Watching," *The Jewish Post* (May 16, 1985).

9 David Matas of Winnipeg was co-chairman.

10 "Rights Conference should be open to public," Letter to the Editor from Bert Raphael, QC, Chairman, Canadian Lawyers and Jurists for Soviet Jewry, *The Globe and Mail* (May 24, 1985). Olivia Ward, "Secrecy at Human Rights Conference is criticized," *Toronto Star* (May 12, 1985).

11 "Closed door aspect of rights conference rapped," *The Canadian Jewish News* (May 16, 1985), p. 14.

12 "Opening statement by the Canadian delegation to the CSCE Meeting of Experts on Human Rights," delivered by Ambassador Harry Jay, May 13, 1985, CJC Archives.

13 Jews, Russian Orthodox Christians, Baptists, Pentacostals, Ukranians and Lithuanians, "Soviets losing patience, U.S. told," *The Globe and Mail* (May 18, 1985).

14 Ibid.

15 John Gellner, "Helsinki: a noble but naive try," *The Globe and Mail* (August 1, 1985).

16 As quoted in *The Globe and Mail* (August 7, 1985), from "International Campaign - Orlov and Sharansky," Bulletin of October-November 1985.

17 CJC's Alan Rose, Martin Penn, Barbara Stern and MPs David Kilgour, Sheila Finestone met with Cy Taylor, Under-Secretary; Pete Walker, Director General for East European Affairs; William Bauer, newly-appointed head of the CSCE Canadian delegation to the 1986 Vienna review meetings. William Bauer interview with the author, August 13, 1991.

18 "Break seen for Soviet Jews," *The Canadian Jewish News* (May 24, 1985), p. 3.

19 David Kilgour interview with the author, August 2, 1989.

20 William Bauer interview.

21 CJC's presentation to the Standing Committee on External Affairs and International Trade at the Public Hearings on the CSCE. Witnesses: Dorothy Reitman, President CJC; Alan Rose, Executive Vice-President, CJC; Martin Penn, National Director,

CCSJ, August 20, 1986. National Archives of Canada, Ottawa, MG 28V133, Vol. 33, file 10.

22 Alan Rose interview with the author, August 2, 1990.

23 "Clark blasts USSR over rights record," *The Canadian Jewish News* (November 13, 1986), p. 1.

24 William Bauer interview.

25 Representing NGOs in Vienna were Barbara Stern, Irwin Cotler, Genya Intrator, Gerald Batist.

26 Remarks by the head of the Canadian delegation, Ambassador William Bauer, December 10, 1986. CJC Archives.

27 Ibid.

28 Ibid.

29 William Bauer interview.

30 Summary of extemporaneous remarks by Ambassador William Bauer at the informal meeting of CSCE heads of delegation, April 19, 1988, CJC Archives.

31 Report on the Moscow CSCE Conference on the Human Dimension, September 10 - October 4, 1991. Sara Frankel, Israeli emissary with the Israeli Consulate, New York 1978-1984.

32 Speech by the Rt. Hon. Joe Clark, Secretary of State for External Affairs, on conclusion of the Conference on Security and Cooperation in Europe Follow-up Meeting, Vienna, Austria, January 19, 1989, p. 5, CJC Archives.

33 Report on the Moscow CSCE Conference on the Human Dimension.

34 Commentary by Barbara Stern, National Soviet Jewry Newletter, CJC Vol. 2, Number 1, Summer 1989.

35 Letter to the Reverend Barry A. Jones, Chairman Board of Advisors, Montreal Inter-faith Task Force for Soviet Jewry, from Alan P. McLaine, Director General, USSR and Eastern Europe Bureau.

Notes, Chapter 21

1 Natan Sharansky, *Fear No Evil* (New York: Random House), p. 270.

2 Ibid, p. 273.

3 Chistopol prison was 800 km east of Moscow and Perm Labour Camp was 320 km east of Chistopol.

4 Ida Milgrom addressed her letters to an official at the Ministry of the Interior of the USSR and the Head of Medical Administration of the Ministry of Internal Affairs of the Tartar Republic. "Update on the condition of Anatoly Sharansky," CJC Archives, 22/1.

5 Letter to Ida Milgrom from M. Klanchich, Deputy Department Head of the Ministry of Health of the Interior Ministry, USSR, March, 1980.

6 Spoken by Cotler at the Sharansky Lectureship, Montreal, April 1980.

7 Barbara Stern interview with the author, October 14, 1990.

8 The motion was raised by the Hon. Flora MacDonald, MP, under Standing Order 43, House of Commons, November 7, 1980, CJC Archives, 22/22.

9 *Fear No Evil,* p. 311.

10 Ibid.

11 Ibid, p. 312.

12 Ibid, p. 322.

13 Present were: MPP Roy McMurtry, MP David Smith, former Toronto Mayor John Sewell, Amnesty International leader Genevieve Cowgill, Anglican Bishop Arthur

Brown, United Church Minister Dr. Douglas Lapp, Father Pat Byrne, Rabbi David Monson of Beth Shalom Synagogue, Rabbi James Prosnit of Holy Blossom Temple and Jewish community leaders Phil Givens, CZF and Sam Grossman, B'nai Brith.

14 "Sharansky's birthday marked by family, mayor," *The Canadian Jewish News* (January 28, 1982), p. 1.

15 Interview with Professor Irving Abella, March 11, 1992.

16 "In absentia," letter from Professor Eric Fawcett, chairman of the Committee of Concerned Scientists, *The Globe and Mail* (June 3, 1982).

17 *Fear No Evil,* p. 336.

18 Ibid.

19 "Mother fears for son's life," *The Gazette* (September 28, 1982).

20 "Force-feeding for Sharansky," *The Canadian Jewish News* (October 21, 1982), p. 1.

21 Co-sponsored by the Ontario Region's Soviet Jewry Committee, B'nai Brith and the Ontario Legislature Committee for Soviet Jewry. Other speakers included: MPPs David Rotenberg, Marion Bryden, Jim Breithaupt and Don Cousens. Legislature of Ontario Debates, Official report (Hansard),October 19, 1982.

22 Motion raised by Flora MacDonald, MP, House of Commons Debates, Motions under S.O.43, Thursday, November 4, 1982.

23 "In light of the fact that Soviet dissident Anatoly Sharansky is currently being force-fed to end his hunger-strike over the legitimate complaint that he is no longer allowed to receive mail or visits from relatives, I move that this government condemn the actions of the Soviets and that it urge that steps be taken to put an end to this flagrant violation of human rights, which is in direct contravention of the Helsinki Accord." Motion raised by Flora MacDonald, MP, House of Commons, Commons Debates, Motions under S.O.43, November 19, 1982, p. 20,817.

24 *Fear No Evil*, p. 347.

25 Ellie Tesher, "Soviets bar family from visit to dissident on hunger strike," *Toronto Star* (January 12, 1983), p. A 10.

26 "Keeping the pressure on," *Maclean's* (February 7, 1983).

27 "Soviet Union put on trial," *Jewish Western Bulletin* (February 3, 1983).

28 House of Commons Debates, January 27, 1983, p. 22,276.

29 "Human Rights – Plight of Soviet Dissident – Anatoly Sharansky," House of Commons Debates, May 26, 1983. p.25,737.

30 "International Campaign – Orlov and Sharansky," Bulletin of May-June 1984, personal files of Herb Landis.

31 Update on Sharansky, March 15, 1984, CCSJ, CJC Archives, 22/1.

32 "Call for Sharansky's hospitalization, community urged," letter to the editor, *Jewish Western Bulletin* (April, 1984).

33 House of Commons Debates, "Human Rights – USSR– plea on behalf of Anatoly Sharansky," March 15, 1984, p. 2,129.

34 Speakers included Canon Garth Bulmer, Rev. Alex Farquhar, Father Irenee Beaubien and Rabbi Ron Aigen.

35 Speakers included Jim Peterson and Alan Rose. A musical tribute was performed by singer Fran Avni. "Personalities participate," *The Canadian Jewish News* (March 14, 1984).

36 "Sharansky and his wife: sad 10 years," *The New York Times* (July 1, 1984).

37 Letter from Professor Israel Halperin to Soviet leader Chernenko, November 18, 1984, personal files of Herb Landis.

38 The message, "May our Lord prepare the hearts of those who can give assent to free

Sharansky and to let His people go," was sent by F.W. Harris, Pender Island, B.C., January 6, 1985, personal files of Herb Landis.

39 Stan and Debby Solomon, Sharansky's cousins, were members of Beth Tikvah.

40 Rabbi Avi Weiss of New York was the scholar-in-residence for the "Sharansky Freedom Weekend." Rally speakers included MPs Gerry Weiner and David Kilgour, "Rally in Metro urges freedom for Soviet dissident," *The Toronto Star* (January 21, 1985).

41 "Wife of imprisoned dissident persists in bid for his release," *The Globe and Mail* (January 21, 1985).

42 House of Commons Debates, "Human Rights – USSR – plight of Anatoly Sharansky," May 15, 1985, p. 4757.

43 On September 18, 1985, "International Campaign – Orlov and Sharansky," Bulletin of December 1985, personal files of Herb Landis.

44 Solomon was accompanied by lawyer Irwin Fefergrad.

45 Moshe Ronen interview with the author, March 25, 1992.

46 Ibid.

47 Text of the letter in an article, "What Gorbachev forgot," Natan Sharansky, *The Jerusalem Report* (July 2, 1992), p. 38.

48 Alan M. Dershowitz, *Chutzpah,* p. 258.

49 "Sharansky is not alone," editorial, *The Toronto Star* (February 12, 1986).

50 *Newsweek* (February 24, 1986), p. 33.

51 Personal recollection of Wendy Eisen.

52 "Soviet Jewry and Canada's press," *Intercom* (March 1986), p. 5.

53 *The New York Times* (February 13, 1986).

54 The Western wall is the holiest Jewish shrine. It is the wall of the ancient temple built by King Solomon.

55 House of Commons Debates, February 11, 1986.

56 Don Cousens, MPP, Hansard official report of debates, Legislative Assembly of Ontario, First Session, 33rd Parliament, February 11, 1986, p. 3997.

57 The premier acknowledged that "Sharansky's effectiveness in fighting for freedom even while behind bars, has provided a beacon for all who are free in this world and all who wish to be free," ibid.

58 "Relatives in Toronto celebrate – Sharansky release met with stunned disbelief," *The Canadian Jewish News* (February 20, 1986), p. 6.

59 "The Impossible Moment," Natan Sharansky, *The Jerusalem Report* (June 13, 1991), p. 22.

60 "Sharansky Tells How He Clung to Psalms Captors Tried to Seize," *The New York Times* (February 13, 1986), p. 8.

61 Irwin Cotler interview with the author, November 16, 1990.

62 Ibid.

63 Ibid.

64 Elaine Dubow Harris, Barbara Stern, Wendy Litwack Eisen.

65 Barbara Stern, interview with the author, February 13,1986.

Notes, Chapter 22

1 Wolf Blitzer, "There are many Sharanskys left behind," reprinted in *The Canadian Jewish News* (February 27, 1986), p. 9.

2 Ibid.

3 Rabbi Moshe Abramov, Evgeny Aizenberg, Yosef Begun, Iosif Berenshtein, Vladimir

Brodsky, Yuli Edelshtein, Nadezhda Fradkova, Evgeny Koifman, Yakov Levin, Vladimir Livshits, Alexei Magarik, Mark Nepomniashchy, Lev Shefer, Yury Tarnopolsky, Anatoly Virshubsky, Leonid Volvovsky, Alexander Yakir, Roald Zelichonok, Zakhar Zunshain, Martin Gilbert, *Sharansky, Hero of Our Time* (New York: Viking, 1986), p. 423-426.

4 *The Edmonton Journal*, January 1, 1986, as reported in the CJCS' *Intercom*, "Soviet Jewry and Canada's Press," Bernard Moscovitz, March 1986.

5 Bruce McLeod, "Jailed Soviet Jews need our letters of support," *The Toronto Star* (January 21, 1986).

6 *The Toronto Sun* (January 29, 1986).

7 "Samantha hears from a refusenik," Jews By Choice, *National Opinion and Post* (September 24, 1986).

8 Genya Intrator, "Jailed for seeking freedom," *The Toronto Sunday Sun* (January 12, 1986). Genya Intrator, "Give Sakharov hope in exile," *The Sunday Sun* (January 19, 1986). Genya Intrator, "Postal rules violated," *The Sunday Sun* (January 26, 1986).

9 Toronto students held an all-day vigil for Lifshitz at Queen's Park culminating in a candle-light ceremony attended by federal and provincial politicians, MPs David Kilgour and Bill Attewell and MPP Marion Bryden. "Students hold an all-day vigil for refusenik," *Canadian Jewish News* (February 6, 1986). Winnipeg's vigil was held January 25 at Beth Israel Synagogue, "Student candle light vigil," *The Jewish Post* (February 6, 1986).

10 MPP David McFadden launched the event, co-ordinated by Judith Bloom, Education Chairman of the Ontario Region's Soviet Jewry Committee.

11 "CHAT students celebrate Refusenik's birthday," *The Canadian Jewish News* (February 20, 1986), p. 3.

12 The panelists included Baruch Gur, director of the Israel Public Council for Soviet Jewry, Leonid Feldman, former Kishinev refusenik and rabbinic student at New York's Theological Seminary and CCSJ chairman Barbara Stern. Flyer for "Soviet Jewry – facts, prospect and rumours," Edmonton Committee for Soviet Jewry, March 26, 1986.

13 The rally was co-ordinated by the Committee for Soviet Jewry, Ontario Region. Chairman Wendy Eisen called upon Ontario NDP leader Bob Rae, MPP Steven Offer, MP Bill Attewell, and Father Ronald Scott to delivered brief messages. National Soviet Jewry director Martin Penn delivered a speech on the deteriorating situation for Soviet Jews." "'Red Square' becomes site of protest," *The Canadian Jewish News* (May 15, 1986), p. 13.

14 "Inter-Parliamentary Conference for Soviet Jewry," report by David Kilgour, April, 1986.

15 From the office of David Kilgour, MP Edmonton Strathcona, "Advance for Release," April 24, 1986.

16 David Kilgour interview with the author, August 2, 1989.

17 Letter to David Kilgour, MP, from V. Bogdanov, Second Secretary, Press and Information, Press Office of the USSR Embassy in Canada, May 7, 1986, personal files of David Kilgour.

18 Letter to The Minister of Foreign Affairs of the USSR, Mr. E. Shevardnadze from Ida Nudel, February, 1986, personal files of Wendy Eisen.

19 Montreal Women's Division of the Canadian Shaare Zedek Hospital Foundation, May 26. Barbara Stern was recognized that day for her untiring efforts on behalf of Soviet Jewry. Speakers included the Hon. Flora MacDonald, Nudel's sister Ilana Fridman, and professor Irwin Cotler.

20 "Sister of Ida Nudel issues plea," *The Canadian Jewish News* (June 5, 1986).

21 Fridman was accompanied in Ottawa by Barbara Stern, Martin Penn and Irwin Cotler. The meeting with Clark was arranged with the full support of the prime minister. Letter from The Rt. Hon Brian Mulroney to Ilana Fridman, June 4, 1986, CJC Archives, 24/7. "Clark asking Soviets to free exiled 'angel' of the refuseniks," *The Gazette* (June 5, 1986).

22 "Excerpts of a letter to Professor Irwin Cotler from the Rt. Hon. Joe Clark," *The Canadian Jewish News* (April 23, 1992).

23 The podium guests were a "who's who" of political and religious power in America.

24 *The New York Times* (May 12, 1986).

25 "Anatoly Sharansky in America," report by Abraham Bayer, National Jewish Community Relations Advisory Council, May 16, 1986, personal files of Wendy Eisen.

26 Ronnie Tessler interview with the author, November 1986.

27 The five families were: Markovskaya, Popok, Elensky, Reznikov, Pevzner. Renee Bellas brought Inna Zarankin, Isaac Blekher, and Fanya Levitsky, the Vancouver half of the equation, to meet with Sharon Wolfe when she visited Vancouver with Prime Minister Brian Mulroney. The Prime Minister's Office pledged to raise the cases of the five families with the Soviets. Renee Bellas interview with the author, May 22, 1992.

28 Nicholls, a non-Jew, had spent the previous year in Israel with her husband, who was on sabbatical. There she learned about Yuli Edelshtein's situation, obtained the transcript of the trial and wrote the play.

29 Moncton, Quebec City, Montreal, Ottawa, Kingston, Toronto, Sault Ste. Marie, Thunder Bay, Winnipeg, Regina, Saskatoon, Edmonton, Calgary, Vancouver. Among the student crusaders were co-organizers, Leora Silver (Toronto) and Eli Cohen (Winnipeg); National Network Chairman, Mimi Estrin (Toronto), Alan Kopstein, Winnipeg, Ilana Krygier (Calgary), Mark Binder (Winnipeg), Dina Zimmerman (Toronto), Stephen Granovsky (Toronto).

30 The students were joined by MPs John Oostrom, Ian Deans, Robert Kaplan and David Kilgour. "Demonstration cites plight of Soviet Jews," *Ottawa Citizen* (May 15, 1986), p. A11.

31 "Refuseniks 'sign' Soviet pavilion guest book," *The Canadian Jewish News* (June 12, 1986), p. 5.

32 "Activities organized for Shevardnadze visit to Ottawa," Committee for Soviet Jewry, CJC Ontario Region, October, 1986.

33 "Canada to press Soviets for reunion of families," *The Toronto Star* (September 26, 1986).

34 The Torontonians included: Janice Atkinson, Nani Beutel, Helen Cooper, Rena Cohen, Joan Dubros, Wendy Eisen. The Montrealers were Barbara Stern, Sima Blitzer, Bertha Stein. "Protesters dog Shevardnadze demanding Visas for Refuseniks," *The Toronto Sun* (October 3, 1986).

35 "'Trust me,' Shevardnadze tells protesters," *The Ottawa Citizen* (October 3, 1986). p. 1.

36 Canadian officials had presented Shevardnadze with ten cases the previous day, including that of Ida Nudel.

37 Personal recollections of Wendy Eisen.

38 Jerry Goodman interview with the author, July 10, 1989.

39 Bill Attewell interview with the author, July 12, 1990.

40 "Chief editor of Pravda accuses Members of Parliament of 'wild accusations,'"

Second part of report by V. Afanasyev, "Eleven days on the other side of the Atlantic," *Pravda* (January 19, 1987), personal files of David Kilgour.

41 Organized by B'nai Brith. (Mayor Bill Norrie of Winnipeg bestowed honourary citizenship on Soviet Jewry refusenik Moshe Abramov of Samarkand, Uzbekistan. A framed certificate dedicated to Abramov was presented to a delegation from B'nai Brith.) "Norrie makes Refusenik honourary Winnipeg citizen," *Jewish Post* (April 24, 1986), p. 4.

42 On that day, many members of those segments of the community joined with the Montreal Inter-Faith Task Force for Soviet Jewry for a prayer service in support of Soviet Jews.

43 Inna Zarankin, Isaac Blekher and Fanya Levitsky.

44 The 123 Torontonians included politicians, journalists, artists, and community leaders. Co-sponsored by the Ontario Legislature Committee for Soviet Jewry and the Ontario Region Committee for Soviet Jewry. "Politicians join call to free Soviet Jews," *The Toronto Star* (December 11, 1986).

45 "Sakharov speaks out . . . the dissident-physicist talks about past persecution and his hopes for a freer Soviet future," *The Globe and Mail* (January 10, 1987), p. D5.

46 Ibid.

NOTES, CHAPTER 23

1 Deans was House Leader for the NDP; Smith, a Liberal, later became Minister of Transport and Small Business; MacDonald, a Conservative, was the Minister for External Affairs in the Clark government.

2 "Soviets Silent on exit visas for Jews: MPs," *The Toronto Star* (September 16, 1982).

3 "Concern voiced for Soviet Jews, MPs in Russia," *The Canadian Jewish News* (September 23, 1982), p. 1.

4 Ian Deans interview with the author, April 11, 1991.

5 Martin Penn interview with the author, August 1, 1990.

6 David Smith interview with the author, June 20, 1991.

7 Flora MacDonald interview with the author, October 1, 1992.

8 As told to David Smith by Ambassador Pearson, David Smith interview.

9 "Moscow presses new crackdown on all dissent," *The New York Times* (October 25, 1982), p. A14.

10 "MPs in Russia . . . Concern voiced for Soviet Jews," *The Canadian Jewish News* (September 22, 1982), p. 1

11 Jim Peterson interview with the author, June 1, 1990.

12 The petition, circulated by Holy Blossom Temple's Soviet Jewry Committee, had been presented to The Hon. John Roberts for delivery to the Soviet Ambassador. "Soviets given refusenik plea," *The Canadian Jewish News* (January 19, 1984).

13 Jim Peterson interview with the author, June 16, 1990.

14 Alan Rose interview with the author, June 13, 1990.

15 Barbara Stern interview with the author, August 1, 1991.

16 Jim Peterson interview.

17 Ibid.

18 "Soviets could back PMs peace push by letting Jews emigrate, says Tory," *The Gazette* (January 27, 1984).

19 Ibid.

20 The group was briefed by Sharon Wolfe. Nelson Riis interview with the author, March 7, 1991.

21 Milton Harris interview with the author, June 25, 1990.
22 "Canadians in Moscow reject talks with anti-Zionist group," *The Sunday Star* (April 21, 1985), p. 22.
23 "Change in the USSR: Prospects for Soviet Jewry," address by David Kilgour to Canadian Lawyers and Jurists for Soviet Jewry, September 27, 1985, personal files of David Kilgour.
24 Nelson Riis interview.
25 MPs reveal what Soviets want to keep hidden," *The Canadian Jewish News* (May 23, 1985), p. 6.
26 Sheila Finestone interview with the author, May 29, 1990.
27 "Twenty thousand Soviets seeks exit visas, MPs told," *The Globe and Mail* (May 15, 1987), p. 2.
28 Ibid
29 Jeanette Goldman interview with the author, August 30, 1989.

Notes, Chapter 24

1 Dr. Gerald Batist interview with the author, July 19, 1989.
2 Ibid.
3 Charny was a mathematician whose research in the aero-space field cost him his job when he first applied to emigrate in 1977; Inna Meiman, who along with her husband was first refused a visa in 1975; and Tanya Bogomolny was married to Benjamin, a refusenik since 1972.
4 International Cancer Patients Solidarity Committee, 1986, CJC Archives.
5 "Cancer patient's families join in protest," *The Canadian Jewish News* (July 10, 1986), p. 8.
6 "Lautenberg of New Jersey," press release, July 14, 1986, personal files of Gerald Batist.
7 CBC "Morningside" interview with Peter Gzowski, May 19, 1987.
8 Dr. Michael Baker, Chief of Medical Oncology at the Toronto General Hospital, Dr. Frederick Lowy, Dean of the Faculty of Medicine at the University of Toronto, Dr. David Kassirer, former cancer patient and member of "Cansurmount," Rev. Dr. Stanford Lucyk, Chairman of the Toronto Inter-Faith Council for Soviet Jewry, and Dr. Gerald Batist.
9 Benjamin Charny's brother Leon, from Boston; Tanya Bogomolny's brother from Montreal; the Braave family of Rochester; and Lea Mariasin's sister from Toronto.
10 Press conferences, 1986, personal files of Gerald Batist.
11 "Doctors call for release of Soviet Cancer patients," *The Gazette* (June 27, 1986).
"New Soviet attitude key to bid for visas for five cancer victims," *The Globe and Mail* (July 29, 1986).
"Soviet Jews still waiting," editorial, *The Toronto Star* (July 30, 1986).
"Toronto doctors try to reunite dying Soviet Jews with families," *The Toronto Star* (July 29, 1986).
"MDs keep pressing to free Soviet patients," *The Gazette* (August 12, 1986).
"Let them have a chance," editorial, *The Gazette* (August 30, 1986).
12 The physicians were from The New England Medical Center, Tufts University School of Medicine, Massachusetts General Hospital, Brigham and Women's Hospital, the New England Deaconess Hospital, Boston University Medical Center.
13 As a further endorsement to their commitment to this issue, free medical treatment was offered by the New England Medical Center to Benjamin Charny, whose

brother lived in Newton, Massachusetts. *New England Medical Center News* (August 21, 1986).

14 *Boston Globe* (August 27, 1986), p. 1.

15 Present were: Senators Gary Hart, Pete Wilson, Allan Cranston, Frank Lautenberg, John Kerry, Paul Simon, William Armstrong, Dennis De Concini; cancer specialists Dr. Bruce Chadner and Dr. Stephen Rosenberg; American delegates to the CSCE Vienna review meetings, Alfonse D'Amato and Ambassador Warren Zimmerman.

16 "Why can't these Soviet Cancer Patients Leave?" *The Washington Post* (September 25, 1987).

17 "Doctor tells of fight to free Soviet cancer victims," *The Gazette* (February 6, 1987).

18 Gerald Batist interview.

19 Ibid.

20 "Doctor tells of fight to free Soviet cancer victims."

21 "Dissident's Ill Wife Leaves Soviet," *The New York Times* (January 19, 1987). p. A9.

22 "Doctor with a mission," *Maclean's* (May 18, 1987), p. 49.

23 "Soviet cancer patient calm amid flood of tears," *The Gazette* (February 9, 1987), p. 8.

24 CBC "Morningside".

25 Benjamin Charny, Sophia Braave, Elizaveta Geishis, Fayina Kogan, David Zolotnitsky, Sheina Schwartz, Mariana Simontova, Edward Erlikh.

26 Letter addressed to Secretary-General Gorbachev from the United States Senate, Washington, D.C., March 23, 1987, personal files of Gerald Batist.

27 International Cancer Patients Solidarity Committee Report, March 31, 1987, personal files of Gerald Batist.

28 "U.S. urged to link Soviet policy on emigration to cancer cooperation, *Los Angeles Times* (April 8,1987), p. 3.

29 Ibid.

30 "What is the Point?" *The New York Times* (March 20, 1987).

31 Ibid.

32 "Doctor with a mission," *Maclean's,* p. 49.

33 Anna Charny Blank was a speaker featured at the NCSJ meetings in Washington in November. She visited Montreal and Toronto and spoke to Soviet Jewry groups, community meetings, and schools. Letter to Ambassador Alexei Rodionov from The Rev. R. L. Scott, November 30, 1987; the Rev. Stanford R. Lucyk, December 3, 1987, personal files of Wendy Eisen.

NOTES, CHAPTER 25

1 Emanuel Litvinoff, editor, *Insight, Soviet Jews* (January 1987).

2 *The Canadian Jewish News* (February 12, 1987).

3 "'Please help,' dissident begs Gorbachev," *The Toronto Star* (January 10, 1987).

4 "Refusenik begins hunger strike," *The Canadian Jewish News* (January 15, 1987). p. 7.

5 Included in the call were Canadian Jewish Congress' Soviet Jewry chairmen: CCSJ chairman Barbara Stern; Toronto co-chairmen Wendy Eisen and Marsha Slavens; Montreal chairman Anna Gonshor; Ottawa co-chairmen Walter Hendelman and Rabbi Bulka; Winnipeg chairman Hillaine Kroft, Calgary co-chairmen David Craimer and Rabbi Jordan Goldson; Edmonton chairman Dr. Mark Keil, Vancouver chairman Rita Cohn.

6 Telephone call to Alexander Ioffe by members of the Toronto Inter-Faith Council for Soviet Jewry, January 11, 1987.

7 "Human Rights, USSR - Plight of Ioffe family," House of Commons Debates, January 19, 1987. Mr. Roger Clinch, Parliamentary Secretary to Minister for External Relations, House of Commons Debates, February 9, 1987, p. 3262.

8 Dalhousie University, St. Francis Xavier University, Université de Moncton, McGill University, Concordia University, Université de Montréal, Carleton University, University of Toronto, York University, University of Manitoba, University of Edmonton, University of Alberta, Simon Fraser University, University of British Columbia. Report of CCSJ, Emergency Campaign in support of Alexander Ioffe, CJC, January, 1987.

9 Atlantic Canada: telegrams were sent by community leadership. Synagogue members were called to action by their rabbis. Ontario and Quebec: Inter-faith Committees telephoned Ioffe and circulated petitions through the churches. MPs telephoned Ioffe from a press conference in the House of Commons and MPPs circulated a petition at Queen's Park. Manitoba: Soviet Jewry leadership co-ordinated activity with university students who demonstrated on campuses. Alberta: Dr. Mark Keil conducted radio interviews and CBC Edmonton filmed and broadcast a telephone call to Ioffe. British Columbia: Mayor Gordon Campbell telephoned Ioffe during a press conference organized by the Vancouver Action Committee

10 Statement by Dr. Gerhard Herzberg, National Research Council, Ottawa, as reported by the CCSJ, Emergency Campaign in support of Alexander Ioffe, CJC Archives.

11 Ibid.

12 Since his release Dr. Ioffe has lectured extensively in Europe and North America and has spent several months in Canada, working in the Department of Mathematics at the Université de Montréal.

13 The coordinator of the Toronto rotation hunger strike, held in Nathan Phillips Square, was Morley Wolfe, Chairman Soviet Jewry B'nai Brith, Morley Wolfe interview with the author, May 29, 1991.

14 Yosef Begun interview with the author, October 8, 1992.

15 "Dissident Begun pledges to keep fighting," *The Gazette* (February 24, 1987).

16 Yosef Begun interview.

17 Natan Sharansky, "Behind the Glasnost facade," *The Jerusalem Post* (October 14, 1987).

18 Sponsored by the Soviet Jewry Committee, Winnipeg Jewish Community Council, Canadian Jewish Congress and Network, *The Jewish Post* (March 5, 1987).

19 Ibid.

20 "USSR - Treatment of Jewish citizens," House of Commons Debates, March 9, 1987, p. 3948.

21 Press release, "Students' Freedom Caravan for Soviet Jewry," Committee for Soviet Jewry, Canadian Jewish Congress, Ontario Region, April 10, 1987.

22 Included in the group were WJC executives Israel Singer, Elan Steinberg and Winnipeg's Sol Kanee. Sol Kanee interview with the author, December 19, 1992.

23 "Gorbachev and the Jews," *Newsweek* (April 13, 1987), p.34.

24 "Two tests of the breadth of Glasnost," *The New York Times* (July 23, 1987).

25 "Shultz to join U.S. Seder in Moscow," *The New York Times* (April 18, 1987).

26 Alan Rose, "Perestroika, Glasnost and Soviet Jews," *Intercom,* CJC Vol. 4, No. 5 (September/October, 1987).

27 Orthodox Rabbi interview with the author, January, 1992.

28 Naomi Jacobs went to the USSR to visit refuseniks in the winter of 1987.

29 "Metro-area group helps win release of jailed Soviet Jew," *The Toronto Star* (May 5, 1987).
30 "Moscow accused of stopping calls," *The Canadian Jewish News* (June 11, 1987).
31 "Freed Soviet dissident meets Toronto cousins," *The Toronto Star* (November 26, 1987).
32 Marsha Slivka interview with the author, May 29, 1991.
33 From 1982 to 1992 the following families were adopted by Holy Blossom Temple: Vasilevsky, Klotz, Tarshis, Yuzefovitch, Lurie, Brodsky, Diki, Svardnovsky, Bronstein, Fulmacht, Lerman, Sorkin.
34 Including: Marsha Slivka, Shirley Hanick, Dorothy Stossel, Ann Moorehouse, Hope Maissner.
35 Contributions came from families and guests of Bar and Bat Mitzvah twins. When a child became a "twin" he was mandated to perform a charitable act which amounted to raising money for the fund – i.e., contributing to a trip, paying for a parcel or directly donating to the fund. Temple members Marsha Slivka, Shirley Hanick, Dorothy Stossel and Rabbi Jim Prosnit travelled to the USSR in 1986. Subsequent trips involved the participation of Rabbi Steve Garten in 1987, and Rabbi David Azen in 1989 and a group of students from Toronto Reform temples in 1990.
36 Marsha Slivka interview.
37 The following synagogues were represented: Adath Israel, Beth Avraham Yoseph, Beth David B'nai Israel, Beth Am, Beth Emeth Bais Yehudah, Beth Haminyan, Beth Tikvah, Beth Tzedec, Holy Blossom Temple, Temple Emanu-el, Temple Har Zion, Temple Sinai. Minutes, Committee for Soviet Jewry, Ontario Region, September 30, 1988, personal files of Wendy Eisen.
38 Ibid.
39 McDougall was Minister of State for Privatization and responsible for the Status of Women. The event was co-sponsored by the Ontario Legislature Soviet Jewry Committee and the Committee for Soviet Jewry, Ontario Region, Canadian Jewish Congress, "Ida Nudel award goes to Barbara McDougall," *The Canadian Jewish News* (May 21, 1987), p. 21.
40 Soviet Jewry Update, Committee for Soviet Jewry, Ontario Region, CJC (May 8, 1987).
41 Marion Bryden, Steven Offer, Donald Cousens
42 The meeting with the wives of Vainshtein and Polansky took place in July 1986, in the presence of the Canadian ambassador to Israel and Marsha Slavens, who co-ordinated the meeting. Barbara McDougall interview with the author, February 7, 1992.
43 Ibid.
44 Halifax, Fredricton, Toronto, Montreal, Saskatoon, Winnipeg, Edmonton, Ottawa and Vancouver.
45 Other speakers included professor and sovietologist Ted Friedgut of Tel Aviv University, Professor Irwin Cotler, former refusenik Alexander Mariasin, Alan Rose, Derek Fraser of the Department of External Affairs and Minister of Justice, Ray Hnatyshyn.
46 *Focus Soviet Jewry,* The Israel Public Council for Soviet Jewry (September 1987), p. 8.
47 Remarks by Natan Sharansky, Massey Hall, September 15, 1987.
48 "Natan credits world Jewry efforts," *The Canadian Jewish News* (September 23, 1987), p. 4.
49 Ibid.

50 External Affairs Minister Joe Clark, Prime Minister Brian Mulroney, Leader of the Opposition John Turner and NDP leader Ed Broadbent.
51 House of Commons Debates, Vol. 129, No. 174, 2nd Session, 33rd Parliament, September 15, 1987.
52 Seated in the front row were members of his Canadian family. The rally was sponsored by the Coalition for Soviet Jewry, comprised of CJC, B'nai Brith, TJC, CZF and 124 affiliated Jewish organizations and synagogues.
53 "Enthusiastic crowd greets hero Sharansky," *The Canadian Jewish News* (September 23, 1987), p. 3.
54 "Introduction of Sharansky," Wendy Eisen, September 15, 1987.
55 "Don't be blinded by Gorbachev's dazzle," *The Gazette* (reprinted from *The Washington Post*) (September 15, 1987), p. B3.
56 *The Canadian Jewish News* (September 23, 1987), p. 4.
57 Personal recollections of Wendy Eisen.
58 *A Hand in the Darkness,* p. 298.
59 Ida Nudel, "From KGB hatred to the free skies of Jerusalem," *Jerusalem Post,* International Edition (October 24, 1987).
60 Ibid, p.303.
61 Ibid.
62 "Ida Nudel welcomed in Israel," *The Canadian Jewish News* (October 22, 1987).
63 Ibid.
64 New immigrants.
65 Personal recollections of Wendy Eisen.

Notes, Chapter 26

1 Carole Moscovitch, National director, CCSJ, Barbara Stern, Jeanette Goldman, Joyce Eklove, Wendy Eisen.
2 NCSJ meeting, October, 1987, personal recollections of Wendy Eisen.
3 "Guardian Angel and the Father come home," *Focus Soviet Jewry*, Israel Public Council for Soviet Jewry (October, 1987), p. 8.
4 "Police break up Moscow refusenik protest," *The Gazette* (reprinted from the *Los Angeles Times*) (December 7, 1987), p. 2.
5 *Focus Soviet Jewry,* The Israel Public Council for Soviet Jewry (December, 1987), p. 1.
6 Among those who attended were MPs Bill Attewell, Sheila Finestone; MPP Steven Offer, Father Barry Jones, Rev. Alex Farquhar.
7 "March by 200,000 in Capitol presses Soviet on rights," *The New York Times* (December 7, 1987), p. 1.
8 Ruth Beloff Begun, "Unguessed routes to Jewish roots," *The Jerusalem Post* (April 5, 1993).
9 "Cotler tells of Soviet Jews emigration crackdown," *The Canadian Jewish News* (February 25, 1988).
10 Letter to Professor Irwin Cotler, Chairman, Interamicus, from Yuli Kosharovsky, February 9, 1988. The letter was co-signed by Yuri Cherniak, Natalia Khasina, Vladimir Kislik, Sergei Mkrtchyan.
11 "Refusenik Action Alert," The Committee for Soviet Jewry, Ontario Region, CJC, February 29, 1988.
12 Moscow, Leningrad, Vilnius, Minsk, Odessa, Kiev, Riga, Bendery and Kharkov.

13 Minutes of a meeting of the Toronto Interfaith Council for Soviet Jewry, March 8, 1988.

14 "Veteran refusenik – Act of Despair," *Focus Soviet Jewry,* The Israel Public Council for Soviet Jewry, Vol. 2 , No. 3, March 1988, personal files of Wendy Eisen.

15 Copy of petition to Mikhail Gorbachev, General Secretary of the Communist Party of the USSR on behalf of Yuli Kosharovsky, March, 1988, personal files of David Kilgour.

16 "Kosharovsky ends protest action," *Focus Soviet Jewry,* The Israel Public Council for Soviet Jewry, Vol. 4, No. 4, (April 1988), p. 8, personal files of Wendy Eisen.

17 "The Toronto Committee to free Elena Keis" was chaired by Hilda Cohen.

18 The JWF delegation included director Carol Seidman, president Etty Danzig, Hilda Cohen, Vicki Campbell, Susan Goldberg, Wendy Eisen. "JWF delegation meets with Soviet Ambassador," *The Canadian Jewish News* (June 30, 1988), p. 18.

19 Report to on trip to Russia, March 15–24, 1988, Nani and Austin Beutel, submitted to the CCSJ, personal files of Nani Beutel.

20 Each travelling companion wrote to Ambassador Rodionov asking for a review of the refusal of my application. Graham Greene of the Department of External Affairs was invaluable in planning the strategy to reverse the decision. On the initiative of Alan McLaine, The Hon. Joe Clark asked the Canadian ambassador to the USSR Vernon Turner to appeal the case to Mr. Sukhodrev, an official of the Soviet Foreign Ministry in Moscow. Through his personal association with Soviet Ambassador Rodionov, Charles Chaplin intervened on my behalf. Letter written to Ambassador Alexei Rodionov from Charles Chaplin, April 5, 1988, personal files of Wendy Eisen.

21 Robert Fulford's remarks to NCJW, May 1989.

22 "A Trip to the Soviet Union – April 10–20, 1988," Irving Abella, John Erb, Robert Fulford, John Oostrom, Wendy Eisen, personal files of Wendy Eisen.

23 Yom Hashoah speech by Irving Abella, Vostryakovo Cemetery, Moscow, April 13, 1988; Jewish cemetery, Leningrad, April 17, 1988, "A Trip to the Soviet Union," submitted to the CCSJ, CJC.

24 "These poems are about my feelings – for myself, my family and my friends who are in refusal. We are forced to be separated from our families and our homeland – how difficult it is to bear. These feelings are a part of my struggle. The support of people all over the world make us proud to be Jews. We must always remember that when one Jew is enslaved, all Jewish people have no freedom. Thank you for remembering us." Elena Keis Kuna, April 1988, recorded on the inside of the original book of poetry by Elena Keis, personal files of Wendy Eisen.

25 Carmella described the challenges of trying to obtain kosher food and travelling monthly to Moscow to the *mikveh* (the ritual bath). Her most serious concern was that her two young sons were threatened with expulsion from school if they missed more Saturday classes for the observance of Shabbat.

26 There were two women's groups. JEWAR was a group of women who planned to emigrate to Israel and JWESR, Jewish Women for Emigration and Survival in Refusal, who were destined for other countries. Report of Trip to USSR, April 10–21, 1988.

27 Press conference held at the Ontario Legislature press room, April 26, 1988.

28 The Beth Tzedec delegation was the first Western group to meet with the Soviet Women's Committee, Genya Intrator interview with the author, March 12, 1995.

29 The brief included relevant background data and recommended that the Canadian government use the CSCE mechanism to resolve cases of long-term refuseniks, poor relatives and prisoners and "desist from participating in the Moscow human rights conference in 1991 until the Soviet Union honours its commitments undertaken in

the Vienna Concluding Document." Presentation to The Rt. Honourable Joe Clark, Secretary of State for External Affairs, Beth Tzedec Congregation Soviet Jewry Committee, chaired by Genya Intrator, September 12, 1989.

30 Letter from Judith Lurie to Wendy Eisen, April 29, 1988, personal files of Wendy Eisen.

31 "Summit: few gestures, few changes," *Focus Soviet Jewry,* The Israel Public Council for Soviet Jewry, Vol.2, No. 6 (June 1988), p. 7.

32 Ibid.

33 Shirley Hanick interview with the author, August 13, 1992.

34 The exhibition, assisted by the Ontario Ministry of Citizenship, was sponsored by the Committee for Soviet Jewry, Ontario Region, Canadian Jewish Congress and the Ontario Legislature Committee for Soviet Jewry.

35 Translated from Russian into English by Michael Sherbourne and Jeanette Goldman.

36 June Callwood, "Secrecy and her son's conscription spell 'no exit' for Soviet refusenik," *The Globe and Mail* (August 24, 1988).

37 "Kwinter's efforts for Refusenik 'didn't hurt,'" *The Canadian Jewish News* (January 5, 1989), p. 21.

38 Audio tape of "Musical Masterpiece at Masada," The Grand Finale of Israel's 40th Anniversary, recorded exclusively in support of Shaare Zedek Medical Centre in Jerusalem, personal files of Wendy Eisen.

39 "PM promises 'better days' to refusenik," *The Toronto Star* (November 23, 1988), p. 2.

40 "Jewish emigré numbers up," *The Ottawa Citizen* (December 23, 1988).

41 "The movement's credo under the test of Gorbachev's regime," Nechemiah Levanon, NCSJ Report, December 1, 1988, personal files of Wendy Eisen.

42 Ibid.

Notes, Chapter 27

1 Michael R. Beschloss, Strobe Talbott, *At the Highest Levels* (Great Britain: Little, Brown and Co. Ltd., 1993), I.F.C.

2 Union of Hebrew Teachers in the USSR, Igud Ha'Morim, founded in September, 1988, had one hundred registered Hebrew teachers and eight hundred students. Shalom magazine, "Machanaim," a cultural and religious club, "The Jewish Information Bulletin," "Jewish Historical Society," "Jewish Book Lovers Club,' "Jewish Students Union," NCSJ *Newsbulletin* (Spring, 1989).

3 "Kwinter's efforts for refusenik 'didn't hurt,'" *The Canadian Jewish News* (January 5, 1989), p. 21.

4 Isi Leibler, "Soviet Jewry – a new Debate," *The Jerusalem Post* (November 30, 1988), p. 4

5 Summary Report: Journey to Moscow, Jack Silverstone, April 4, 1989, personal files of Father Barry Jones.

6 The United States, Great Britain, France, Australia and Canada.

7 "Culture centre a new start," *The Canadian Jewish News* (February 23, 1989), p. 1.

8 "Lobbying for Soviet Jewry must go on: Stern," *The Canadian Jewish News* (March 23, 1989).

9 The names were supplied by Leah Machison, a friend of Judith Lurie's mother in Israel, who was working on the Luries' behalf in Israel and by Jacques Lurie of Philadelphia.

10 "What will you be doing on January 25, 1989?" letter to Soviet Jewry advocates and

supporters of the Lurie family from Shirley Hanick, Chairman, Committee for Soviet Jewry, Holy Blossom Temple, December 27, 1988.

11 "Four go on hunger strike," *The Canadian Jewish News* (March 16, 1989), p. 15.

12 A forum of Canadian Jewish Congress' Twenty-second plenary assembly, Sunday May 7th, 1989, Queen Elizabeth Hotel, Montreal.

13 Ibid.

14 "Situation for refuseniks is still bad, Raphael says," *The Canadian Jewish News* (June 8, 1989).

15 Grigory Kanovich, "A Jewish Daisy," *Komsoml'skaig Pravda* (October 5, 1989), translated into English by Sonia Bychkov, personal files of Wendy Eisen.

16 Kanovich was the guest at an Ontario Region Soviet Jewry committee meeting in October 1989.

17 Brenda Barrie interview with the author, November 13, 1990. "Family reunited in Canada after Soviets grant exit visas," *Globe and Mail* (May 1, 1989), p. 1.

18 A coalition of forty-seven national Jewish organizations and three hundred local American Jewish federations and community councils.

19 Co-sponsored by Adath Israel Congregation Soviet Jewry Sub-Committee; National Council of Jewish Women (Toronto Section) and the Ontario Region Committee for Soviet Jewry, Canadian Jewish Congress. Taking part in the program were: Rabbi Erwin Schild, Joyce Eklove, vice-chairman of the CJC committee, Janice Rotman-Goldman and Karen Fingrut, co-chairmen of the Adath Israel Soviet Jewry committee and Mindy Rosenberg, chairman of the World Jewry Committee of NCJW. "Conference supports Jackson-Vanik waiver – Soviet Jewry stance changed," *The Canadian Jewish News* (June 29, 1989), p. 1.

21 Ibid.

22 Letter to members of the Montreal Inter-Faith Task Force for Soviet Jewry from Father Barry A. Jones, October 12, 1989, personal files of Father Barry A. Jones.

23 "Jewish marchers see glasnost as rallying point for hope," *The Ottawa Citizen* (October 23, 1989), p. A4.

24 Ibid.

25 Plan of activities in the former Soviet Union 1994, The Jewish Agency for Israel, Office of the Chairman of the Executive, The Unit for the CIS and Eastern Europe, submitted to the Board of Governors of the Jewish Agency, October 1993.

26 Personal recollections of Wendy Eisen.

27 Present were representatives of the National Conference on Soviet Jewry, Union of Councils for Soviet Jewry, World Jewish Congress, B'nai Brith International and the CJC.

28 The Zionist Forum was created by Natan Sharansky to assist newcomers from the Soviet Union in Israel. Headquartered in Jerusalem with branch offices throughout the country, the Forum is made up of Russian-speaking staff who provide assistance to clients in finding job opportunities, directing them to professional re-training courses and interceding on their behalf with the various government ministries.

29 Ibid.

30 The delegates paid tribute to Nobel laureate Andrei Sakharov, a great champion of human rights and Jewish rights, who had died in Moscow during the days preceeding the conference. Alan Rose communicated greetings on behalf of the CJC and Prime Minister Brian Mulroney. The Honourable Justice Ted Matlow interview with the author, May 29, 1993.

31 Mikhail Chlenov, Jewish Cultural Association Moscow; Joseph Zissels, former Prisoner of Conscience from Chernovtsy; Roman Spektor, Alexander Shmukler, Leonid Stonov, cultural activists from Moscow; Vladimir Dashevsky, head of

Moscow's religious community; Boris Kelman, head of the Leningrad Society for Jewish Culture; Samuel Zilberg and Gregory Krupnikov head of Riga's Latvian Jewish Cultural Society.

32 "Jews meet in Moscow first time since Czar," *The Canadian Jewish News* (January 5, 1990).

NOTES, CHAPTER 28

1 The JDC is funded by the American United Jewish Appeal and, to a small extent, by the United Israel Appeal of Canada; The Jewish Agency for Israel (JAFI) began by establishing offices in six republics and by 1994 operated out of thirty-one offices in fifteen republic. Plan of activities in the former Soviet Union, JAFI, October, 1993. The "Law of Return" entitles any person with at least one grandparent to make aliyah, personal files of Wendy Eisen.

2 The Honourable Justice Ted Matlow, co-chairman of the Committee for Soviet Jewry, Ontario Region of CJC. Alan Rose, executive vice president of CJC. Rabbi Martin Cohen of Beth Tikvah Congregation in Vancouver. Benjamin Maissner, cantor of Holy Blossom Temple, visited Samarkand with his wife, Hope, vice-chairman of Holy Blossom Temple's Soviet Jewry Committee. There, the cantor conducted a Hebrew class for self-taught Hebrew teachers and performed a concert of Hebrew, Ladino and Yiddish songs. "Jews of Samarkand want close ties to Canada," *The Canadian Jewish News* (January 11, 1990).

3 Roma Bross had lived in Samarkand during WW II. Josef Schechtman was born in the USSR. They taught beginner and advanced Hebrew lessons and the writings of Jewish poets. "Mission to Samarkand – June-August 1991," submitted to the CCSJ by Roma Gelblum Bross, personal files of Wendy Eisen.

4 As reported in *Newsbreak*, National Conference on Soviet Jewry (January 10, 1991), p. 3.

5 Michael R. Beschloss and Strobe Talbot, *At the Highest Levels.*

6 "Russian Jews expected to leave," *The Canadian Jewish News* (November 4, 1993).

7 Jewish Agency activities in the former Soviet Union were directed by Baruch Gur from 1992–1995.

8 *Hotline,* Keren Hayesod United Israel Appeal, January 1995.

9 The Great Soviet Exodus," *National Geographic* (February 1992).

Index

Abella, Irving, 194, 251, 252-253, 255
Abella, Rosalie, 256
Abbey, Monroe, 8, 34, 42
Abramov, Moshe, 170
Abramovich, Felix, 98
Abramovich, Mark, 54, 77
Abramovich, Pavel, 98, 137
Abram, Morris, 236, 247
Adath Israel Synagogue (Toronto), 239, 264
Afanasyev, Victor, 212-213, 221
Afghanistan, Soviet invasion of, 110, 116, 141 146, 186, 243, 247
Ahs, Josef, 93
Ain, Steve, 46
Airst, Celia, 45
Alexander II (czar), 2
Alexander III (czar), 3
All-Canadian Rabbinic Conference (1964), 18-19
Altman, Anatoly, 33, 111, 114
American Academic Committee on Soviet Jewry, 51
American Association for the Advancement of Science, 152
American Jewish Conference on Soviet Jewry, 20
Amnesty International, 124, 153
Andriefsky, Felix, 92
Andropov, Yuri, 170, 171, 196
Anshei Minsk Synagogue (Toronto), 149
Anti-semitism, 2ff.
Anti-Zionist Committee (USSR), 162-163, 177, 220
Applebaum, Albert, 45
Appleby, Ron, 207
Appoloni, Ursula, 112
Arnett, Peter, 246
Arthurs, Harry, 242
Aspen Institute for Humanistic Studies, 147
Association of Jewish Publishers of New York, 164
Atlantic Jewish Council, 174-175
Attewell, William (Bill), 199, 202, 212, 213, 221-222, 235, 247
Atwood, Margaret, 208
AUCCTU. *See* Central Council for Trade Unions
Avigur, Shaul, 10, 28-29
Azbel, Mark, 86, 93, 120

Babi Yar (massacre), 136
Balcan, George, 71
Ballard, Harold, 206
Bar-On, Ruth, 37, 94, 270
Barthos, Gordon, 211
Batist, Dr. Gerald, 223-226
Bauer, William, 186-188, 189, 227
BBC, 31, 226, 259
Becker, Rabbi Lavy, 56-57
Begin, Menachem, 38, 108, 111
Begun, Boris, 220
Begun, Ina, 161
Begun, Yosef, 49, 94, 95-96, 108, 120, 135, 138, 161-162, 167, 183, 206, 207, 210, 211, 220, 233-234, 240, 248, 266, 270
Beilinson, Dolores, 164
Beilis, Mendel, 4
Believe Me, Sister (Elena Keis), 256
Bellas, Renee, 209-210
Ben-Gurion, David, 7, 9, 10, 12

Berenshtein, Inna, 220
Berenshtein, Josef, 176, 183, 187, 211, 220
Bergelson, Dovid, 8
Berger, David, 237
Berger, Ruth, 67
Berton, Pierre, 125
Beryozka dancers, 69-70
Bessin, Hyman, 40
Bessner, Morton, 207
Beth Israel Hospital (New York), 225
Beth Israel Synagogue (Halifax), 155
Beth Israel Synagogue (Vancouver), 149
Beth Shalom Synagogue (Ottawa), 241
Beth Shalom Synagogue (Toronto), 239
Beth Tikvah Synagogue (Toronto), 123, 147, 198, 199
Beth Tzedec Congregation (Toronto), 13, 16, 48, 255
Beutel, Austin, 251
Beutel, Nani, 251
Bialik High School, Soviet Jewry Committee (Montreal), 105-106, 119-120
Bikel, Theodore, 45
Binder, Sharon, 152
Birnbaum, Jacob, 20
Birobidjan, 5. *See also* Pale of Settlement
Blood accusation, 4. *See also* Jewish conspiracy theory
Bloom, Judith, 235
B'nai Brith, 53, 107, 157, 213, 233. *See also* League for Human Rights
Bogdanov, V., 207-208
Bogomolny, Tanya, 223-228
Boshevik Revolution. *See* Communist Revolution
Bolshoi Ballet (tour, 1974), 67-68, 69, 76
Borenstein, Sylviane, 58, 59
Bosley, John, 164
Bowker, Alan, 189
Braave, Rima, 223-227
Brailovsky, Irina, 137
Brailovsky, Leonid, 105-106
Brailovsky, Victor, 105, 110, 136-137, 151-152, 153-154, 240, 270
Breithaupt, Jim, 156
Brezhnev, Leonid, 21, 26, 49, 60, 62, 73, 75, 104, 121, 125, 162, 171, 242
Brind, Yuli, 65
British Broadcasting Corporation. *See* BBC
British Parliamentary Committee for the Release of Soviet Jewry, 168
British 35s, 64-65, 74
Broadbent, Ed, 202
Broadbent, Lucille, 164
Bronfman, Andrea, 65
Bronfman, Edgar, 152, 203, 236, 261
Bronfman, Edward, 57, 215, 237
Bross, Roma, 269
Brussels Conference (1971). *See* World Conference on Soviet Jewry
Bryden, Marion, 156, 177
Bulka, Rabbi Reuven, 173, 180, 265
Bund, 4
Bush, George, 171, 247, 260
Butman, Hillel, 111, 114

Cable News Network. *See* CNN
Cafik, Norman, 101-102, 126, 127
Caged (Elena Keis), 271
Caiserman, H. M., 4
Caccia, Charles, 102
Calgary Committee for Soviet Jewry, 53, 155
California Institute of Technology, 80
Callwood, June, 166, 256-257
Canada-Russia hockey series (1972), 57, 251
Canadian Academic Committee for Soviet Jewry, 51
Canadian Association for Labor Israel, 16
Canadian Bar Association, 58
Canadian Broadcasting Corporation. *See* CBC
Canadian Cancer Society, 227
Canadian Committee to Save the Life of Anatoly Sharansky, 198
Canadian Committee for Soviet Jewry, 53, 63, 88, 100, 115, 134, 157, 161, 216
Canadian Conference of Catholic Bishops, 124
Canadian Hadassah-Wizo, 43, 54, 68, 76, 112, 231
Canadian Jewish Congress, 4, 8, 12, 16, 17, 21-22, 38-39, 60, 65, 97-98, 105, 107, 112, 133, 142, 153, 156, 185, 186, 215, 235, 251, 262. *See also* World Jewish Congress
Canadian Jewish News (Toronto), 46, 110, 250
Canadian Labour Congress, 122, 128-129, 131, 175

Canadian Lawyers and Jurists for Soviet Jewry, 82, 147, 168, 192-193, 212
Canadian Manufacturers' Association, 45
Canadian Parliamentary Group for Soviet Jewry, 88-89, 102, 168-169, 173-174, 185, 197, 202, 207, 213, 215, 217, 249
Canadian Zionist Federation, 53, 107, 157
Carlucci, Frank, 245
Carr, Shirley, 122
Carter, Jimmy, 119, 121, 128, 146
Cartan, Henri, 197
CBC, 59, 75, 129, 225, 232, 259. *See also* names of specific programs
CCSJ. *See* Canadian Committee for Soviet Jewry
Central Council for Trade Unions, 128
Central Intelligence Agency. *See* CIA
Chabad Lubovitch, 268
"Charges in the Final Form" (against Sharansky), 127
Chaplin, Charles S., 76
Charny, Benjamin, 223-227, 228, 229-230
Charny, Leon, 227
Chernenko, Konstantin, 171, 174, 177, 197, 198
Chernobilsky, Boris, 93
Chernoglaz, David, 82
Chistopol Prison, 114, 190-191, 193, 194, 195, 198, 203, 233
Chlenov, Mikhail, 252-253, 260, 266
Choral Synagogue (Moscow), 19, 22, 137
Christian Embassy, 180
CIA, 121, 128
CIS. *See* Commonwealth of Independent States
CJC. *See* Canadian Jewish Congress
Clarfield, Mark, 39, 42
Clark, Joe, 112, 177-178, 184, 186, 188, 202, 208, 211, 212, 227, 255, 258, 264
CLC. *See* Canadian Labour Congress
CNN, 246
Cohen, Lyon, 4
Cohen, Rabbi Martin, 269
Cohn, Rita, 209-210
Cold War, 51, 219
Collenette, David, 173
Collenette, Penny, 164-165, 166, 173
Combined Jewish Appeal, 63
Committee of Concern for Soviet Jewry, 27
Committee of Concerned Scientists for Soviet Jewry, 88
Committee for Soviet Jewry, Ontario Region, 53
Commonwealth of Independent States (CIS), 269
Communist Party, 9; abolition of, 269. *See also* International Communist Party
Communist Revolution (1917), 4, 266
Community Hebrew Academy of Toronto, 206
Concerned Sterns for Shtern, 96
Confederation of Jewish Organizations and Communities in the USSR (the Vaad), 266
Conference on Confidence and Security-Building Measures and Disarmament in Europe (Jan., 1984), 170
Conference on Security and Cooperation in Europe, 60-61, 183, 185, 186, 188, 189, 219, 260
Congregation Beth Tikvah (Dollard des Ormeaux, Quebec), 239
Congress Bulletin (Canadian Jewish Congress), 61
Congressional Wives for Soviet Jewry, 164-175, 171
de Corneille, Roland, 149
Cotler, Ariella, 203
Cotler, Irwin, 13, 20, 35-36, 123, 130-131, 137, 139-141, 147-148, 157, 165, 184, 186, 191-192, 192-193, 194, 196, 203, 242, 243, 248, 262, 263
de Cotret, Robert, 174
Cousens, Don, 202
CPGSJ. See Canadian Parliamentary Group for Soviet Jewry
Crosbie, Jane, 164
CSCE. *See* Conference on Security and Cooperation in Europe
CTV, 113

Davidovich, Yefim, 71
Day of the Soviet Jewish Child (Toronto), 115
D'Amato, Alfonse, 227
Deans, Ian, 167, 215, 217
"Declaration of Solidarity with Soviet Jews," 32
Decter, Moshe, 18, 20
Delbruck, Max, 80

Delworth, W. T., 60, 101
demokratsia, 260
Dershowitz, Alan, 196
Desmarais, Lucille, 164
Le Devoir (Montreal), 22
Diefenbaker, John, 16, 19, 22, 72
Dinitz, Simcha, 30
Dinstein, Dr. Yoram, 60
"diploma" tax, 49-53
Disenhouse, Sheldon, 142-143
Dobrynin, Anatoly, 152, 172
"Doctors Plot," 8
Dolnik, Solomon, 24-25
Douglas, Tommy C., 84
Dragunsky, David, 162
Dreyfus case, 3
Drinan, Father Robert F., 121
"dropping out." *See* neshira
Dubianskaya, Elena, 218
Dubow, Elaine, 91, 117
Dymshitz, Mark, 32, 33, 35, 111

East-West summits. *See* U.S./Soviet summit meetings
Eban, Abba, 151
Eagleson, Alan, 206
Edelshtein, Yuli, 174, 187, 207, 210, 211, 237-238, 247, 270
Edelsteins for Edelshteins, 237, 238
Edelstone, Gordon, 237
Edelstone, Selma, 237
Edmonton Journal, 206
Edmund Burke Society, 45
Educational programs to the Soviet, 159-160, 163
Eggleton, Art, 193
Eiran, Amos, 52
Eklove, Joyce, 159
Elbert, Inna, 233
Elbert, Lev, 136, 167, 233, 240, 270
Eliav, Pinchas, 13
Eliashiv, Arlazar, 105
Ellis, Roberta, 153
Em l'Em (Mother to Mother), 271
Erb, Rev. John, 251
Eshkol, Levi, 3
Essas, Ilya, 163
European Inter-Parliamentary Conference for Soviet Jewry (Berne, 1986), 207
Executive Council of Australian Jewry, 261
Exodus (Uris), 27, 77, 181
Expo '67 (Montreal), 42
Expo '86 (Vancouver), 209-210
Export-Import Bank Bill (U.S.), 78

Fabiola, Queen (of Belgium), 87
Farquhar, Rev. Alexander, 144
Fawcett, Eric, 88, 122
Federenko, Nikolai, 25
Federov, Uri, 33, 35
Fedorchuk, Vitaly, 171
Fefergrad, Irwin, 263
Feffer, Itzik, 8
Feld Carr, Judy, 45
Feldman, Alexander, 65
Feldman, Leonid, 77, 90, 270
Fields, Rabbi Harvey, 158
Filer, Sam, 58, 82, 123
Finestone, Sheila, 42, 173, 176, 202, 219-220, 221
Fisher, Dan, 140, 141
"Flight to Freedom" (1975), 83-84
Fogel, Shimon, 174-175
Folkshtime (Yiddish newspaper, Warsaw), 11
Fonda, Jane, 172, 244
Ford, Gerald, 79
Fosdick, Dorothy, 51
Frankel, Sara, 157
Fraser, John, 94-95, 149, 241
Freidgut, Theodore, 155
Fridman, Ilana, 81, 172, 208, 243
"Friends of Goldshteins," 83
Fuga, Olga, 153
Fulford, Robert, 251
Furman, Aliyah, 253
Furman, Lev, 239, 253
Furman, Marina, 253

Gaisan, Nathan, 38
Garber, Michael, 13, 17-18, 20, 21-22
Garvis, Miriam, 58
Gates of Brass (docudrama), 180
The Gazette (Montreal), 92, 97, 106, 109
Gelber, Nahum, 58
Georgian State Song and Dance Ensemble, 41
Gerber, Rabbi Don, 125
Gilbert, Martin, 100, 103, 163-164, 240
Gillen, Sister Ann, 87
Ginzburg, Alexander, 121, 122

glasnost (openness), 182, 221, 222, 237, 245-259, 260, 263
Glass, Barbara, 69
Glass, Irving, 88
The Globe and Mail, 113, 124, 125, 256
Gold, Dr. Phil, 224
Goldberg, Arthur J., 101
Goldfarb, Alexander, 79-81
Goldfarb, David, 230
Goldman, Jeanette, 54, 152-153, 160, 221-222, 239
Goldmann, Nahum, 12, 16
Goldschlag, Klaus, 73-74
Goldshtein, Grigory, 83
Goldshtein, Isai, 83
Goodman, Brian, 134
"Good Morning America," 202
Gorakoff, Boris, 76
Gorbachev, Mikhail, 166, 177, 180, 181, 184, 199, 205, 206, 207, 210, 212, 213, 220, 224-225, 227, 228, 231, 232, 242, 246, 249, 258, 260, 269
Gorbachev, Raisa, 200
Gorst, John, 121
Gotlieb, Allen, 247
Gottlieb, Calvin, 8, 122
Granovsky, Stephen, 234
Gray, Charlotte, 143, 144
Gray, Herb, 72-73, 84, 124, 127
Greater New York Conference for Soviet Jewry, 63, 111
Gromyko, Andrei, 6, 50, 170, 178
Grossman, Larry, 202
Group of 15 (France), 87, 109
Gruda, Michael, 39
Gzowski, Peter, 225
Gur, Baruch, 269
Gurwitz, Sergei, 65

Hadassah-Wizo. *See* Canadian Hadassah-Wizo
Hall, Emmett M., 83, 121, 134
Hallward, John, 144
Halperin, Grace, 59
Halperin, Irving, 59
Halperin, Israel, 88, 197, 198
Hammer, Armand, 230, 243
Hanick, Shirley, 256, 261, 264
Harcourt, Michael, 156, 168
Harker, John, 122, 131, 175
Harris, Ethel, 219
Harris, Milton, 207, 215, 219-220
Harris, Sydney, 44, 50, 53
Hart, Gary, 227
Hartman, Rabbi David, 12-13
Hayden, Tom, 172
Hayes, Saul, 12, 13, 18, 39-41, 60-61
Hebrew Immigrant Aid Services, 91, 150-151
Hebrew University (Jerusalem), 29, 90
Helsinki Agreement. *See* Helsinki Final Act
Helsinki Final Act, 60-62, 73-74, 100, 103, 115, 118, 122, 125, 131, 147, 173, 179, 183, 184, 187, 188-189, 199
Helsinki Parliamentary Committee, 100, 102, 125
Helsinki Review conferences (1977, 1980, 1986), 101-104; (1989) 188-189
"Helsinki Watch" group, 100-101, 120, 127, 184
Hechtman, Rabbi Isaac, 56
Hershon, Goldie, 142
Herzberg, Dr. Gerhard, 152, 232-233
Herzl, Theodor, 3
Herzog, Chaim, 246
Heschel, Rabbi Abraham Joshua, 16, 19
HIAS. *See* Hebrew Immigrant Aid Services
Hineini (Reform congregation[s]), 250
Hirsch, Rabbi Richard, 250
Histadrut Society Humanitarian Award, 16
Hitler, Adolph, 5-6
Hofstein, Dovid, 8
Hollywood Reporter, 76
Holocaust, 6; Irving Abella's speech (Moscow), 252-253
Holy Blossom Temple (Toronto), 34, 158-159, 238, 256, 264
Hughes, Barry Conn, 78
L'Humanité (French communist daily), 33, 196
Hyman, Ralph, 110

Ida Nudel Humanitarian Award, 152-153, 161, 166, 208, 239-240
Ida Nudel in Exile (film), 113
Ingram, Peg, 153
Institute of American and Canadian Studies (Moscow), 146, 215
Institute of Planning and Production (Moscow), 81

Interamicus (organization), 248, 262
International Book Fair (Moscow), 163-164, 236
International Campaign to Free Yuri Orlov and Anatoly Sharansky, 197, 199
International Cancer Patients Solidarity Committee, 224, 230
International Committee for the Release of Anatoly Sharansky, 121-122, 125
International Communist Party, 11
International Conference of Parliamentary Spouses for Soviet Jewry (April, 1984), 171
International Foundation for the Survival and Development of Humanity, 262-263
International Helsinki Federation for Human Rights, 248
International Olympic Committee, 109
In Touch (supplement, *Canadian Jewish News*), 250
Intrator, Genya, 39, 49, 58, 80, 117, 123, 160, 206, 255
IOC. *See* International Olympic Committee
Ioffe, Alexander, 137, 219, 232-233, 271
Ioffe, Dimitry, 232-233
IPCSJ. *See* Israel Public Council for Soviet Jewry
Irlin, Dr. Yosef, 223
Israel Philharmonic Orchestra, 250, 257
Israel Public Council for Soviet Jewry, 37, 94, 100, 175, 270
Israeli Women for Ida Nudel, 111
IWIN. See Israeli Women for Ida Nudel
Izvestia (USSR), 24, 120

Jabotinsky Prize, 162
Jacobs, Naomi, 178-179
Jackson, Helen, 164, 165
Jackson, Henry M. (Scoop), 50-53, 78-79, 129, 162, 165
Jackson-Vanik Amendment, 52, 78-79, 127, 179, 264, 269
JAFI. *See* Jewish Agency for Israel
Jamieson, Don, 76, 95, 107, 110, 126
Janner, Greville, 168
Javits, Jacob, 19, 50
Jay, Harry R., 184-185
JDC. *See* Joint Distribution Committee
JDL. *See* Jewish Defence League
Jerusalem Report (Israel), 272
JEWAR. *See* Jewish Women Against Refusal
Jewett, Pauline, 112
Jewish Agency for Israel, 265, 268, 269
Jewish Community Council (Montreal), 56
Jewish conspiracy theory, 3. *See also* Blood accusation
Jewish Cultural Association (Moscow), 260
Jewish Defence League, 38, 41-42, 45, 46, 87
Jewish General Hospital (Montreal), 224
Jewish Minorities Research Bureau, 18
Jewish Reporter (Toronto), 31
Jewish state, creation of (1947), 6
Jewish Student Network (York University), 131, 210-211. *See also* York University
Jewish Telegraphic Agency, 172
Jewish Theological Seminary (New York), 270
Jewish Voices from the Soviet Gulag (booklet), 113
Jewish Women Against Refusal, 235, 249, 255, 262
The Jews of Russia, their History in Maps and Photographs (Gilbert), 103
The Jews of Silence (Wiesel), 22
Jews in the USSR (samizdat journal), 110, 151
Jobin, F. L., 155-156
Johnston, Don, 167
Joint Distribution Committee, 268
Jones, Father Barry, 97-98, 126, 144, 265
Joseph Wolinsky Collegiate (Winnipeg), 234
Joyal, Serge, 86, 165
JWF. *See* Toronto Jewish Women's Federation

Kahane, Rabbi Meir, 38, 87
Kaminsky, Lasal, 82
Kampelman, Max, 103-104, 163
Kanovich, Grigory, 263
Kaplan, Robert, 58, 83, 84, 86, 87-88, 125, 127
Karchev, Konstantin, 236, 251
Katz, Mara, 228
Kaye, David, 182

Kayfetz, Ben, 13, 31, 35
Kazakov, Yasha, 26, 28-29, 30, 31-32, 272
Kedmi, Yasha. *See* Kazakov, Yasha
Keil, Dr. Mark, 206
Keis, Elena, 249-250, 252, 253-254, 256-258, 271
Kelman, Efim, 206
Kemp, Joanne, 164
Kennedy, Edward, 228-229
Kent, Charles A., 27
Kfar Blum (kibbutz), 9-10
KGB, 8, 26, 49, 64, 174, 205, 209, 218-219, 234, 241, 242, 243, 250, 252, 254
Khachturyan, Armen, 206
Khnokh, Leib, 33, 87, 111
Khnokh, Yigal, 87
Kholmiansky, Alexander, 174
Kichko, Trofim, 19
Kiev Opera and Ballet Company (tour, 1974), 68-69
Kilgour, David, 173, 178, 80, 183, 185, 198, 207, 211-212, 219, 221
King, Audrey, 164, 173, 218-219
King, Fred, 173, 176, 207, 218-219
Kirkpatrick, Jeane, 163
Kirov Ballet, 69
Kirshblum, Eliezer, 239
Kissinger, Henry, 49, 51, 78
Knowles, Stanley, 40
Kochubievsky, Boris, 26, 28
Kogan, Zinovy, 250
Kol Yisroel (radio), 28, 31, 55, 91
Kondrashev, Sergei, 104
Korey, William, 60, 103
Kosharovsky, Inna, 249
Kosharovsky, Yuli, 94, 246, 248-249, 252, 253, 262, 271
Kosygin, Alexei, 21, 24, 25, 40, 41, 42-46, 48, 51, 133
Koudriavtzeff, Nicholas, 69
Kowalsky, Vladimir, 76
Kravtsov, Boris, 248
Krushchev, Nikita, 9, 11, 21
Kuna, Giorgi, 250
Kurchatov Atomic Institute (Moscow), 79
Kushnir, Alexander, 174
Kussner, Sheila, 224-225
Kuznetsov, Anat, 271
Kuznetsov, Eduard, 33, 35, 79, 111, 114-115, 271
Kuznetsov, Rudolf, 172, 243
Kvitko, Leib, 8
Kwinter, Monte, 257, 260

Lacey, Rev. Msgr. M. P., 125
Ladispoli (Rome), 150, 264. *See also* neshira (dropping out)
Landis, Gloria, 123
Landis, Herb, 122-123, 180, 198
Landis, Noah, 122-123
Landsberg, Michele, 113, 208
Lautenberg, Frank R., 225
Layton, Irving, 147
Lazerte, Alan, 180
League for Human Rights (B'nai Brith), 149
Leddy, Mary Jo, 208
Lefortovo Prison, 97, 121, 124
Lehman, Herbert H., 8
Leibler, Isi, 261, 262
Leikina, Meita, 249-250
Leland, Rev. James E., 206
Lenin, Vladimir, 4
Leningrad (ship, demonstration at), 13
Leningrad (show) trials, 32-36, 40, 41, 54, 77, 87, 111, 113, 152
Lerner, Dr. Alexander, 57, 62, 120, 134, 139-141, 157, 216, 237, 246, 271
Lerner, Tina, 155
Lerner, Tova, 8
Levanon, Nechemiah, 9, 21, 28, 31, 37, 63, 98, 150-151, 258-259, 271
Levich, Dr. Benjamin, 50, 134
Levin, Arye, 261
Levin, Rabbi Yehudah Leib, 14, 56
Levine, Boris, 56-57
Levine, Rabbi Daniel, 155
Levinson, Sender, 110
Levitt, Gregory, 160
Levy, David, 129
Lewin, Sam, 19
Lewis, Anthony, 229
Lewis, David, 22, 61
Lewis, Roz, 235
Lewis, Stephen, 125, 178-179
Lifshitz, Vladimir, 187, 206, 211, 240
Lipavsky, Sanya, 120
Lishkat Hakesher, 10, 37, 63, 149-150, 268, 272
Lokshin, Osip, 222
Long Island Committee for Soviet Jewry, 247

Los Angeles Times, 129, 139, 141
Lubarsky, Lazar, 97, 162
Lubianka Prison, 8
Lucyk, Rev. Stanford R., 143-144, 171
Luntz, Alexander, 88
Lurie, Emmanuel, 261
Lurie, Judith, 249, 252, 255, 261

Ma'ariv (Israel), 15
McCurdy, Howard, 221
McDermott, Dennis, 128
MacDonald, Flora, 107-108, 112, 115-116, 141, 161, 208, 215-217
Macdonald, H. Ian, 194
MacDonald, Lynn, 207, 218-219
McDougall, Barbara, 239-240
MacEachen, Allan J., 74, 165
McGibbon, Pauline, 152-153
McGill University (Montreal), 20, 241
McGonigal, Pearl, 153
MacGuigan, Mark, 103, 154
McKay, Dr. Robert, 147
McLaine, Alan, 157, 207, 262
McLeod, Bruce, 206
McMurtry, Roy, 115
Magarik, Alexei, 187, 205, 240
Maissner, Benjamin, 269
Makarov, Alexei, 209
Malenkov, Georgi, 9
Maloney, Arthur, 83, 134
"Man and His World." *See* Expo '67
Marchais, Georges, 196
Marchenko, Anatoli, 214
Mariasin, Alexander, 144, 228
Mariasin, Faina, 228
Mariasin, Lea, 223-225, 228
Markish, Esther, 123
Markish, Peretz, 8, 123
Marmur, Rabbi Dow, 158, 238-239
Martin, Paul, 17, 18
Marx, Karl, 5
Matlow, Ted, 266, 269
Matroskaya Tishina Prison, 95
"May Laws," (1982), 3
Medjuck, Frank, 155
"Meet the Press," 202
Mehta, Zubin, 257
Meiman, Inna, 223, 227
Meiman, Naum, 220, 228
Meir, Golda, 7, 29, 30-31, 38, 50, 55, 86, 87-88, 87-88, 94, 137, 150
Meirovich, Rabbi Harvey, 239
Mendelevich, Josef, 33, 35, 84, 111, 114, 152, 157, 199-200
Metzenbaum, Shirley, 164
Mikhoels, Solomon, 6, 260-261
Milgrom, Ida, 123, 127, 139, 190-191, 193, 194, 195, 197, 201, 203, 220
Miller, William, 58
Ministry of State Security (USSR), 8
Mirkin, Anatoly, 163
Miroshnichenko, Boris T., 34
Mitterand, François, 180
Montand, Yves, 257
Montreal Committee for Soviet Jewry, 53, 66, 83
Montreal General Hospital, 224
Montreal Inter-faith Task Force for Soviet Jewry, 97, 126, 144, 179, 265
Montreal Star, 69, 217
Montreal 35s, 66-68, 72, 73, 74, 94, 96, 105, 109, 117, 138, 195
"Morningside," (CBC), 225
Morris, Nomi, 256
Morris, Joe, 122
Moscow Book Fair. *See* International Book Fair
Moscow Institute for Economic Planning, 95
Moscow News, 15
Moscow State University, 155
Moscow Yiddish Theatre, 6
Mosser, Mary, 232, 251
Moynihan, Daniel, 85
Mulroney, Brian, 173, 179, 185, 211, 235, 258
Murzhenko, Alexei, 33, 35

Nashpitz, Mark, 81, 82, 218
Natan Sharansky Lectureship in Human Rights, 241
National Committee for Soviet Jewry (France), 63
National Conference on Soviet Jewry, 52, 63, 151, 155, 236, 245, 264, 265
National Council of Jewish Women, 53-54, 110, 115
National Council for Soviet Jewry (Great Britain), 50, 63
National Council of Women, 124
National Interreligious Task Force on Soviet Jewry (Chicago), 87

National Union of Israeli Students, 29
Navon, Ofira, 164
Navon, Yitzhack, 164
NCJW. *See* National Council of Jewish Women
NCSJ. *See* National Conference on Soviet Jewry
Neilson, Erik, 166
Nelson, Rev. Sidney, 126
Nepomniashchy, Mark, 142
neshira (dropping out), 91, 94, 150-151, 264
Netanyahu, Benjamin, 209
Netzer, Tzvi, 150
Network. *See* North American Jewish Students Network
New England Medical Center (Boston), 225, 230
Newman, Peter, 146
The New York Times, 28, 31, 32, 51, 80, 119, 128, 158, 217, 229
Next Year in Jerusalem (Avital Sharansky), 132
Nicholls, Hilary, 210
Nixon, Richard, 49, 51, 78, 93, 118
Nixon, Robert, 143, 202
North American Jewish Students Network, 178
Notre Dame de Sion, Catholic Sisters of, 167
Novosti (international press agency), 150
Nudel, Ida, 81-82, 104, 106-108, 111-113, 116, 134, 148, 152-153, 160-161, 166, 167, 172, 185, 186, 187, 207, 208, 210, 211, 216, 221, 231, 239, 243-244, 247, 271
Nurgitz, Nathan, 261

O'Connell, Martin, 100, 125
OLCSJ. *See* Ontario Legislature Committee for Soviet Jewry
Olympic Games. *See* Summer Olympics
Ontario Legislature Committee for Soviet Jewry, 156
Ontario Rabbis Council for Soviet Jewry, 239
Oostrom, John, 251, 253
"Operation Exodus," 267, 268, 270
Orah (magazine), 231-232
Orlikow, David, 196
Orlov, Yuri, 100, 121, 122
Orzy, Rick, 142-143, 263
Ottawa Committee for Soviety Jewry, 53, 125
Ottawa Jewish Bulletin and Review, 173
Ottawa 35s, 67
Ovsishcher Committee (Beth Israel Synagogue, Vancouver), 149
Ovsishcher, Lev, 148-149

Palatnik, Raisa, 64-65, 271
Pale of Settlement, 2
Pamyat (anti-semitic organization), 236-237, 266
Paris conference (1960), 12
Paritsky, Alexander, 155
Parliamentary Group for Soviet Jewry. *See* Canadian Parliamentary Group for Soviet Jewry
Parliamentary Spouses Committee for Soviet Jewry, 156, 164-165, 173
Pearlson, Rabbi Jordan, 251
Pearson, Geoffrey, 195, 216
Pearson, Lester B., 18, 19
Peck, Gregory, 257
Penn, Martin, 100, 138-139, 153-154, 166-167, 183, 186, 215-217
Penson, Boris, 33, 111, 115
The People's Court of the Volgogradsky Region (Moscow), 107
Pepin, Lucie, 21
Peres, Shimon, 201, 246
perestroika (restructuring), 182, 222, 251, 260, 263
Perle, Richard, 51, 52
Perm Labour Camp, 190, 191, 193, 220
Peterson, David, 195, 202
Peterson, Jim, 155, 168-169, 172, 197, 217-219
Pevsner, Valery, 209, 210
Pidyon Shevuyim (redeem the captives), 48
Pilkey, Clifford, 125
Pipeline to the USSR (newsletter), 156
Plaskov, Avi, 29
Plaut, Rabbi W. Gunther, 34, 43-44, 46, 125, 128
Podgorny, Nikolai, 21, 33
Pogroms: first wave (1881-1884), 2-3; second wave (1903), 3-4; third wave (1919), 4
Polansky, Mark, 240
Polisuk, Ted, 58

Pollack, Allan, 73
Pollack, Ruth, 112
Polsky, Victor, 49, 58, 69, 78, 82
Pomerant, Joe, 123, 125
Popov, A.Y., 19
"The Position of Soviet Jewry, Human Rights and the Helsinki Accords," 183
Potma Labour Camp, 54, 75, 76, 82
Pozdnyakov, Uri, 165
Pravda (USSR), 79, 163, 170, 212-213, 221
Preminger, Otto, 38
La Presse (Montreal), 70
Prestin, Misha, 96
Prestin, Vladimir, 49, 96, 146, 240
Prisoners of Conscience. *See* refuseniks
Prisoners of Zion. *See* refuseniks
Proctor, John, 194
Prossin, Ben, 235
The Protocols of the Elders of Zion (1895), 3
The Province (Vancouver), 168
Prussakov, Valentin, 24-25

Quebec Bar Association, 58
"Quirks and Quarks," 232

Rabinovich, Lilia, 264
Radio Canada, 226
Radio Liberty (New York), 31, 91, 259
Rae, Bob, 202
Rager, Yitzhack, 64, 65-66
Rais, Carmella, 254
Rais, Vladimir, 252, 254
Raphael, Bert, 58, 82-83, 110, 124, 212, 263
Raphael, Stan, 263
Rather, Dan, 226
Ratner, Judith, 243
Raviv, Zvi, 29, 30
Rawlings, Jay, 180
Rawlings, Meridel, 180
Reagan/Gorbachev talks. *See* U.S./Soviet summit meetings
Reagan, Nancy, 200
Reagan, Ronald, 170, 181, 188, 201, 212, 226, 246-247, 255
Rebecca Sieff award, 112
Rechetov, Yuri, 261, 265
refusenik, 47ff.
Regan, Carol, 164
Reichmann, Albert, 237, 258
Reitman, Cyril, 237
Reitman, Dorothy, 186, 237
Resnick, Sam, 57
Resolution 3379, 85
Ribicoff, Abraham, 19, 50
Richler, Dr. Avrum, 75-76
Richler, Mordecai, 131
Richter, Glenn, 20
Ridgeway, Rozanne, 245
Riis, Nelson, 173-174, 219-220
Ritchie, A. E. 34
Roberts, John, 72-73, 84, 86, 89, 127, 158
Roberts, Peter, 218
Robertson, John, 84
Robinson, Marthe, 165
Rogers, R. Louis, 103, 104
Ronen, Moshe, 199, 234-235
Rose, Alan, 35, 60, 61, 101, 102, 103, 122, 166, 183, 186, 207, 218-219, 266, 269
Rosenberg, Rabbi Stuart E., 13-17, 18-19, 20, 21, 22, 23
Rosenne, Meir, 12, 13
Rosenshtein, Grigory, 138
Rosnovsky, Anna, 249-250, 257-258
Rotenberg, David, 156
Roth, Sheila, 138
Roth, Stephen, 60, 103, 138
Route to Freedom, an experience of escape from the Soviet Union (refusnik board game), 133
Rubin, Janice, 256
Rubin, Vitaly, 100, 120
Rudenko, Roman, 130, 140
Russian Contemporary Art Exhibition (1975), 70-71
Russian Jewry, oppression and persecution of, 3-7, 146, 163-164, 167, 205
Russian Revolution. *See* Communist Revolution
Rustin, Bayard, 86-87
Ryan, Claude, 22

Sadowski, David, 39, 42
St. Michael and All Angels Church (Toronto), 251
Sakharov, Andrei, 146, 178, 213-214
Salansky, Naum, 94-95, 147
Salsberg, Joseph B., 11, 13, 55
SALT II treaty. *See* Strategic Arms Limitation Talks
samizdat literature, 24-25, 27, 33, 110, 151. *See also* names of specific publications

Satok, David, 88
Saturday Night (magazine), 251
Sauvé, Jeanne, 165, 166-167, 212
Schechtman, Josef, 269
Schifter, Richard, 255
Schwartz, Dr. Robert, 226
Scott, The Most Rev. Edward W., 125
Scriavin, Georgyi, 233
Shaar Hashomayim Synagogue (Montreal), 241
Shaare Zedek Hospital Foundation, 208
Shakhnovsky, Valdimir, 239
Shamir, Yitzhack, 246, 261
Shapiro, Ben Zion, 167
Shapiro, German, 92
Sharansky, Anatoly (Tolya), 59, 73, 94, 97, 100, 108, 114, 116, 117-132, 137, 139, 167, 178, 183, 190-204, 205, 208-209, 220, 241-243, 247, 271, 272
Sharansky, Avital, 117, 120, 122, 123-124, 130, 132, 184, 190-204, 209, 241, 271
Sharansky, Boris, 122-123, 132, 190
"The Sharansky Case," (report, Cotler), 130-131
Sharansky Lecture(s), 192-193
Sharansky, Leonid, 127, 137, 139, 193, 195
Sharansky, Natan. *See* Sharansky, Anatoly
Sharett, Moshe, 3, 7
Sharp, Mitchell, 35, 40, 42-46, 50, 60-61
Shastokovsky, Ilya, 135, 216
Shazar, Zalman, 3
Shecter, Debbie, 133-134
Shecter, Max, 134
Shenhar, Shmuel, 262
Sherbourne, Michael, 47, 80, 109, 120, 257
Shevardnadze, Eduard, 188, 208, 211-212, 241, 243, 250
Shibayev, Alexei, 128-129
Shifter, Richard, 185
Shipler, David, K., 128
Shmuckler, Alexander, 260
Shnirman, Simon, 222
Shoham, Rabbi Sidney, 126
Shomer Achi Anochi (organization, Israel), 109
Show trials. *See* Leningrad (show) trials
Shpeizman, Yuri, 228
Shperling, Dov, 27, 28-30
Shroeder, Pat, 108
Shtern, Dr. Mikhail, 67, 96-97
shtetls, 2
Shtiglitz, Misha, 117
Shultz, George, 170, 171, 227, 236, 244, 245
Shumiatcher, Barbara, 149
Silver, Leora, 210
Silver, Nat, 13
Silverstone, Jack, 261
Simard, René, 164
Simms, Rev. Dr. John, 126
Singer, Israel, 152, 266
Six Day War (1967), 25, 27
Slavens, Marsha, 54, 240
Slepak, Maria, 105, 107
Slepak, Valdimir, 39, 49, 58, 78, 94, 105, 106, 107-108, 120-121, 133, 135, 207, 245-256, 247, 266
Slivka, Marsha, 158, 239
Slovina, Leah, 27, 28-29
Smith, David, 102, 153-154, 164, 168, 196, 215-217
Smith, Frederick N., 144
Smith, Heather, 215
Smith, Hedrick, 80
Smuckler, Connie, 133
Sofinsky, Vsevolod, 185
Sokolov, A. P., 15
Solidarity March for Soviet Jewry: Toronto, May 1981, 155; May 1982, 161
"Solidarity Sunday for Soviet Jewry," 208-209
Solomon, Debby, 123, 202
Solomon Mikhoels Cultural Centre (Moscow), 260-261
Solomon, Stan, 123, 199
Soviet Academy of Sciences, 51, 232, 233, 258
Soviet Congress of People's Deputies (Lituania), 263
Soviet cultural events, demonstrations/boycotts, 69-72
Soviet-Israel Friendship Society (Baltic), 260
Soviet Jewry. *See* Russian Jewry
Soviet Jewry Committee (Vancouver), 167
Soviet Jewry Committee of Edmonton, 206
Soviet Jewry School Kit, 105, 106
Soviet prisons, surviving in, 113-115. *See also* specific prisons
Soviet Trade Unions, 175

Spektor, Roman, 260
SSSJ. *See* Student Struggle for Soviet Jewry
Stalin, Josef, 5, 6, 7, 11
The Status of the Soviet Jewish Community (hearings, May 1984), 172-173
Steering Committee for Soviet Jewry (Toronto), 155
Steinman, Ned, 98
Steinsaltz, Rabbi Adin, 258
Stern, Barbara, 67, 71, 96, 100-101, 102-103, 117, 122, 177, 186, 203-204, 207, 218-219, 241, 261
Stern, Isaac, 257
Strategic Arms Limitation Talks, 116
Student Struggle for Soviet Jewry, 20, 42, 63, 87, 98, 109
"A Study of Jews Refused their Right to Leave the Soviet Union," (1980), 102-103
Summer Olympics: 1976, Montreal, 70, 92; 1980, Moscow, 108-110

Talisman, Mark, 52
Tanenbaum, H. Wayne, 57
Tangrey, Beverley, 153
Taratuta, Aba, 216, 240
Taratuta, Misha, 135
Tarnopolsky, Yuri, 163
Team Canada (1972), 57
Technion (Haifa), 271
Tekoah, Yosef, 31
Tel Aviv University, 270
Temple Emanu-El (Palm Beach, Florida), 270
Temple Sinai (Toronto), 251
Tessler, Ronnie, 209-210
Thant, U, 26
They Came to Stay - the Soviet Jewish Experience in Israel (United Jewish Appeal), 91-92
The 35s (Women's Campaign for Soviet Jewry), 64-74, 76, 96, 97-98, 109, 271. See also British 35s, Montreal 35s, Ottawa 35s, Toronto 35s, Winnipeg 35s
Tifereth Beth David Jerusalem Synagogue (Montreal), 191-192
Tonks, Alan, 262
Toronto Inter-faith Council for Soviet Jewry, 171, 249, 251
Toronto Jewish Women's Federation, 249, 250, 256
Toronto Star, 15, 125, 144, 206, 211, 256
Toronto 35s, 72, 74, 195
Toronto Women's Federation, 39
Toth, Robert, 129
Trade Reform Act (U.S.), 51, 52, 79
Traders of Souls (Soviet film), 93-94, 120
The Trial of Anatoly Sharansky (play), 131
The Trial of Yuli Edelshtein (play), 210
Tritt, Bracha, 142
Trobiansky, Yosef, 265
Trotsky, Leon, 4, 5
Trudeau, Pierre Elliott, 39-41, 44, 73, 124-125, 130, 166, 173, 195, 196, 241
Tsirlin, Evgeny, 108, 112, 113
Tsitlionok, Boris, 81, 82, 94
Tsitverblit, Yitzhack, 136
Tsukerman, Inna, 156
Tsukerman, Vladimir, 160, 165
Turner, John, 202
Turner, Vernon, 251
Tytherleigh, Mike, 168

UCSJ. *See* Union of Council for Soviet Jews
Union of Council for Soviet Jews, 63-64, 109
Union of Hebrew Teachers (Soviet), 260
Union of Orthodox Jewish Congregations, 268
Union of Soviet Socialist Republics. See USSR
United Israel Appeal, 63
United Jewish Appeal, 63
United Synagogue of Conservative Judaism, 268
United Talmud Torah's Hebrew Day School (Montreal), 105
"Unity Week for Soviet Jews" (Montreal, May 1981), 155
Universal Declaration of Human Rights (1948), 24, 53, 74, 175
Uris, Leon, 27, 77
Urman, Stan, 66
U.S./Soviet summit meetings, 181, 199-200, 203, 246-247, 255
U.S. Trade Bill (1972), 49, 78
Uspensky, Inna, 252, 262

the Vaad. *See* Confederation of Jewish Organizations and Committees in the USSR

Vaad L'Hatzolas Nidchei Yisroel (organization, New York), 160, 163

Vainshtein, Leonid, 240

Vancouver Action for Soviet Jewry, 149

Vanik, Charles, 52

Vasilevsky, Anatoly, 158, 238

Vasilevsky, Natasha, 158, 238

Vesty (newspaper), 271

Visas, process of applying for, 25

Vogel, Wolfgang, 200, 203

Voice of America, 41, 226, 259

Voice of Israel, 259

Vokhenblat (Cdn. Yiddish weekly), 11

Volvovsky, Leonid, 181

Voronel, Alexander, 78

Wadell, Ian, 167-168

Wagner, Claude, 61

Walker, John, 22

War of Independence (Israel, 1948), 6-7

Washington Post, 28, 119

Waxman, Henry, 229

Weil, Simone, 162, 163

Weinberg, Henry H., 237

Weiner, Gerry, 198

Weizmann, Chaim, 3, 139

Weismann Institute of Science (Israel), 80-81, 271

Wenick, Martin, 264

Western Wall (Jerusalem), 7, 108, 201

Whelan, Eugene, 166

Wiesel, Elie, 22, 46, 247, 261

WIN. See Women for Ida Nudel

Winnipeg Committee for Soviet Jewry, 53

Winnipeg 35s, 74

Wolfe, Sharon, 134-138, 142, 174, 215-217

Wolfson, Alla, 264

Women for Soviet Jewry, 39

Women's Campaign for Soviet Jewry. *See* The 35s

"Women's Petition for Human Rights" (1975), 72, 89

Women for Ida Nudel, 112

Women's Federation of Allied Jewish Community Services, 42

World Conference on Soviet Jewry: Brussels, 1971, 37-38; Brussels, 1976, 85-88, 258-259; Jerusalem, 1983, 163-164

World Jewish Congress, 12, 152, 236, 261, 266

World Jewry Committee, 54

World Presidium on Soviet Jewry, 62, 85, 94, 101, 103, 109, 171, 184

World Union of Progressive Judaism (Reform), 250, 268

Yacovlev, Alexander, 165

Ya'hav, Yona, 29, 30

Yeltsin, Boris, 260

Yerushalaim (magazine), 270

Yom Kippur War (1973), 54-55

York University: hunger strike, 1977, 124-126; confers honourary degree, Sharansky, May 1982, 193-194, 242

Zagladin, Vadim, 221

Zaks, Eliahu, 138-139

Zalmanson, Israel, 33, 114

Zalmanson, Sylva, 33, 54, 66, 75-77, 114, 271

Zalmanson, Vulf, 111

Zambrowsky, Rabbi S. M., 18

Zarecki, Mark, 34-35, 41

Zeitz, Rabbi Mordechai, 147

Zelichonok, Roald, 221

Zerker, Sally, 153

Zhdamovich, Vadim, 174-175

Zilberg, Samuel, 266

Zimmerman, Warren, 227

Zionist Congress (Basel, 1897), 3

Zionist Forum, 270, 271, 272

Zionist Organization of Canada, 40

Zissels, Yosef, 266

Zittrer, Jack, 57

Zivs, Samuel, 162